FAMILY

ROSA GRASSI
1890-1976
M. 1908

MARGRIT
BIEVER
M.1980

(Previous husband Philip Biever.
Children: Annie Biever Roberts,
Phoebe Biever, Philip E. Biever)

PETER
MONDAVI
1914-

BLANCHE
M.1950

MARCIA
MONDAVI
1947-

MICHAEL
WILLIAM
MOREY
M. 1970
D.1972

TIMOTHY
MONDAVI
1951-

DOROTHY
REED
M.1976
D.1997

THOMAS
BORGER
M.1980

HOLLY
PETERSON
M. 1997

CARISSA
ELLEN
MONDAVI
1977-

CHIARA
MONDAVI
1978-

CARLO
CESARE
ROBERT
MONDAVI
1980-

DOMINIC
MONDAVI
1981-

DANTE
MONDAVI
1984-

MARC
MONDAVI
1954-

PETER
MONDAVI JR.
1958-

THE
HOUSE OF MONDAVI

THE
HOUSE OF MONDAVI

THE RISE AND FALL OF AN
AMERICAN WINE DYNASTY

JULIA FLYNN SILER

GOTHAM BOOKS

GOTHAM BOOKS
Published by Penguin Group (USA) Inc.
375 Hudson Street, New York, New York 10014, U.S.A.
Penguin Group (Canada), 90 Eglinton Avenue East, Suite 700, Toronto, Ontario M4P 2Y3,
Canada (a division of Pearson Penguin Canada Inc.);
Penguin Books Ltd, 80 Strand, London WC2R 0RL, England;
Penguin Ireland, 25 St Stephen's Green, Dublin 2, Ireland (a division of Penguin Books Ltd);
Penguin Group (Australia), 250 Camberwell Road, Camberwell, Victoria 3124, Australia
(a division of Pearson Australia Group Pty Ltd);
Penguin Books India Pvt Ltd, 11 Community Centre, Panchsheel Park,
New Delhi – 110 017, India; Penguin Group (NZ), 67 Apollo Drive, Rosedale, North Shore 0745, Auckland,
New Zealand (a division of Pearson New Zealand Ltd);
Penguin Books (South Africa) (Pty) Ltd, 24 Sturdee Avenue, Rosebank, Johannesburg 2196, South Africa

Penguin Books Ltd, Registered Offices: 80 Strand, London WC2R 0RL, England

Published by Gotham Books, a division of Penguin Group (USA) Inc.

First printing, June 2007
10 9 8 7 6 5 4 3 2

Gotham Books and the skyscraper logo are trademarks of Penguin Group (USA) Inc.

LIBRARY OF CONGRESS CATALOGING-IN-PUBLICATION DATA
Siler, Julia Flynn.
The house of Mondavi : the rise and fall of an American wine dynasty / Julia Flynn Siler.
p.   cm.
Includes bibliographical references.
ISBN: 978-1-592-40259-5 (hardcover) 1. Robert Mondavi Winery—History. 2. Vintners—United
States—Bibliography. 3. Mondavi family. 4. Family-owned business enterprises—United States—Case
studies. 5. Wine industry—United States—Case studies. I. Title.
HD9379.M66S56   2007
338.7'66320092273—dc22
[B]   2007004326

Printed in the United States of America
Set in Janson Text
Designed by Spring Hoteling

For my family, with love

CONTENTS

AUTHOR'S NOTE

This narrative account is based on 525 hours of interviews with more than 250 people and an examination of tens of thousands of legal and corporate documents. The landmark case of *Robert Mondavi v. C. Mondavi & Sons*, which was tried in 1976, alone runs to 10,059 pages. Likewise, the depositions and filings in the lawsuits involving former Mondavi executive Gary Ramona well exceed that page count. Dialogue and direct quotations come from those documents as well as oral histories, letters, memoirs, and the recollections of participants. On March 29, 2005, the author interviewed Robert G. Mondavi. Because Mr. Mondavi, who was then ninety-one years old, was unable to clearly recall events, the author decided not to use the material from this session. It was the last formal interview that Mr. Mondavi granted to a writer, according to his spokesman Harvey Posert.

Over a period of two and a half years, the author interviewed all of the principle family members involved in the events leading to the sale of the Robert Mondavi Corporation, seeking to understand how and why a seemingly "takeover proof" family-controlled company was sold over the objections of several key family members. The author conducted extensive in-person interviews with Mr. Mondavi's two sons, Michael and Timothy, and his wife, Margrit Biever Mondavi, returning to them repeatedly for clarification and fact-checking. Marcia Mondavi Borger, Mr. Mondavi's daughter, participated in only two short telephone interviews. The author also conducted lengthy interviews with current and former Mondavi executives and board members, including nonexecutive chairman Ted Hall, chief executive officer Greg Evans, and directors Sir Anthony Greener and Philip Greer. Memories and interpretations of events sometimes conflicted in this complex family and corporate saga. In such cases, the author has attempted to note differences in perspectives so that readers can weigh the evidence themselves. The result is the inside story of America's leading wine dynasty, in all its brilliance and destructiveness.

THE
HOUSE OF MONDAVI

PROLOGUE

Blaze, June 5, 2004

Robert Mondavi glided through the oak-studded grounds of the Meadowood country club in an electric golf cart. The ninety-year-old vintner's craggy profile looked as if it belonged on a Roman coin, but his dashing Western wear—a red-and-white-checked shirt, drawstring tie, black broad-brimmed bolero hat, and leather vest—prompted a few double-takes from the khaki-clad volunteers setting up for that day's wine auction. The aging emperor of Napa Valley also wore a faint frown.

Four decades earlier, Robert Mondavi had become famous for praising the benefits of fine wine to a nation that preferred Coca-Cola and cocktails. He had tirelessly sermonized that food and wine were at the heart of the good life, that in an age of fast food, wine was a healthy and civilizing force with sacred traditions, and that Napa Valley wines belonged in the company of the world's best. Along the way, this son of an Italian peasant became the patriarch of America's fine wine trade.

His passion had paid off: In time, Napa Valley wines took their place alongside those from Bordeaux as the world's finest, and a new wine-and-food culture leapfrogged from America's coastal cities to the heartland. Along the way, he and his children had become fabulously wealthy by selling stock in the family business to the public.

But that was long ago. Now, his company's reputation for producing high-quality wines had eroded and the House of Mondavi itself was rent by conflict. In the 1960s, a family feud had erupted, leading to a sensational court battle that created a decades-long split between the brilliant pitchman, Robert, and his introverted younger brother, Peter. These tensions were threatening to end Robert's dream of creating his own American wine dynasty in the image of Europe's Antinori and Rothschild families. On the eve of the wine trade's most glamorous annual event, Robert's family was on the brink of losing control of the company.

The auction tent hummed with Schadenfreude as the Mondavis' rivals and acquaintances experienced a delicious thrill in witnessing the troubles of the valley's most prominent family. Two days earlier, a front-page story in *The Wall Street Journal* had revealed the Mondavis' personal and business turmoil, after the Robert Mondavi Corporation's board had ousted Robert's eldest son, Michael, as chairman and put him on an indefinite leave of absence from the company. The move, which neither his father nor his siblings had opposed, had publicly humiliated the volatile Michael and left the company in the hands of nonfamily members for the first time in its history.

But Robert had a more troubling secret. Only his immediate family and a handful of his closest advisors knew that it was the patriarch's own financial overreaching, as well as his determination that his offspring would head the company, that had undercut the family's control of the Robert Mondavi Corporation. Whether it was hubris or simple financial miscalculation, Robert's philanthropic commitments had led him and his children into a crushing struggle with the company's board of directors. The nonagenarian's own financial situation had begun to look precarious.

Robert still commanded a large measure of loyalty and respect, which the Mondavis hoped would be reflected during the sale of Lot 11, their offering. It was a showcase for the family's craft and a treasure trove of its most sacred winemaking achievements, far removed from the mass-market Mondavi brands sold at Costco and Safeway. The lot contained nine bottles of Mondavi's finest Oakville Reserve Cabernets, made from coddled grapes aged for three years in French oak barrels. Robert's granddaughter Chiara had hand-painted and then etched the golden silhouettes of grapevines on each bottle.

For years, Mondavi wines had been among the top sellers at charity auctions such as this, a point of pride in the family. For while they might please millions of customers with affordable table wines, America's leading wine family could also produce wine lots that sold for hundreds of thousands of dollars, more than Robert himself had earned from the company's entire first year of production back in 1966. A few months earlier, at Florida's Naples Winter Wine Auction, a lot of four large-size bottles of Mondavi's 1997 Cabernet Sauvignon Reserve had sold for $190,000, reflecting Robert's role that year as the event's honored vintner. Lot 11's price would not only signal the Mondavis' prestige but also the family's continuing power in America's wine industry. "This lot should do really well," predicted the celebrity chef Michael Chiarello in front of a camera for his cable television show *NapaStyle*.

Robert limped into the white tent, leaning heavily on his cane as his wife, Margrit, gently guided him to his seat at the front. He was still an icon but in the past year had come to seem physically smaller than he had been before, shrunken in his stylish clothes. The hearing aid in his left ear could not pierce the cocoon of deafness that surrounded him, and his once-famous charisma had diminished. His mind had begun to slow in a way that alarmed some family members as he was beset by a fog of mental confusion that seemed to be thickening each day. More worrisome, Robert seemed to have lost some of the optimistic spirit that had buoyed him for so many decades.

Anticipating that her husband would tire easily after recent surgeries, Margrit stayed by his side. With her ageless blond effervescence, she offered friends a smile and a cheek to kiss as the couple waited for the bidding to begin. In her late seventies, she was a striking woman who carried her small frame with grace. She wore a drawstring linen pantsuit in the color of the Spanish moss that draped the valley's oaks. Although she had lived in Napa Valley for more than four decades, her English remained softly accented by her childhood in Switzerland.

Auctioneer Fritz Hatton started the day's bidding.

"Fasten your seat belts because heeere . . . weeee . . . goooo!" whooped Hatton, shuffling sideways across the podium. With his gourmand's belly spilling out of his trousers and his pianist's hands sweeping rapidly back and forth as if he were playing arpeggios, Hatton kicked up his heels with a flourish.

Below him, a group of vintners also took flamboyant measures to ramp up the excitement. Wearing a Hawaiian shirt and Birkenstock sandals, Roger Trinchero, whose family's Sutter Home Winery first became famous for its easy-to-drink blush Zinfandel, whipped out a squirt gun in one hand and a can of Silly String in the other. He incited bursts of laughter at his table as he began spraying guests. The air inside the white tent grew warm. Then, minutes into the auction, some two thousand wine lovers shifted their attention to the podium as Hatton started the bidding for Lot 11.

"Five thousand, there it is. . . ."

"Ten thousand. . . ."

An awkward silence followed.

The bidding had stalled and hushed tension gripped the crowd. After decades of serving as a global ambassador for Napa Valley wines, promoting them in countless tastings and events, Robert Mondavi had built up deep reservoirs of goodwill. No one wanted to see the old king humbled by a low sale price for his family's choicest wines. Yet, the most sophisticated wine buyers were no longer paying top dollar for Robert Mondavi Cabernets. The Mondavi reputation had slid a few years earlier after his younger son Timothy's winemaking style came under fire from such influential critics as Robert Parker and *Wine Spectator*'s James Laube. By the late 1990s, wine connoisseurs had moved on to small production cult wines such as Screaming Eagle, Harlan Estate, and Dalla Valle Vineyards that were wildly expensive—$200 a bottle was not unusual—and hard to get.

"Fifteen thousand . . ."

"Twenty . . ."

Volunteers with big foam index fingers—the type that fans wave around at football games—pointed in the direction of bidders to draw Hatton's attention to rival paddles. Paddle 253—held by Jess Jackson, the seventy-four-year-old proprietor of Kendall-Jackson Wine Estates—was bidding against paddle 5, held by construction heir Ron Kuhn. A sharp negotiator who had had a legal run-in with the Mondavi family a few years earlier, Jackson wore a placidly earnest look on his face. With a net worth estimated by *Forbes* magazine at $1.8 billion, he was one of the wine industry's few billionaires.

"Forty thousand . . ."

"Fifty-five thousand . . ."

Hatton looked around for any bidders to top the previous bid. There were none. Robert seemed confused by the slowing bids. Shadows crossed his face. Would his family suffer further dishonor by such a low price?

"Sold . . . to Jess and Barbara Jackson! Thank you very much," exulted Hatton.

Excited volunteers—known as the Hoopla Committee—surrounded Jackson, a towering man with a silver crown of hair. Some of them tossed up fluorescent green "Napa Valley Donor Dollars"—with each bill in the denomination of fifty million dollars, bearing the slogan "In Wine We Trust." Across the room, Robert Mondavi's bald dome and aquiline profile was unwavering amid the flutter of the play money.

Despite the manufactured gaiety, the moment was poignant for the onlookers at the auction that day who understood the drama playing out in the Mondavi empire. A lot offered by Napa's most famous family was bought at a fire sale price by one of their company's fiercest rivals from neighboring Sonoma County. Was the bid symbolic of Jackson's rising strength in the industry and Mondavi's fading glory? Was it a kind gesture aimed at sparing Robert from further humbling? Or was it a foreshadowing of what was to come—with Jackson and other potential predators at that very moment eyeing Mondavi's many attractive properties?

Jess Jackson grinned broadly for the news cameras, photographers, and fellow bidders who surrounded him. He stood up from his table as Robert hobbled unsteadily toward him. The two men grasped hands, at least an eight-inch height difference between them. The Hoopla Committee surrounded both of them and their images were projected simultaneously onto the ten monitors mounted in the tent.

The men soon parted and returned to their seats. The bidding day had just begun and more highly sought lots were ahead. Of keen interest to many of the high-flyers who'd come to Napa that weekend was Lot 17, a "flight" of three bottles of Screaming Eagle Cabernet Sauvignon from the 1995, 1996, and 1997 vintages. A wine industry newcomer would have difficulty seeing why such a humble-looking offering—presented in a rustic box, with the brand name and an image of the namesake raptor burned into the wood—could generate such excitement. But Screaming Eagle, owned by Jean Phillips and produced by the winemaker Heidi Peterson Barrett, was America's most collectible wine.

Expectations ran high. Almost immediately, the bidding leapt into the six figures, with paddles shooting up left and right. The most intense back and forth took place between paddles 511—held by Edward Weltman, a defense attorney from Long Island, New York, and paddle 32, held by a Chinese electronics magnate, M. K. Koo.

"One seventy," shouted the British auctioneer David Elswood.

"One eighty. One ninety."

"Two hundred," Elswood said, gesturing at Weltman, who was wearing a white polo shirt and reflective sunglasses.

"Two twenty," pointing at Koo, who was sitting in the very back of the tent, with a clear line of sight to the center of the podium.

"Sold at two twenty!"

Over the loudspeakers, the Steve Miller Band's 1976 hit, "Fly Like an Eagle," reverberated throughout the tent. The music's deafening beat became a physical presence, roiling the hot air inside the canvas. The Hoopla Committee swarmed around the inconspicuous-looking Chinese man, as did the television cameras. Koo, wearing glasses, a baseball cap, and a plaid, long-sleeve button-down shirt, stood up, grinned widely, and raised his champagne flute in a toast for the cameras.

As winemaker Heidi Barrett and vintner Jean Phillips came to congratulate Koo, Robert Mondavi and his fair-haired son Timothy tilted their heads back to watch the excitement at the other side of the tent projected on one of the video screens. With the Screaming Eagle lot positioned so closely to the Mondavis' offering it was hard for anyone to ignore the fact that tiny, upstart wineries had overshadowed the big, venerable names, such as Beaulieu and Beringer, which had put Napa Valley on the map. The prices paid for the California cult wines left those pioneering vintners—people who had been in the valley since the 1960s and, for the Mondavis, since the late 1930s—shaking their heads.

Robert and Timothy stared up at the screen, silent in the midst of the raucous celebration of the bid. They seemed isolated, as the Hoopla Committee and television cameras moved elsewhere. For that moment, the Mondavis were no longer the center of attention. When the spotlight returned in the months to come, it would blaze mercilessly on the dismemberment of their empire.

PART ONE

FOUNDATION

CHAPTER ONE

The Valley, 1906–1952

In February of 1906, a quiet twenty-three-year-old Italian named Cesare Mondavi climbed aboard a steamer moored in Antwerp called the *Vaderland*. After a rough, twelve-day crossing of the Atlantic in steerage class, he landed at Ellis Island in early March and then ventured west to the harsh mining country of Minnesota to join his brother and other young men from his small village in central Italy. His childhood home on the outskirts of the medieval town of Sassoferrato and his new home in Minnesota's Iron Range were an ocean apart, but they bore one similarity: Both were rocky, unforgiving terrains where a man's character would be tested as he struggled to earn a living.

Cesare Mondavi's first job in America was in the mines, hauling iron ore. He labored hard and lived frugally for two years before returning to Sassoferrato in 1908, where he courted a local girl named Rosa Grassi. The daughter of peasant farmers, she had briefly worked as a domestic. Known in her family as a *testa dura*, a "hardhead," Rosa also had a sweet face, a cheerful disposition, and a gift for cooking. She readily accepted the proposal of marriage from the serious, intelligent Cesare, for although he, too, came from peasant stock and completed his formal schooling by about age nine, he was an avid reader and perhaps the first member of his family to learn to write his name.

To marry, Cesare and Rosa traveled from their respective farmsteads to the Piazza del Castello, the center of the old town of Sassoferrato. They made their way down a cobbled alleyway to the Catholic church, where they wed on November 8, 1908. After a brief honeymoon at a nearby cottage, Cesare and the seventeen-year-old Rosa boarded a steamer, where they were directed seperately to the men's and women's sections in steerage class, with a hundred or so berths and only a single toilet. Rosa, who had never traveled by sea before, was sick most of the time. When they finally arrived at Ellis Island, a freezing rain pelted them and slush slowed their way to the train that would carry them west, to Ely, Minnesota. In later years, Rosa would recall how Cesare had told her back in Italy that, in America, their lives would be easier. During difficult times in later years, she'd sometimes mutter under her breath, "*Che uno scherzo brutto*," or "What an ugly joke."

Soon after, Cesare Americanized the family's name by changing it from "Mon-dah-vee" to "Mon-day-vee." Since his brother, Giovanni, also lived nearby, the change may have been a source of some confusion. But Cesare and Rosa struggled along in their new lives until tragedy struck; Giovanni was killed in a mining accident, leaving behind a widow and two children. Not long after his brother's death, Cesare quit working in the mines, just as he and Rosa were starting their own family. Mary, their eldest, was born in 1910, Helen in 1912, Robert in 1913, and Peter fourteen months later, in 1914. With four children born in four years, it is likely that Cesare and Rosa decided that the meager wages for such dangerous work were not worth the risk.

Cesare became business partners with the Brunettis, another Italian family. Together, they opened a small grocery store in Virginia, Minnesota, that stocked fresh pasta, Italian sausages, olive oil, and wines. The store did well, and eventually Cesare sold his part of the business and bought a saloon. Catering to Italian immigrants, it gave them a place where they could sip familiar-tasting wines, speak their own language, and temporarily escape the scorn they felt as newcomers.

To supplement the family's income, Rosa began taking in boarders— often as many as fifteen or more immigrant miners at a time. The small clapboard house where the Mondavis and their boarders lived had three bedrooms and only one bathroom, with no heat except a wood-burning stove in the kitchen. She worked hard—cooking two hot meals and packing lunches for them each day, while cleaning, laundering, mending, and ironing. During the harsh Minnesota winters, Rosa would hang the miners' wet overalls on lines strung across the small rooms to dry. She normally rose at four-thirty each morning and went to bed shortly before midnight.

Rosa was a strict taskmaster with the men who boarded in her home. She forbade gambling, drunkenness, filth, and vulgarities. Boarders who broke her rules faced her wrath. One evening after dinner, with the children within hearing distance, one of the men began spewing obscenities. "I warned him once—on such matters I never warned anybody more than once—and he continued his obnoxious behavior," Rosa recalled nearly five decades later. "So I rushed at him with a quart bottle in my fist. Fortunately, he beat me to the door or I should have broken the bottle on his head. He never entered my house again."

Drinking was a part of everyday life in the Mondavi household. Rosa and Cesare allowed each of their boarders to keep a fifty-gallon wooden wine cask in their basement, printing their names on them so they could tell the casks apart. Before dinner, the men would pour some of their wine from the cask into a carafe, bringing it to the table to accompany their supper.

For the most part, Cesare and Rosa continued to live in a world of fellow Italian immigrants. The family spent Sundays with other Italian families, attending church and picnicking at lakes and parks. The men would gather after work to drink wine and play bocce. Cesare and Rosa spoke Italian all their lives, though eventually they both learned English. "I'm sure when they went to bed at night, they dreamed in Italian," says one of their grandsons.

Although Italian was spoken almost exclusively in the Mondavi home, it was only daughter Helen who would become fluent in it. Peter remembered throwing the languages together in a sort of Italian-American patois. After starting school, some of the other kids called Robert a "wop" and a "dago" on the schoolyard. He became determined not to give them an excuse to call him names again. He refused to speak his parents' native tongue.

*   *   *

In 1919, Congress passed the Volstead Act, which marked the beginning of Prohibition. Under its rules, families were permitted to make two hundred gallons of wine per year for their own use and wineries were allowed to continue making wine for sacramental purposes. The Mondavis were already making their own wine. They drank it at most meals—watered down for the children and a tablespoon of red wine in coffee for the adults' breakfasts. And as distilleries were shuttered, Prohibition opened up vast new business opportunities for the wine trade.

Because Minnesota did not have the climate or soil for growing wine grapes in large quantities, the Italian-American Club of Virginia, Minnesota, sent Cesare to California to purchase some on its behalf. In 1919, the same year Prohibition came into effect, Cesare climbed aboard a train and traveled west to Lodi, a flat, fertile agricultural town in the Central Valley that had only incorporated in 1906, the year San Francisco was devastated by an earthquake and fire. Just south of Sacramento, it was known for flame-red Tokay grapes, a sweet table variety. Cooled by ocean breezes blowing in through the Carquinez Straits, Lodi enjoyed a climate of warm days and cool nights similar to the one Cesare and Rosa had left when they'd emigrated from the Marche region of Italy, northeast of Rome. It was also centrally located for buying and shipping grapes. Not only was the weather an improvement over Minnesota's but class and cultural prejudices against Italian immigrants in California were less corrosive than in the Midwest.

Recognizing these advantages, Cesare decided to move his family to California. As their smoke-bellowing train transported the family across the Great Plains and the desert into California, climbing the Sierra Nevada mountain range and descending into California's fertile San Joaquin Valley, Peter, the youngest member of the family, gawked out the window, marveling at the strange scenery. Rosa, who had barely learned to read or write, crocheted during the journey. Cesare, in his dark three-piece suit, read the newspaper, while the girls quietly read novels and the boys played tag through the train's narrow aisles.

Their journey west in 1923 was a sign of the Mondavi family's future. On the long train ride, two of the children got separated from the rest of the family. The train they were traveling in stopped at one of the big cities along the way. Part of the family ended up in one car, while the rest was in another. In later years, the siblings would remember it differently. Robert, who was ten or so at the time, recalled that it was he and one of his sisters who got separated from the rest of the family when the train they were riding made a stop. Peter remembered that he and Robert got separated from everyone else.

Both boys were frightened. But Robert, as the older brother and dominant personality, had the presence of mind to call for help. "I screamed bloody murder until the railroad people came to the rescue," he recalled. "They halted both trains and got us reunited. I can just imagine my parents saying to each other, 'That Bobby, always going off in his own direction!' " Rosa burst into tears when the family was finally reunited.

The family's life in Lodi revolved around Cesare's grape and fruit whole-saling business and the Italian-American community. With Cesare's shrewd business skills and Rosa's energy and resourcefulness, it didn't take long for the Mondavis to rise in Lodi's social hierarchy. They started in a modest house but soon traded up to a six-bedroom, two-and-a-half-bath home on West Pine Street, just a few blocks from Lodi's old downtown and once owned by the former president of the local Farmers and Merchants Bank.

Built in 1917, it was an example of the Arts and Crafts movement of the time, with low roof lines, wood gables, and a broad porch flanked by large square posts. Every spring, lilac-colored wisteria blossoms covered the house's delicate pink exterior. In the cool, dark basement, Rosa had lined the shelves with glass jars of peaches, green beans, and other fruits and vegetables she'd grown in her garden and preserved, as well as home-made sausages, dried herbs, and wine. Rosa, who had a habit of slightly lowering her eyelids over her hazel-green eyes before she began to speak, made sure there was always an abundance of food at the table.

The Mondavis sent their children to St. Anne's Catholic School and then Lodi Union High School. At the same time, the Mondavi home became a base for a number of newly arrived immigrants and on Sundays the women in the family would set Rosa's enormous oval dining table with as many place settings as it would fit, knowing that visitors would fill each place before the day was over. The family sometimes called Lodi "Little Sassoferrato" because Cesare had helped so many people from his and Rosa's hometown come to the U.S. by sponsoring them and offering them jobs. One fellow immigrant, who came to live with Cesare and Rosa at their boardinghouse in Minnesota and then followed them to Lodi, was Peter Bellardinelli, whom the Mondavi kids came to call "Uncle Pete."

Although sparing with words, often expressing himself with nods and a slight upward tilt of his chin, Cesare cut a memorable figure around town with his large broad nose and a penchant for broad-brimmed Borsolino hats. As one family member tells it, people used to call him "Cesare the Phantom" and "the headless horseman" because of how he disappeared behind the wheel when he drove his large DeSoto. All that could be seen of him from the outside was his hat: He was so short he'd have to peer through his steering wheel to see the road.

However comical he might appear behind the wheel, Cesare was also highly respected because he offered fair prices, paid his bills, and honored his agreements, which were often made with a handshake. His office was in the front of the West Pine Street home and was dominated by a dark, heavy wooden desk. No one dared enter it without being invited, except his grandchildren. "My cousins and I were always welcome there and we loved to sit in his big, deep leather chair," says his grandson Michael. "He'd smoke his stogies and we'd try to chew the ends a little bit as kids." Tucked in the corner of his office was a brass spittoon, which he used to spit in from his desk. Cesare spoke English with a heavy Italian accent and when he talked, everyone listened. If Robert or Peter or perhaps a member of Lodi's extended Sassoferrato community ventured into his study and made the case for a business investment or some other venture, Cesare would listen carefully and ask a question or two. Then he would pronounce his decision. That ended the issue and people who knew Cesare knew not to argue with him. He was the undisputed paterfamilias.

Cesare's good reputation soon reached beyond the Italian-American community of Lodi. Long before Robert was old enough to get a driver's license, Cesare had entrusted his eldest son with the responsibility of driving Rosa, his sisters, and his younger brother around town in the family's Studebaker. One time, a police officer pulled him over after he'd made an illegal U-turn. The officer asked him whether he had a driver's license. Robert admitted he didn't. Then he asked who his family was. Robert answered that he was the oldest son of Cesare Mondavi.

The officer's attitude changed instantly. Knowing Cesare as one of Lodi's most respected citizens, the officer told Robert his father was "good as gold." He then let him off with a warning, gently suggesting he get a permit if he planned to drive. Robert never forgot the lesson he learned that day about the value of a good reputation.

From the time Robert was thirteen, the Mondavi boys helped their father with the business during the summers. Cesare paid them $1.25 for every hundred boxes they nailed together—the same wage he paid his adult workers. The boys could make $25 for a good day's work and Cesare set the boys' earnings aside in a special account for them. With the other odd jobs they did for Cesare, the boys together saved close to $15,000, Robert wrote, an enormous sum of money for those days.

On one occasion, Robert and Peter held a competition to see who could nail together the wooden grape shipping crates fastest. Robert had an overwhelming need to prove he was the best, even in seemingly small tasks, and set about studying the way the workers nailed together the boxes to come up with his own efficient assembly line. With a helper to prepare the slate, he trained all summer, seeking to improve his time. The day came for the final showdown. Robert nailed together more than two thousand boxes—winning the competition and declaring himself the world champion.

The box story became part of Robert's personal mythology, revealing, as he told it over and over, the early manifestation of a competitive drive that he would later bring to the production and marketing of wines. In his darker moments, Robert would also bring up the story to illustrate how Peter could never keep up with him.

For the most part, the Mondavis thrived during Prohibition. Like the Gallos and Franzias, they shipped grapes from California to family wine-makers back east. Thick-skinned varieties such as Alicante Bouschet, which were considered "shipping grapes," sold at double or even triple prices, soaring to $50 per ton from the $10 to $20 that they had sold for before Prohibition, reflecting the surge in demand from home wine-makers and others. Attracted by such ripe opportunities, organized crime entered the business. There is no evidence that the Mondavis were directly involved in bootlegging, and Cesare even rebuffed an offer from Chicago mobsters to get involved in their business, according to one grandson. But it is likely that at least some of the grapes he sold were used to make bootleg wine.

The grape market plunged in 1926 because of overplanting, but that proved a short-term problem as Cesare continued to ship grapes east. When the stock market crashed in 1929 and the Great Depression began, Cesare's business ran into trouble. He came to his sons, who were nailing boxes together at the time, and asked them to loan him back much of the

$15,000 he had paid them for their summers of work. Cesare promised, in return, to put them through any college they chose.

The boys loaned him the money and their father honored his promise. By the time that Robert, and then Peter, was ready for college, his business had recovered enough so that Cesare was able to send Robert and Peter to Stanford University. With little or no formal education themselves, Cesare and Rosa placed a high value on education for their sons. But they sent their two daughters to secretarial school, reasoning that it would give them a set of skills to fall back on. They decided their sons—though not their daughters, who would presumably marry—would have the finest educations money could buy.

Although Robert had inherited a business sense from his father and volcanic energy and drive from his mother, he lacked confidence as a student: "I never felt I was very smart; in fact, I always had a bit of an inferiority complex in that regard." But he was a hard worker and was intensely determined. He played on the football team at Lodi High—even though he weighed only 140 pounds and had short legs. In his senior year, the team made it to the regional championship.

In the yearbook for his senior year of high school, Robert chose as his motto: "An honest man is as good as his bond," perhaps reflecting his growing realization that Cesare's business success had as much to do with personal integrity as with the fruits he sold. Wearing his hair slicked back, a solemn suit and tie, and an intense gaze, the young Robert Mondavi was already stacking up the accolades himself: He was on the honor roll in three of his four years, captain of the football team, and class president his senior year, as well as a member of the International Club and Scholarship Society.

His brother chose a very different motto: "He is kind," referring to himself somewhat awkwardly in the third person. His yearbook photo also shows an intense young man who also wears his dark his hair combed back with oil. But his softer, more rounded jawline contrasts with Robert's angular profile, making him look much younger. Unlike his older brother, the younger, sweeter Mondavi son eschewed self-promotion. He was as quiet and introspective as Robert was voluble and outgoing. His sister Helen once came upon Peter praying on his knees in his bedroom when he was about seventeen. Yet his list of accomplishments was nearly as lengthy as Robert's: class president, Scholarship Society, honor roll in three of four years, and a member of the football team his last two years.

In addition, he exhibited an early interest in chemistry and studied Spanish as a member of the "Los Ameoles" club.

Cesare and Rosa encouraged their sons' high aspirations, even in the midst of the Great Depression. Paying for two sons to attend the West Coast's leading private college was certainly no small feat. A 1931 article in *Time* magazine described Stanford as "predominantly a rich man's college" with "one of the finest Pacific Coast golf courses, two lakes, a polo field as well as two great gymnasiums and many a smaller playing field and game court" in addition to its ninety-thousand-seat football stadium. "More than half [the men] own automobiles. Some fly their own planes," the *Time* article continued.

Stanford drew mostly white Protestant young men from upper- and upper-middle-class backgrounds. As first-generation Italian-Americans and Catholics, the Mondavi boys stood out. That may explain why they lived together in the Phi Sigma Kappa fraternity. At Stanford, Robert again excelled in sports—playing on the rugby team, where his wiry strength and speed served him well. He learned to drink beer and Scotch, and found teachers who urged him to look beyond the strict teachings of his Catholic upbringing and to think for himself.

"Throughout my boyhood, I had always been motivated, first and foremost, by fear," wrote Robert in later years. "I was always afraid of failing to win approval, afraid of falling short. I was convinced, too, that I was not as intelligent as many of my peers. My first year at Stanford, though, I had a wonderful professor of religion and philosophy who opened me up to another way of seeing and thinking. 'Use your own damn head!' he would urge me. 'You are just as intelligent as anyone, if you open your mind and your heart.'"

His confidence grew. Robert studied economics and business during his first three years of college and thought at the time he might become a lawyer or businessman—a reliable upward path for an immigrant's son. But during his junior year his father asked him if he was interested in the wine business. Through his contacts with grape growers and wholesalers, Cesare had become convinced that a new market for California wines was about to open up now that Prohibition had been repealed.

That was a contrarian view. Prohibition had left America's wine industry in a shambles. Only 130 or so California wineries had survived, down from more than 700 before the "noble experiment," and the wines hurried onto the market in 1934, often by speculators with little winemaking experience, were probably the worst ever produced in the nation's history. Sweet, fortified wines dominated the market and wine as a beverage became associated with "winos" on skid row. Many of the wines shipped in the years after repeal were spoiled and nearly undrinkable. The fine wine market, such as it was, was tiny and dominated by French producers. Against this backdrop, Cesare believed that Americans would eventually start drinking drier table wines with their meals, in the European fashion, and saw a great opportunity in fine, high-quality wines.

In that respect, Cesare was decades ahead of the curve.

Napa Valley, barely thirty miles long and, at its widest, just five miles across, stood apart from California's other grape-growing regions, as Cesare saw it. He had motored through most of the state on his buying trips and believed that Napa Valley, which was just north of San Francisco, had the greatest potential for producing fine table wines.

As a buyer, he was experienced in judging the quality of the grape berries coming from the Central Valley and coastal regions versus those from Napa, with its porous, well-drained soils in the southern end of the valley and reddish, volcanic soils from Mount St. Helena on the northern end. Cesare found he could buy Napa grapes for nearly the same price as those from the Central Valley and sell them to winemakers for much more.

Napa's winemakers had once known great days. Before the microscopic scourge phylloxera destroyed many vineyards starting in the late nineteenth century, Napa wines such as Beaulieu and Charles Krug were winning accolades from New York and abroad. Yet, by the early 1930s, many of the valley's vineyards had been pulled out and replanted with prune trees and walnuts. More than 232 California wineries had closed in the mid-1920s. By the 1930s, more than 400 of the 700 cellars that were bonded at the start of Prohibition had closed. Napa was not as well known for its wines as it was for its overcrowded, Gothic-style asylum for the insane.

At the same time, wine consumption in the United States more than doubled during the Prohibition years, from roughly 60 million to 150 million gallons, surging due to the loophole in the Volstead Act that permitted families to make wine at home for their own consumption. Moreover, the perception of wine as a beverage of southern European immigrants—the so-called dago red and dago white—or as a luxury that the very wealthy imported from France, was starting to fade. At the same time many of Napa's vineyards disappeared, wine was on the verge of entering mainstream American culture as Americans ventured abroad and returned home with more worldly tastes.

Robert thought seriously about entering the fine wine business. It wasn't long before he took him up on the offer. In part, he was respectfully following Cesare's wishes, for children of immigrant Italian families, that "the sun would rise and set" on their parents, Robert explained. "They could make no mistake." As well, for students graduating from college during the Depression years, jobs were scarce.

So Robert took a chemistry course in his senior year at Stanford, hoping that it would help him make wine. He graduated from college in 1936—the first member of his immediate family to do so. A photo from the time shows Robert in his black cap and gown, between his mother and father, his arms over their shoulders, towering over them in height (even though he himself was just over five foot eight) and beaming. Cesare and Rosa, grown stout over the years, have solemn expressions on their faces. That summer, he took what he called a "crash course" in viticulture, the growing of grapes, and enology, the making of wine, from two professors at the University of California at Berkeley.

Toward the end of the summer, Robert made his way north to the hamlet of St. Helena, then a sleepy farm town about three-quarters of the way up the Napa Valley where many of the streets were still unpaved. There he began working for a friend of his father's named Jack Riorda, who ran a bulk wine business that came to be called Sunny St. Helena Winery. Shortly before Robert arrived, Cesare had purchased an interest in the business.

Robert worked through his first cycle of winemaking, laboring as a low-paid "cellar rat" and serving as Riorda's assistant. During that time, Sunny St. Helena made what was known as "tank wine," simple young wine that wasn't aged first in oak barrels but instead shipped directly to customers in railroad tanks. The winery didn't grow its own grapes but instead bought them from growers each year.

Robert felt at home in the valley, where a number of Italian immigrant families had settled. By 1937, four years after repeal, more than forty wineries were operating again in Napa County. Many were run by Italian immigrants with names such as Molinari, Rossi, Martini, and

Garibaldi. Slowly, the valley's winemakers recovered from Prohibition, but some blended in pre-Prohibition-era wines with newer juice to give their wines some "age." The result: Napa's reputation as a winemaking center suffered, undermining the good reputation it had earned during the Gilded Age.

In 1940, Robert married his high school sweetheart from Lodi, Marjorie Declusin, who had also attended St. Anne's Catholic School and Lodi Union High School a year behind him, in Peter's year. Her chosen motto in the senior yearbook: "Give Yourself a Pat on the Back." Marjorie was a sporty young woman, playing volleyball, hockey, swimming, tennis, and basketball. Like Peter, she, too, was a member of "Los Ameoles." But although Marjorie's father was also a local fruit buyer, her family's social status was a few notches above the Mondavis'. Marjorie's mother, an Irish-American educator and a ranking golfer at the local Woodbridge Golf and Country Club, had not welcomed Robert Mondavi's courtship of her daughter. Robert recalled in his autobiography that she did not think much of Italians. But eventually he won her over.

Auburn-haired and soft-spoken, Marjorie fell in love with the boy who was included among "The Honored Great" in his high school yearbook in 1932. After their wedding, Robert managed to visit most of his father's bulk wine accounts while on his honeymoon; even in the earliest days of their marriage, the wine business intruded on their private life. Robert and Marjorie settled in St. Helena, in a small house at 931 Charter Oak Avenue, with an old-fashioned front porch and modest lawn.

While Robert began his business career, Peter completed his studies at Stanford. Throughout his childhood, Peter had loved making model airplanes and thought he might become an engineer. But after having a persuasive conversation with his father, and being a dutiful son, he decided to join his father and brother in the family's new venture. So after graduating from Stanford in 1937, he went on to graduate studies in enology at the University of California at Berkeley, studying under Professor W. V. Cruess, who was highly regarded in the field.

It was there that Peter began research on cold fermentation, a process well-known in Germany and that would soon prove to be a breakthrough in the U.S. wine industry, because it made possible the production of exceptionally crisp, fruity white wines. After graduating, Peter worked briefly at the Acampo Winery and Distilleries, a cooperative in the Central Valley where his father was president, before serving in the army air corps in England during the Second World War. Robert, meanwhile, had won exemption from military service because he was growing grapes and overseeing a small truck farm that grew tomatoes, agricultural products considered vital to the war effort.

As Riorda and the Mondavis grew Sunny St. Helena—expanding from five hundred thousand gallons to more than a million gallons within a few years—Robert began tinkering with ways to improve the wine. His inability to be satisfied with "good enough," which would later lead to conflict, was already in play. This part of his character also sowed the seeds of conflict: A perfectionist who was seldom satisfied with the efforts of family members, he found it impossible not to criticize and to leave well enough alone.

In 1937 he had first set up a primitive wine lab underneath Jack Riorda's house, where he would draw off samples and test the various batches at the end of the day. Later, he turned an old water tower behind his house into a small lab. He had water and gas installed and lined the tower with pine boards—transforming it into a place where he could continue with his experimentation year-round.

When Jack Riorda died in 1940, Robert became the winery's manager. As the U.S. entered the Second World War, the wine industry, like many others, was forced to grapple with labor shortages and rationing of food and materials. By 1942, vintners were advertising in *The St. Helena Star*, the local paper, seeking workers to do the tedious and low-paid job of pruning vines. Because rail tankers were being used to ship war materials across the country, they weren't available for bulk wine shipments. So, many wineries began bottling their wine, rather than shipping it in bulk: Shipments of munitions that came from the East in boxcars could be filled with bottled wine for the return trip. Bottling wines also helped control quality, particularly beneficial because at the time some unscrupulous winemakers and wholesalers, faced with huge demand for their product, were diluting wines with water or even apple juice.

In 1943, Robert learned that the old Charles Krug property—one of the oldest wineries in Napa—was up for sale. Spread over 147 acres just north of the town of St. Helena, the Krug Ranch was ideally situated on the floor of the Napa Valley. It also had a well-known name and a rich heritage. Charles Krug had been a Prussian immigrant who established the first winery in the Napa Valley in 1861—just eleven years after California had become a state. In 1892, after Krug's death, the Moffitts, a socially prominent San Francisco family, bought the property. For years, they summered there in a pair of large, single-story cottages surrounded by lawns and trees.

The Moffitt family held on to the ranch through Prohibition and the Great Depression, but by the early years of the Second World War it had fallen into disrepair. Because there were no family members interested in running the winery, the property had been leased out to Louis Stralla, who reputedly had made money during Prohibition by operating a gambling ship outside the three-mile limits in southern California. Stralla grew grapes on the property and produced what he called "heavy paisano red," which he sold by the tankload until 1940, when his lease ran out. By 1943, no wine was being made at Krug.

On a Friday, Stralla, along with Paul Alexander, the Bank of America's man in St. Helena, tipped off Robert that the Moffitt family had decided to sell the shuttered winery. On Saturday, Robert headed off to Lodi, aiming to convince his father to buy the place. At that time, Robert didn't have the money or the credit to make such a big purchase on his own. So he carefully laid out the case to Cesare. Father and son met alone in the den of the home on West Pine Street: Cesare was sitting back, puffing on a little Italian cigar. Robert argued that the price was reasonable and that the family could quickly recover its investment by labeling Sunny St. Helena's bulk wine as Charles Krug wines and selling them for a higher price.

Cesare listened quietly, then said, "You know, I'm happy. I don't have to get any bigger than what we are."

That was all Cesare said. He then climbed the stairs to his bedroom.

Rosa was listening to the conversation, too, as she worked in the kitchen.

Then, in a glimpse of the salesmanship that would later make Robert Mondavi famous, he privately petitioned Rosa.

The next morning, before Robert could say a word, his father asked him how soon he wanted to leave for St. Helena to visit the Charles Krug Winery.

Although she was seldom invited into Cesare's den when the men were discussing business, Rosa, it seemed, had wielded her influence overnight.

Peter had arrived home late that Saturday night, after the conversations about Krug, on a short furlough from his military duties. The next day, on Sunday, he joined Robert and his father in their trip to St. Helena to take a look around the Krug Ranch. They liked what they saw. The three men then ventured to James K. Moffitt's office on Monday, with Peter, wearing his air force uniform, and his father and brother.

Moffitt at the time was the epitome of old San Francisco's society: a director of the Crocker First National Bank, a regent of the University of California, and a wholesale paper magnate. As an Italian immigrant with his first-generation American sons, Cesare must have felt a bit intimidated at the prospect of meeting with Moffitt in his impressive offices at the Crocker Bank. Robert had had trouble sleeping for a few nights before. The men entered Moffitt's sumptuously appointed office suite and began chatting, accompanied by the banker, Paul Alexander.

"Gee, how wonderful it is to have two boys who will carry on your business," Moffitt said to Cesare. Moffitt himself had one child—a daughter—who was not interested in the wine business. "It's so wonderful to be able to pass something like this on."

The telephone rang and on the other line was a rival buyer for Krug from the Midwest. The conversation between Cesare and Moffitt had not advanced beyond generalities and they hadn't discussed specific purchase terms. Yet, Moffitt signaled to the caller that he was not interested in negotiating with anyone else.

"I'm sorry, I just sold the property to Cesare Mondavi," Moffitt said.

Robert was stunned by Moffitt's words. All of a sudden, it seemed that his family might actually be able to buy Charles Krug.

Moffitt hung up the phone and he and Cesare began discussing interest rates for a loan to buy the property. They quickly agreed on a sale price of $75,000 for the winery, the buildings, and surrounding acreage. Afterward, the Mondavis were Moffitt's guests at the Old Poodle Dog, an infamous French restaurant in San Francisco's financial district that served food downstairs and was said to have private rooms for sexual trysts upstairs.

Cesare imposed a single condition on his sons in buying the ranch: Robert and Peter must agree to work together to build the business. They readily assented to Cesare's condition, but their promises would prove impossible to keep.

In 1943, another momentous event occurred. Robert and Marjorie had their first child—a boy who was born on January 23 at the St. Helena

Sanitarium. They named him Robert Michael, and he became known as Mike.

With Peter still serving in the air force, Robert took on the task of turning his family's purchase of Krug into a success. But after being starved of capital investment for many years, the winery was in shambles. Although the stone exterior was intact, the interior walls were crumbling and the floors were dirt. There were cracks in the wall dating back to the earthquake of 1906. Before the Mondavis could start making wine there, they needed to build new supports for the structure and cement the floor immediately.

Finding the materials to do this—in the midst of wartime shortages—wasn't easy. So in the first few months after buying the old Krug place, Robert made many trips between St. Helena and San Francisco. Frustrated at not making much progress, he camped at the War Board in San Francisco daily for an entire week until he finally managed to persuade the federal agency overseeing supplies for private industry to let him buy lumber, steel, and cement to restore the old winery building. During the Mondavis' first crush at Krug in the fall of 1943, the cement floors were still drying.

Within a year, the Mondavis had recouped the $75,000 purchase price. During the war years, the price of bulk wines was frozen at 28 cents a gallon but the price of bottled wines could fluctuate and thus could be sold for much more per gallon. They decided to sell their better wine under the Charles Krug label because the name was well known and happened to be the same as that of a famous champagne house in France. The family also decided to launch a lower-priced wine under the CK label, initially using the bulk wine from Sunny St. Helena to fill the bottles. Robert's idea of bottling bulk wine from Sunny St. Helena and selling it for more worked beautifully.

Krug's reputation soared after Peter Mondavi returned from the war. Assigned to working production, Peter resumed the work he'd begun at UC Berkeley in cold fermentation. Krug began producing distinctive wines that won medals at the California State Fair and other wine competitions. The family resisted producing sweet wines, which were still the top sellers in the 1940s and 1950s, and instead focused on drier wines from specific varieties of grapes. The Mondavis won their first gold medal in 1949 at the California State Fair for its Traminer white wine, a crisp, early drinking varietal that's better known now as Gewürztraminer. By the mid-1950s the winery was receiving national attention. *Life* magazine, for one, staged a tasting in which its judges chose Krug's Traminer as the best of the lot, rating it "remarkable," "surprisingly clean," and "the best California white wine." The "Mondavi boys"—as they came to be called—were on a roll. Robert's marketing savvy in entering Krug wine in competitions and Peter's technical prowess were a winning combination.

The *Life* article was followed by stories in *Newsweek* and *Consumer Reports*. The publicity helped them sell more wine and when the family finally paid off the original loan that had allowed them to buy Charles Krug, they celebrated by hosting a potluck supper for themselves and their workers. They dug a fire pit in front of one of the houses and roasted a wild pig that the ranch's caretaker had shot earlier that morning. The workers' wives brought casseroles to share and the Mondavis laid dozens of bottles of wine down the center of wood tables covered with red-and-white cotton tablecloths. Toward the end of the evening, the usually taciturn Cesare rose from his seat to toast his children's contributions to the success of the winery (in those early years his daughters helped out as well, with Mary keeping the books and Helen working as Robert's secretary).

Raising his wineglass, he made a spare but eloquent toast to the efforts of his four children. "*Elena, Maria, Roberto e Pietro, bravo, bravo. Grazie e ti amo.*"

CHAPTER TWO

France, 1943–1963

Soon tourists began seeking out Charles Krug. The Mondavis became one of the first wine families in the valley to open up a visitors' center to let people sample wines on the grounds. They also quickly embraced a new craze called the "wine-tasting party"—hosting one in 1958 on the Krug grounds with the Northcoast Prestige Wine Society. Though 1950s America was still a beer, milk, and whiskey-drinking nation, wine consumption was rising, in part because of the postwar drop in import duties aimed at helping the European wineries get back on their feet. Also, some returning GIs had developed a taste for fine wine while stationed in Europe.

The winery also attracted a little Hollywood glitter when crews used the grounds of Charles Krug as well as many other Napa Valley sites to film *This Earth Is Mine*. Starring Rock Hudson, Claude Rains, and Jean Simmons, the movie had a steamy plot involving the travails of three generations of a Napa Valley winemaking dynasty. In it, the patriarch, played by Claude Rains, stubbornly insists on crafting his family's fine wines the time-tested way, while his grandson, played by Rock Hudson, pushes to boost profits through questionable business practices. Conflict arises among the family members and romantic complications ensue.

It was a story line that would become familiar to many of Napa's winemaking families in later years.

Meanwhile, the Mondavis were producing what they hoped would become the third generation of their own business dynasty: Marcia Anne was born in St. Helena to Robert and Marjorie on July 16, 1947, and their youngest child, Timothy John, was born April 11, 1951. Robert and Marjorie's three children grew up on the Charles Krug ranch, using the tanks and wine barrels as their playground. They wore rubber boots through much of the winter and walked on the wooden planks laid out between the buildings, to avoid the dark mud. Michael Mondavi recalled that from the time he was about three, the winery's cellar master would baby-sit him, a memory that reflects the fact that his father was constantly working and traveling in those days.

In the meantime, Peter had married a divorcée named Blanche, who had a young daughter from her first marriage. Within a few years, the couple had two sons as well: Marc, who was born in July 1954, and Peter junior, who was born in January 1958. Because Robert had been at Krug from the very beginning, he and his family occupied one of the two rustic homes on the ranch. The other, known as the "brown house," was set aside for Cesare and Rosa, who continued to live on West Pine Street in Lodi but often visited their children and grandchildren in St. Helena.

Slowly, changes began taking place in the way Robert and Peter ran the winery. As early as the 1940s, they arranged blind tastings of Krug and Mondavi wines against other brands for the winery staff, an innovation at the time. In 1951, they took that same idea and expanded on it. At an annual "Tastings on the Lawn," which was open to the public, the family compared Krug wines against rivals on the ranch's spacious lawn. Robert's philosophy from his earliest days at Krug had been to do only minimal advertising for its more expensive wines, focusing instead on urging people to taste them and decide for themselves. It was this hands-on, intensely personal and local marketing that would become the hallmark of the "boutique" winery movement of the 1960s and 1970s.

Soon after, the family converted an old storage shed on the ranch into a hospitality room—painting the walls white and setting out some tables. In the early 1950s, tasting wines at a winery was a novel idea. The Mondavis served cheese and crackers along with their wines, and on some weekends hundreds of people would flock there. Napa Valley became a weekend getaway for San Franciscans and for even the occasional movie star, such as Clark Gable. Krug's innovative tastings were part of the first small groundswell of interest in visiting the Valley.

During this time, the Mondavis launched one of the first winery newsletters, "Bottles & Bins." Written by their tour guide, Frank "Paco" Gould, in a breezy style and published sporadically ("Uncorked and poured from time to time" was its motto), the newsletter offered recipes and chat about Charles Krug wine, as well as news from Napa Valley. By 1952, it was being mailed to seven thousand wine lovers across the country. Gould, who sported a beret and was a frequent traveler to Europe, became a legendary public relations man who helped elevate the Napa Valley above other grape-growing regions.

With Gould's help, Charles Krug became better known. And the ranch, with its massive oaks, graceful lawns, and wisteria and orange trees, was slowly becoming more than the Mondavis' home and workplace; it was now also a tourist attraction. The family would return from church on Sundays to find visitors wandering in their homes and across their lawns. In turn, the Mondavi kids would have fun with the tourists, spying and shooting peas at them while crouched on the catwalks of the Redwood Cellar, an enormous, four-story cupola-topped building where the family stored and bottled its wines.

Although they had come from the Central Valley and had started in the bulk wine business, the Mondavis had begun distinguishing their wines from the product that was most commonly served in American homes through their tastings, concerts, and newsletters. At that time, most American wines were sold in jugs, quality was marginal by today's standards, and consumption was minuscule. Sweet wines were still more popular than dry table wines and winemaking in the U.S. remained, for the most part, a low-margin commodity business dominated by the Central Valley's bulk wine producers—Italian Swiss Colony in Asti, Roma Wine Company in Lodi and Fresno, and Ernest and Julio Gallo in Modesto. The Napa Valley had only a few big names: Inglenook, Beaulieu Vineyard, Beringer Brothers, Louis Martini, and, increasingly, Charles Krug.

Driving to work from his home in town, Peter would veer off the main road and turn right onto a dirt lane that led to the Krug Ranch and its grand rows of Dutch elm trees leading to the winery. Flanked by Howell Mountain to the east and the Mayacamas to the west, its properties' vast vineyards seemed to disappear when they were shrouded in the winter mist.

On days when such otherworldly beauty took hold, it was not difficult to believe the old stories about its past. In one of these tales, a daughter of Charles Krug had been secretly buried on the grounds, after being impregnated by a Chinese laborer. The girl's bones are said to lie beneath a stone statue that had long stood between the ranch's two homes, the one occupied by Rosa and Cesare when they visited from Lodi, and the other where Robert and his family lived. The legend is that her ghost still haunts the ranch, unable to achieve its final rest.

By the late 1950s, the Mondavi family was struggling to keep its own skeletons buried. As Peter each day drove past the home where his brother, Robert, and his family had lived nearly rent-free for more than a decade, his resentment began to build. Although Robert's home was very modest by today's standards and had no central heat for the first twenty years he lived there, its bucolic setting of lawns and massive oaks was grander than the one-story colonial that Peter and Blanche had built for themselves across from St. Helena's middle school on a small corner lot.

It was a discrepancy that was impossible to ignore. But Peter's resentment and jealousy toward his brother grew for other reasons as well. Peter felt that Robert got all the credit for Krug's success, while he seemed to get very little recognition for making the wine. Newspapers and magazines photographed Robert, while ignoring Peter. Robert also drove a nicer car, earned a higher salary, and was invited to glamorous events. But the reasons for the tension between the brothers went deeper than just press attention or perceived slights. It had its roots in a business crisis that nearly toppled Charles Krug shortly after the end of the war.

Peter had been stationed in England, which suffered terrible food shortages during the war. Rosa sent him eggs that she dipped in paraffin wax over and over again to try to protect them during the journey from California to the United Kingdom. For long stretches, London came under nightly air attacks from the Germans, and some members of the Mondavi family feared that Peter would not survive the war.

When Peter returned to the States to join Krug in 1946, he found the adjustment difficult. His confidence was shaken and he was initially confused by the hodgepodge of grape varieties then under production at Krug. "I was wondering if I was fit for anything anymore," Peter recalled.

Robert would later claim that he had to teach Peter everything about winemaking from scratch when he returned from England. Because the brothers never formally sat down and decided who would do what, they slipped back into the roles that they'd had as children: Robert, the dominant older son, and Peter, the quiet and reserved younger child. As employees of a family business, their roles were unequal. As the older brother who had been working at the winery from the start, Robert held the title of general manager, making him his brother's boss.

Perhaps a rupture was inevitable, considering the brothers' opposing personalities. Robert was a natural salesman and promoter and outwardly never seemed to lack self-confidence. His family used to joke that he could "wear a grape stake down just by talking," and when his sister Helen was his secretary, she would urge him to reel in his loquaciousness by jokingly asking him: "Bobby, are you dictating a letter or writing a book?" With a tight, compact body set on bowed legs, dark complexion, and piercing gaze, Robert was attractive to women, despite a nose that was a little too pronounced and a high-pitched voice that could grow tiresome over a long evening. Men found him charismatic and likable.

His brother left a very different impression. Soft-spoken and methodical in his decision making, Peter could appear slow or indecisive. But he tended to be the more analytical of the two Mondavi boys and was the one who was more comfortable with academic learning. He was restrained in his manners and more comfortable grappling with technical details than making sales calls or entertaining visitors. With his rimless spectacles, he looked bookish, as well as slightly feminine with his pale, round face and full lips.

Never much of a traveler after his experiences during the war, Peter preferred to stay close to home. He only spent about a week a year in New York on business. Robert would get up to greet visitors and warmly shake their hands or embrace them, Peter would stay behind his desk, seemingly uncomfortable with physical contact. Family-oriented and on the quiet side, Peter could also be stubborn. Once he made up his mind, he seldom changed it.

Although Robert had put several people in place who were officially in charge of making the wine, Peter slowly began to take on more responsibility, eventually becoming production manager. He again began applying the lessons about cold fermentation he'd learned at UC Berkeley—the colder the temperature at which white wine was fermented, the fruitier and better the quality. He took his attention to detail so far as to throw big blocks of ice in the winery's cooling tower during a heat wave, to make sure the temperature of the fermenting juice didn't rise too high.

But Peter's cautiousness would clash with Robert's ambition to improve the quality of Krug wines.

It wasn't long before Peter gained some ammunition for what would become a bitter campaign against his brother.

The winery had turned a modest profit in its first few years but ran into serious difficulties after the war. Because of surging demand after World War II, the price of bulk wines had tripled, shooting up to $1.50 a gallon. In mid-1946, the Mondavis were locked into sales contracts with a number of the eastern wine distributors that Cesare had done business with for years. To supply the wine to these important customers, Robert agreed to make large grape purchases from local growers. He also bought an extra hundred thousand gallons of wine at $1.25 a gallon.

As Peter remembers it, his father had warned Robert not to buy all those grapes. But Robert had in fact discussed with Cesare the big commitments he was making and got the go-ahead from him. By February of 1947, prices for bulk wines plunged radically to 50 cents a gallon and the eastern distributors broke their contracts. As a result, the Mondavis were stuck with a loss of some $371,000—driving Krug to the brink of financial disaster.

Instead of suing these important, long-standing customers and risking the possibility of losing their business in the future, the Mondavis chose to absorb the full loss. More strikingly, they also made the tough decision to stick by the promises they had made to their growers and pay them full price for their grapes—demonstrating a personal integrity that would be remembered for years afterward.

But that integrity came at a high cost: Robert and his father scrambled to sell inventory and slash expenses. Despite the belt-tightening, by December of 1947, Krug was struggling under the enormous $600,000 debt. The Mondavis worked hard to bring that down and within the year, they had reduced the amount by nearly two-thirds, to $230,000.

Still, that reversal was one of the reasons that the Bank of America eventually forced Krug to warehouse its receipts—a form of financial control which meant that each time the winery wanted to sell wine, it had to seek permission from the bank to do so. Charles Krug remained in this humiliating state of financial restraint from the early 1950s until 1961, requiring family members to make trips to the warehousing office to get receipts to satisfy their bankers at the St. Helena branch of the Bank of America.

Robert's mistake infuriated Peter, who remained bitter about it for years afterward. "That decision by Bob set us back ten to fifteen years," Peter says, recalling the incident some six decades later. "When the banks got tough on him [Robert], I gave him my full support—I told him we'd work it out. But as things got better, he got more active, more expansive in what he wanted to do. He got his confidence back—he's a salesman. He was on the promoter side and the rest of the family was on the more conservative side."

In the late forties, shortly after the near disaster with the grape contracts, Peter turned to Cesare to vent his rage. In a meeting with Cesare and Robert in the high-ceilinged "great room" of the home on the ranch, where his father and mother stayed on weekends and in the summer, Peter demanded that his brother be removed as general manager and that the two of them be put on equal footing at the winery.

The Mondavi patriarch, who was sitting at the family's large dining table, responded quietly but firmly.

"If you bring this up one more time, I will fire you," he warned Peter.

Then, Cesare turned to his older son.

"If you makes another mistake like this," he said, "he won't have to ask me to fire you."

Cesare had a quiet authority that neither son dared to challenge. But the relationship between Robert and Peter steadily worsened through the 1950s. Robert complained that the wines Peter made were oxidized—giving them an off flavor. Robert also noted that the weekly in-house professional tastings on Monday evenings had come to a halt. As well, Robert claimed that Peter was unable to delegate responsibility and had failed to do the quality checks that might have avoided such problems as oxidation. Peter, in turn, wanted Krug to remain a small wine operation, blaming the quality problems on his brother's quest to expand production too quickly. Peter also felt that Robert was spending too much on promotional and business expenses as he traveled around the country.

The head-butting between the brothers reached a turning point in

1958, when reports started coming in from the sales staff in the field that Krug's wines were flat-tasting and oxidized. Customers had begun to complain. At the same time, Peter's production staff was struggling to meet delivery schedules and the morale of employees at the ranch was at a low. This time, Robert turned to his father in a bid to halt what he considered the desperate deterioration in Krug's operations. Cesare sided with his oldest son and not only gave Robert overall control of the winery's operations as general manager but also put him in charge of production personnel—an area that had been Peter's realm.

Peter was infuriated. In September 1958, he left the winery operations for five months, calling on various company accounts and doing public relations work. His time away from the ranch could have served as a cooling off period between the brothers. But when he returned to the winery in February 1959, he was just as angry as before. The seeds of Peter's bitterness and resentment toward Robert had begun to germinate.

During this time, Cesare's physical and mental health had begun deteriorating. While behind the wheel of his DeSoto, he slipped into a diabetic coma as he was heading to Fresno to meet some growers. His car veered out of control, jumping the curb and hitting and killing an elderly female pedestrian. Cesare himself was badly injured in the crash, breaking his nose, ribs, and both legs, as well as losing many of his teeth. He spent months in bed and suffered from guilt for what had happened. It was a tragedy that would shadow this proud immigrant man for the few remaining years of his life.

Cesare had always been a man of few words. But he almost never spoke after the accident and spent the rest of his life virtually in mourning because of the death. Michael Mondavi, who was then approaching adolescence, also remembers his grandfather as becoming deeply somber after the tragedy. He relied more and more on "Uncle Pete," who served as a driver, handyman, friend, and later the vineyard foreman at Krug. At the end of the work day, the deeply reserved Cesare would settle into his rocking chair on the front porch of his Lodi home and silently nurse his Old Fashioned.

Cesare turned over all of his business interests to Robert, perhaps earlier than he might otherwise have done, because of the auto accident. He traded in his DeSoto for a Cadillac and asked Uncle Pete or someone else to drive him when he went on business trips. He also voluntarily sent the victim's family money and paid them visits. But his decline continued. In mid-November of 1959, Cesare suffered a heart attack. After two weeks in the St. Helena Sanitarium and Hospital, the same place where five of his grandchildren had been born, Cesare died on the cold afternoon of Sunday, November 29, 1959, at age seventy-six, as a tule fog shrouded the vineyards. That evening, Rosa sat at the head of the table as the family silently ate their strawberries in red wine.

The local newspaper, *The St. Helena Star*, marked Cesare's passing with only a small obituary, perhaps because the family was not socially prominent at that time. But during the Requiem High Mass that was held at the St. Helena Catholic Church three days later, Cesare's casket bearers included Paul Alexander—the banker from the St. Helena branch of the Bank of America who had helped him buy the Charles Krug Winery. During the long service, Rosa was overcome with grief. The black-clad widow of Cesare Mondavi threw herself on her husband's coffin, crying and wailing. Cesare was buried at Holy Cross Cemetery—the first family member to be buried in the Mondavis' newly established family crypt.

After Cesare's death, Rosa inherited control of the winery, becoming its president. Charles Krug had been held by a family partnership, C. Mondavi and Sons, with Cesare and Rosa owning 40 percent of the stock, their two sons each owning 20 percent, and their daughters each owning 10 percent. The difference in shares reflected Cesare's view of the relative contributions that each of his offspring had made to the business: He had considered Robert's and Peter's to be equally important, while his daughters—who were married and living elsewhere in California—were not deeply involved in its operations.

In late 1959, Helen moved herself and her teenage children, Serena and Peter, from Beverly Hills to the San Francisco suburb of Hillsborough. Long divorced from her children's straying father, Henry Ventura, she moved to be closer to Rosa and the rest of her family. Yet, in the rainy spring of 1960, not long after they had unpacked their boxes, Helen suffered the first of a series of emotional collapses.

Not only did Cesare's death shake Helen and the rest of the Mondavis' emotional terrain, it also created a leadership vacuum in the family. Without their father to arbitrate between them, Robert and Peter's disagreements began to build upon each other and their arguments became more and more frequent. "Slowly, the pot began to boil between the two boys," says Peter Ventura, Helen's son. "But this time, there was nobody to take care of it."

Rosa tried to step into that role. But she consistently seemed to side with Peter, the baby of the family. She insisted that Robert treat Peter as an equal in the business, even though Robert was older, more experienced, and had been Peter's boss for more than a decade.

Having been cast in a lesser role all his life grated on Peter. Throughout his childhood, he had lived with the nickname "Babe." To his dismay, his identity as the youngest in the family clung to him through adulthood. Peter strongly disliked the name and had tried to convince the family to stop using it when he went to Stanford, but his request was ignored. To this day, some people in the Mondavi family, as well as longtime Napa Valley residents, continue to call him "Babe" or "Uncle Babe."

In addition to being older, Robert was also more driven than his younger brother. That became clear in 1962, when Robert took his very first trip to Europe in what would be a pivotal moment for the Mondavis and the history of winemaking in California. Over several weeks, he and Marjorie visited forty-eight wineries—at company expense—including many of the continent's great wine-producing estates in Bordeaux, Burgundy, Tuscany, and Germany's Moselle region. Robert couldn't help but compare the Europeans' focus on handcrafting their wines and using small oak barrels to add depths of flavor and complexity with the American focus on technology and mass production. Held against the European wines he had tasted, he realized that not only his family's tank wines, but also its better table wines, were still far outclassed.

Robert and Marjorie also got their first taste of the good life on that trip. The couple traveled to a small village outside Lyons. Shaded by plane trees and graced by a walled garden scented by the northern Rhône, their destination was La Pyramide in Vienne, one of the world's greatest restaurants. Under owner and chef Ferdinand Point, La Pyramide was the training ground for many of France's most famous cooks, including Paul Bocuse and Pierre and Michel Troisgros. As they settled into their seats, savoring the thought of the meal ahead of them, their waiter brought their first course, a sole from the Saône River that was "floating in butter," as Robert described it. "The sole was light, delicate, and full of flavor—we finished it all," despite having had a large breakfast a few hours earlier. The couple moved on to their next course, a chicken Alexandria, and then the desserts. They ate everything but felt better than when they had arrived. The food was full and flavorful but not over-powering or heavy, and accompanied by wonderful wines. Robert real-ized that Krug's wines could also be made with the same lightness and subtlety.

It was a life-changing meal for Robert, a far cry from the sturdy, home-cooked meals and rough wines that he'd grown up with in Min-nesota and Lodi. For the first time he had experienced the subtle and graceful pairing of foods and wines in course after course. For years after-ward, he would retell the story of how dining at La Pyramide just once had changed his thinking about what a sublime experience eating fine food and drinking gracious wines could be. He returned from that trip convinced that his family should aim higher and produce truly fine wines, rather than the jug variety that they had mostly sold. Robert was con-vinced that conditions in California for producing fine wines was equal to or perhaps even better than in Europe. By adapting techniques and learn-ing from the Old World, he felt certain that California winemakers could improve their quality.

In part, Robert was swept up in the Francophilia that engulfed America in those years. It was a time when Jacqueline Bouvier Kennedy, the glam-orous first lady, became a trendsetter by wearing fashions designed by Chanel, Givenchy, and Christian Dior, prompting her husband to intro-duce himself at a press luncheon as "the man who accompanied Jacque-line Kennedy to Paris." Likewise, the American food world fell in love with France. In 1961, when McDonald's and other fast food chains were multiplying and many Americans were drinking Coca-Cola and eating TV dinners, *Mastering the Art of French Cooking* became a best seller.

The book's coauthor, a Californian living in Paris named Julia Child, led the charge, bringing a new awareness of food and wine into many homes. A few years later, in 1966, a young American student named Alice Waters would have a similar revelatory dining experience at a country inn in Brittany, just as Robert had had at La Pyramide. When Waters opened Chez Panisse in Berkeley in 1969, she would consciously model it on the French cooking she had found so inspiring during her time abroad, par-ticularly its use of fresh local ingredients.

But while worldly Americans were embracing all things French during that period, Robert was ahead of his time compared to many of his fellow winemakers, who continued to sell relatively low-quality bulk wines and saw no reason to change. In the early 1960s, as the wine historian Paul Lukacs has written, the overwhelming majority of American wines being produced were either "misery market" fortifieds, such as Thunderbird and Ripple, or undistinguished table blends, helping to explain why President Kennedy's decision to order U.S. embassies around the world to serve only American wines in the early 1960s came as a shock to the wine world. With a few exceptions—wines made by Beaulieu Vineyards, Inglenook, Louis M. Martini, and Charles Krug—the American wine industry still churned out oceans of mediocre juice.

Against that backdrop, Robert's aspiration to produce even higher quality French-style wines put him on the cusp of a powerful trend. Even though some of Krug's profits and most of its sales came from its lower-priced CK line, Robert had years before befriended the valley's preeminent champion for quality, John Daniel, who became a mentor.

With his characteristic enthusiasm, Robert pushed hard for changes when he returned home to St. Helena. He felt an evangelical fervor about his beliefs and was not particularly diplomatic with the family about communicating them. He didn't present his family with a plan to discuss: Instead, he returned from Europe and declared a new vision he intended to follow—a vision that would in coming decades ultimately shift the balance of power from the great châteaus of Burgundy and Bordeaux toward the new world.

He did not mince words about the areas that he felt were most lacking at Charles Krug: the way it made wine. Because production was Peter's realm, Robert's effort to make the changes he wanted was interpreted as criticism by Peter. Even though Peter, too, was trying to produce better wines, he resented the unilateral way his brother was pushing it.

"I was working like a dog, and he'd come back from a trip and tell me I was doing everything wrong. Meanwhile, he was out promoting, overspending, overprojecting, never catching up with any of his projects. He was uncontrollable!" Peter would say. "There was a big difference between my brother and myself and I did what I could, but it never satisfied [Robert]. . . . I devoted my whole life to this business, for better or worse, but I couldn't satisfy him. He always criticized."

Robert knew that his brother was bridling at his suggestions, but attributed this to what he perceived as Peter's deeply rooted conservatism and stubborn resistance to change. To Robert, it just didn't seem as if Peter shared his ambition to create world-class wines. Underlying this resistance was Peter and his wife Blanche's insistence that more of Charles Krug's profits should be distributed to themselves and other shareholders, instead of being reinvested in marketing and promotion. Peter and Blanche gradually won Rosa, Mary, and Helen, at least initially, to their side of the argument. In effect, while Robert wanted to invest to expand the business, the rest of the Mondavis preferred to keep it as a small family enterprise that paid them larger dividends.

William Bonetti, a longtime California winemaker who worked at Charles Krug in the 1960s, recalled that Robert Mondavi used to say, "One bad wine in the valley is bad for every winery in the valley. One good wine in the valley is good for everyone." Robert maintained that Napa Valley winemakers were in it all together and would be better off cooperating rather than withholding ideas from one another. He set the tone for the cooperative spirit of sharing ideas, equipment, and facilities that helped fuel the valley's explosive rise to fame. It was a spirit that would be largely pushed aside by fiercer competition in the 1980s and 1990s.

It was that reasoning that led Robert to call André Tchelistcheff, the storied winemaker for Beaulieu Vineyard and the one man in Napa Valley who held the secrets to making the greatest French-style wines, to ask him to consult for Charles Krug. A diminutive Russian émigré who had escaped the Revolution after serving as a White Russian cavalry officer in 1918, he had been educated in the best wine school in France and then hired by Georges de Latour, the worldly Frenchman who owned Beaulieu, after meeting him in Paris in 1938. Tchelistcheff had brought a level of precision and skill to winemaking that was unknown at that time in the valley. Tchelistcheff's custom of wearing a white lab coat to work reflected his exacting standards. He was known to gallantly begin kissing a woman's hand at an introduction and proceed with small kisses up to her elbow but was also nicknamed "Stalin" by some of the winemakers who found him intimidating.

"I said, 'André, why don't we form a group of people?'" recalled Robert. "'Let's bring in Louis Martini, Inglenook, Beringer Brothers. Let's have a little seminar, a group where we could meet and exchange the ideas of winemaking so that we can further the cause of winemaking by all of us.'"

That led to the formation of the Napa Valley Technical Group in the 1950s. Although Tchelistcheff was open to the idea of swapping information, some fellow winemakers expressed concerns. "After about the third meeting, one or two of the people said, 'Gee, we're giving away all our secrets.'"

One of those people was Peter. As Krug's assistant production chief Bonetti recalled it, Peter was one of the people who felt it was imprudent to share too much information with competitors. Bonetti felt that Peter was so concerned about keeping his production techniques secret that he cut himself off from learning from other winemakers, comparing the stance to China's decision to build the Great Wall. There were only a few dozen wineries in Napa during the mid-1960s, and unlike later years when the wineries would compete aggressively against one another, the Mondavis and other Napa Valley winemakers at the time were struggling to produce enough wine to meet the surging demand. Against that backdrop, the willingness to share production information with rivals was a key philosophical difference between the brothers.

Likewise, although Peter was ostensibly in charge of production by the early 1960s, Robert retained a keen interest in everything that went on in the winery and cellars. Robert was as far from a hands-off manager as could be, which undoubtedly irked Peter and others. Particularly at times during the year that Peter was in Lodi, supervising the original family business of shipping grapes back East, Robert would keep a close eye on production in his absence. It was Robert, then general manager, who hired Bonetti to serve as assistant production manager under Peter in 1961.

"I remember [Bob Mondavi] used to follow me, watching the temperatures, and watching the fermentation every morning," Bonetti recalled. "I would say, 'Well, tomorrow we have to start at six o'clock,' and by six o'clock, Bob Mondavi was there." Intensely focused and hard working, Robert seemed tireless to people who worked for him, driving them as hard as he drove himself.

Yet while the company had spent heavily on public relations and promotion, it scrimped on the unglamorous production side of the winery, which was Peter's area. The original winery, known as the Redwood Cellar and dating back to 1861, was badly in need of updating. The last big renovation had been in 1957, when the winery installed glass-lined tanks that were better for storing wine than stainless steel, which developed a metallic taste in the vintages. But in the mid-1960s, Krug, like many other wineries, was still fermenting its wine in open-topped tanks, which meant that bugs and other contaminants could fall into it.

The ranch's vineyards were also in a sorry state. They were a mix of old, obscure grape varieties—most of which were no longer popular. Although replanting had gone on in the early years, the fiscal restraint that Krug operated under during the 1950s made replanting difficult. By the mid-1960s, there were still many acres on the ranch that were long overdue for being pulled out entirely and replanted with better varieties.

The few improvements that had been made circled back to public relations. Not long after Robert and Marjorie's trip to Europe, in 1963, Robert decided to upgrade the image Krug presented to its customers. It brought in a plush, reconditioned railroad dining car to serve as a supplementary tasting room. Built in 1914, the car had traveled for years between San Francisco and Reno on the Southern Pacific line and now had a view of the family's vineyards from its windows. In a Saturday evening ceremony with champagne, the Mondavis christened it "Rose of the Vineyard," in honor of the family matriarch who had become the company's largest shareholder after Cesare's death.

It was not a successful venture, though, perhaps because of the railcar's tendency to heat up during the summer months. With a semicircular bar in the center of the seventy-five-foot carriage, some family members later dubbed it "Mondavi's Miscarriage." But although the carriage was not a hit, the winery's popularity as a tourist destination continued to grow, with seventy thousand people visiting the winery in 1964, up from fifty thousand in 1960.

The Mondavis also began making a few key production changes. During his trip to Europe, Robert had discovered that French winemakers used small, 50- to 300-gallon oak barrels to store and age their wines. In contrast, when the Mondavis bought Charles Krug, they had also bought huge, old-fashioned redwood tanks. The original tanks, which were decrepit with age, were soon replaced—but also with redwood tanks, which were then used for many years to make the everyday wine, the smallest holding 9,600 gallons and the largest more than 36,000 gallons. Such large redwood tanks were typical for Napa at that time.

Winemakers in the valley were beginning to realize that aging wines in redwood was not ideal because of the risk of oxidation and discoloration. As well, oak imparts a subtler flavor to wine than redwood. So

Robert wanted to invest in new barrels. But the brothers initially disagreed on the kinds of barrels they should use. Robert wanted fresh French oak barrels, which were more expensive than the used oak barrels Peter had initially preferred. Peter's choice, while not as flavorful, would have saved money. Robert, as general manager, won the argument and Krug ended up placing an order for 125 barrels of different oaks with Demptos, a famous Bordeaux-based barrel maker that had been supplying the world's leading winemakers since 1825.

The winery tried out the wines in the different barrels and learned that the origins of the wood, as well as how it had been toasted, or aged, made a big difference in how the wines ended up tasting. So Krug started aging some of its wines in smaller oak barrels in 1963, a key step in giving them the complexity that Robert had discovered in the European wines. Although Sonoma County's Hanzell, a hobby winery owned by the forest products executive James D. Zellerbach, had led the way nearly a decade earlier, Charles Krug became the first large-scale California winery to age wine in French oak. As with cold fermentation and the tastings on the lawn, the brothers in later accounts disagreed over who had played the leading role in each of these innovations.

CHAPTER THREE

East of Eden, 1963–1965

In 1963, the tense relationship between the brothers would explode over a mink coat. Robert and Marjorie received a gold-embossed invitation from President Kennedy and his glamorous wife, Jackie, to join them at a state dinner at the White House in honor of the president of Italy, scheduled for November. The Mondavis had been invited as prominent Italian-Americans and Robert, to the dismay of the rest of the family, had assumed the honor was only meant for him and his wife. After they had accepted the invitation, it quickly became a source of concern: What would Marjorie wear? And how would Robert, who then earned around $24,000 a year, be able to afford it?

The couple went shopping together at what was then the most sophisticated department store in San Francisco: I. Magnin and Company. Initially, they didn't find anything that was quite right—until a saleslady suggested that Marjorie try on a mink coat, with the wildly expensive price tag of $5,000. It fit beautifully and the Mondavis felt it was just the right thing for the event—but the couple decided against buying it because it was so expensive. As weeks passed, Marjorie still hadn't found a coat to wear, and they returned to I. Magnin to discover that it had gone on sale and its price had dropped 50 percent. Even so, the $2,500 price tag was a huge amount for a family with three young children.

Robert decided to buy the coat and put it on his company expense account, with the intention of scrimping and saving in other areas to pay back Charles Krug. While that decision may have been defensible in the sense that it was important for the couple, as representatives of the family business, to look their best at the White House, Robert's decision to expense the coat without getting approval from the rest of the family first was hardly diplomatic.

When Peter and his wife, Blanche, heard about the purchase, they were stunned. Blanche, who was a divorcée with a young daughter when Peter married her, rode her second husband hard on how his brother seemed to get all the invitations and take all the glamorous trips while she and Peter stayed at home. On top of Robert and Marjorie's trip to Europe and their lunch at La Pyramide, this seemed to be more evidence of Robert's irresponsible spending. Envy, too, may have played a role in Peter and Blanche's perspective on the purchase: Why, after all, had Robert and Marjorie been invited and they had not? And why had the company paid for Marjorie's expensive mink coat while not paying for one for Blanche?

The issue simmered as Robert and Marjorie's trip to the White House for dinner was postponed after President Kennedy's assassination. Robert and Marjorie did eventually attend a state dinner in honor of the slight, white-haired president Antonio Segni of Italy and his wife two months later in the company of such notables as baseball star Joe DiMaggio, composer Gian Carlo Menotti, and pundit Walter Lippmann. As the first state dinner hosted by the new president Lyndon Johnson and his wife, Lady Bird, the White House presented what one observer described as a "musical program of probably the greatest extremes ever witnessed at a presidential dinner"—a rendition of Verdi, followed by a rousing hootenanny. Marjorie looked elegant in the mink coat that would later touch off a family furor.

Despite the mounting tension between their fathers, Rosa held the family together, and her grandchildrens' memories of the 1960s are happy ones, particularly of the summers they spent together on the ranch and in Lodi. The extended family stayed in touch with its Central Valley roots, even after Cesare's death. During Lodi's annual harvest festival, the Mondavis would gather at Rosa's home on West Pine Street to watch the festival parade. The grown-ups would sit on the porch and steps, while the cousins would perch on the roof above them to get a better view.

The families spent much of the summer together in Lodi, where the heat could rise to an oppressive 103 or 104 degrees during the day. But when they were on the family compound at the Krug Ranch, they'd head to the Napa River, where they'd catch frogs, and fish for sunfish and perch with bobbers. On the Fourth of July, the Mondavis often spent the evening with the Martini family at their nearby winery, the children running around the woods in the pitch-dark night while their parents sipped their drinks and had their own supper, serenaded by the sound of crickets and bullfrogs. For a night out, both Peter and Blanche and Robert and Marjorie were regulars at the square dancing clubs that thrived in St. Helena in the 1960s, a vestige of rural simplicity.

Prunes were still the primary crop and St. Helena's schools sometimes closed during those years to allow children to help out with the harvest. The town's population was just a few thousand people and while it was safe—the Mondavi kids would ride their bicycles to school along St. Helena's elm-lined Main Street and gather after school and on weekends at the A&W Root Beer stand—it also had its prejudices. Robert's eldest son, Michael, was a little embarrassed to tell people his family was in the wine business, because it was then still mostly an immigrant occupation.

Whether she was in Lodi or at the ranch, Rosa spent most of her day in the kitchen, humming happily as she made delicious homemade gnocchi—potato dumplings—with dark, rich sauces made from the quail, duck, and even robins that the boys would shoot from the trees for her. She would strip the meat from the jack rabbits that the boys caught for her: They considered them pests since they'd nibble from the low-hanging grapes. Rosa would also sometimes kill a chicken herself. She'd swing it above her head and then stab it with an ice pick, draining its blood into a pot. Always frugal, she would boil the blood and serve it as a side dish with bacon and onions.

"Nonna," as she was known, never got her driver's license and so, to do her marketing, she would have her sons or grandsons, once they were old enough, drive her to St. Helena to visit the butcher, the baker, and the other merchants in town.

During the Christmas season, the Mondavi cousins would take turns driving Rosa to St. Helena's Main Street, where the shopkeepers would offer their customers cookies, punch, and wine in the back of their stores. "Everyone was speaking Italian" back then, Peter Jr. recalls. Peter, who is known in the family as "Pete," had begun working at the winery when he was eight, unwrapping wineglasses from tissue paper that would be part of the Christmas gift baskets that the winery sold. His older brother, Marc, would assemble gift baskets on the third floor of the creaky and vast Redwood Cellar as a kid.

Every Easter, the Mondavis would stage elaborate egg hunts on the grounds of the ranch—with the older cousins hiding eggs in the gardens or in the Redwood Cellar if it was raining. With catwalks, spiderwebs, and a cupola with a 365-degree view of the vineyards, the winery offered plenty of places for the children to hide and search for colored eggs. The extended family gathered around the table at three P.M. every Sunday for a large home-cooked meal Rosa prepared. The adults might not lay their napkins on their laps and wipe their mouths to finish until four or five hours later. In between courses, the kids would play bocce ball on the lawn. After the meal, someone would usually bring out an accordion; they'd literally roll up the rugs and dance on the wooden floors.

One summer, Timothy and his cousin Marc built a track for Timothy's new gas-fired go-cart. They raced it around the ranch. "We tore up the lawns and got chewed out for it," says Marc. "It's a wonder nobody got killed." Marc says that Nonna, his father, Peter, and Robert seemed to take turns disciplining the boys. Nonna would pull out her yardstick and wave it around threateningly, thwacking the boys with it every now and then.

The cousins spent hours each day during the summer in the swimming pool. And while the Mondavi kids were not brought up to feel they were wealthy, they enjoyed certain amenities. Although Rosa did all the cooking, she had a full-time housekeeper who would serve the family, many of whom worked at the winery, their several-course lunch each day. In good weather, they'd eat under the spreading oaks, on a rollaway table covered in a red-and-white checked tablecloth, near the front door of Nonna's home. If woodpeckers began making a racket during lunch, Peter, Michael, and sometimes their cousin James would get their BB guns and try to shoot them—at least until their grandmother put a stop to that practice.

"Stop shooting the house, boys," she'd admonish, gesturing with both hands, with a smile on her lips. By then in her seventies, Rosa was broad-hipped and full-bosomed, favoring wash-and-wear jersey dresses and plain, comfortable shoes. She kept the waves of her thick gray hair pinned behind her ears and wore a thin wedding band. She cooked, gardened, and ran the home where she and her brother, Nazzareno Grassi, lived together after Cesare's death. For fun she'd play *scopa*, an Italian card game, and black jack, occasionally cheating to win. When she was dealing, she'd stack the cards in her favor, then slap her winning combination down and proclaim, "Blacka Jacka!" She also loved to watch Lawrence Welk, and attended the monthly dinner dance at the Native Sons of Italy Hall in St. Helena.

Not every aspect of the Mondavi grandchildren's lives was so idyllic. Michael struggled as a student in St. Helena's public school system and spent little time with his father, who traveled constantly. "I was a bad student in a bad school system," Michael says, explaining why his parents decided to send him to a boarding school in the Ojai Valley in the sixth grade. From that time on, Michael traveled back and forth between school and the Krug Ranch.

Michael moved on to Bellarmine Preparatory, a Jesuit high school, where he joined the football team and played offensive guard. He was a fearless player who wouldn't hesitate at going up against boys much bigger than he was, even though by his final years in high school he was a well-put-together six-footer with an athletic build. Although Michael was outgoing, he didn't often let on that he was from a family that was well off.

Bellarmine was an academically rigorous prep school, with two to three hours of homework per night. Perhaps because of the heavy workload, students liked to blow off steam by pulling pranks, such as lifting up someone else's VW and sticking it between two trees. The acronym for the school disciplinary approach was JUG—an acronym for "Judgment Under God." Students would say they "got JUGged," meaning they'd been disciplined by a teacher. Most of the time punishment entailed memorizing a passage of a text or an obscure snatch of poetry. Day students, who made up about half of Bellarmine's student body, were known as "day dogs."

At his graduation from Bellarmine, Michael recalls receiving several awards, including one for being his class's most improved student. When his father, who attended the ceremonies, learned of the award, he commented, "Oh, my God, I didn't think you had it in you." Robert's cruel remark stung his son, though later Michael would say he didn't think his father intended to wound him. "I think it was his lack of understanding of how to be a father," Michael says now. "One thing you can say is my father never had an excess of sensitivity. It just was not in his DNA."

By 1965, all three of Robert and Marjorie's children were away at college or boarding high schools. Michael, then in his early twenties, was in his final year at the University of Santa Clara, a Jesuit college on the Peninsula just south of San Francisco. Marcia, eighteen in 1965, was completing her senior year at Santa Catalina School for Girls in Monterey, a boarding school, and had been accepted into the University of Santa Clara. Timothy, just fourteen then, was in his first year of Bellarmine Prep.

Michael, Marcia, and Timothy were all boarders. But during the summers, they would return to the ranch and work at the winery. Michael, in particular, began working in Krug's repair shop from eighth grade on and then, when he turned eighteen, worked for several summers alongside his cousin Peter Ventura as a "cellar rat," as Cesare had—doing the toughest, dirtiest jobs there were in the winery. "My father's instructions to Mike Bertolucci, who was the cellar master then, was to give me the dirty jobs and the hard jobs and if I came home and complained, then Mike was doing a good job," Michael said.

Wearing boots and coveralls, they'd scrub the tops, insides, and underneath the huge redwood tanks, encrusted with years of layered sugars, yeast, and mold, where many of Krug's wines were still made. They also played the occasional prank, particularly on the staffers in lab coats who tested the wine. One time, they took the car of one of the lab workers and, with the help of six or eight other workers, lifted it and placed it sideways on a truck ramp so the owner couldn't drive off. Another time, the cousins poured the contents of their buckets over the side of a tank they'd been cleaning on one of the main tour alleys, accidentally drenching a female tourist in the fermenting juice and muck. After their paychecks were docked to pay to clean the dress, the cousins never did that again.

Robert was ambitious for his children and particularly for Michael.

But that may not have been the only reason they were off at boarding schools and college during this time. Robert and Marjorie's marriage was strained by his intense focus on work. At family dinners, Robert would spend the entire meal talking about the winery, despite his sister Helen's suggestion that he leave work behind for a few hours and talk about something other than business. But she seldom succeeded in shifting the conversation away from the family business.

Robert was also a perfectionist who held his family to what they saw as impossibly high standards. Always very sparing with compliments, Robert would focus on the one gold medal out of ten that Peter's production innovations at Krug had not won—rather than on the nine that they did. He'd begin with a compliment, saying, "Gee, Peter, this wine is wonderful, but . . ." followed with criticisms.

His children and wife didn't escape his barbed comments either. Indeed, it took a long time for Michael to understand why his father was so harshly judgmental. "He wasn't picking on you; he was measuring everything against the image of perfection that he carried in his mind—but had never experienced." To Robert, what others viewed as his critical eye, he viewed as his drive to raise the business and the family to a higher level.

Marjorie, to all outward appearances, seemed to simply absorb or ignore her husband's criticisms. With an apron tied around her waist and dressing a salad on the oilcloth-covered kitchen table, Marjorie worked hard to develop her skills as a cook, which could never match those of Robert's mother, Rosa. She'd spend hours in her modest kitchen, with curtained windows and a view out to the garden, tidying up the dishes before calling the family to gather around the dinner table for the evening meal. Robert would take his place at one end of the table and Marjorie at the other, and Robert would begin carving the roast. Marjorie was hoping the meal would please her husband.

"An absolutely beautiful dinner, Marj, but the prime rib could have used more salt," he would say. Or, if she'd prepared a leg of lamb, he'd begin by saying, "Gee, Marj, it was great but . . ." and then launch into wide-ranging criticism for twenty minutes.

Always elegant, Marjorie would look at Robert and smile, maintaining her composure. Around the dinner table, with family and friends present, Marjorie would not strike back. Her restraint in the face of her husband's criticism earned her a reputation for being gracious and lady-like. But Marjorie coped with her hurt feelings in other ways. As early as the 1950s, she was drinking heavily and at one point, family members staged what would now be called an intervention to try to help her with the problem. By the 1960s, people outside the family began to realize Robert's wife was an alcoholic. "Marj was an alcoholic because Robert pushed her that way," says the wine historian William Heintz, echoing the sentiments of other people in the valley, particularly those who ended up siding with Peter in disputes between the brothers. "She couldn't keep up with her husband."

Meanwhile, a vivacious Swiss woman named Margrit Biever, who wore her hair in a thickly braided blond pigtail draped over one shoulder, had joined Krug in the early 1960s, leading tours and helping with public relations. Because the winery was a small operation at that time, Margrit (pronounced Margaret) caught Robert's eye. They danced together at Krug's annual employee Christmas party and Margrit remembers that one of the false eyelashes she was wearing had fallen off without her knowing it and was resting on her cheek. Margrit, who was married and had three children of her own, was also able to connect with the Mondavi family through her interest in food and wine as well as her ability to speak Italian. In some respects, she had gifts similar to Rosa's, including her ability to prepare a beautiful meal and to bring people together at the table.

The tension at the Mondavis' dinner table during those years may have been heightened by Robert's roving eye. Michael, for one, believes his mother had sensed the attraction between her husband and his sparkling, buoyant employee almost from the beginning. Peter's wife, Blanche, noticed, too, her brother-in-law's cocky behavior. That gave her another reason to be critical of most everything that her husband's older brother did—including his constant traveling and tendency to focus al-most solely on work even at home, which seemed to amount to neglect-ing his wife and children. Meanwhile, Marjorie's drinking problem worsened as her marriage began to unravel. So when Peter, Rosa, and other members of the family expressed their views that Robert was un-controllable, they may have meant his private life as well as his expense account.

*　*　*

In early October of 1965, Robert went to Lodi to talk with Peter. The headlines were dominated by Pope Paul VI's visit to the United States and the airwaves were filled with the Beatles' new hit, "Love Me Do." To protest the Vietnam War, student activists had staged the first public burning of a draft card.

Closer to home, there were also big changes taking place; Lodi, the once sleepy town where the Mondavi boys had spent much of their youth, was growing explosively. Highway 99, the site of Cesare's tragic accident in the 1950s, had become a four-lane expressway. A new middle school had opened earlier that year to accommodate the waves of new-comers to the area. In June, voters had passed the first municipal bond measure in forty-four years to fund a new building for the police and fire departments, as well as a new courtroom and sewage treatment plant. But despite the growth, Lodi kept up some of its oldest traditions, including the harvest-time grape festival, which had been held almost every year since 1907.

But on that crisp autumn morning after harvest, as the leaves on the grapevines were reddening, the brothers began to argue over Robert's spending and, specifically, his decision to put Marjorie's mink coat on his company expense account. Peter had once again accused Robert of spending too much company money on travel and promotion. Then Peter, uncharacteristically, exploded and accused Robert of taking money from Charles Krug in order to buy the mink coat, since he doubted that Robert could afford to repay it. Robert was enraged by the implication; his younger brother had dared to call him a thief and a swindler.

"Say that again and I'll hit you," Robert warned him.

Peter said it again.

Then he gave him a third chance. "Take it back."

"No."

Robert swung and struck his younger brother hard. Then he did it again.

By one account, the brothers—both in their fifties by then—ended up wrestling on the ground, dust and curses flying. At some point, Robert had his hands around Peter's neck and throttled him, leaving purple marks on his throat.

When Rosa saw the bruises, she demanded he tell her where he'd gotten them. At first, Peter insisted he didn't know. Then he claimed he had run into a door. Although he was a grown man with children of his own, Peter would always be Rosa's youngest child, in need of her protection as she saw it. Eventually Peter told his mother about how Robert had hit and tried to choke him. That news was the breaking point for Rosa.

After all the years of mounting conflict, the fact that the brothers had come to blows precipitated a family crisis. If this had been merely another argument between the Mondavi boys that had gotten out of hand, that would have been one thing. But it was much more. It was the future of the business itself.

Both sides gathered their armies. Rosa, in her role as matriarch, quickly conferred with the rest of the family about what to do about Robert. She also turned to a prominent San Francisco lawyer, Joseph L. Alioto, who would eventually serve as that city's mayor. A year or two earlier, Alioto had joined the board of the Mondavi family's company at Robert's suggestion. One of his key skills was speaking Italian, which helped in communicating with Rosa, whose Italian was better than her English. As well, the family had brought in Fred Ferroggiaro, who was then chairman of the finance committee of the Bank of America and was a member of the family company's board, to try to mediate the dispute between her sons. Rosa also tapped the well-known management consultancy McKinsey and Company to help the family through the crisis.

Robert had met the McKinsey consultant Douglas Watson on a transcontinental Pan Am flight earlier that year from San Francisco to New York. The men spent the entire six-hour flight talking about the wine industry and how it was changing. Watson was struck at the time by Robert's almost evangelical conviction that Krug's future lay in transforming itself into a high-quality, premium wine producer.

Watson quickly grasped that the young vintner's ambitious vision was sharply at odds with the philosophy of some of his other wine clients, including the California Wine Association, a trade group of mostly Central Valley wine producers who shipped their wines back east. Soon after that conversation, Robert hired McKinsey to review Krug's marketing strategy and prepare a ten-year growth plan. He hoped that the white-shoe firm would agree with him that Krug's future was in the fine-wine business.

Watson and his team interviewed the winery's employees and examined Krug's costs. In 1965, the company had earned a pretax profit of $201,000—almost ten times greater than a year earlier. That fact alone would seem to have bolstered Robert's position as head of the family business, since Krug was booming. Robert had asked McKinsey to weigh in on a relatively simple strategic question: whether Krug should drop its less expensive CK label, which sold most of its wines in half-gallon and gallon jugs, and focus instead on its higher-end Charles Krug wines. McKinsey concluded that the winery should focus on its more profitable Charles Krug label wines.

In the course of that study, the McKinsey consultants discovered a swirling cauldron of bitter family emotions. They soon saw that Robert's brash style had alienated the other family members. It didn't take long before they discovered that a majority of Krug's shareholders, Rosa, Peter, Mary, and at that point Helen, believed that Peter should replace Robert as general manager. And although McKinsey's initial assignment was to see if they could find a better way to structure Krug, when Robert punched Peter in Lodi in the fall of 1965, they ended up in the midst of a war, since the majority of Robert's family had turned against him.

Several months after their final report had been delivered and the engagement completed, Watson and his team again met with members of the Mondavi family. This time, though, he met only with Rosa and Henry Ventura, who was married to Rosa's daughter Helen at the time, at McKinsey's offices on 100 California Street in the heart of San Francisco's financial district. The meeting took place on a Saturday morning. Rosa had turned to Watson and the other consultants because she wanted advice on how to handle her battling sons. Over several hours, the McKinsey men talked through the various possibilities to end the feud once and for all.

To Watson, it seemed as if Rosa had already made up her mind to fire Robert. Diplomatically, the consultant suggested that the family instead ask Robert to take a paid six-month "leave of absence." Watson was hoping that that might cool the family's heated emotions down, allowing Rosa and the rest of her children to see that Robert's contributions to the business outweighed his mistakes in family diplomacy. Rosa decided to take his advice.

A day or two later, Rosa summoned Robert and other members of the family to her home on the ranch. Joining them was Fred Ferroggiaro. As the other members of the family filed out of the room without asking Robert about the dustup between him and Peter, Ferroggiaro delivered the news: Robert must take a six-month leave of absence with pay and would no longer be general manager of Krug. Although Ferroggiaro attempted to present the leave as a "cooling-off period," Robert was furious and shocked at having been blindsided by his mother and siblings. He felt betrayed by his family.

Robert's ouster was formalized at a board meeting of Krug that took place on November 11, 1965, in the main dining room of Rosa's home, with its enormous dining table that could seat twenty. It was a stormy event, with shouting and fists pounding on tables. After hearing the news that all the shareholders of the company with the exception of Robert had decided that Peter should become general manager and Robert should be put on leave, two directors—the company lawyer Webster Clark and an auditor named Harry Meade—objected to Robert's removal. Outvoted, they both ended up resigning in protest instead.

Not long after that meeting, Robert's son Michael learned that there would be no position for him at Krug either. As a senior at the University of Santa Clara, Michael had been planning to join his father and uncle at Krug after a trip to Europe in the summer after his graduation. Instead, Rosa had let it be known that Michael would not be working for the family business. It was a crushing blow—made worse coming from his grandmother. In later years, Michael would struggle to understand why Rosa would do such a hurtful thing to him. The explanation he came up with was that Rosa, for many years, had herself been excluded from any business matters by her chauvinistic husband and was not equipped to handle it when she was forced into that role. Cesare's attitude had been that business was not for women. Indeed, when one of the women in the family would go into Cesare's office in Lodi, all conversation would stop.

Robert, in turn, interpreted Rosa's decision to ban Michael from working in the business less charitably. He simply saw it as her way of making sure that Peter's children would inherit the ranch.

Rosa later denied that she had banned any of her grandchildren from working for Charles Krug. She explained in a court deposition, through an interpreter, that the tensions between her sons had begun years earlier.

"Before dying, my husband asked me to go in between the two brothers and try to make them agree," she said in the deposition. "I answered him: You are not able to do that. How do you think I will be able?" Cesare urged her to try anyway, but her efforts failed. Three and a half months later, her husband died.

To be sure, Rosa was more comfortable preparing food in the kitchen and feeding her family and guests than mediating disputes between her sons. Barely literate and with little or no formal education, she was ill equipped to halt the feud that was brewing. She developed the habit of sucking breath in through her thin lips and letting it out again in a staccato fashion that signaled to her family that she was upset or anxious. At night, she would weep in her bed.

Outwardly, her response to their fighting over the years had been to insist that the boys try to get along, as if they were schoolchildren again. She was a forceful, hardworking person who didn't fear much in her life. Indeed, a few months before Robert and Peter had their tussle, a fire started on the third floor of the winery. Neither of her sons was around at the time. In a moment captured by *The St. Helena Star*, Rosa donned a fireman's jacket and hose to help put out the blaze.

But after the fisticuffs in Lodi, she realized that she could no longer cope on her own with her sons fighting. So she picked one son over the other. Rosa's choice: Peter, the baby of the family who she felt needed more of her protection. Recalling that decision during her deposition, she would explain that she tried to consider all of her children's interests, and perhaps she felt that Robert was better able to fend for himself. "With everybody, because I was—for everything. Sometime I am a mother to everybody. I am the mother of all of them."

Yet, what the Mondavi brothers needed at Charles Krug was not a mother, but a mediator who could help them work out their disagreements quietly and quickly. That didn't happen, despite the efforts of Joe Alioto and others.

However he might rationalize Rosa's reasons, Robert was especially furious that Michael had been banished from working at Charles Krug. Like his own father, he had implicitly embraced the idea that his eldest son would follow in his footsteps and inherit his role as leader of the family business. It was an echo of the ancient system of primogeniture— land going to the firstborn son—that still exists in many rural societies and was certainly the norm in Sassoferrato at the turn of the century, when Cesare and Rosa emigrated to the U.S.

From Robert's perspective, his father's idea had been to build a business for the entire family, including his son Michael. He tried to explain to his mother that his son had wanted to join the business since he was a boy, but Rosa told him he couldn't because of what she termed a "difference of opinion." Rosa refused to be specific with Robert about what that difference was, but, of course, it was Robert and Peter's inability to get along with each other at Krug.

"I then said to her, 'If that's the case, Mother, what I will do, I'm going to build a winery.'"

CHAPTER FOUR

To Kalon, 1965–1966

Robert Mondavi liked to do his thinking in the vineyards. During his most troubled days, he'd carry a folding card table and a chair between the rows of trellised vines at the Charles Krug Ranch. He'd find just the right spot, surrounded by foliage and out of sight of his mother, who lived just three hundred yards away from his and Marjorie's home. By taking shelter in the vineyards, he also managed to stay out of Peter's way. It hadn't taken his younger brother long to seize control of the winery and move into Robert's corner office. Unfolding his table and setting it upright onto the gravelly clay loam, Robert would sit there and ponder, sometimes for hours.

At age fifty-two, Robert Mondavi had no job, almost no savings, and private school tuition to pay for two of his three children. The home on the Krug Ranch where he and his wife and children had lived for more than two decades didn't solely belong to him: Peter, Rosa, and the rest of the family were co-owners, since the home was an asset of the family business. And while Robert owned a stake in the Charles Krug Winery and C. Mondavi and Sons, as part of the family partnership his father had

set up before his death, there was no quick or easy way to turn his holdings into cash. As a result, Robert's financial situation looked grim, even
desperate.

A restless person, with deep reservoirs of energy and ambition,
Robert was initially knocked flat by his family's decision to put him on
leave. Ostensibly a "cooling off" period for both sides, Robert's forced
vacation, instead, deepened his anger and left him dispirited. To make
matters worse, when he asked his mother to clarify what his future might
be with Krug, he was repeatedly put off with vague and unsettling responses such as "Be a good boy—then we'll see." Yet, the signs were not
good. As early as January of 1966, Peter had begun openly telling people
outside the family that Robert's leave was permanent and that he would
no longer be part of the business.

For more than two decades, Robert had poured himself into the
Charles Krug Winery with the conviction that he was building something lasting. He had made the classic trade-off for men of his generation
by focusing intensely on work while ignoring his family's individual
dreams and needs. At family meals, Robert would almost exclusively talk
business, scarcely listening to his wife and his children. His eldest son,
Michael, would later recall, "I can't remember any times my father did
not talk about wines from the time I was in diapers through this moment.
Every meal we had at home—lunch, dinner, even breakfast sometimes—
had wine involved." Believing that his sons would inherit and build upon
his work at the winery, he'd placed business discussions at the core of
most family interactions over the years.

So Rosa's abrupt decision to bar Michael from joining the family
business infuriated Robert. From junior high through college, Michael
had spent every summer and holiday working at the Charles Krug winery. He tended the vineyards, washed barrels, manned the pumps, and
tested samples in the lab. With Robert traveling almost constantly, and
wholly focused on work when he was home, Michael found that the only
real way to spend time with his father was to work alongside him. And so
he did. Even in his senior year at Santa Clara University, where he ma-
jored in business, he made the five- or six-hour round-trip commute
twice a week to St. Helena during harvest season, often hitchhiking to
save the bus fare.

Michael knew from an early age that he would join his father and uncle in the wine business. Although Michael would later say that his father

and mother had "outsmarted" him and his siblings by telling them that they should not enter the wine business unless they really wanted to, Robert's actions suggested that he fully expected his firstborn son to work alongside him when he was done with college.

Robert began his campaign to recruit Michael early. In the summer of 1961 at the Sutter Club in Sacramento, Robert invited Maynard Amerine, the famed UC Davis professor of viticulture and enology, to lunch with him and Michael to discuss Michael's future. The dining room of the mission-style private men's club, with its wood-beamed ceilings and antiques, was a suitably solid setting for a discussion of the young heir's future.

Then just eighteen years old and about to begin his senior year at Bellarmine, where other Italian-American wine families, including the Sebastianis and Franzias, also had sent their offspring to be educated, Michael spent much of the meal listening to his father talking about the future of California's wine industry. Robert eventually came around to his real purpose: He declared that Michael should go to UC Davis to study wine.

Amerine quietly disagreed.

Michael's first reaction was panic: Had the eminent professor somehow discovered his mediocre grades?

"Why not?" asked Robert. "He's been working in the cellars and the vineyards all his life."

"Because you can teach him more than I can," replied Amerine. "His biggest job will be learning how to make a profit." Instead of Davis, Amerine advised Michael to study business at Santa Clara University, where the professor's friend headed the business school. "That lunch was worth about two years in college," Michael now says.

Michael took Professor Amerine's advice, majoring in business and with a minor in sales. After college, the plan was simple and appealing: He would go to work at Charles Krug. But first, he'd undergo a glamorous finishing. His expectation had been that his father would arrange for him to serve an apprenticeship at one of France's grand châteaus, spending six months or a year absorbing the subtleties of centuries-old methods of blending and aging fine wine. Next, he would cross the Channel to spend a year or two in London, working for the wine merchant Harvey's. He'd then return Stateside to enter a graduate business program and earn an MBA.

By late 1969 or early 1970, he would have been beautifully groomed to help his father elevate Charles Krug into a producer of truly fine, European-style wines. It was perhaps not a coincidence that during his postcollege years, this plan would have Michael safely occupied in work outside the U.S. and thus out of the draft board's reach. Who could argue with such an elegant and practical solution?

It would also give his progeny a good head-start in the race to succeed Robert and Peter at Krug. As the first of the next generation of Mondavis to announce his intention to enter the business and thus claim his birthright, Michael was a threat to Peter's plans for his two sons, who were much younger than Michael and not even close to settling on careers yet. That may have been another reason for the subsequent battle between the brothers: They were engaged in the early skirmishes of what would become a dynastic war of succession.

Whatever the cause, the family conflict destroyed Michael's short-term plan for a grand European tour and his longer-term plan to join Charles Krug. Not only was it unclear whether Robert could count on a salary from Krug past the six-month leave period; it did not seem likely that he would be able to offer his eldest son a job, as Michael had expected. So, just before Thanksgiving, Robert telephoned each of his children at their schools and asked them to come home because he had something important he needed to discuss with them. Returning to the now embattled family compound, the three children retreated into Robert and Marjorie's home to hear what their father had to say. Sitting them down, Robert explained how he had been put on a forced leave of absence with no guarantee that at the end of the six months he would be allowed to return to the family business. The mood was somber, as Michael, Marcia, and Timothy listened. Robert then laid out his plan to build a winery—warning that they might have to go through at least five and perhaps even ten years with little cash to spare. "I wanted them all to think of this very seriously, that we would not have the standard of living that we were accustomed to before," said Robert later. His children returned to school in Santa Clara, south of San Francisco, and considered what their father had told them. About six weeks later, they met again and they all agreed that, as a family, they were willing to make sacrifices, if they had to, for the new venture.

Decades later, Robert would say that he wanted to set up a winery out of a sense of obligation to his eldest son. "Since Mike wanted to be in the business, I would establish the Robert Mondavi Winery for Mike," he recalled, adding that Michael's first name was also Robert. Perhaps naively, in the face of his brother and mother's attitudes, Robert recalls that his initial plan was to set up a small, fifteen- to twenty-thousand-case winery, ostensibly for his eldest son, while he continued to work for Charles Krug.

But, given Robert's vaulting ambitions, it is unlikely he ever really intended the winery to be Michael's alone. Timothy was still an adolescent at the time and Marcia was in her sophomore year of college, so perhaps it is not surprising that he did not include them in explaining his motives in later years. But it is more believable that Robert was hedging his bets. He must have realized by early 1966 that he'd better begin working toward opening up a winery of his own, as the friction between him and the rest of his original family was intensifying—despite his efforts to extend olive branches.

In the early months of his leave, Robert had approached his mother to ask if she would like to acquire a 25 percent interest in the new winery he planned to open in exchange for investing $25,000. Rosa, who was standing over the sink in her kitchen, asked Robert, "Will I be able to vote my stock?" Robert gently said no. "What I'm offering is a form of nonvoting shares," he explained. Rosa flatly turned him down. Likewise, Robert's repeated efforts to get Rosa or the other family members to clarify his status failed as well.

So it is not difficult to believe that by the summer of 1966, Robert wanted to build a winery named after himself in part to prove to the rest of his family that he was right and they'd treated him wrongly. Robert brought up the subject of his new winery's name over coffee one afternoon at his mother's home on the ranch. He came into the kitchen, where Peter was also sitting, and announced his plans to call it the "Robert Mondavi Winery." Peter immediately protested, arguing that Krug had used the Mondavi name on its labels from the beginning and that using it would confuse wine buyers.

Robert countered that he planned to use the original, Italian pronunciation of the name and that consumers would catch on to the differences between the two brands. Rosa, who was listening quietly to her sons' argument, then rose from her chair and swiftly extended her hand across the kitchen table, slapping her eldest son on the cheek. Tears filled Robert's eyes as he suffered this smarting, silent rebuke from his mother.

* * *

Several of the family's closest friends offered to back Robert's new winery. Bill and Ina McCormick Hart, who square-danced with Robert and Marjorie, were among the first to realize there was a serious rift in the family. The Harts, who had inherited a fortune in Kern County oil, approached Robert and said, "Bob, we know that there is a difference with the family here and if there is anything we can ever do, we would be very happy to support you in any venture that you would want to go into." Robert initially declined their offer, hoping the problem would resolve itself. He told them, "Well, no, we will resolve our differences."

But after Rosa had let Michael know he wouldn't have a job at Krug, Robert realized he needed help. He took the Harts up on their offer and borrowed $50,000. The Mirassou brothers, fourth-generation Santa Clara County winemakers who had hired Robert as a consultant to help them transform their bulk wines into something finer, cosigned a note so that Robert could borrow $100,000 from the Bank of America, which was then the leading agricultural lender in California. Another $50,000 came from two growers in the valley who had sold grapes to the Mondavis for many years: Fred Holmes and Ivan Shoch, who each lent him $25,000 in exchange for shares in the new winery, as well as assurances that Robert's winery would buy their grapes. So, altogether, Robert had raised $200,000 in start-up capital and had retained 50 percent of its equity. He managed to do this entirely with other people's money.

Robert's ability to raise funds to start a new winery was a reflection of the goodwill he'd accumulated over the years, particularly with valley grape growers. It is not a stretch to imagine that Fred Holmes and Ivan Shoch remembered the bad times in 1946 when Robert and his father chose to honor their commitments to buy the growers' grapes, rather than break the contracts as others did.

Robert's friendship with Ivan Shoch was crucial in helping him purchase perhaps the most storied vineyard in Napa Valley: To Kalon, which is the Greek term for "most beautiful." Planted in the 1870s by Hamilton W. Crabbe, who came to California in the 1850s looking for gold, this fertile stretch of vines near the hamlet of Oakville is one of the oldest vineyards in the valley. Crabbe had taken cuttings of "noble varietals" from France and planted a wide variety of grapes in his vineyard. He built To Kalon into a national brand that had developed, by the late 1880s, into one of the valley's largest and most successful wineries, capable of producing four hundred thousand gallons a year. As Crabbe joked to one visitor, To Kalon may mean "most beautiful" in Greek, but "I try to make it mean the boss vineyard."

When Crabbe died, the estate was sold to the E. W. Churchill family. The winery reopened after Prohibition ended in 1933, selling only bulk wines, but then burned to the ground in 1939. Four years later, a wealthy San Francisco real estate tycoon named Martin Stelling Jr. bought a large parcel of it. Sensing an emerging market for premium varietals, Stelling began planting many of the 600 acres he owned there with Cabernet, Chardonnay, and Sauvignon Blanc grapes.

Stelling died in a car wreck in 1950 and the property was overseen by a trustee. Its foreman was Ivan Shoch, who eventually approached his old friend Robert Mondavi about buying part of the famous old vineyard. In 1962, the Mondavis purchased nearly 500 acres of the Stelling Estate, including most of the original 359 To Kalon acres, for $1.35 million. The purchase, which *The St. Helena Star* called "the most outstanding real estate transaction in Napa Valley for many years," meant that Krug had the grapes to produce an additional 240,000 gallons of premium wine annually, almost doubling its output. The Mondavis held the property under the name of the parent company that Cesare had formed, C. Mondavi and Sons, and they knew the vineyards well: They'd been buying Cabernet Sauvignon grapes from To Kalon since at least the early 1950s.

When the reality that he had been expelled by his family from Krug had really begun to sink in, Robert turned his sights to the remaining few acres of To Kalon that his family didn't own. By then, the property had become embroiled in a complex development plan. In 1966, with Shoch's help, he bought a tiny, 11.6-acre parcel of that historic vineyard. While that wasn't nearly enough land to grow the grapes to supply the twenty-thousand-case-a-year winery he envisioned, a condition of Shoch and Holmes's investment was that Robert would buy their grapes for his new winery. The spot was ideally located, as well. It was close to Highway 29, the main artery through the valley and the route that most tourists took as they headed toward Beaulieu, Charles Krug, and other well-known wineries. With his keen instinct for public relations, as well as knowledge from his years at Krug of how much more cost-effective word of mouth was over traditional advertising, the location was superb for attracting visitors.

Cradled at the base of the hills and blessed with healthy vines and lush greenery, the land Robert felt an immediate connection with possessed a unique calmness and beauty. He intuitively knew this was the place he wanted to build his winery.

Robert's soaring ambitions were evident in his choice of design. After traveling in Europe and staying with the wine expert Alexis Lichine at his Château Lascombes in the Médoc, and other grand estates, Robert saw that his French counterparts had created veritable palaces. While Robert's tight finances wouldn't permit him to build a Versailles of wine, he sought out a singular Californian talent—Clifford May. Robert had never forgotten the elegant, mission-style complex in Menlo Park, California, that May had designed for *Sunset* magazine. Robert visited it as part of a Wine Institute event in the early 1960s. Low slung, understated, and with a gentle reference to California's colonial history, May's project for *Sunset* perfectly captured the zeitgeist of California in the 1960s, with its architectural focus on casual indoor/outdoor living.

Robert got in touch with *Sunset*'s longtime publisher, L. W. "Bill" Lane Jr., to ask him which architect had designed the magazine's new campus. Lane told him it wasn't an architect at all but a designer named Clifford May, a bon vivant with a beautiful young wife who regularly piloted his own plane down to Mexico to collect artifacts. Lane had left a message for May that Robert Mondavi was interested in talking to him about his new winery. Lane later told him, "Bob, you know, Cliff May was so excited by my message that he called me back at three o'clock in the morning!" Robert felt the same and hopped on a plane with Shoch and Holmes to visit May at his office in West Hollywood. The negotiations got started almost immediately, as May asked Robert how big he planned to make his winery. May's fees were high; he charged 12 percent of a project's construction costs rather than the typical 10 percent. And although Robert's initial plan was to start producing a modest twenty thousand cases a year, he expected to expand rapidly. He didn't have much to spend on a new building. His worry was that if May designed a winery for him that could produce fifty thousand or even a hundred thousand cases a year, he would have blown his budget before he sold even his first bottle of wine. The men went back and forth.

"Well, Bob, how big is your winery going to be?" May asked.

"It's going to be a small little winery to start with," Robert answered.

May then asked how big it would eventually become. Robert didn't want to reveal his plan, worried that he'd charge too much. After sparring for twenty minutes or so, they found a compromise.

"Listen, Cliff, if I built a winery that big, I wouldn't have enough money to put into the winery," said Robert.

So May said, "I'll tell you what. I'll make a deal with you. I'll design it that way and I'll only charge you for what you build. Eventually, if you enlarge, you will pay me then."

They struck a deal. Not long after, May jetted up to Napa in a private plane, landing on a tiny private airstrip near Inglenook that locals called jokingly "Rutherford International." Holmes, Shoch, Robert, and his son Michael picked him up at the airport and took him to look at three possible building sites.

May asked him what qualities he wanted the architecture of his winery to convey.

"I want the building to declare, 'Here is a heart and soul,'" Robert answered. "I want something that tells people this is not a factory, this is a home."

His response may have reflected his desire to build a new dwelling for himself, since he had been banished from the family winery and faced possible exile from the Krug Ranch. It also reflected a willingness to break with convention. Clifford May's design for the new winery was a startling change from the grand Victorian mansions and stone castles that housed the area's leading wineries at the time. May was a leading proponent of the California ranch-style home that exploded across the state's burgeoning suburbs in the 1950s and 1960s.

He was also a sixth-generation Californian who traced his roots to José María Estudillo, a commander of San Diego's Presidio who died in 1830, and May's vision for Robert's winery had its origins in the early history of the state. The building's silhouette would be close to the ground, with an archway separating the modest public façade from the more expansive, private space, defined by two wings of veranda expanding outward, broken by carved wooden doorways and decorative wrought-iron grills. Its low profile would be broken by a soaring bell tower, reminiscent of the Spanish missions that were built throughout California in the 1800s. Through the archway, the vista would open onto an expanse of vineyards and the Mayacamas Mountains. May masterfully balanced the warm and welcoming goal of a public façade that visitors would first see against the feeling of a privileged, exquisitely maintained country estate.

At the time when Robert expressed a desire to build a winery that felt like a home, the valley was experiencing the first rumblings of corporate interest in traditionally family-owned wineries. In 1964, John Daniel, head of Inglenook and a descendant of its founder, Gustave Niebaum, sent tremors through the valley when he sold the winery to United Vintners, a large cooperative that itself was part of Allied Grape Growers. There were many reasons that Daniel sold out, but among them was his belief that he lacked a family successor, since neither of his daughters seemed ready to take over the winery when he was gone. In 1966, as Robert was starting his winery, many of the valley's longtime vintners could see change was coming. Not only was a generational turnover taking place, but corporate interests began clashing with a small but growing tribe of urban refugees who'd given up higher-paying jobs and moved to the valley to make wine and live close to the land. It was also a time when hippies roamed the streets of San Francisco's Haight-Ashbury district and were venturing north to Mendocino and other rural northern-California counties to live in communes.

For Robert, that arrival of United Vintners and the rumors of big liquor companies on the prowl added to his sense of urgency to get construction under way quickly. "I wanted to be in the market before other people came in. I realized that the big companies were beginning to come in and wanted to invest big money. Not having that kind of money, I knew that time would be of the essence and that is why I wanted to get started that first year." He had another reason for moving quickly as well. Plans were afoot to turn the old Stelling estate into a Palm Springs–like luxury resort and housing project, with a model winery at its heart. By agreeing to build that model winery, Robert got his first pick of the parcels in the proposed development.

Although he publicly supported the controversial plan, he would later explain that he doubted it would ever win approval from the county. His fear was that if United Vintners or Seagram caught wind of the plan, the price would soar. Shoch, who was friendly with the Stelling trustees and the project's developer, went to work as Robert's emissary. They quickly cut a deal. Robert and his partners got a prime piece of land for the future home of the Robert Mondavi Winery.

Construction crews broke ground on July 16, 1966. *The Napa Valley Register* that month was dominated by news of the killings of eight student nurses in Chicago, preparations for the Gemini 10 spaceflight, and dispatches from the war in Vietnam. On the cultural front, the paper reported that "Pool House Is the Newest Status Sign," as well as the news that "Frank Sinatra, 50, to Wed 21-Year-Old Mia Farrow." In local news, there was a photo featuring Miss Napa County cradling a shotgun—a promotion for an upcoming turkey shoot to raise funds for the Yountville Volunteer Firemen. A three-bedroom, split-level home in north Napa listed for $17,500. Perhaps auspiciously, the groundbreaking also took place on the birthday of Marcia, who turned twenty that day.

It was a frantic time for Robert, who continued consulting for the Mirassou family and the Guild Winery in Lodi, earning a retainer of $1,000 a month from each. He also oversaw construction, ordering barrels and other equipment for his new winery. Michael helped when he could, but on June 18 he had married a fellow student he'd met in Santa Clara named Isabel Alcantara, the daughter of a Spanish-speaking stockbroker who had been stationed in Panama as a plainclothes U.S. Army officer, leading some family members to conclude he had been an American spy. The couple exchanged rings in a Catholic ceremony at Holy Cross Church in Santa Cruz, California, not far from where they went to college.

Escorted down the aisle by her father, Isabel wore a sophisticated gown of imported Dupioni silk and elbow-length sleeves of French guipure lace. A dark-haired beauty whose loveliness was set off by the six bridesmaids' pink organza gowns, Isabel carried a bouquet of lilies of the valley and orchids. Although Isabel's sister Joleen was her maid of honor, Marcia Mondavi was also a bridesmaid. Michael's best man was his friend Peter A. Stern. After a brief honeymoon in Hawaii, Michael enlisted in the army reserves and was occupied through November with training.

With Michael gone for much of that summer and fall, Robert realized he needed some help. He found that help through his old friend André Tchelistcheff, who was aware that a young winemaker named Warren Winiarski had just parted ways with Lee Stewart and his highly regarded Souverain Cellars, a pioneer in the budding "boutique" wine movement.

Winiarski was casting about for a new opportunity. Robert, Michael, Ivan Shoch, and Winiarski met in one of the partners' homes, where they spread Clifford May's plans for the new winery over the table.

Although Michael participated in some of the early planning, he mostly stayed in the background. Robert's son struck Winiarski as a clean-cut college kid: He wore his hair slicked back and a button-down shirt open at the collar. Although he was polite, Michael otherwise didn't make much of an impression on the winemaker. Far more memorable was Robert's enthusiasm, which swept them all up and ultimately convinced Winiarski, who then had a wife and two young children to support, to join the fledgling enterprise.

Robert couldn't resist announcing his new venture to the newspapers. On July 21, 1966, *The St. Helena Star* ran a story on its front page that confirmed "the long rumored report that Robert Mondavi and his associates will build a new winery in the valley." The *Star* also reported that John Daniel Jr., the well-regarded valley vintner who was a former president of the Wine Institute, had placed the first order for Robert's first vintage, telephoning in a request for five cases. Several other papers reported that Robert had not severed business relationships with his family enterprise, C. Mondavi and Sons. His family's decision to force him to take a leave had certainly hemmed him in; yet Robert surely could not have been so blind to the possibility that announcing a new winery would heighten tensions with his family.

To Peter, Robert's plan was a serious threat. By going so far as to set up his son in his own winery, particularly one that used the Mondavi name in it, Robert would be targeting many of Charles Krug's customers. Peter's overriding desire was for Robert to completely sever his ties with Krug, leaving the way open for his own sons, Marc and Peter junior, to inherit the business.

Rosa also objected to her eldest son's plan to build a new winery. "Bobby, don't do this," she pleaded to him, siding with Peter. Although Robert's new winery was arguably at that point only a small competitive threat to Krug, it provided a perfect excuse to Peter for firing his brother. Acting for Rosa and the rest of the family, Peter turned to Krug's new, high-powered general counsel, Joe Alioto.

Balding, bull-shouldered, and as crisply tailored as he was sharp-tongued, John L. Alioto was a force to be reckoned with as the feud between the

Mondavis gained momentum. Fred Ferroggiaro, a top officer at the Bank of America, had recruited Alioto to Charles Krug as a director and as general counsel in late 1965. By that time, Alioto had built a reputation as an unbeatable litigator. His raw magnetism and wide-ranging intelligence had impressed jurors and voters for many years. To Rosa, he was someone strong enough to stand up to her eldest son.

Born and raised in San Francisco's North Beach neighborhood, Alioto was a product of the city's vibrant Italian-American immigrant community. During Prohibition, he had stomped grapes in his family's backyard to make homemade wine. His father, who had emigrated from Sicily at the age of nine, ran a successful wholesale fish market in downtown San Francisco. During the summers, Joe would rise before dawn to work at his father's fish business, and then hurry off to the nearby courthouse to watch the great trial lawyers of the day make their arguments. From an early age, he was drawn to the operatic drama and eloquent orators of the court.

A star debater as an undergraduate at St. Mary's College, Alioto graduated magna cum laude and won a scholarship to Catholic University of America Law School in Washington, D.C. He then joined the Justice Department's antitrust division in San Francisco, which was flexing its muscles under Roosevelt's New Deal administration. One of the first big cases he brought was against the wine industry, alleging that between 1938 and 1942 it had fixed prices in sweet wines—then the dominant wine sold. In prosecuting that case, he took on some of the biggest wineries of the day, including the Roma Wine Company, Petri Wine Company, Italian Swiss Colony, and the Wine Institute, as well as the powerful Bank of America, which financed many of them.

Alioto scoured documents and subpoenaed witnesses, eventually discovering a series of memos that helped him to win the case. "The entire wine industry was simply a cartel, a huge cartel, dominated by the Bank of America," he concluded. He had sought permission from his superiors at the Justice Department to file criminal charges against the group, but eventually, after allegations of grand jury tampering, was forced to file a civil complaint instead. Alioto's effort resulted in a voluntary dissolution of one of the key wine associations, the California Cooperative Wineries.

But Alioto made his name and personal fortune in a series of antitrust cases that he brought against big organizations as a private attorney. Although in later years he liked to characterize his work as defending the "little guys"—individuals and small businesses that had been hurt by anti-competitive practices of big business—he represented some big names, as well, including the movie mogul Samuel Goldwyn.

A cultured man who, to unwind, would hum "O Mio Babbino Caro" from Puccini's opera *Gianni Schicchi* and quote Dante and St. Thomas Aquinas to illustrate his points, Alioto was fifty years old and in his prime when he joined Charles Krug's board.

Robert never forgot the advice that Alioto gave him as they walked across the ranch's lush lawn together in November of 1965. Robert had just learned that his family was forcing him to take a sabbatical from his job at Charles Krug. Alioto, who even then must have realized that a lawsuit was likely, had counseled him to hire the best lawyer he could find. What was Alioto's explanation for advice that would not seem to be in Rosa and Peter's best interests?

"So we don't steal you blind," Alioto said.

But very quickly Alioto dropped any pretense of serving as an objective mediator as he was drawn into Rosa's powerful orbit. Krug's board meetings took on a pleasurable aspect for him, since they were generally concluded with a home-cooked meal served by Rosa in her dining room. Robert and Peter would both attend these luncheons. The lunches were a temporary cease-fire.

Despite Rosa's habit of spending most of her time during board meetings in the kitchen, preparing the meal, it didn't take long for Alioto to grasp that the power in the family lay with her as the company's president. His allegiance was firmly with the Mondavi widow, perhaps in part because his longtime law partner Richard Saveri had drawn up Cesare's will for him many years before. Alioto's goal was to help Rosa protect the family business against the consequences of a bitter sibling rivalry that threatened to tear it apart.

Alioto's later descriptions of the family drama playing out at the Krug Ranch resonated with Old Testament pathos. Rosa, in his words, had meted out "old-world punishment" to her eldest son, declaring that he should be "exiled" for six months from the business. He had quickly grasped that Rosa had made up her mind to fire Robert from the very beginning and had no intention of allowing him to return from his expulsion. "There isn't any question that the mother did in substance fire him, even though she paid him his wages," Alioto said.

In early 1966, Alioto arranged to meet Robert, who was returning from a trip to Los Angeles, at the San Francisco Opera. They enjoyed the performance and talked afterward. As Alioto recalled it, he tried to convince Robert to rejoin Krug. But Robert instead told him that he planned to open his own winery. The issue simmered as rumors began swirling in the valley about Robert's new project. But it was further newspaper coverage that brought the family's anger to a head. On August 4, 1966, Alioto sent Robert a searing letter that excoriated him for starting a new winery.

"Dear Bob," it read. "You are familiar with the fact that I made a considerable effort to ameliorate the unfortunate situation that developed in your family. I did tell you, however, that the moment you went ahead to a point of no return on the construction of a winery in the Napa Valley that [sic] all chances of success in restoring family unity would be gone. Your mother and Peter have told me that you have begun construction of your winery and I believe that inevitably it can only be called a competitive winery."

Alioto then went on to inform Robert that his employment at the family business was being terminated as of July 31, 1966. His severance pay would be a paltry one-month consulting fee in the amount of $2,000. Alioto made particular note of the newspaper announcements of Robert's new winery, calling them "unfortunately worded," and insisted that Robert stop using the Mondavi name in his new venture. Alioto then laid out the further details of Robert's firing: While the family would permit him to continue living in his longtime home on the Krug Ranch, it would be putting Robert's utility and telephone bills in his own name. Robert, in turn, must return all his company credit cards and begin paying his own membership fees and country club bills.

Alioto struck one small conciliatory note. "I say again as I have previously told you that I am genuinely sorry that I was unable to patch up this serious rift; and while I know you have a difference of opinion about it, I am convinced that the existence of the new winery is an insurmountable obstacle in the whole matter." The letter was signed, "Very truly yours, Joe."

Alioto's icy letter stunned Robert. "I couldn't sleep for three months because I spent twenty-nine years of my life, every day, working and creating something," he later recalled. Even years later, Robert couldn't bring himself to believe that his mother had acted coldheartedly or with malice toward him. Nearly two decades later, he continued to maintain that "this was really an unfortunate misunderstanding. I knew that my mother didn't want to hurt me. I saw her practically every other day, or every third day. I lived right across the way, went to her, explained the differences in that regards. Unfortunately, we couldn't resolve the difference. There were honest misunderstandings in the thing."

Far from simple misunderstandings, Robert's estrangement from Rosa and other family members deepened further. Although he and his family still lived on the Krug Ranch, the Robert Mondavi family was no longer invited to sit at the table with the rest of the Mondavis at family meals at "the brown house," Rosa's home, although he continued to enjoy her lunches at board meetings. On holidays, Rosa would cook one of her spectacular feasts of roast lamb, cappelletti, "little hats" of ground meat and spices, and verdure—spinach or chard sautéed in garlic and oil. First, she would serve the Peter Mondavi family, her brother, and other relatives and friends at her house. Then, carrying a tray of food, she would walk over to Robert's home across the way and hand him the same meal through the door, without staying to eat with them.

PART TWO

CONSTRUCTION

CHAPTER FIVE

Crush, 1966–1972

T he first few months at the Robert Mondavi Winery were chaotic. Carpenters, masons, plumbers, electricians, and the winemaker, Warren Winiarski, were all working on top of one another. By late summer, there were walls, but still no roof, catwalks, or ladders to reach the tops of the new stainless steel fermenters. Parts were missing and there was no place to do any lab work—let alone a lab technician to do it. Since there were no desks or offices or tables, Winiarski worked from a clipboard. Robert, who had a small office in a trailer, was seldom in one place for long. Winiarski would see him early in the morning and late in the day; the rest of the time, he was a whirlwind of energy, conferring with the builders, making deals for grapes, consulting, and purchasing equipment.

Robert's energy was infectious and his aspirations heady. But he was strongly motivated to start making wine. Fired from Krug without any significant severance pay, Robert was under severe financial pressure. With construction costs mounting, he sought to produce cash flow as quickly as possible. So he set an ambitious timeline. He was determined to bring in the harvest that first year and crush grapes to make the Robert Mondavi Winery's first vintage. From groundbreaking to crush, he had two, or perhaps three, months at most. Although Robert had probably not fully formed his intentions for the new winery in 1966, even by then the people who were helping him to make it happen recognized that his dreams were lofty. "It was not meant to be a small winery and it was not meant to be a family winery. From the beginning, the Robert Mondavi Winery was meant to reach out," says Winiarski.

Once again, the friendships that Robert had built after twenty years in the valley came to his rescue. William Bonetti, by then the production chief at Charles Krug, helped Winiarski with some lab work, allowing him to come over and use the Krug lab to run simple analytical tests of the fermenting juice, as well as to borrow equipment and chemicals. Winiarski had assumed that Bonetti had gotten Peter's implicit, if not explicit, permission to help out his brother, but it wasn't exactly clear, since neither brother had spoken openly to Winiarski of the simmering feud.

Krug also crushed grapes for the Robert Mondavi winery's first year, sold it yeast, bottles, and a labeling machine, and loaned the new winery a bottling machine free of charge. As a safety net, Peter and Rosa agreed to pay Robert a $9,000-a-year consulting fee after he was fired, although he never performed any consulting services for Krug. While they didn't welcome Robert as a competitor, they also didn't want him to fail. As Peter later explained, "We felt that he needed some support from the family inasmuch as he ventured, and we wanted to see him make a success of what he was doing." Louis Martini and the winemakers at Beaulieu also pitched in to help out their old friend.

And when the time came to design the winery's first label, Robert again turned to people he had worked with at Krug: a well-known local printer named James E. Beard and a graphic designer named Mallette Dean. Dean had done beautiful work over the years for Krug, including a delicate woodcut of a farmer tending grapevines that had graced the masthead of the Krug newsletter "Bottles & Bins."

The label the pair created for the new Robert Mondavi Winery captured its spirit centered around Dean's wood engraving of the Cliff May building, with its elegant arch and wings. But Dean struggled with a lack of vertical balance in the frame, which he eventually corrected by adding a flank of poplar trees to the scene. In the real setting, a series of trees planted on the walkway had failed to flourish in the 1970s, so eventually, to match the reality to the image on the label, the winery ended up planting poplar trees where Dean had imagined them. Dean's label for the Robert Mondavi Winery quickly became one of the iconic images of Napa Valley.

The cool weather that year also came to Robert's aid, pushing harvest back by several weeks. Fieldworkers picked the last Cabernet grapes on Veterans Day, November 11, in a season marked by tule fog and cool evenings that often cloaked the valley until ten or eleven in the morning.

To the astonishment of some of the friends and rivals who'd called him crazy, Robert managed to make wine that first year. In 1966, the new Robert Mondavi Winery crushed about 490 tons of grapes—even though there was nothing even close to resembling a building on the site yet. By the time the crush rolled around, there were only concrete slabs on the ground, foundations for the fermenting tanks. In the open air, Robert pumped the juice from the fermenting tanks into other tanks. As summer became autumn, workers were plastering the walls of the newly erected building, even as Warren Winiarski made the wine.

Returning to the rituals and ceremonies of the Roman Catholic Church, Robert marked his winery's first crush of the grapes surrounded by his immediate family and his most supportive friends on a sunny morning in mid-September. Robert halted the whirl of painting, plastering, and sanding for a few hours. On a concrete platform surrounded by dirt, a group of a few dozen people gathered on the north side of what would become the winery. Father Levinus of the nearby Carmelite monastery, wearing a long black robe that fell to his ankles and a white cassock over that, faced the gondola that held the grapes. Marcia Mondavi, with her short-cropped dark hair and a ladylike knee-length skirt and sleeveless blouse, bowed her head and clasped her hands together. The priest began his benediction in English sprinkled with Latin words.

In the background, Winiarski operated the lift that raised the gondola filled with grapes and tipped them into the hopper. From there, the fruit moved along a conveyer belt to the crusher. The mechanics of the moment only hinted at the deeper transformations that would take place as the grapes moved toward their transfiguration into wine. The atmosphere was solemn: There was no round of applause or cheering as Robert's partners Fred Holmes, Bill Hart, and Ivan Shoch stood watching, their families beside them. Also present was Charles Daniels and two of his sons. Daniels had been distributing Krug's wines since the 1940s and was close friends with Robert. He wanted to support him in his new venture and offered to distribute his wines when they were released in the spring of 1967, even though he knew that support would infuriate Peter.

For growers such as Holmes and Hart, crush is a moment of death as well as birth. The life that they have nurtured from bud break through harvest is coming to an end; another is about to begin. "There is a death taking place here," reflects Warren Winiarski, who later became one of the valley's most famous winemakers. "It's the death of the grape. I never saw a grower sad, but solemn. They're glad that it's happening but it's a mixed feeling. They've worked all that season to make these grapes what they are and now they are being crushed, being destroyed in order to be reborn into a different substance. They're glad but also a little bit mindful of destruction."

But that moment of solemnity passed. Robert said a few words about a new beginning. The group included workmen clad in overalls and hats to shield them from the sun. Marjorie began pouring the white wine that had waited for the group beneath a folding card table in a plastic tub filled with ice. Looking cool and elegant, with her blond hair pinned into a chignon, Marjorie, like her daughter, had dressed for the heat, in a conservative A-line skirt that stopped just below the knee and white flats, even though miniskirts and go-go boots were shocking the nation elsewhere.

After the ceremony, the Holmeses, Shochs, and Mondavis gathered for a group photo in front of the grape-filled gondola. The adults held long-stemmed wineglasses. Robert smiled at Marjorie. Timothy, fair-haired and with the gangly look of a teenager, wore black-and-white-laced Converse sneakers. Then just fifteen years old, he, too, held a wineglass in his hand. Marcia, looking contemplative, sat below the row of standing adults. Perhaps in a foreshadowing of the family drama to come, Robert's elder son was absent on that momentous day.

The new Mondavi winery was the most significant to be built in the valley since Prohibition, and with barely three dozen bonded wineries operating in the valley at the time, the groundbreaking marked a key turning point. "The construction of the Robert Mondavi Winery marks the effective beginning of American wine's rise in both quality and prestige," wrote the wine historian Paul Lukacs. "What happened there helped ignite the revolution in American tastes. It also helped change broad public attitudes toward wine in general and American wine in particular."

That fall, however, the significance of Robert's bold new winery—a venture that some dismissed as "Robert's Folly" and others as an example of his hubris—seemed to offer concrete proof of the fissure between the proud and talented Mondavi brothers. Fellow vintners watched the rising feud between Robert and Peter with a mixture of sympathy and dismay. After all, Robert was building his winery just five miles south of Krug on Highway 29. The brothers were barely on speaking terms. Other vintners in the valley didn't talk about it much; mostly, they looked the other way.

But what also caught everyone's attention and provoked some amused comments was that almost as soon as he started his own winery, Robert began pronouncing his surname differently than Peter, Rosa, and the rest of the family. He restored it to "Mon-dah-vee," which was how the name was pronounced before Cesare had Americanized it after immigrating to the U.S. Meanwhile, Peter and the rest of the family continued to pronounce their last name as they always had done: "Mon-day-vee."

However slight the change, the new pronunciation had the intended effect of distinguishing Robert from his younger brother. When his long-time friend Charles Daniels asked Robert why he'd changed it, Robert explained with a straight face: "That's the proper Italian pronunciation." Daniels also recalled that around that time, some people in the valley began asking, "What is it with this Mondavi business?" referring to the rift between the brothers and Robert's startling decision to Europeanize his last name. Robert never formally announced the change in pronunciation; it just spread through usage. In later years, his sister Helen would even jokingly introduce herself as "Helen Mon-dah-vee Mon-day-vee."

And soon enough many people—and especially newcomers to the valley—started referring to the entire family as "Mon-dah-vees"—a galling, frequent reminder to Peter of Robert's linguistic coup over the rest of the family.

The Robert Mondavi Winery's growing reputation was built on fine wines, meaning expensive wines made almost exclusively from Napa Valley grapes. It was also built on Robert's gift for hiring talented winemakers. Keeping those winemakers was another matter, though. For Robert faced an ongoing problem: With one son in the business and another likely to join, the family would always get the credit for the elegant wines that were produced at Oakville, even though it was often the staffers doing much of the work. And although Robert would pay employees 10 to 15 percent above other wineries' wages and offered such perks as weekly wine tastings, there was a ceiling to any career ambitions that a staffer without the last name Mondavi might entertain at the winery. The family openly acknowledged this.

Michael, upon his return, worked hard and earned just $650 a week. To try to drum up business, he would sometimes drive slowly down Highway 29 from Rutherford to Oakville, waiting for cars to stack up behind him. Driving a pickup truck borrowed from his father-in-law, he'd then slowly make the right-hand turn into the winery. When a car or two followed him, as they often did, he'd jump out of his truck and stick out his hand, saying, "Hi there, I'm Michael Mondavi. Would you like a tour?" Yet, Michael also clearly enjoyed an advantage because of his last name, even joking about it at times. On meeting Michael for the first time for a job interview, one applicant asked if he minded that the applicant's wife also worked at the winery. Robert's elder son leaned back in his chair and grinned: "Nepotism can be a good thing."

But this practice carried a sizable cost for the company: Ambitious employees often ended up quitting for better opportunities elsewhere. The first to go was Warren Winiarski, the academic refugee from the University of Chicago. Winiarski worked through the first two crushes at the Robert Mondavi Winery, amid the chaos of construction, and left shortly before the third in 1968.

This first year, Winiarski did much of the lab work himself as well as supervising crush, fermentation, and aging of the reds. Michael was doing his National Guard duty for much of the first year as the Vietnam War raged, so Winiarski took his guidance from Robert. In terms of the day-to-day production, Winiarski was in charge, without any sort of directions in terms of style from either Robert or Michael to produce, for example, Bordeaux-style wines. Because so much else was going at the winery—completing construction, negotiating grape contracts, and selling their first year's wine—Winiarski was left mostly to his own devices. Yet by 1967, Michael had returned from the National Guard and become, in title at least, the winemaker at Mondavi.

That proved frustrating for Winiarski, who, despite his differences with Lee Stewart, had embraced his old boss's style of paying close attention to even the seemingly most minor details of winemaking. Michael, in turn, had no formal training in enology or chemistry and while he had absorbed a general understanding of winemaking from his days as a cellar rat at Krug, he was not by nature highly detail-oriented. So when incidents occurred in Winiarski's second and third years at Mondavi, such as Michael taking the valves off the tanks and not replacing them, thus inadvertently exposing the wine to air, Winiarski started to wish he had more control. "There were things he didn't see because he didn't care," says Winiarski. "He liked wine but it wasn't his passion."

Winiarski had borrowed money in 1965 to buy fifteen acres of his own up on Howell Mountain, where he hoped to plant a vineyard. His first season in 1967 was a disappointment but he didn't give up. The following year, his plans to start a vineyard of his own started to come together. So, hoping he could support his family as a freelance winemaker and consultant, he announced he was quitting the Robert Mondavi Winery, shortly before the crucial time of harvest. As Winiarski tells it, Michael was not happy about the timing of his departure. But "I didn't come to California to be the number-two man in a two-man winery," recalled Winiarski, referring to his relatively short stay at Souverain Cellars. "The same thing was true at Mondavi." While Winiarski learned an extraordinary amount at both places, he bridled at working under someone else. "Everyone who is devoted to making something wants to have control of the material—finally and completely—and that couldn't happen there because of Mike and Robert. It was their material," meaning it was ultimately their grapes, yeast, barrels, and wine.

It didn't take long for Robert to recruit Winiarski's replacement: a talented Croatian immigrant named Miljenko "Mike" Grgich, who was then working at Beaulieu Vineyard for André Tchelistcheff, the quality-driven winemaker who demanded high standards of cleanliness and precision from his staff. Tchelistcheff was about to retire, but ironically his own son had applied for his job, which seemed to suggest that Grgich was unlikely to become the next winemaker at Beaulieu, the most revered producer of fine wines in the valley. Robert knew of Grgich's situation and thought he might be looking for a new position. So the men arranged a chat in the fall of 1968, just a few weeks after Winiarski had left.

Grgich made the short, two-mile drive down Highway 29 and met with Robert on a wooden bench, near the Robert Mondavi Winery's mission-style arch. It was a sunny fall day and Robert's enthusiasm was infectious, as he explained to Grgich his dream of making French-style wines with the newest and most technologically advanced equipment available. Robert also explained that his son recently had returned from duty in the National Guard and was the vice president of winemaking. "I need someone to help my son Michael, who is very young," Robert told Grgich. While his job title would be head of quality control, in fact he would run the winemaking operation for the family and be the actual winemaker, in a deus-ex-machina fashion. In return, Robert offered Grgich the opportunity to build his reputation as one of the finest winemakers of his generation.

"Mike, if you join my company, I'll make out of you a little André Tchelistcheff!" he promised him.

It was an irresistible offer, made more so because of Robert's evident passion to make the Robert Mondavi Winery America's finest. Grgich accepted and got to work, introducing—among other methods he had learned at Beaulieu—malolactic fermentation, a technique that lends a soft, buttery quality to wines by converting hard malic acids into soft lactic acids. Every Monday, led by Robert, the staff would have their own blind tastings of Mondavi wines against the best from France. It entered into company legend that the winery was California's largest importer of French grand crus because of these competitive tastings. Robert showed up at the winery nearly as early as Grgich, at six or seven each morning during crush, to taste the progress of the fermenting juice from the barrels or discuss a technical issue with his winemaker.

The very first Cabernet Grgich made for the winery, the 1969, was entered in a blind tasting—which meant that the wine labels would be hidden from the judges—against several other Cabernet Sauvignons from California. Organized by the *Los Angeles Times*'s wine writer, Robert Lawrence Balzer, the judges, who included Tchelistcheff and Robert, had made most of the wines being tasted that day. When the judges voted the 1969 Robert Mondavi Winery Cabernet as the very best, that decision led to a rush of favorable publicity for the young winery, catapulting it overnight into the ranks of such revered wines as those made at Beaulieu.

Though Grgich had made the wine, Robert took credit for it. The Balzer tasting, as it came to be known, was the first big publicity breakthrough for the winery, sending its sales soaring. It helped attract the attention of the European wine trade, which, a few years later, in 1976, would organize a blind tasting that would have an even more significant impact on Napa Valley.

Yet Grgich, like Winiarski before him, grew frustrated with the fast pace of growth and attendant chaos at the winery. In contrast to the orderly calm of Beaulieu, where experiments took place one at a time, allowing the winemakers to gauge their success before proceeding to the next step, everything seemed to happen at once at Mondavi. Some people in the valley began calling Robert's place the "test-tube winery" because of its rapid embrace of new ideas and technologies. Robert would credit the quality of the wines one year to his new roto-tanks, automated fermentation tanks that would rotate at the push of a button, and then the next year attribute it to a centrifuge, his latest purchase. The following year, he'd have forgotten all about the new tanks and the centrifuge and enthuse over a new type of filter. "He was just charging forward. For me it was a little faster than I would do myself," Grgich said.

The fast-moving atmosphere was driven, in part, by the leap in demand for Robert Mondavi wines. The winery was crushing five hundred tons of grapes in Grgich's first harvest in 1969; four years later it was crushing five thousand tons, or ten times as much. "[Robert] was so successful that I, as a precision winemaker, could not take care of all his wines; it was just too much wine for me." So Grgich asked Robert to hire another winemaker to handle the lower-quality wines, while Grgich would tend to the Cabernet and Chardonnay. Robert resisted Grgich's plea.

"Mike, I know you can handle it," Robert said.

"I know I cannot, because I am not happy if some mistake comes and I cannot control it. I want to have total control and perfect wines," Grgich explained in the thick Croatian accent he never lost, echoing the desire for control that Winiarski also felt. Although Grgich hired an assistant, Zelma Long, after his first two years on the job, the workload for both of them was extremely heavy. At the same time, though the Mondavis left day-to-day control over the winemaking to Grgich and Long, they were not generous in acknowledging their contributions to the winery and instead claimed the glory for themselves. To Zelma Long, "it was always the family member that was the winemaker."

At around that same time, two men from Los Angeles approached Grgich with a plan to revive Château Montelena. They offered him complete control plus a small equity stake. When Timothy graduated from

UC Davis, there would soon be three Mondavis actively involved in the business and Robert had made it clear he would not offer a nonfamily staffer shares in the winery. Grgich accepted the Château Montelena job as its winemaker in 1972. The Mondavis had lost another talented winemaker.

Mondavi would reap the benefits of having employed Winiarski and Grgich several years later, when a young Englishman named Steven Spurrier, who owned a wine shop in Paris called the Caves de la Madeleine, and an adjacent wine school, organized a blind wine tasting of French and California wines. On May 24, 1976, Spurrier brought together nine French judges with impeccable wine credentials, recalls George Taber, the sole journalist who covered the tasting that day at Paris's Intercontinental Hotel. The labels were covered so the judges would not know if they were drinking a wine from America or France. About halfway through the tasting, Taber realized the judges were getting confused. They were identifying California wines as French. As Taber wrote later,

> Raymond Oliver, the owner and chef of the Grand Véfour restaurant in Paris, one of the temples of French haute cuisine, swirled a white wine in his glass, held it up to the light to examine the pale straw color, smelled it, and then tasted it. After a pause he said, "Ah, back to France!" I checked my list of wines twice to be sure, but Oliver had in fact just tasted a 1972 Freemark Abbey Chardonnay from California's Napa Valley! Soon after, Claude Dubois-Millot of GaultMillau, a publisher of French food and wine books and magazines, tasted another white wine and said with great confidence, "That is definitely California. It has no nose." But the wine was really a 1973 Bâtard-Montrachet Ramonet-Prudhon, one of Burgundy's finest products.

The French judges ended up picking two California wines as the best at that day's tasting. They were a 1973 Château Montelena Chardonnay, made by Mike Grgich, and a 1973 Stag's Leap Wine Cellars Cabernet Sauvignon, made by Warren Winiarski. These Californian upstarts beat such fabled producers as Haut-Brion, Mouton-Rothschild, and Meursault-Charmes. *Time*'s modest June 7, 1976, story, written by Taber and headlined "Judgment of Paris," announced "the unthinkable happened: California defeated all Gaul." The tasting represented a turning point for California's wine industry. For the first time, the wine establishment, rooted in Europe and the East Coast, began to take California producers seriously.

Although Robert's own wines were not chosen for the tasting, his cash-strapped winery shared the glory, since it had been one of Grgich's and Winiarski's training grounds. Although neither had been able to tolerate for very long their lack of control at Mondavi, their alma mater nonetheless reveled in the attention, becoming known as "Mondavi University"—an experimental hotbed producing not only America's finest wines but also some of its finest winemakers.

In the spring of 1967, Joseph Alioto took a trip to Paris, a city he had loved all his life. One evening, he went to dine at the famous Parisian restaurant Maxim's with his newlywed son, John, and John's wife, Madeleine. When their French waiter asked the party what they would like to drink, Alioto replied that he'd like a bottle of Charles Krug Cabernet Sauvignon. The waiter looked confused, so Alioto explained that Charles Krug was a very fine California wine.

"Monsieur," said the waiter, drawing himself up in a haughty manner, "we only use California wines for cooking."

The group from San Francisco laughed at the waiter's dismissal of their state's product and drank Bordeaux with their meal instead. California wines were not considered good enough by many Europeans to be included on the wine list of one of their fine restaurants. And indeed, the leading California wineries at the time were consciously patterning their winemaking styles on French models.

At about the same time that Alioto was visiting Paris, Robert invented a faux French name as a way of glamorizing the everyday Sauvignon Blanc grape. Much of the wine made from the Sauvignon Blanc grape in those days was of poor quality, but Robert took the crop provided by his growers and aged it in French barrels. Modeling it after herbaceous whites from the Loire Valley, as well as softer, oak-aged ones from Bordeaux, Robert transposed what was known as *blanc fumé* in France, and marketed it, in a twist, as Fumé Blanc. It was the first of many such marketing coups for Napa's newest winery.

When Alioto returned from his trip, his focus on Charles Krug began to wane as he got swept up in a mayoral race. After an electrifying fifty-five-day campaign, he was elected in 1967 to the first of two four-year terms as mayor of San Francisco. After only six months in office, the city's ebullient new mayor began jockeying for a vice presidential spot alongside Hubert Humphrey on the 1968 Democratic ticket. Although U.S. senator Edmund Muskie of Maine got the nomination, Alioto delivered Humphrey's nomination speech at the Democratic National Convention that year. He then turned his sights to running for governor of California, but was knocked out by a devastating 1969 article in *Look* magazine that alleged that he had mafia ties. It took him more than a decade of wrangling in the courts, but Alioto eventually forced *Look*, in 1980, to pay $350,000 in libel damages.

The mafia allegations were not Alioto's only worry in 1969. That same year, he was indicted for kicking back a legal fee. Alioto eventually won a civil trial stemming from that charge and a judge dismissed related criminal charges brought by the federal government, but Alioto's legal and personal woes ultimately drained the energy from his administration. The fact that Rosa and Peter's champion had plenty of troubles of his own as he moved more deeply into politics and headed toward a bizarre and bitter end to his first marriage would all prove a fatal disadvantage to "Mama Mondavi" and her youngest son when their family feud exploded in court.

Charles Williams made a linguistic faux pas when he interviewed for a job at the new Robert Mondavi Winery in 1970. A tall, straight-talking man who'd been born and raised in Lodi, Williams walked into Robert's office, stuck out his hand, and called him "Mr. Mon-day-vee," which is how the family's name had always been pronounced back home in the Central Valley. Williams realized his mistake when Robert chuckled good-naturedly and pronounced his name "Mon-dah-vee." Propping his feet on his old wooden desk and leaning back in his chair, Robert was relaxed during the chat, spending most of the time talking about himself and his business philosophy. The two men hit it off. "I fly by the seat of my pants, but I fly so fast and so low, nobody notices," Robert confided in Williams, before offering him a job.

Robert was being candid. The early years of the Robert Mondavi

Winery were indeed fast-paced and chaotic. What Robert had originally envisioned as a small, 20,000-case winery for his son rapidly outgrew that modest vision. In 1967, the winery sold 2,579 cases of wine. The following year, its case sales nearly quadrupled. They tripled in 1969 to more than 30,000 cases. By 1973, they had tripled once again, approaching an astonishing 100,000. That growth, however, did not correspond with steadily rising profits.

From the very beginning, Robert spent freely on such state-of-the-art equipment as jacketed stainless steel tanks, Austrian-made rotating dejuicer-fermenters, known as roto-tanks, and expensive French barrels. While the Robert Mondavi Winery quickly gained a reputation as being technologically advanced, it didn't have the careful planning and administrative controls that more established wineries relied upon. As a start-up, decisions were often made on the fly and were not carefully thought through—the same unruly entrepreneurial energy fueling the explosive growth of nearby Silicon Valley at the same time.

An early example of this start-up mentality occurred when a flood of growers sought to sell their grapes to the new winery. Robert wouldn't refuse and ended up crushing more than a thousand tons of grapes in 1967, more than twice as much as the previous year. He faced a difficult choice: selling all the extra wine he'd made or letting his contracts with these new growers lapse, opening the way for them to sell their grapes to rival wineries. Instead, he and his partners decided to look for an outside investor.

Ironically, the partner for the man who would soon make the words *fine wine* and *Napa* synonymous came from the brewing industry, and specifically the Sick's Rainier Brewing Company, a relatively small, family-owned brewery based in Washington State. Rainier was looking for a way to diversify its interests in a related field that was not yet dominated by a few industry giants, as the brewing industry was even then by Anheuser-Busch and Coors. Its advance scout in Napa Valley was Alan Ferguson, the grandson of Rainier's founder and its president and CEO at the time.

Nicknamed "Ferg," Rainier's chief executive had just sold the company's baseball team, the Seattle Rainiers, and had $12.5 million in cash to invest. He learned through Chuck Daniels, Krug's longtime northern-California distributor, that Holmes and Shoch were getting nervous about ever seeing a return on their $25,000 investments in the Robert

Mondavi Winery and were somewhat unnerved by Robert's large ambitions for the business. They realized he wasn't satisfied with just running a model winery for their real estate project, but more ambitiously wanted to compete with his brother.

After visiting a number of Napa Valley wineries, Ferguson paid a call on Robert Mondavi in the spring of 1967. During that visit, Robert explained his philosophy of "being the best, not the biggest" and spoke convincingly of the growing market for fine wines. Ferguson raised the possibility of Robert selling out to Rainier entirely, but Robert was not interested. Still, the two men developed a good rapport. From Robert's perspective, he was bringing in another family operation as a partner that shared his drive to excel in quality.

Ferguson went back to Seattle and drafted a proposal to Rainier's board. In February of 1968, Rainier's directors approved a deal to buy out Shoch and Holmes's stake and leave Robert with management control. Robert had insisted on this after his banishment by Rosa and Peter, since he was determined never again to repeat the experience he'd had of being ousted at Krug. Both Robert and Michael Mondavi agreed to work under management contracts. In order to obtain the capital they needed to grow their winery, they gave equal say in it to Rainier. The bargain was that Rainier, in turn, would provide the cash to help them rapidly grow their young company. Rainier's goal was for the Robert Mondavi Winery to eventually sell two hundred thousand cases a year—an ambitious goal, considering that Mondavi's sales had barely topped ten thousand cases in 1968. Charles Krug, in contrast, was selling more than half a million cases of wine a year by then. But Rosa and Peter still viewed Rainier's backing as a threat, since the Seattle company was proposing an enormous, twentyfold increase in sales over the decade, a goal that would certainly test Robert's stated belief that growth did not have to come at the expense of quality. Considering the valley's small size and how quickly news traveled, Robert's family almost certainly knew of his plan.

Was sibling rivalry fueling Robert's drive to build a bigger operation? Or did he simply need a deep-pocketed investor if the winery was to keep its creditors at bay? As the head of a family enterprise himself, Ferguson was no stranger to the emotional undercurrents that influence so many business decisions. He entered into the arrangement with Robert and Michael with a full understanding of the family politics at play. He realized there was a simmering feud between Robert and the rest of his family and knew that this feud could well erupt into a legal battle that would challenge everything from Robert's right to use his own last name on his wine labels to Robert's equity stake in Krug. He may have hoped that by buying an investment position in Krug, he could help pave the way for family reconciliation.

But Ferguson, a good judge of character, also recognized that the same ambition that fueled Robert's entrepreneurial drive also led him to spend freely and without self-restraint. One example of this was Robert's stance on the construction of the columns of the new winery. To save money, Cliff May had suggested they could be made of boards covered in chicken wire and then stuccoed. But where quality was at stake, there was no choice. Robert insisted the walls be solid, even though that meant they'd cost more.

Knowing this, Ferguson installed Daniels as vice president and treasurer of the Robert Mondavi Winery and senior vice president in charge of vineyards. Daniels also became the third member of the winery's executive committee, along with Robert and Michael. Daniels also was instrumental in helping the young winery purchase an additional 230 acres of the To Kalon vineyard after he learned that the Stelling heirs wanted to cash out, as well as helping to buy another 550 acres nearby through a new subsidiary called Robert Mondavi Vineyards and Company. Some old-time farmers viewed the well-dressed Daniels suspiciously, referring to him as one of the unwelcome breed of "suede shoe boys" coming to the valley. But Daniels helped put the pieces in place for the Robert Mondavi Winery's breathtaking ascendancy as Napa Valley's most innovative winery, with its success adding fuel to the Mondavis' smoldering family feud.

Although he'd been reelected to the board of C. Mondavi and Sons continuously through the 1960s, Robert had no longer bothered to go from late 1966 onward; it was clear to him that he was not welcome. Joe Alioto generally attended the meetings both as a director and as C. Mondavi and Sons' general counsel in the early years, but Robert was barred from having his own legal counsel at the meetings and denied even the most basic information about Krug's operations and finances.

But not long after Rainier bought into his winery, Robert began attending board meetings at Charles Krug again. The impetus for his return was the possibility, at least in Robert's mind, that Rainier might serve as a buyer for any Krug shareholders who wished to sell out to it on a fair basis.

Often held around the long wooden dining table in Rosa's great room at her home on the Krug Ranch, the family board meetings were called to order by the Mondavi matriarch. Then, she'd turn the proceedings over to Fred Ferroggiaro or Joe Alioto and promptly disappear into the kitchen to continue rolling pasta and simmering sauces. As it turned out, the real discussions among the "majority directors" often had already taken place out in the garage before the formal meeting even began.

Decisions that the "majority directors"—meaning Peter, Rosa, Mary, and at first Helen—had taken would then be announced to the larger group, consisting of Robert, Michael, and Robert's attorney, Cliff Adams. If Robert objected, Alioto's tactic was simply to cut him off as he started to speak, refusing to allow him to ask questions or make suggestions concerning Krug's operations.

The bitterest moments of these tense and unhappy gatherings often involved the feast that would take place afterward. Throughout the meetings, wonderful smells of roasting meats and sautéed garlic would drift into the great room, making the directors' mouths water as the midday meal approached. Generally, Michael, Cliff Adams, Alioto's associate Rick Saveri, and any other lawyers who were present in the room sat in chairs behind the table where the principals were seated. When the time finally came, "it was very clear that Bob and Michael were not welcome to stay for lunch," says Cliff Adams. The small band supporting the sole "minority director" would rise from their chairs, leave Rosa's home, and walk the short distance across the lawn to Robert's house, where Marjorie would have prepared the midday meal for them.

Robert tried to soften Rosa's position, often wandering into his mother's kitchen in the early mornings before the other directors had arrived, ostensibly to have a cup of coffee with her. But his attempt at approaching Rosa as a mother rather than as a company president did not produce any visible détente in the boardroom.

If anything, the situation grew worse. Minor issues, such as Peter's refusal to authorize payment for maintenance or repairs to the home on the Krug Ranch where Robert and his family still lived, took on a life of their own. In turn, when Robert delivered his sales pitch to wine buyers, explaining that he wanted to make wine that would "stand in the company of the world's best," Peter and other members of the family interpreted it to mean Krug was lackadaisical about quality. Misunderstandings like these became symbolic of the much larger ways in which communication between the Mondavi brothers was breaking down.

In 1972, Peter made an explosive move. At his initiative, the "majority" directors approved a new family partnership. The new entity boosted the payout to the participating family members—to everyone, that is, except Robert. The complex scheme, which involved shifting company profits to the new paper partnership, led to what would become perhaps the longest and most brutal inheritance battle in Napa history.

The Mondavi family partnership had begun in 1943, when Cesare had set up an entity called C. Mondavi and Sons. Its assets consisted of Cesare's various business interests, including the Charles Krug Winery. The patriarch had envisioned the partnership as being a vehicle for all of his children and grandchildren—not simply for one branch of the family. That wish was expressed in the partnership's paperwork:

"Whereas the said Cesare Mondavi has formed the said partnership for the purpose of assisting his sons who are general partners, and his daughters who constitute the limited partners herein, *in building up an estate for them and their children.*"

The next event had occurred four years later, in 1947, when the C. Mondavi and Sons partnership transferred most of its assets into a newly created corporation in exchange for ten thousand shares of stock. That meant that the old family partnership's main asset was its shareholdings in the corporation. Typical of closely held family companies, the expectation was that the shares would be gifted or willed to the next generation of Mondavis. In case a shareholder decided to sell or transfer shares to an outsider, the partnership's bylaws gave the shareholders right of first refusal to buy each other's shares at book value. This restriction was added in case Cesare and Rosa's daughters decided to sell their stock after they married.

In the late 1950s, Cesare and Rosa had gifted some additional shares to their children. The shareholdings shifted again after Cesare died in 1959, when his interests went into a trust, controlled by Rosa. By the early 1970s, the ownership of Charles Krug hadn't changed very much from Cesare's original plan:

But what had changed in the intervening decades was a phenomenal

Cesare Mondavi Trust	1,200 shares or 12%
Rosa Mondavi	1,200 shares or 12%
Robert Mondavi	2,400 shares or 24%
Peter Mondavi	2,400 shares or 24%
Mary Mondavi Westbrook	1,400 shares or 14%
Helen Mondavi Ventura	1,400 shares or 14%
Total	10,000 shares or 100%

spurt in the value of those underlying shares. By the early 1970s, Napa Valley had left behind its rural past of prune trees and walnut orchards. It was becoming a glamorous destination for urban refugees, as well as a hunting ground for conglomerates seeking diversification. In 1971, Switzerland's Nestlé bought Beringer, and two years later Pillsbury snapped up the small but prestigious Château Souverain. By then, the value of vineyards and well-known brands in the fine wine industry far outstripped their book values.

Charles Krug had a book value—the value of its assets as carried on the balance sheet after depreciation—of around $6.5 million in the mid-1970s. But its actual value was at least three times that much—and probably far more, if the offers batted around by potential buyers were a reliable guide. Put differently, while the book value of shares in the family partnership was worth around $650 per share, their market value was probably far north of $2,000 per share. With Rosa, Robert, and Peter each controlling 24 percent of the shares, the book value of their interests was around $1.56 million.

Conservatively estimated, the company's market value approached $5 million, and possibly much more. For Robert, who had been sorely cash-strapped ever since his banishment from Krug, that paper wealth was agonizingly close yet hard to reach. Robert could only sell to the family and only at book value. What Cesare had envisioned as being reasonable—never having imagined the huge run-up in values or the possibility that his sons wouldn't get along—had become unconscionably unfair in the intervening decades to a family member who wanted to sell out.

* * *

Two years after Rainier entered the picture as an investor in his brother's winery, Peter agreed to meet with the brewing company. In April of 1970, Peter led Alan Ferguson and Charles Daniels on a tour of the Krug winery. Although Peter made it clear he wasn't interested in selling at that time, the three men discussed the family's cash problems and the estate tax issues that would arise upon Rosa's death. Ferguson and Robert were also invited by Rosa to have lunch. Rainier's interest in Krug later led to inflammatory charges by Peter and his lawyers that Ferguson and his company were out to "bulldoze Mother," "capture the fine wine market," take over Krug, and destroy their winery. But the truth was that Krug was simply too big and too expensive for Rainier to seriously consider buying.

In the meantime, far bigger companies than Rainier's had caught a whiff of the family troubles at Charles Krug. Peter had been approached on several occasions about selling out, but he had until then rebuffed such inquiries. It was not until the Schlitz Brewing Company of Milwaukee, Wisconsin, approached the family that they realized that the true value of their shares might be much greater than their paper worth. On September 3, 1971, a Schlitz representative sent a letter that dangled a tempting offer before the Mondavis:

"Peter, you and your family may tailor this offer to best fit your situation. Part cash—part stock, management contract—whatever you deem reasonable—and with you as the controlling factor in the production of all wine."

Peter did not immediately reject Schlitz's offer, so the big Midwestern company began courting Fred Ferroggiaro, who offered it counsel on how to woo the Mondavis and even agreed to present Schlitz's offer to the Krug board in December. But the corporate minutes of that meeting make it clear that Rosa rejected the idea of a sale almost immediately. Peter, Mary, Helen's son, Peter Ventura, and Fred Ferroggiaro all supported the matriarch by voting with her, while Robert abstained. At the same time, everyone in the family except for Robert voted yes on a motion by Peter to further restrict family members from pledging their stock. Robert's was the sole no vote on that motion.

Six days later, Robert wrote a letter to his sister Mary, who was the company secretary, asking for a written copy of the motion that had been passed: His request implies that Peter and the rest of the family had kept the dollar value and specific terms of the Schlitz offer secret from him.

They had several reasons for keeping quiet. Schlitz was offering $32 million for Krug, which meant that Robert and Peter's stakes—at least theoretically—were each worth $7.68 million. But the Schlitz offer was alarming as well. Rosa, who was then eighty-one, owned shares worth some $3.84 million and controlled a trust with an equal value. When she died, the estate taxes on those shares would be high. The new awareness of the family's wealth carried with it a fear that they'd have to sell off vineyards or other estates to make the payment when the time came. Peter immediately asked Krug's outside accountant to investigate the estate tax problem.

After the lean years of the late 1950s and early 1960s, Krug's after-tax earnings had been rising fast. Between 1967 and 1971, its profits had more than tripled to $875,000 from $237,000. The accountant advised Peter that "since Napa Valley wines have attracted nationwide attention, they may presently be considered a glamour industry, and accordingly its stock would have a relatively high [price to] earnings ratio." Assuming that the Internal Revenue Service chose to use this method of determining the value of the family's shares, the Mondavis were facing a potentially crippling tax bill when the time came.

One strategy for cutting that bill would be to reduce the size of Rosa's estate through gifts to her children or grandchildren. Another possibility was to dampen Krug's earnings by stepping up the winery's program for repairs and maintenance, planting more vineyards, and hiking salaries. Peter and Rosa ended up adopting a two-pronged plan: slash Krug's reported earnings and build up Rosa and Peter's liquid assets so Rosa's family could pay the inheritance tax.

Despite being rebuffed by the board, Schlitz remained in the background that spring, reiterating its desire to consummate a "marriage between the Mondavi and the Schlitz families." Meanwhile, though, a new suitor had appeared: the Quaker Oats Company. Peter had turned down its proposal as well, indicating that the family would entertain no thoughts of selling until it had worked out its potential estate tax problems.

Further complicating the matter were Rosa's feelings. As Alioto recalled it in later years, Rosa was dead set against ever selling the Charles Krug Winery, no matter how high the price. When he broached the idea with her—Rosa barely five feet tall and Alioto towering over her at more than six feet—her stance was unshakable.

"Mrs. Mondavi," Alioto said, "you really ought to think about this seriously, particularly in view of the dispute that's going on. That's one way of settling it."

"But my Cesare always told me never to sell the winery. Never to sell the winery!"

"Yes, I know," said Alioto. "But when he told you that, he was thinking that maybe somebody might offer you the same kind of terms on which you bought the winery, might offer you a couple of hundred thousand dollars payable over five years or ten years. They're offering you thirty-two million dollars in cash, and you really ought to think seriously about it."

Rosa paused for a moment. She finally said, "Mr. Alioto, what am I going to do with thirty-two million dollars? Right now I have this winery. I enjoy inviting my friends to my Sunday lunches and maybe we'll just keep it the way it is. . . . Can I do anything more or be any happier than I am right now?"

In later years, Alioto could never forget Rosa's stubborn insistence on keeping the winery, regardless of how much money she might get. Alioto realized that Mama Rosa felt she had no need for more money. "It was just the dispute that was driving her crazy," he concluded.

CHAPTER SIX

Gunslingers, 1972–1975

To solve the looming estate tax problem, Peter put his head together with his accountants' and lawyers' and hit upon a drastic plan. They would immediately terminate the old C. Mondavi and Sons partnership and create a new one in its place to be called C. Mondavi and Company. As a sop to Robert, they offered him a token 10 percent limited partnership in this new entity. Peter and his lawyers would later argue that his reason for unilaterally dissolving the old partnership and creating a new one where Robert's interests were slashed was that Robert had been competing with Charles Krug in lining up grape contracts in the Central Valley. But in the letter that Peter wrote to Robert dated September 26, 1972, urging him to quickly sign the documents necessary to carry out this plan, he never mentioned the supposed competition from Robert that would later be a key issue in defending his actions.

Buried in the fine print of the new partnership's legal documents was an even more troubling fact. Robert would be shut off from any means of participating in Krug's profits, which would be diverted to the other members of his family instead. The plan also radically tilted the share ownership of the new partnership: Rose would get 30 percent, Peter 30 percent, Mary 15 percent, and Helen 15 percent, with Robert's stake just 10 percent—and a limited interest at that. But perhaps the most painful part of the proposal was the condition that the general partners—Rosa, Peter, and the two sisters—"would have the right to purchase all or any portion of the interest or shares of any limited partner [there was only one, namely Robert] his heirs or personal representatives on thirty days' notice for the *nominal amount of his share of capital, together with his share of the profits up to such a date—with no payment to be made for goodwill.*"

It was an outrageous suggestion, particularly in view of the Schlitz offer for Charles Krug. Behind the dry language of a business partnership, Robert's mother, brother, and sisters were trying to cut him out of the profits and value of the family business that he had helped start and had labored on for more than two decades.

Understandably, Robert refused to sign the papers. But soon afterward, Peter, Rosa, Mary, and Helen formed the new partnership anyway, excluding Robert entirely. By doing so, Peter and Rosa boosted their shares in the company even more to 35 percent, while Mary and Helen's stayed at 15 percent each. On paper, his mother and brother had wiped out Robert's interest entirely and divided it between themselves.

Helen, though, had begun to have her doubts. She had not been involved in the discussions leading up to the formation of the new partnership and Mary, as corporate secretary, simply presented her with the papers to sign. Helen, who was on the phone at the time the papers were laid before her, refused. Straightaway, she called her son, Peter Ventura, who by then was a practicing attorney in Bakersfield. Peter talked with his mother. Helen then handed over the phone to Mary, who spoke with Peter and then handed it back to her. Peter warned his mother that she would find herself a limited partner like Robert unless she signed. It was a heavy-handed threat from the family directed at a woman who was struggling with emotional problems at the time. On her son's advice, Helen signed.

A new personality entered the fray a few years before the "majority directors" began their efforts to squeeze Robert out of his inheritance. Citing rules prohibiting elected officials from being involved in alcohol-related businesses, Joe Alioto stepped down from C. Mondavi and Sons' board in

August 1969 and asked his son John to take his place. Then in his mid-twenties, John was running a family steamship business. As he recalled the request, his father phoned him, explained the problem about not being able to serve as C. Mondavi's chairman any longer, and asked him to serve as a director instead. "You're the business guy, so I want you to do this for me," John Alioto recalled his father telling him. Although John tried to talk him out of it, explaining he was far too busy for such a commitment, Joe Alioto wouldn't take a no.

John's father didn't keep him entirely in the dark about the family feud. He summed up the personalities neatly, describing Robert as "the guy with flair" and Peter as the "steady plodder" who ran the business. As John Alioto recalled it later, his father had sized up the situation as a personality clash between brothers. But the most important thing Joe Alioto communicated to his son concerned his clear role on the board, which was to support "Mama Rosa" and her younger son. "Your job is to vote with Peter and Rosa," he instructed.

By 1972, John Alioto started to worry that he had waded into treacherous waters. A meeting on November 17, 1972, was the first gathering of the board since Peter had informed Robert of the plan to dissolve the old partnership. Eventually, the explosive subject of the relationship between the old partnership and the corporation arose.

Peter Ventura moved that the corporation buy and operate the old Lodi partnership, which he and Robert supported as a way to liquidate their branches of the family's interests. Peter Mondavi objected on the grounds that it would "constitute an untold financial burden and entail yet another several million dollars of borrowing" and "would cause cash flow problems."

The motion was voted down. Rosa was brought into the room from the kitchen, where she was cooking, to cast her vote. John Alioto—following his father's instructions—voted with Rosa and Peter. Robert was the sole dissenting vote, since even Peter Ventura, whose allegiances between the two brothers wavered in the early days of the fight, cast his vote with his grandmother and against his uncle Bob. While it was clear that this loss infuriated Robert, he remained politely restrained and businesslike during the meeting. Even when he voiced his objections, saying, "You can't do this to me," he kept his temper in check.

Only afterward did Robert's bitterness emerge. The meeting had concluded and he sat down in front of Rosa's large stone fireplace to have a quiet word with Fred Ferroggiaro. Robert turned to John Alioto and said, "You're doing a good job for your client, you're cutting me out."

That meeting was a turning point for John Alioto. He had grown up as one of Joe Alioto's six children and couldn't escape dinner conversations about court trials. So it didn't take long before he realized the feud would erupt into a lawsuit—and that agreeing to do for his dad this seemingly simple favor was going to cost him a lot in terms of time and reputation. He demanded and received legal indemnification from Krug in return for serving as a director. "My father had thrown me into the midst of a lion's den," he says. "He knew it was going to result in litigation."

After Peter, Rosa, and the rest of the family set up the new partnership in 1972, Adams advised Robert to go to court. Suing his own mother, brother, sisters, and the high-powered Bank of America executive Fred Ferroggiaro was not something Robert took lightly. But after mulling it over for weeks, he came to the conclusion that a lawsuit was the only way he could protect his and his children's birthright.

Adams drafted Robert's first complaint on November 21, 1972, and filed the suit on December 11, about two months after Robert had learned of the plan to form the new partnership and a few days after learning of Peter and Rosa's intention to sack him from C. Mondavi and Sons' board. It sought a supervised dissolution of the new partnership and a full accounting of its assets. It also asked for an injunction to halt the board from firing him. Robert had dropped a bombshell on his family and would feel the emotional repercussions of naming his mother Rosa in the lawsuit for the rest of his life.

The complex case moved slowly. Peter, Rosa, and the other defendants answered Robert's charges and filed a barrage of cross-claims of their own on February 2, 1973. Adams countered by filing a petition on June 13, 1973, in San Joaquin County Superior Court seeking removal of Rosa and Peter as trustees of the Cesare Mondavi Trust. In a hearing, the flamboyant court veteran Joseph Alioto ran rings around the tweny-six-year-old Adams. The judge dealt Adams a blow: He decided to remove both Robert and Peter as trustees, leaving Rosa alone in that role. That laid the groundwork for pitting son against mother.

At the conclusion of the hearing, the judge came down from the bench to pay his respects to the famous Joseph Alioto, who was then running for California governor. The judge was Italian, Alioto was Italian, the Mondavis were Italian, and so everybody started speaking Italian, leaving Adams at sea as the interpreter stopped interpreting.

It rapidly became clear to both Adams and Robert that he needed a lawyer with more experience in court. So as they drove back from Stockton, Robert and Adams discussed hiring a litigator. And not just any litigator: He had to be the toughest, wiliest courtroom gunslinger they could find, since he'd be facing Joseph Alioto, who seemed bulletproof.

Adams interviewed more than half a dozen attorneys before narrowing the field down to three. One candidate, John Martel, was, to put it mildly, unconventional. The son of a state dairy inspector, Martel had grown up in the Central Valley town of Modesto. Because of his family's modest means and his father's limited ambitions for him, Martel graduated from public high school and Modesto Junior College. On his own initiative, Martel then went on to the University of Oregon on a partial basketball and track scholarship, where he studied business administration until the Korean War intervened midway through his junior year. He joined the air force and became a pilot, training to fly missions over Korea but never getting the chance: He received his orders for Korea the day the truce ending the war was signed. Young and aggressive, Martel was devastated that he wouldn't see combat. He had hoped to get over there and drop bombs on cows and rice paddies.

With three years of paid tuition coming to him from the GI Bill, Martel decided to enter Boalt Hall School of Law at Berkeley. Not long out of law school he found himself trying murder cases. Eighteen months later, he jumped to a leading private defense firm, Bronson, Bronson and McKinnon, where his pay inched up an additional $50 to $400 a month; the hours were as long, but the challenges were different. Then in 1964, at the urging of Frank Farella, a friend who also had worked at Bronson, Bronson and McKinnon, he joined Tom Elke, Farella, and Jerry Braun at a young firm that became Farella, Braun and Martel. There he continued his courtroom winning streak, capped by a case in 1968 in which a Richmond, Virginia, jury awarded his client in an antitrust case the highest monetary judgment in the state's history. The case was later overturned, but it gained national attention.

But by the mid-1970s, Martel was beginning to feel burned out. So he took a break and explored his creative side by writing songs and performing them at local clubs. In mid-April of 1975, he took a three-month sabbatical and traveled to Los Angeles, where he put together a backup band. With original songs titled "Stoned and Alone," "Unwanted Child," and "Handwriting on the Wall," he was good enough to earn bookings at the Troubadour in Los Angeles and the Palomino Club in West Hollywood. In publicity photos from the time, he bears a striking, if somewhat dissolute, resemblance to the actor Tom Selleck. With his dark, shoulder-length curls, mustache, and casual charm, Martel played under the stage name "Joe Silverhound" and wore tattered blue jeans and Western-style button shirts onstage. One of his songs, "Survivor," won an American Songwriters Award.

Because Martel hoped to land a contract with a big record company, he kept his other life as a lawyer under wraps while he was pursuing his music career. He was juggling several complex cases, including defense of a subsidiary of the Bank of America in Washington, D.C., while performing weekends fronting a trio at the Blue Crystal Lounge in San Francisco. He was drinking a lot—regularly tossing down multiple shots of tequila offered by fans between breaks at the clubs—and leading a complicated life as a single man. His marriage to his first wife had ended in 1969, undermined by his long hours at work. His personal life at the time was "somewhere between a shambles and a shipwreck."

Several months before his sabbatical and departure for Los Angeles, Martel had received a call from Adams asking if he'd be interested in meeting a vintner from Napa Valley named Robert Mondavi. Martel said he would, and in early August of 1974, Robert and Cliff Adams visited Martel at his firm's offices in the Russ Building at 235 Montgomery Street, a neo-Gothic structure that had towered over San Francisco for four decades as the city's largest office building. Robert and Adams passed beneath vaulted ceilings, with hand-chalked colors between the ribbings, and walked through an entryway resembling that of the *Chicago Tribune* building. A frieze of mythical creatures stared down at them as they stepped into the elevator and pressed the button to take them to the penthouse on the thirty-first floor.

Martel, who was wearing a suit and had trimmed his hair for the occasion, met them at reception and led them to his office. It was well-appointed, with oak parquet floors and exposed brick walls. The two visitors sat facing Martel's desk. A framed photograph of Martel's muse, Jerry Garcia, and a cartoon drawing of two lawyers with their guns drawn at each other hung on the wall. Beyond his desk was a sweeping view north of Coit Tower, Alcatraz, and, on a clear day, the southernmost tip of Napa County, a commanding view intended to impress his clients.

Martel already had some inkling of the personalities involved in the mounting conflict at Charles Krug. Before the meeting with Robert and Adams, Martel had rung his friend Jack Davies, owner of the Schramsberg Winery, whom he had known for years. Martel knew the case was going to be explosive and wanted to gauge what he was getting into if he agreed to take it on. He probed Davies for his perspective on the feud between the Mondavi brothers, which by then had become grist for gossip in the valley.

"Well, they're both very difficult," Davies said. "But if I had to pick, I'd rather work with Bob Mondavi: You can trust him."

With that in mind, Martel listened closely to what Adams and Robert had to say on their first meeting. Martel had seated his visitors so that they were sure to see his "ego wall," covered with honors he had received. Martel's firm was a relative upstart in the San Francisco legal scene with only seven partners and ten associates, and thus was not an obvious choice. Martel knew he faced competition from more established litigators in town, all eager to represent Robert.

After a forty-minute meeting, Robert finally stood up, signaling the end of the interview. He and Martel shook hands and then Robert got a shrewd glint in his eyes as he sized up the forty-three-year-old lawyer.

"John, I like the cut of your jib," said Robert. "But I have one last question. Why should I hire you instead of all the other lawyers I've met?"

Martel barely paused before answering, never breaking his eye contact with Robert or loosening his grip. The two men stood in the doorway, still clasping hands.

"Because I don't lose cases and I don't intend to start with yours," Martel said.

Robert's use of a nautical term amused Martel, since it seemed to him that his client had probably never been on a sailboat, let alone handled a jib. Yet Martel didn't care what Robert's background was, what he looked like, or whether he knew the difference between a yawl and a ketch. His dreams of landing a recording contract had subsided. Martel had become single-minded in his effort to land this dynamic first-generation Italian-American vintner as a client. In turn, what struck Robert and Adams about Martel was his strong drive to win. "Here was the guy who really wanted to beat Joe Alioto," says Adams.

The interview ended and Robert and Adams left the Russ Building. They quickly agreed that Martel was the gunslinger they'd been looking for.

On the other side, Alioto was flexing his legal muscles on the rest of the Mondavi family's behalf. A year and a half before this meeting, Peter and Rosa and the other defendants had countersued Robert. On February 2, 1973, they charged him with breaching his fiduciary duties to the old partnership by competing with it and usurping partnership and corporate opportunities. Worse, they argued that Robert had engaged in an antitrust conspiracy with Alan Ferguson and Rainier to monopolize the wine business and eliminate Charles Krug as a competitor.

Given the relative size and market power of the two wineries, it was a tenuous argument tailored mainly to suit Alioto's antitrust specialty. With Rainier's help, the Robert Mondavi Winery had grown to case sales of a hundred thousand in 1973, while Charles Krug's case sales that year topped a million, more than ten times as much. Yet Robert had to take it seriously, since the argument was being made by the formidable Joseph Alioto, known nationwide as "the King of Antitrust."

Alioto and his team didn't let up on the pressure as discovery started. They claimed that Robert, with Rainier's backing, had become a powerful and "intolerable" competitor to Krug; that he sold wine that competed with Krug's offerings and supposedly purchased grapes in the Central Valley and North Coast of California in competition with the rest of his family, offering growers $25 to $50 more per ton than Peter while still serving as a C. Mondavi and Sons director.

"At all times that plaintiff was promoting this detrimental competition, he was attending meetings of the Board of Directors of defendant corporation, accepting partnership distributions and participating in the partnership business as a general partner," Alioto maintained. "As such, he had full access to both the sensitive pricing information discussed and disseminated at meetings of the corporation or partnership as well as their books and records"—a claim that was patently false, as the judge hearing the case would later declare. Alioto also argued that the rest of the family "had no legal obligation to subsidize a competitor."

One touchy issue that Alioto attempted to evade, by muddying the waters, was the question of which brother was the better businessman—a question Robert had first raised in pushing for dissolution. Alioto attacked the idea that Robert was a more competent businessman than Peter by emphasizing how shaky the finances of the Robert Mondavi Winery were despite its rapid growth. In 1975, said Alioto, the Robert Mondavi Winery showed a net loss (after taxes) of $729,000, while Charles Krug showed a net income for that same year of $97,246. Both operations—the young Robert Mondavi Winery and the more established Charles Krug Winery, he argued, were both "presently experiencing serious financial difficulties."

Unintentionally, Alioto's argument undercut his contention that Robert's money-losing winery posed a serious competitive threat to Krug. But he was right that it was on shaky financial ground. With his legal costs piling up, high interest rates, and a bulk wine surplus weighing down the industry, Robert's winery lost three quarters of a million dollars in 1974, and even more in 1975. In the meantime, new wineries were cropping up everywhere across the valley, encouraged in part by the apparent success of the new Mondavi winery on Highway 29. The Napa County Planning Department was flooded with architectural plans for new cellars or remodeling plans for the old "ghost" wineries that had been abandoned during Prohibition. Grape prices began climbing as two of California's largest lenders, the Bank of America and Wells Fargo, predicted that Americans would be drinking far more wine by the end of the decade.

To the outside world, Robert's tightened financial straits were not evident. At sales functions, Robert was "as good a pitchman as anyone's ever seen," according to Ted Simpkins of the fast-growing distributor Southern Wine and Spirits. Robert made sales calls all day, going on to dinner with customers at night, and eventually rolling into his hotel around midnight—finally ending his day after reminding Simpkins to pick him up again the next morning at seven A.M. Simpkins and others found him exhausting.

Robert put on a great show, but his young company's footing was not nearly as solid as he suggested. In earlier years, it had been able to buffer its bottom line by selling off bulk wine. But when the bottom fell out of that market, the Robert Mondavi Winery was in a bind. The Molson Brewing Company, which owned 49 percent of Rainier, began to wonder if it would ever see a return on its investment. "The Canadians were getting very impatient," recalls Cliff Adams.

Molson expressed its concern by summoning Robert to Seattle to meet with the company's chief financial officer shortly after the Robert Mondavi Winery reported its disastrous 1974 loss. Robert brought Michael and Cliff Adams with him to the meeting, where the winery's poor record-keeping and accounting systems came under fire. Robert would later blame the situation in part on an accountant he wasn't happy with. But his own unchecked spending, his inability to stick to a budget, and his refusal to submit expense accounts also worried Molson.

The crisis reached a head when Molson attempted to seize control of the company from Robert and Michael. Because of modifications that had been made to the partners' operating agreement in 1972, Molson couldn't strip Robert of his leadership role. Yet the Canadian brewer did win one key concession: It forced the Mondavis to install Alan Ferguson as the company's overseer, sitting just down the hall from Robert at the winery. Charles Daniels's friendship with Robert grew strained, since he became increasingly identified as being Rainier and Molson's man at the winery.

Considering the desperate cash crunch that the Robert Mondavi Winery was facing, it didn't help that Robert also lost the sizable monthly support he had been receiving from his family. Six months after Krug filed its cross-claim against Robert in February of 1973, and shortly after the conclusion of Krug's fiscal year, Peter and Rosa finally decided to terminate Robert's contract as a consultant to Krug, which had been worth $9,000 a year to him. "After almost six and a half years of patient indulgence," the family decided "to discontinue the financing of a competitor (albeit a son) from the proceeds of the family operations," Alioto said in the pretrial briefing.

Peter and Rosa were fighting battles on other fronts. Struggling with the same bulk wine market crash as Robert and the rest of the industry, Krug decided after the 1974 harvest to break contracts with growers to buy grapes from them at a previously set price. What had been a seller's market suddenly became a winery buyer's market, and Peter attempted to take advantage of this by insisting on paying less for the grapes—thus damaging Krug's important relationships with growers. It was a step that Robert and Cesare had refused to take in the late 1940s.

Andrew Pelissa, a dairy-farmer-turned-grape-grower in the valley, as well as a number of other growers, filed a complaint against Krug with the California Department of Agriculture's Bureau of Market Enforcement. Pelissa and others were so outraged by Peter Mondavi's actions that they refused to sell grapes to him the following year, and began selling to his brother Robert and other vintners instead. In a letter dated September 8, 1975, from Pelissa to Robert, the grower explained,

> It is our feeling that C. Mondavi and Sons is no longer a family controlled operation, but rather is solely controlled by your brother, Peter. We find doing business with Peter impossible as he has seen fit to blatantly break [his] written contract with us.

Pelissa then went on to write that he had decided not to deliver any grapes to C. Mondavi and Sons "as long as it means dealing with Peter."

Peter's actions would end up forcing the younger Mondavi son to contend with an additional legal morass, and when the dispute came out in the trial, it would undermine his lawyers' efforts to portray him as a man of integrity.

As the case moved toward trial, Robert wrote Cliff Adams on August 8, 1975, informing him that he wanted John Martel to take over the case. Martel and his team—a young partner named Victor James "Jim" Haydel III and a recent graduate from the University of Chicago named Bruce R. MacLeod—swung into action, brainstorming different strategies. They decided to come out with all guns blazing, adopting a far more aggressive approach to the case than Adams had taken.

Their plan was to ask the court to dissolve Krug as a corporate entity on the basis of general mismanagement. Robert and Adams had initially rejected the notion of trying to dismantle the venerable family winery, in part because they didn't believe it could be done. Later, however, as the remaining goodwill dissipated between the feuding parties, Robert changed his mind and gave Martel the green light. This would turn out to be one of the most important decisions of his life.

The firm filed amendments on July 17, 1975, against Robert's family and Krug's board of directors, charging them with a breach of fiduciary duties and seeking involuntary dissolution of the winery on the grounds of mismanagement. "It was a very tough, scorched-earth strategy," Martel says. There were few, if any, cases where it had worked. They also sought a temporary restraining order against Peter and the others to stop the new partnership from distributing profits. "If we'd won, it would have been a devastating blow to the other side," Martel recalls.

But on February 13, 1975, Joseph Alioto dazzled the court and Martel failed to convince the judge to grant the order. Although he didn't admit it to his client, Martel, like Adams, was beginning to feel outgunned by San Francisco's powerful mayor: "I felt I had been run over by a truck at that hearing and had forgotten to even take down the license number." Not long after Martel's defeat, Alioto had called to invite him for a chat, explaining that this fight between the Mondavis was really not good for the company or the family and claiming he'd really like to see it resolved.

Martel made the trip from the Russ Building to the mayor's office, in City Hall. As he entered Alioto's inner sanctum, his footsteps echoed on the polished stone floors. The sheer size of the rooms made Martel feel as if he were walking into a throne room, approaching a king. Alioto did not rise from his large chair behind a fortress of a desk. Martel's chair had been strategically positioned lower than the mayor's—a move to make his visitors feel diminished in his presence. Alioto then proceeded to lecture Martel at length about why he should advise his client to drop his case.

"Joe, I thought we were here to talk settlement," Martel said.

"Yeah, settlement in this case is simple," growled Alioto. "You quit."

Martel left the meeting furious and even more determined to beat his adversary in court. He and his team dived more deeply into the case, interviewing witnesses, arguing motions, and preparing to launch a new discovery attack. By April of 1975, the time for Martel's long-planned three-month musical sabbatical arrived. With Robert's uneasy consent, Martel turned over the case to Jim Haydel and Bruce MacLeod and left for Los Angeles, guitar and chord charts in hand. Haydel characterized Martel's absence to the judge in a letter as "an extended vacation," never elaborating that the purpose of Martel's break was to front a rock 'n' roll band in L.A.

Meanwhile, MacLeod set up camp in the "Rose of the Vineyard," the reconditioned railcar that the brothers, in happier days, had set up as a tasting room and had named after their mother. The car was filled with boxes of documents that Krug had been ordered to produce by the court, and in the summer the heat beat down on the metal car, melting MacLeod as he pored through thousands and thousands of sheets of paper.

But one day, buried in that mountain of documents, he made a crucial discovery: a dozen handwritten internal memos that criticized the quality of the bulk wines that Krug was purchasing. They would prove invaluable when it came time to attack Peter's credibility and management skills on the witness stand. He felt that rare lawyer's rush: In this sweltering old railroad car, he had discovered what could be a stunning piece of evidence.

Euphoria swiftly passed, however. For MacLeod was having less success in other areas. In what he'd later describe as the "most frustrating day in my life," he deposed "Mama Mondavi" in the "little brown house," her home on the Krug Ranch. Rosa and her attorneys had insisted to MacLeod that as she spoke only Italian, she preferred a specific woman interpreter who was also a personality on a local Italian-American television show.

MacLeod would ask Rosa a question through the interpreter and then the elderly woman would answer, speaking at length in Italian. The interpreter would beg her to stop, explaining that she couldn't keep up anymore. After the first few questions, it became clear to MacLeod that Rosa was talking about something entirely different from what he'd ask. When he tried to steer her back to the point, her attorney, Richard Saveri, would protest: "Wait! She hasn't finished her answer!"

Adams had suffered a similar experience with Rosa back in December of 1973, when he took her deposition. In this case, Adams deposed Rosa in Joseph Alioto's offices in San Francisco with all four of her children present, as well as an interpreter.

"How long has this dispute between your sons existed?" Adams had asked her then.

"Irrelevant!" claimed Saveri, chiding Adams for "keeping Mrs. Mondavi for this inquisition."

Again and again, Saveri interrupted Adams's questions and Rosa, in turn, claimed not to know the answer to even the simplest questions because, she said, she could not read English.

But from Adams's frustrating encounter, one theme emerged from the transcripts: Rosa's simmering anger toward her firstborn child.

For example, when Adams asked her if she understood the complaint, Rosa had said, "I think that [Robert] wanted to do to me bad things but for motive I don't know."

"What bad things?"

"He wished to force me to sell the winery," answered Rosa, never explaining during the deposition why she felt Robert was trying to force her to sell Krug, but making it clear that her eldest son had gone against the wishes of her husband and the rest of the family.

Most strikingly, in both of the depositions she gave for the case, the barely educated grandmother managed to outsmart Robert's lawyers. "Rosa probably spoke pretty good English, but she didn't let on," says MacLeod. She "pulled that strategy off to perfection."

Around that same time, however, Peter proved less circumspect than his mother. During a deposition taken by Richard Saveri, Peter vented his frustration and sheer rage at Robert over what he perceived as the unfairness of his older brother's having gotten to live on the ranch over the years while he and his family lived in town. This was in response to a straightforward question from his own lawyer Saveri about Peter's proposed purchase of twenty acres of land on the Krug Ranch to build a home. It was an issue that had been discussed at a board meeting and was relevant to the allegations of self-dealing that his siblings had made against him. But the question triggered Peter's rage and this spontaneous venting:

> Now, my brother has a home he lived in all of his life, one time for a long, long time. He paid practically no rent, I guess, for a long time. He paid nothing, then he finally paid a piddly sum. I had to build my own home. I had to. He didn't pay for a goddamned thing. He got everything for nothing.

Peter then went on to rail against his sister Helen for what he considered her leaning on the family for money:

> Do something for everyone else, but don't ever do anything for yourself. Take care of everyone else, but don't do it for yourself or your own family, but undermine your own family before anybody else . . . in 1974, December of 1974, with Helen bitching for more and more money, I—we sent money down to her. What did I have to do? I have to cosign a note in which—no one knows about it—otherwise she would never have gotten that money. She wanted to borrow money for speculation in the cattle feed business to save on income tax.

What I have to do—she pestered my mother till she was teary-eyed, and then she finally had to plead upon me—and where am I going to get the money?—so they called the Bank of America. You know who had to go down there.

A few months later, Peter's simmering resentment toward his siblings would reach a full boil in court.

CHAPTER SEVEN

Judgment, 1975–1976

Returning from his sabbatical, Martel began to prepare Robert for the witness stand. But he quickly realized he had a problem on his hands: Robert would either respond too quickly, saying the first thing that popped into his head, or answer defensively. He'd begin his answers with a windup such as "The simple fact was . . ." and weave long and elaborate trails of intersecting defensiveness and self-justification.

Martel would later joke that Robert would react to even the most direct questions—such as "What is your name?"—by answering defensively, "Well, it's Robert Mondavi, but I didn't have anything to do with that, really. . . ." But he knew that if Robert answered questions that way on the stand, Alioto would demolish Robert Mondavi and his case. So he decided to go out on a limb.

Martel asked if Robert would mind his phoning someone for help with their problem. He wanted to consult a psychiatrist he had used as an expert witness in previous cases. Robert readily agreed and Martel walked from the conference room on the thirtieth floor, where they had been working, to his office on the thirty-first and got the doctor on the phone, asking if he could buy a half an hour of his time. The psychiatrist agreed and Martel summarized the history of the Mondavi family's troubles—the immigrant Cesare buying the Charles Krug Winery and insisting that his two sons work together, Robert and Peter's escalating disagreements, their fight and Robert's subsequent ouster, his formation of the Robert Mondavi Winery and the critical praise it had received for the quality of its wines, and Robert's attempt to dissolve the winery his father had created.

It didn't take long for the doctor to diagnose the problem. He suggested that the cause of Robert's defensiveness was his guilt over having defied his father's wishes that the family work together, his attempt to dismantle his father's life's work, and, worst of all, having succeeded in making even better wine than his father ever had. Martel hung up the phone and headed back down to the conference room.

"Bob, are you up for this?"

"Yes, go ahead," Robert told him.

Robert might be feeling guilty, Martel told him, from having achieved so much more than his immigrant father had and for betraying his father's wishes that his sons work together in the family business.

"Oh, my God," said Robert. From that moment on, he began answering questions simply and directly.

But Martel still had to grapple with another problem: Robert's tendencies to interrupt and to answer too quickly. Martel's solution was an old-fashioned shopkeeper's bell. Martel would tap on his "Pavlovian" bell to signal every time Robert began to answer the question too quickly, often even before it had been asked. The device managed to cure Robert of both his bad habits.

Meanwhile, Alioto tried again to prevent the case from going to trial. This time he summoned Cliff Adams to his office in City Hall and made an offer that initially might have seemed attractive to a cash-strapped vintner such as Robert: The family would pay him $3 million for his stake in Charles Krug if he promised to drop all claims against them. As the two men walked together up Sutter Street, Alioto warned that the trial would tear the family apart and suggested that Robert was just as culpable as Peter in the whole mess. Apprised by Adams of Alioto's offer, Robert again rejected Alioto's offer. The stage was set for the long-awaited war of the wineries.

* * *

The trial was set to begin in May, 1976. Both of Napa's superior-court judges had recused themselves from the case, citing potential conflicts of interest. So the court had brought in a "circuit rider" named Judge Robert D. Carter—a veteran judge from Stanislaus County who, after undergoing a successful coronary bypass operation, traveled around the state, stepping in to handle lengthy or complex cases. Instead of a jury, the judge would decide this case. When Judge Carter pulled into downtown Napa and parked his silver Airstream near the courthouse to hear *Mondavi v. Mondavi*, he was in for one of the longest, most closely watched, and complex cases in Napa County history.

In anticipation of a long trial and large crowds, the case took place in a double-wide trailer that had been converted into a large temporary courtroom. Joseph Alioto represented Rosa, Peter, Mary, and the Krug directors. On the other side, John Martel, his longish curls hinting at his other life as a rock musician, represented Robert. The opening statements were, respectively, described as bombastic and intense by a reporter who covered the trial. Robert's supporters sat on one side of the courtroom or sometimes in the jury box, while Peter's sat stone-faced and silent on the other side. Rosa, then eighty-six, remained at home, where she took long naps on the porch. The courtroom was packed, as friends, rivals, reporters, and the simply curious waited for the story of the Mondavi family's feud to unfurl fully in public for the first time. As one lawyer observing the scene recalled, the opening round histrionics "made the Scopes trial look like a cotillion intermission."

Robert reached out to his mother, who had been struggling with pancreatic cancer in the year leading up to the trial. He'd slip quietly into Rosa's house toward the end of the trial, kissing her on the cheek and sitting down for coffee with her in the mornings, before the trial day began.

According to one account, during one of these visits mother and son began arguing in Italian, their emotions rising. Rosa fell off her chair. As a friend rushed to help Rosa, Robert stood looking down at his ailing mother, stunned into inaction by what had happened and perhaps worried about what effect the fall might have on her. He helped his mother up and the two of them got her into her bed. After Robert had gone, Rosa expressed her despair: "I have two sons. One has short legs and he is a saint. One has longer legs and he is a devil."

* * *

Before dawn on July 4, 1976, soon after this incident, Rosa Mondavi died of heart failure in her home. She suffered what appeared to be a stroke, described as a "cerebro-vascular" accident, soon after the trial began. The editor of *The St. Helena Star* couldn't let the date pass unnoticed in an editorial. He called Rosa and Cesare "living testimonials to the very core of the Declaration of Independence, the right to the opportunity to use one's own potential to the very best of one's ability." Neither the *Star's* nor the other local obituaries of Rosa mentioned that she died in the midst of a lawsuit that was ripping her family apart.

But the feud was impossible to ignore at her funeral service. Anthony Cook captured the scene in an article he wrote for *New West* magazine:

> The first awkward moment came after the Lord's Prayer. Monsignor William Serado, pastor of the St. Helena Catholic Church, stood before the tightly packed congregation of 250 mourners and offered a blessing for the dearly departed, Rosa Mondavi: Let us offer each other the sign of peace. Almost in unison, the mourners shifted their eyes to catch a glimpse of Rosa's two sons and two daughters, standing in the first three pews with their families. What would they do? Time stopped, as the morning sunlight filtered through the stained-glass figure of St. Helena, the mother of Constantine. Then, reluctantly, Rosa's children exchanged tentative, embarrassed handclasps. The moment passed, and they turned away from one another to stare straight ahead at the altar. . . .
>
> Father Sixtus Cavagnaro, a close friend of Rosa's during her last years, stood up to speak. His words were Italian, and they rolled forth with an intensity that riveted even the few in the crowd who couldn't understand a word. Father Sixtus pointed to Rosa's coffin. Signora Mondavi is gone, he said. So what good does this greed do? Let your mother rest in peace. Stop this family war before you are all six feet under!
>
> As the service drew toward its end, the brothers, Robert and Peter, sat like stone. A group of mourners approached the bier. Joseph Alioto bent to grasp a handle. His friend, Fred Ferroggiaro, reached for the other. Then Rosa's brother, Nazzareno Grassi, joined them, along with Andrew Johnson, manager of the

Rosa and Cesare Mondavi on their wedding day in 1908, in Sassoferrato, Italy.
(Courtesy of the Charles Krug Winery)

The Cesare Mondavi family.
Baby Peter is held by his father,
and Mary and Helen stand behind
Robert. (Courtesy of the Charles Krug
Winery)

Rosa Mondavi with her children, 1920, Virginia, Minnesota. (Courtesy of Peter Ventura)

The Mondavi family outside their Walnut Street home in Lodi, California, 1922. (Courtesy of Peter Ventura)

Cesare Mondavi with sons Robert, left, and
Peter, in front of their Lodi home.
(Courtesy of Peter Ventura)

Rosa with her adolescent children in Lodi,
1920s. (Courtesy of Peter Ventura)

Peter, left, and Robert, right, looking dapper
in suits, with their cousin Joe Maganini in the
center. (Courtesy of Peter Ventura)

Stanford graduate Robert Mondavi poses
with parents Cesare and Rosa in 1937.
(Courtesy of Pate International)

The Mondavi family purchased the Charles Krug Winery in 1943. (From right) Peter, Rosa, Cesare with shovel, and Robert, with Krug workers in the background, gather for a groundbreaking ceremony. (Courtesy of the Robert Mondavi Winery)

Charles Krug's float in the "Early Days Harvest Festival," circa 1948. (Courtesy of Peter Ventura)

Rosa and Cesare Mondavi on the dance floor in the late 1950s. Cesare died in 1959, leaving Rosa in sole control of the Charles Krug Winery. (Courtesy of the Charles Krug Winery)

Peter and Rosa at the Charles Krug Winery.
(Courtesy of the Charles Krug Winery)

The Mondavi family and supporters gather for the first harvest in 1966 at the Robert Mondavi Winery. Marcia is kneeling at left; Tim is kneeling at right; and Robert is standing second from the right. (Courtesy of the Robert Mondavi Winery)

The first "blessing of the grapes" at the Robert Mondavi Winery. (Courtesy of the Robert Mondavi Winery)

Robert supervises a grape stomp at the first harvest. (Arlene Bernstein for Pate International)

The now-iconic Robert Mondavi Winery building and tower, seen under construction in 1966. (Courtesy of the Robert Mondavi Winery)

Robert Mondavi, left, hand-delivers the first case of wine from his new winery to partners John Daniel Sr. and Fred Holmes. (Courtesy of the Robert Mondavi Winery)

Michael Mondavi awaiting delivery of new winemaking equipment for the Robert Mondavi Winery. (Courtesy of Pate International)

Robert Mondavi, with eldest son Michael on his right, in the barrel room.
(Courtesy of Pate International)

St. Helena branch of the Bank of America. These were the pall-
bearers, all picked by Peter. The four carried Rosa's coffin down
the blue carpet, past her friends and family and out into the July
heat. Rosa's children followed at a distance, girding themselves
for the last rites at the family mausoleum.

There were separate receptions held on the grounds of the Krug
Ranch following the service.

Rosa's death weighed heavily on Peter, who had always been very close to
his mother. Afterward, he seemed to change, becoming angrier and even
more resentful of Robert. Rosa's death and the court battle also took its
toll on Helen Ventura. The younger of Robert and Peter's two sisters had
decided to switch her allegiance to Robert, away from the rest of the
family. She filed her own suit for dissolution of the family company by
piggybacking on Robert's request. Helen had learned that there'd be no
place at Charles Krug for her son, Peter Ventura. Seeking to cash out her
shares in the company, she hoped that by separating business and family
matters, the Mondavis might ultimately come back together as a loving
family, rather than as warring business partners.

Another reason Helen decided to back Robert was what she perceived as the shoddy treatment she and her son had received from Peter
and Mary, stating in court documents that Peter "dominated and controlled" the family shareholders who supported him while limiting information to those who didn't. Robert, in turn, had surely done his best to
convince his sister to side with him: Helen had heard some of the key
conversations between Peter and Mary concerning their brother's shareholdings in Krug and her testimony could strengthen his case.

Rosa's death, coming as it did in the middle of the trial, was a major
blow to Helen, a warmhearted woman who loved her mother and her siblings. But Helen's suffering from the family's legal implosion had begun
long before that. About a decade before, around the time of Robert's expulsion from Krug and when Helen was living in the house she'd built on
the Krug Ranch, she grew despondent. Elsa Maganini, who had known
Helen and considered her a friend since the 1940s, maintained that she
was close to having a nervous breakdown.

Helen tried to kill herself by taking an overdose of sleeping pills in
the mid-1960s, around the time of Robert's expulsion from Krug.

She survived and after the school year ended she pulled her children out of Santa Clara University for a Roman holiday, of sorts. Helen, Peter, and Serena departed for Italy, where they initially lived in a hotel suite and were chauffeured around town, then were cooked for and waited upon in a private apartment, with her family back in California paying the bills. They spent eighteen months in Rome, but returned at her family's request when the tensions began escalating even further. Helen's emotional problems had eased when she was abroad, but returned in full force when she came home.

By 1975, as *Mondavi v. Mondavi* was heading toward trial, Helen's lawyer had produced a letter from her doctor in West Los Angeles to explain why she had ignored questions from the Alioto team and would not appear for her deposition, which had been scheduled for mid-December at her lawyer's office in Bakersfield.

In a letter dated December 9, 1975, Dr. John P. Moffat, her attending physician, wrote to the court to explain Helen's problem.

> Mrs. Ventura has been undergoing office psychiatric consultations for emotional problems of Depression and other related psychological symptoms. Her previous history indicates hospitalization for the above problem.
>
> I have been seeing her on a 1–2/week basis since June 1975 with gradual progress. A key factor in her slow progress has been her deep tied emotional problems with her biological family which I understand now is in litigation proceedings. The effect of this unresolved family affair has seriously undermined progress in her resolving her depression.
>
> A premature legal interrogation at this point would seriously harm Mrs. Ventura's psychological progress and may well precipitate intense suicidal feelings and impulses.

He went on to strongly recommend that the court not force Helen to undergo a "legal interrogation" at this time. But that doctor's note only helped her avoid being questioned for a few months more. On April 5, 1976, the Alioto team finally received written answers from Helen and her lawyer to their interrogatories. She then had been scheduled to appear in court on July 6, 1976, to testify as a witness in the case. Her lawyer, Bruce F. Bunker, told the court that her appearance would not be possible because of Helen's precarious mental condition. The judge ordered that Mr. Bunker produce documents relating to Helen's hospital admissions as a psychiatric patient, including history and examination record for each admission and her discharge summary, as well.

Helen suffered another emotional collapse shortly before Rosa's death, and at one point during the court battle, Helen also completely stopped communicating with some members of the family. She ended up in the hospital more than once. Joseph Maganini, who was Helen's second cousin, in retrospect, expresses skepticism about the causes of her emotional problems. "The only thing wrong with Helen was nothing that money wouldn't cure," says Joseph years after the trial and after Helen had died.

The court battle resumed five days after Rosa's funeral. Martel and Bruce MacLeod had moved into a two-bedroom condominium at the nearby Silverado Country Club, which the winery had rented for them. With the trial normally starting at ten A.M. and running until four P.M., Robert's lawyers were working around the clock to prepare for the next day. Martel would return from court in the late afternoon and he and MacLeod would change into their running clothes and run around the golf course together.

As they jogged, Martel would tell MacLeod what had happened in court and who was scheduled for the following day. They would then return to the condo, eat frozen dinners, and go back to work. At ten or so, Martel would go to bed and MacLeod would stay up late into the next morning, poring through documents and preparing areas of questioning. To unwind, he'd uncork one of Mondavi's reserve Chardonnays, polish it off, and collapse into bed. Martel would wake up to find MacLeod's suggested themes and supporting documents for the next day's attack.

Joseph Alioto and his partner Richard Saveri, in turn, commuted between San Francisco and Napa during the trial, arriving in front of the courthouse in a long black chauffeur-driven limousine. From the outset, there was distrust, gamesmanship, and ill-disguised animosity between the two lead attorneys. Alioto's habit of creeping up behind Martel and reading documents over his shoulder annoyed the younger attorney, who would ask Judge Carter to order Alioto back to his seat.

One day, Martel took matters into own hands. The court was resuming after a lunch break and Martel could tell that Alioto was getting close, since his love of garlic-laden lunches clearly announced his approach. He waited until Alioto had come up behind him, then, acting as if he didn't know his opponent was near, spun suddenly and "accidentally" drove his elbow into the famous attorney's solar plexus. But Alioto did not budge and simply smiled. To Martel "it was like hitting a car door."

Even so, Alioto's cross-examination of Robert didn't yield the solid gains that the famous attorney had hoped for. Robert had made it through several days of testimony and cross-examination, holding up well under the pressure. Yet it hadn't been easy.

Sometime during that period, his nephew Peter Ventura recalls spending a fitful night with Robert and Marjorie at their home on the ranch during the trial as he lay sleepless in one of the twin beds in Michael's childhood room. He heard a strange thumping noise and wondered what it could be. Finally, he realized that Robert was hitting the soft part of his fist against the wall as he paced the hallway outside the room where Peter was trying to sleep. He knew that because he could hear his uncle repeating over and over, "Only the strong survive, only the strong survive, only the strong survive."

Robert had survived Alioto's tough questions, and his lawyers and sons exulted in his performance on the witness stand. On the late afternoon after the last day of cross-examination, Martel was sprawled out on a chaise in back of the condo, watching the ducks on the pond just outside the back door. He was alone and in running shorts, though he felt too exhausted from the day to run. Michael and Timothy Mondavi came walking up along the pond, having apparently circled the condo upon finding the front door locked. They wore their usual khakis and short-sleeved shirts and were grinning widely.

"This is for getting Dad through these past weeks," Michael said, and Timothy handed the lawyer a magnum of their reserve Cabernet. The brothers were proud of the wine and Martel was touched by their surprise appearance. They were effusive about the way their dad had successfully duked it out with one of the great cross-examiners of all time. The three men laughed about the shopkeeper's bell and the quick-fix, telephonic visit with the shrink.

Alioto's client, Peter, had a much tougher time of it on the witness stand. Martel systematically broke him down, laying bare the intense sibling rivalry he bore toward his brother and the lack of any substantive evidence of wrongdoing on Robert's part. One key issue in the case concerned Peter's allegations that Robert competed against the family company by wooing away grapes and growers in the Central Valley from the old partnership by paying them more than Krug was willing to pay. Yet, when pressed for the source of his information, Peter couldn't provide specifics. Oliver Tecklenberg, Peter's employee and "man on the scene" in the Central Valley, couldn't back up the story. Peter's own testimony on the issue revealed to the judge the depths of his hatred of Robert. One example of this involved the grape contracts that Robert had allegedly taken away from Krug.

"What prices he paid for the Thompson Seedless, I don't know. But I imagine it was well above market," said Peter, who was on the witness stand.

"Why do you imagine that?" asked Martel.

"Well," said Peter, "that is how he operates."

"What do you mean when you say this is the way he operates?"

"He pays well above market in whatever he does," replied Peter.

"Why does he do that?" asked Martel.

"Well, some people are geared that way. He's a promoter."

"What is he promoting when he pays a hundred-dollar premium?"

"Well," said Peter, finally goaded to anger, "he's promoting himself, his ego, and his greed. And he thinks that he's the God Almighty in the wine industry."

Another key moment involved Krug's bulk wine purchases. All along, Alioto and Peter had contended that the high markup in prices of the wines sold by the new partnership to Krug—the same partnership that had cut Robert out of any profits from his corporate stock—was justified by the wine's high quality. MacLeod's sleuthing proved it was not. He'd managed to piece together the precise route of the grapes sold by the new partnership. He'd discovered the paper trail documenting where individual loads of grapes were grown, crushed, blended, and ultimately transformed into wine. He struck gold with his discovery of documents that proved that at least some portion of the blended wine Krug was selling had alcohol levels too low to be classed under California regulations as real wine. Martel used that to his advantage: With a dramatic flourish, he accused Peter of peddling grape juice.

Girded with MacLeod's discovery, Martel challenged the witness directly.

"So that there's no mistake about it, sir, I am about to show the Court that some of your wine wasn't really wine at all," Martel said.

The courtroom exploded. After a half day of systematic questioning, during which Martel filled up a huge chalkboard with scribbled dates, vineyard locations, vat numbers, and chemical data, Peter was confronted with evidence that some of his juice could not be classified as wine under the state of California's rules. Although it was mainly a semantic argument on Martel's part, since Peter could blend lower-quality wine to bring it up to state standards, it was a blow for the defense.

Another revealing instance was the sale by the new partnership—the one from which Robert had been excluded—of 226,373 gallons of dry red wine from the Lockford Winery at $1.16 a gallon. Soon after, the new partnership sold the same wine to Krug for $1.45 a gallon—a $.29-per-gallon markup—apparently as a way to funnel money from Krug to the new partnership, bypassing Robert. Yet even before the sale was made to Krug, Peter had written to the manager of the Lockford Winery complaining of its poor quality; he had sold to his own winery a wine he apparently knew was inferior.

More damning to Peter's case was a sale between the new partnership and Krug that Robert had tried, but ultimately failed, to block. On February 17, 1975, at a temporary restraining hearing, Robert tried to halt a sale of 168,816 gallons of dry red wine by the new partnership to Krug for $1.05 a gallon. The court turned down Robert's request for a restraining order and the sale went through based upon Peter's testimony that the 168,816 gallons were "high quality wine," words that he would later regret. For during the trial, Martel produced a letter written by Peter almost seven weeks before the injunctive hearing stating that there was a serious problem with a large portion of that wine and it was not even usable.

Peter's dismal performance as a witness was reflected in his deteriorating physical condition on the stand. At the start of his cross-examination, he chose to stand, explaining to the court that his back was more comfortable in that pose. But as the cross-examination continued day after day, he was forced to bring a specially outfitted corrective chair resembling a sling into the courtroom to help relieve his pain. "By the time we'd been through some of those transactions with him, Peter could hardly sit up. He had basically collapsed," recalls MacLeod.

As Martel destroyed Peter's credibility, Alioto sensed that the case

was turning against them. He tried to prepare his clients for the possibility of defeat. Alioto warned Peter, "It doesn't look good."

Meanwhile, Peter's lead attorney was preoccupied with other matters
during much of the trial, courting the beautiful and dynamic younger
woman who would eventually become his second wife, Kathleen Sullivan,
daughter of New England Patriots owner William "Billy" Sullivan Jr.
During the trial, rumors of their affair hit the *San Francisco Chronicle* and
Martel couldn't resist ribbing his Roman Catholic counterpart one day in
the hallway at a break.

"So how are things progressing with Ms. Sullivan?" he asked.

Alioto, as Martel had hoped and expected he would, blew up.

"Those sons of bitches! I'll tell you this, I'll sue the *Chronicle* when
I get through with this trial and within the year I'll own that fucking
newspaper!"

"So I take it, Joe, you're telling me this isn't true?" Martel asked him.

"Of course it is not true," Alioto declared. "What do you think?"

But Martel knew that every lunch hour Alioto would disappear into a
local floral shop and arrange to have flowers delivered wherever Sullivan
was staying. Alioto's troubled domestic life had made the papers even before then, when his first wife, Angelina, disappeared for eighteen days
"visiting missions." After a police search, she turned up, explaining that
she had meant to "punish" her husband for his neglect. Angelina filed for
divorce in 1975 and the estranged couple spent the next three years
wrangling over an estate she valued at $8.7 million. In 1978, soon after
their divorce was finalized, Alioto, who was then sixty-two years old, wed
the thirty-five-year-old Kathleen Sullivan.

Alioto may have been distracted—he ended his second term as San
Francisco's mayor in early January 1976—but his warning to Peter about
losing the case was prescient. On August 12, 1976, Judge Carter handed
down a decision, written with the spare eloquence of a Steinbeck novel,
that was a scathing condemnation of Peter, Rosa, and Mary. Finding that
they'd engaged in a "deliberate and calculated execution of a scheme to
defraud Robert," the judge found them guilty of fraud, abuse of authority, and persistent unfairness to minority shareholders. He also ruled
that Krug's "majority" directors—Peter, Rosa, Mary, Helen, John Alioto,
and Fred Ferrogiaro—were guilty of much the same thing.

At the same time, he concluded that "Krug is no longer the family corporation originally envisioned, but instead has in reality become a corporation for Peter and his family." With that reasoning, he ordered the sale of the Charles Krug Winery so it would no longer divide the family—the largest dissolution of a profitable business ever ordered by a California court at the time.

Judge Carter's decision handed Robert a complete moral vindication. "If one thing is evident from this entire litigation, it is the fact that Robert Mondavi is not and never has been a man of greed," wrote the judge. Even so, he awarded him additional damages totaling more than half a million dollars in cash and another $489,451 in attorneys' fees. As for Peter's "defensive afterthought" that "Rainier sought to capture the fine wine market and take over and destroy the Krug Corporation," he ruled them "simply unfounded charges and totally lacking of evidentiary support in this case."

From his written decision, Judge Carter viewed Robert as a man of integrity who had been deeply wronged by his family, while Peter fell far short of that, as his treatment of growers, self-dealing, and inconsistencies to the court demonstrated. Afterward, some observers of the Mondavi brothers would compare them to Cain and Abel, describing their problems as a case of modern sibling rivalry.

CHAPTER EIGHT

The Heirs, 1976–1978

Robert had a knack for hiring good people and one of his smartest hires was his first bookkeeper, a woman named Elaine Clerici. An imposing, big-boned figure in wire-rimmed glasses who was perhaps a few inches taller than Robert, Clerici was meticulous about keeping track of every penny spent by the company. She would challenge such mundane expenses as sending socks and underwear out for laundering while on a business trip, insisting that there was no reason they couldn't be rinsed in a sink at night instead. She sat right outside Robert's office and wouldn't hesitate to bring even the slightest possible malfeasance to his attention.

By the end of the trial, Clerici was headed for a collision with her boss. Robert was so cash-strapped that he was borrowing money from the company to buy groceries. When Clerici caught on to what was happening, she took it upon herself to make sure Robert accounted for every penny. "You're going to have to give me a receipt, or you're not going to get reimbursed," she barked at him. Other people who worked for Robert also sensed his financial worries. He regularly complained that he didn't have enough money to buy a color television. Partly in jest and partly because he knew his client was truly broke, Cliff Adams gave Robert a color TV as a Christmas gift in 1976. "Although he thanked me, I don't think he got the joke," Adams later said.

To foot his legal bills, Robert had pledged his C. Mondavi and Sons stock to borrow a quarter of a million dollars. He ran through that sum quickly and couldn't pay his lawyers through much of 1975 and 1976. By the time of the decision in August of 1976, Robert owed more than $140,000 to his lawyers, even though Martel and his team had agreed to a reduced rate. If Judge Carter had not ruled in his favor, Robert could have been in serious financial trouble and might even have lost the winery.

Instead, the court's decision dramatically improved the fortunes of the Robert Mondavi family. By valuing C. Mondavi and Sons at $46 million, the court put Robert's stake at more than $10 million. And by awarding him more than half a million dollars in compensatory damages as well as his legal costs, Judge Carter gave Robert a shovel to dig himself out of his financial hole. The ruling meant Robert was liquid again: The banks would loan him more, based on his valuable stake in C. Mondavi and Sons.

Robert later said the three-month trial was one of the worst experiences of his life. But Robert's refusal to back down had given him, Marjorie, and their three offspring undreamed-of financial freedom. The trial that began just before the Fourth of July—the culmination of more than a decade of bitter wrangling—had assured Robert and his family of their financial independence. But it also left an indelible mark on Cesare and Rosa's children and grandchildren.

The lengthy trial and the ensuing publicity made the Mondavis famous for their feuding. On Friday, August 13, *The Napa Valley Register* splashed the decision in Robert's favor on the front page. Inside, it ran a story headlined "Mondavi—A Dynasty Torn and a Family Divided," summarizing Judge Carter's lengthy opinion as "retelling an age-old conflict" of brother versus brother.

The Mondavi feud also hit the national news. *The Wall Street Journal*, *Time* magazine, *BusinessWeek*, and other publications covered the story. The brothers voiced their respective negotiating stances as well as their shifting emotional states to reporters. "It doesn't seem fair," Peter complained to one interviewer shortly after the ruling, as he sat in his cluttered, outdated office with portraits of Cesare and Rosa staring down at him from the walls. "One man can force you to sell what you've worked for your whole life."

Peter had cause for worry. Judge Carter's order that C. Mondavi and Sons be sold and the proceeds of the sale distributed proportionately among the irreconcilable shareholders multiplied the financial pressures on him. It also threatened his dream of passing on the business his own father had founded to his two sons, Marc and Peter junior. If C. Mondavi and Sons were auctioned off to the highest bidder, Peter and his family, like the other branches of the family, would end up with millions in the bank, but they'd lose Napa Valley's oldest operating winery.

The alternative: Peter could try to buy out his siblings. To do that, he would have to borrow heavily, possibly burdening the winery with debt for years to come.

Less than eighteen months earlier, Peter's plan to ensure a legacy for his two young sons had seemed certain. In early 1975, Rosa gave much of her stock in the family company to Peter's two sons, who were then twenty-one and seventeen. Her gifts transformed Marc and Peter junior, two of her seven grandchildren, into millionaires and assured that Charles Krug would stay under the control of Peter's branch of the family. Rosa and Peter hadn't told Robert or Helen's families about the stock gifts when she made them, nor did she reveal that she had taken steps to keep her fortune out of their hands. The other side of the family first learned of Rosa's gifts to Peter's sons at the trial. Not only did that deepen the already existing divide between the four branches of the Mondavi family, they also caused Peter an enormous tax headache that would take seven years to resolve.

The tax problems arose almost as soon as Rosa died. The Mondavi matriarch had named Peter and Mary coexecutors of her estate. After her passing, but before the court had issued its decision, Peter and Mary filed tax forms valuing the shares Rosa had gifted to Marc and Peter junior at $370 per share. Judge Carter issued his ruling soon after that filing and it laid out in precise detail the steps they had taken to try to minimize the taxable value of their mother's estate. By stating that the value of Krug was vastly more than the heirs had let on, Judge Carter's decision unleashed the wrath of the tax authorities on the siblings' heads, with both the Internal Revenue Service and the controller's office contending that the shares that Rosa had left to Peter's sons were worth $4,074 per share—eleven times as much as Peter and Mary had reported.

At the same time, Peter and Mary were wrangling with the remaining portions of Rosa's estate. In late November of 1975, around the time that Rosa was diagnosed with pancreatic cancer, she changed her will for the last time. With Richard Saveri and his brother Guido as her witnesses, Rosa revoked all her former wills and signed a new one that expressed her unalloyed fury at Robert and Helen by writing them and their heirs out of the bulk of her fortune. She gave a mere $3,000 in cash to Helen and $1,000 each in cash to Robert, Michael, Marcia, and Timothy Mondavi, and the same amount to Helen's adult children, Serena and Peter Ventura.

Although the language was legalistic, Rosa clearly expressed her wrath in the document. "I have intentionally made no other provision in this Will for my son Robert Mondavi and my daughter Helen Mondavi Ventura," the will stated. It also contained a provision that if any of Rosa's heirs attempted to challenge the will on any grounds whatsoever, they'd automatically get only $1.00 each.

All of the jewelry, silverware, china, and furniture in Rosa's home on the ranch went to her loyal daughter, Mary, as well as the home in Lodi and the Bijou Pines cottage near Lake Tahoe in the Sierra Nevada Mountains. The bulk of her fortune, including all of her interest in the trust created by her husband, Cesare, in C. Mondavi and Sons, went to Peter alone, with her partnership interest in Mondavi Properties, a holding company formed by Peter and Mary in 1966 to purchase one hundred acres of prospective vineyards, to Mary's sons, Henry C. Fink and James E. Fink.

Although he had achieved the large goal of assuring a legacy for his two sons, the cost to Peter in terms of loss of reputation and financial pressures was steep. His frustrations and anger surfaced in the dark month of November, when the directors of C. Mondavi and Sons met in the law offices of Joseph Alioto on Sutter Street in San Francisco. It was the first meeting of the board since Judge Carter's devastating decision. With Alioto presiding and his partner Richard Saveri taking the minutes, the directors elected Peter as the new president of the corporation, taking Rosa's place. Then, they elected Alioto as chairman, since he was no longer San Francisco mayor and even though he was struggling through a brutal, highly publicized divorce from his wife, Angelina.

Peter Ventura arrived at the meeting late, missing the elections of officers. Since he and his mother had switched sides and allied themselves with Robert, Ventura was treading onto hostile territory. Alioto's law offices were filled with dark, richly carved Italianate furniture. A letter had informed him of the meeting's date and time, but it was clear he was not welcome. When the next item of business rolled around—a move to fire Krug's longtime accounting firm, John F. Forbes Company—Ventura demanded an explanation for this move.

Alioto archly informed the younger man, who was then practicing law in the Central Valley, that Forbes worked for Robert Mondavi and thus had a conflict of interest. Ventura pressed him to explain further and Saveri spoke even more bluntly: The firm had "betrayed them at trial," he fumed. The vote to sack the firm was nearly unanimous, with Ventura as the sole objector.

The next contentious issue had to do with boosting Peter and Mary's salaries. Alioto, according to the minutes of the meeting, contended that since they were taking on additional responsibilities, they should earn more. But Ventura recalled his uncle explaining that it was because he and Mary were no longer receiving salaries from the partnership as a result of Judge Carter's decision that they needed raises. The salary hikes passed, with Peter's jumping to $75,000 from $48,000. Again, Peter Ventura cast the only vote against the pay hikes.

Then the group reached an even more emotionally fraught issue: Peter Mondavi sought to rent the "brown house," the home that Rosa had lived in on the Krug Ranch, for $150 a month, the same favorable terms that Rosa had enjoyed. Since Robert paid $550 per month for his home and Helen Ventura paid $500 for hers, Ventura objected. Alioto and the rest of the board voted in favor. The subject of Robert's delinquent rent also came up: He owed the corporation $7,500 plus utility payments. The directors agreed to send Robert a letter, demanding that he pay up.

Ventura then broached the question of Peter's deteriorating relations with growers. Peter shrugged off the problem, explaining that Krug had "lost miscellaneous growers because it refused to pay unreasonable prices." Although Ventura expressed concern that Krug wouldn't have the grapes it needed because it had lost so many growers, his uncle assured him it would, even though neither he nor his sister Mary planned to sell grapes from the vineyards they personally owned to Krug that year, as they had done in the past.

The meeting ended on a sour note. Several weeks later, in what seemed like an act of petty retribution toward the nephew who had challenged him, Peter sent a letter to Helen, Ventura's mother, and to Serena Ventura, his sister, to inform them he was kicking them off the ranch. Dated November 29, 1976, on the same day that Cesare had died seventeen years earlier, it read:

> Dear Helen:
>
> You undoubtedly received word from your son that my family and I are moving into Mother's home, which means that while [sic] the white house will also be fully occupied with furniture other than yours or Serena's and will be lived in by others. This of course means both homes will be fully occupied.
>
> In view of this, we must, of necessity, move all of your's [sic] and Serena's furniture out of the white house before these coming Holidays.

The letter then went on to ask where Helen would like her furniture shipped, since the garages were full. It also went on to advise her that she would be billed for expenses "following corporate [sic] rules." It was cc'd to Serena as well.

With this cold letter, Peter severed ties with the older sister who had turned against him in the court fight. But for Helen, her brother's rejection deepened the already severe depression that she had been struggling with for years, as her family of origin unraveled.

Always the peacemaker and perhaps a bit naively, Helen had hoped to reach out to all of her siblings over the holiday season. She chose her favorite family photographs from happier times in Lodi, the ranch, and at Bijou Pines, and ordered copies of a set of the photos for each of the four branches of the family. The gifts were meant as a peace gesture and her intention was to try to convince her brothers and her sister to let go of the recent past and reunite in their memories of Rosa's wonderful feasts and Cesare's quiet authority.

But Helen's effort failed. She had left the four sets of family photos in Rosa's old home, which was now Peter and Blanche's. Helen never had the opportunity to retrieve them or to give them to her brothers and sister. Another source of pain for her was that Rosa had explicitly willed all of the old-fashioned china and silverware and knickknacks that held so much emotional resonance for Helen to her sister. Mary had no intention of sharing any of it with Helen.

Yet, Helen herself stepped away from an opportunity to become more deeply involved with Robert's side of the family. At some point after Judge Carter's ruling, he asked her if she'd like to become an investor in his winery. Pained by the years of litigation and some of the moves made by her brothers during the settlement talks, she told him that she would never be a partner with either of her brothers again. That forceful stand, however, didn't ease her emotional problems. Helen made another attempt at suicide, again by overdosing on pills. She did not succeed this time, either, but struggled with depression and feelings of being unloved for decades afterward.

Serena Ventura, who was closer to her mother than Peter was, did her best to take care of Helen over the years. But neither of Helen's children found him- or herself able to escape the emotional fallout, even after their mother died. Their anger and sense of betrayal over having been effectively disinherited by their grandmother was compounded by the coldness they felt from Peter and Mary's families for many years. Even at Rosa's funeral, they felt shunned by that side of the family. It was impossible to ignore the sense that they had been the losers in the battle, particularly as the fortunes of the Robert Mondavi family soared. Of the four branches of the Mondavi family, Helen's may have suffered the most.

As the holiday season passed and 1977 began, Peter struggled with mounting problems of his own. Alioto's firm was trying to convince the appellate court to toss out Judge's Carter's decision and grant a new trial. But when Judge Carter issued his final judgment on February 9, he instead threw out the entire board of directors—including Peter, Mary, and Joseph Alioto—replacing them with a triumvirate of court-appointed directors/receivers. After hearing from Robert's counsel about the contentious November board meeting, Judge Carter took this radical step to make sure the competitive and financial position of Krug didn't worsen during the period when the appellate court reviewed his ruling.

Judge Carter chose the former McKinsey consultant Douglas Watson, who had impressed him during the trial with his intelligence and level-headed testimony, to head the triumvirate as its chairman and serve as chief executive of C. Mondavi and Sons. The judge then allowed each brother to choose his representative. Robert's pick was Harry G. Serlis, a brilliant, quirky wine marketer whom Robert had first gotten to know through the Wine Institute, the San Francisco–based trade association. Peter chose Charles A. Lane, a tax attorney who'd worked closely with Joe Alioto over the years. From the start, the receivers were factionalized, with Watson and Serlis pitted on some issues against Peter's representative Lane.

The first shot in what would become an eleven-month-long war took place in late March. The receivers unanimously voted to fire Mary and Helen, since they were earning salaries but doing very little work. That didn't prompt a protest from either side, but on May 3, Watson and Lane moved to fire Peter as president, arguing that his presence was disruptive. To the judge, Watson described a series of problems at Krug that were spinning out of control. Peter had deferred maintenance at the old, oak-shaded winery for so long that a Wine Institute safety consultant had recommended immediate remedial work costing more than $125,000. Morale was terrible and several key employees, including the winery's controller, quit during these months.

Watson had also found that the dispute between Peter and local grape growers was threatening the winery's entire production that year. Krug was facing a July 1 deadline to respond to a market enforcement action that arose from the charges of ten growers that it had breached its grape purchase contracts for the 1974 harvest. If it didn't, it could lose its processing license, meaning that it would be prohibited from producing wine from the 1977 harvest. Because of Krug's bad relations with growers, it was uncertain whether it could get all the grapes it needed that year. With this looming uncertainty, Peter and Mary tried to use their grapes as a negotiating chip with Watson and his brother. Piling on the complications, the IRS claimed that the company had underpaid taxes and wanted it to pay up—resulting in negotiations on that front as well.

But perhaps the final straw involved Peter and Blanche's move into Rosa's old home. In November, when the subject had come up with the previous board of refurbishing the home, Peter had explained that he planned to use part of the house as an office. But when Watson and Serlis discovered that he had charged the corporation $23,000 for furnishing it, they kicked the expense back to Peter, insisting it was personal. Relations between Peter and Watson went from bad to worse as Watson became convinced Peter was holding conferences with growers and employees behind his back, sometimes meeting surreptitiously in the office where Watson worked at the ranch.

Watson convinced Judge Carter to keep Peter out of the winery. Blanche was furious at what she considered Peter's rough treatment. Peter's lawyers fought back. They petitioned the court to fire Watson, implying that he had taken a trip to New York to visit his daughter at company expense. Watson later successfully explained to the court that he'd paid for the trip himself. But the result of these skirmishes was to put pressure on both sides to negotiate a settlement.

By September of that year, they had agreed on the terms of a cease-fire. To avoid dissolution or a forced sale of Krug, Peter agreed to turn over cash and properties worth some $11 million and to drop his appeal. Robert, in turn, got some hundreds of acres of the most valuable vineyards in the valley, including much of the old To Kalon holdings, in return for agreeing to drop any further legal action and for permitting Peter to buy Charles Krug. When Judge Carter issued an order to discharge the triumvirate of receivers on December 20, 1977, Watson felt an enormous wave of relief knowing he'd never have to work with Peter Mondavi again.

The Robert Mondavi Winery attracted attention in the early years for its striking architecture and gleaming, stainless steel fermentation tanks. It also drew a group of gifted outsiders to the valley: people who were changing their lives, starting over, or struggling for a place to fit in. The talent was well above the pay scale, which started at about $3 an hour in the mid-1970s for tour guides. But money generally wasn't what attracted people to work at the mission-style winery off Highway 29. It was a sense that something unusual was happening there: a sense of openness, of being part of a food and wine movement stretching from Berkeley's Chez Panisse and beyond.

One of the misfits who landed at the winery in the mid-1970s was Norman Mini, a writer who'd been a member of the artist colony that sprang up around Big Sur in the 1950s and 1960s. Henry Miller immortalized Mini in his 1957 book *Big Sur and the Oranges of Hieronymous Bosch*. "I sensed that he had suffered deep humiliations. I did not look upon him then as a writer but as ... a failed strategist, who had now made life his battleground ...," Miller wrote about him. "One felt that he was cut out for bigger things, that he had taken to writing in desperation, after all other avenues had been closed off. He was too sincere, too earnest, too truthful, to ever be a worldly success."

A short statured man who stood perhaps five feet four in his shoes with a Roman-style haircut shagged in the front, Mini loved good wine and made it himself. He was opinionated on most subjects and intolerant of what he considered ignorant questions by the people he led on tours of the winery. He appointed himself Robert's conscience on matters of wine quality. Mini was no fan of Michael's, simply because Michael leaned toward the business side of the winery. He found Robert's other son's softer approach and love of winemaking more appealing. During the tour guide's "happy hour" conversations after work, Mini was often the first to weigh in on what became known as "the brother question"—Michael and Timothy's fraught relationship.

He did so loudly at a "crush" party in the early 1970s. The tradition marking a successful harvest is an ancient one, but Mondavi was famed for its wild bacchanalias. Margrit and her staff would make a big pot of soup, accompanied by bread and cheese. Wine would flow. In those years of flowing caftans, long hair, and relaxed attitudes toward marijuana, Mondavi's "crush" parties were exuberant and energy-infused—with employees toking on joints in the back room and slipping off to the vineyards together in uninhibited expressions of free love. "If only the vines could speak!" was a joke that staffers would share among themselves afterward; spouses were explicitly not invited. The parties were cathartic. After fourteen-hour days during the grape crush, everyone from the winemakers to the cellar rats was ready to loosen up.

Toward the end of that particular party, Mini rose unsteadily to make what some of his colleagues remember as a prophecy of further troubles ahead for the Mondavi family. Like many of the employees at that point in the evening, he was well into his cups. Mini made the same point he had repeated to the other Mondavi staffers: Timothy, a person with the soul of a poet, was headed toward conflict with his brother, just as Robert had clashed with Peter. "Tim, the poet, is going to be sorely challenged here," predicted Mini. He was one of the few nonfamily employees to speak of his worries about this imminent family collision in a company-wide gathering, but others saw it coming as well.

Mini's end at the winery came not long after that fateful harvest party, ostensibly because he had insulted one too many guests on his tour. As the guides used to joke, Mini got his "cake and moscato"—the traditional send-off party after losing his job. His firing wasn't directly related to his prophecy at the harvest party, but it can't have helped that he was willing to speak publicly about what many others also saw. Like the ancient seers who prophesied ill omens to the Roman emperors, Mini found his career quickly coming to an end.

Timothy always seemed cut from a different cloth than the rest of his family. With his long, fair hair and beard, his looks fit in with the other back-to-the-land seekers who were moving to Napa in the 1970s. A photograph taken of him in 1971 shows a gangly young man in his early twenties whose blond hair is parted to the side, surfer-style. Sporting scraggly sideburns and wearing a college student's striped T-shirt, he presents a tentative smile for the camera. He's standing next to Michael, who looks a generation older. Michael had not even turned thirty at the time the photo was taken, but his button-down shirt, his carefully trimmed black mustache, and his confident smile make him look far more mature.

Instead of going to the private college in Santa Clara where his brother and sister had gone, Timothy struck out on his own and became the first Mondavi to attend the publicly funded University of California at Davis, a school then known mostly for its agricultural research. He steered clear of joining the university's well-known Viticulture and Enology program until well into his freshman year. When his father realized that Timothy hadn't signed on, he asked him why.

As Robert later recalled to a wine historian, his son expressed the desire for a different way of life than the kind imposed by his father's hard-driving work ethic, which got him started at six A.M. and often meant entertaining business guests until midnight. "Well, Dad, I want to be creative," answered the younger man. "You are working all the time. I would like to have things of my own, my chickens, my horses. I don't want to work seven days a week."

When his dad challenged him to explain himself further, Timothy said "Yes, I want to work. But I'd like to have something that would give me personal satisfaction."

Robert answered "Tim, we can make wines here for the next, not one, but three or four generations, and we'll always learn. This is a very complex thing. There's [sic] over four hundred elements in wine. Each and every year is a different year. So, Tim, if you want to be creative, we are just getting started in the business. And you can go on and on."

The summer between his freshman and sophomore year, Timothy headed off on a backpacking trip to Europe with his friend Steve Taplin. Although his father had given him the names of a dozen or so top wineries to visit, he only stopped by two or three. Yet the trip was eye-opening for the youngest Mondavi, who, according to his father's telling, realized that some of the vintners created their own ways of living on the land, combining grape growing with raising vegetables, chickens, cows, and horses. On that trip, he also saw that the life of a winemaker could be a very good one. "Dad gave me an important perspective: 'Listen,' he said. 'No matter what business you're in, there's always going to be turmoil.'" Timothy came back and enrolled in the enology course, fulfilling his father's wish.

Timothy's fellow student in the Davis program, Harry Wetzel III, recalls him as being "always a little more serious than I was about his scholastics." He had a good grasp of biochemistry and came into the program, unlike Wetzel and some other students, with some practical experience in winemaking. During summers in the early 1970s, he would good-humoredly help the winemaking staff with such tasks as taking a physical inventory of the wine. When Timothy graduated from Davis with a bachelor's degree in fermentation science in 1974, he did not immediately join the family business. Instead, he headed off to South Africa, where he worked on experimental programs at Stellenbosch Farmers' Winery. He learned more about winemaking and was befriended by Francis Bayly, the South African who was in charge of quality control at the winery. Timothy was very well liked by the staff and showed an impressive knowledge of winemaking.

Timothy also had a frightening experience during his sojourn abroad. Driving at night over a mountain pass after a day of collecting wine samples, Timothy ran head-on into a camper van. Exhausted by the long day, he had forgotten that South Africans drive on the left side of the road. Nobody was hurt, but the episode could have been tragic for a by-then famous wine producer's son.

Although Timothy didn't broadcast his concerns at the time with professors or fellow students at Davis, he had doubts about joining the family business. Michael had been there since the winery's founding in 1966, so he would have eight years of seniority on him. He also wanted to avoid the kind of sibling squabbling that his father and his uncle experienced at Krug. Timothy was interested in architecture, marine biology, and the sciences and didn't want to experience a repeat of the pattern of fighting with his own brother, Michael.

Yet despite his misgivings, he decided to join his father and older brother full-time at the Oakville winery in 1974. He arrived at a time when the winery's reputation for making superb wines was taking off, in large part due to the efforts of Warren Winiarski, Mike Grgich, and Zelma Long. But to the winemakers, it was clear the family was keeping a spot warm for Timothy to take when he matured into a full-blown wine-maker. At first, it didn't seem to some longtime Mondavi employees as if Timothy was really committed to the job; he partied a lot, flirting with female employees, and did not take things too seriously.

But it didn't take long before Timothy turned serious. His attitude may, in part, have reflected his changing life circumstances. On July 30, 1976, not long after the *Mondavi v. Mondavi* trial had ended and before Judge Carter issued his decision, Timothy married the woman he had be-come very close to, Dorothy Reed. Six and a half months later, their first child was born, whom they named Carissa Ellen. Suddenly, Tim had a family to support.

Marcia's path to the family winery was less direct than either of her brothers'. In a lighthearted moment, she described herself as "the rene-gade daughter who had to have a little time to play before settling down." To be sure, she had little time to play during her high school years, which she spent at Santa Catalina, a strict, Catholic all-girls boarding school where the students wore skirted uniforms during the week and white shirtwaist dresses and round lace "doilies" on their heads for church on Sunday. Freshmen lived in dorms with linoleum floors and curtains to partition one student's living space from others'. The girls were required to take four years of Latin, and every Sunday morning they practiced handwriting using wide-nibbed calligraphy pens.

Marcia arrived on the campus of Santa Clara University just as her brother Michael was beginning his senior year. By then, Michael was the proverbial "big man on campus"—a football player, member of the Busi-ness Administration Association, the Society for the Advancement of Management, the Ski Club, and the Kappa Zeta Phi fraternity, which sponsored the "Man of the Semester Award," given to the student who epitomizes the "Santa Clara Man's image." Like her brother, Marcia also joined the university's ski team, which hosted often rowdy trips to the

Sierra Nevadas during school holidays. In the span of the seven years that Michael and Marcia were on campus, the university itself underwent tumultuous change. In Michael's freshman year, the college admitted its first class of women; by the time Marcia got there, half her class was female.

Some of Santa Clara's male students were actively opposed to women on campus. Not only did at least one sports columnist for the college paper argue against allowing women to sit in the main students' section at football games, but in ongoing discussions of the so-called sex "integration" issue, a Santa Clara sociology professor at the time argued in print that ". . . coeducation is also highly desirable for the purpose of mate selection." By the time Marcia graduated in 1969 with a bachelor's degree in social science, the Vietnam War was raging and ethnic awareness and activism were growing on campus. In January of that year, the Black Students Union, Mexican-American Students Committee, and the Students for Democratic Action stormed the university's cafeteria to demand the administration recognize them as viable student groups and establish ethnic studies courses. Students also staged a sit-down over dorm curfews in Marcia's senior year.

Although she graduated from college during this period of rising social consciousness, Marcia followed the traditional route for a young woman of the upper middle class: She began working toward earning her teaching credentials. She taught elementary school and participated in a program for underprivileged children near San Jose University. In 1970, when she was twenty-two, she married Michael Warren Morey, who had been ahead of her at Santa Clara. Their winter wedding took place on January 24 at the St. Helena Catholic Church, followed by a reception at the winery in Oakville.

It was an elaborate affair for hundreds, spilling out from the Vineyard Room onto the lawns. Marcia, whose shoes were custom-made to match her white gown, looked happy as a young bride, with her strong features framed by her dark hair in a Marlo Thomas *That Girl*-style flip. But some close family friends of the Mondavis were less impressed with her groom, who seemed overwhelmed at initial gatherings by Marcia's talented and emotional family. After two years, Marcia realized the marriage was a mistake. The couple separated on July 2, 1972, and Marcia and her mother took an extended trip to Europe. When they returned, Marcia turned to the winery's attorney, Cliff Adams, to handle her divorce.

It shouldn't have been complicated; there was little property to split up and Marcia wasn't seeking alimony. But Morey, who came from a devoutly Catholic family, refused to respond to the legal summons in the case and pushed for an annulment of the marriage instead. At that time, divorced people were not allowed to remarry in the Catholic Church and a lengthy list of conditions had to be met for a marriage to be annulled. Initially, that caused some difficulty due to hesitance about the terms.

Eventually the couple worked out the details so that they finalized the legal dissolution of their marriage in June in the state of California, as well as receiving an annulment from the Church. The marriage, which had lasted two years, five months, and eight days, did not produce any children. Marcia successfully petitioned the judge to legally restore her maiden name, Marcia Anne Mondavi.

To begin afresh, Marcia became a stewardess for Pan American Airlines, based out of Miami. The job satisfied her travel bug and was a way for her to see the world. But it didn't take long before the glamour of the job began to wear thin. Sensing his daughter's discontent, Robert asked Harry Serlis to try to convince her to join the winery. It had long been Robert's dream that all three of his children work with him. Their effort succeeded and Marcia worked for a time at the Oakville winery, but in 1976, she moved back to New York as the winery's eastern sales representative. Her return to New York occurred around the time *Mondavi v. Mondavi* was heading toward trial in Napa.

Coming from a sheltered background and having grown up on the family compound at the Krug Ranch, for Marcia, the move to Manhattan initially came as a shock. "I'm a slow mover," she told an interviewer who met her in New York in 1977, after less than a year on the job as eastern sales director. "When I first arrived here it took me four hours to get enough courage to take a ten-minute subway ride to the bank."

Well before Marcia arrived, her father had established many key relationships with restaurant owners and distributors in New York. In 1972, he signed on House of Burgundy, which carried mostly French and Italian wines at the time, as the company's New York distributor. Robert was tenacious in his efforts to get his wines included on the top restaurants' wine lists, including a lunch at Le Cirque with House of Burgundy's owner, Robert Fairchild. Even though there were already perhaps eleven bottles of wine on the table, Robert ordered even more, as well as his own. It was Robert's sheer persistence that helped Mondavi break into those exclusive wine lists. Unlike the more laid-back European wine-makers, who treated their annual visits to the New York market more as state visits than as marketing opportunities, the Mondavis and other California winemakers aggressively courted New York restaurants.

Eventually Marcia found that, like her father, she had a talent for promotion and the composure to make cold calls on potential customers. She began by knocking on the doors of the city's top restaurants, urging them to place her family's wines alongside the French wines that were more familiar to East Coast oenophiles. She met the most resistance from French restaurants, which insisted that their customers expected only French wines. "Madame, we do not serve any California wines in our restaurant. And we will only do so over my dead body!"

Marcia initially felt discouraged. In frustration, she once confided to her father that she felt she was not cut out to be a salesperson. He bolstered her confidence by explaining that her job was to educate and build relationships, not just to sell cases. Eventually Marcia helped place Mondavi wines on the lists of The Four Seasons, Windows on the World, and Quo Vadis.

Marcia also began organizing "component tastings"—a program adopted from the University of California at Davis that sought to explain the different flavors in wine by breaking them down into their basic ingredients; sugar, yeast, and alcohol. In this, as in many other areas during the 1960s and 1970s, the Robert Mondavi Winery was not as much an innovator as an early adopter of ideas, helping to spread them through the industry. Marcia and Michael together presented the idea of component tasting to the Wine and Food Society in New York. The president of the London branch attended that presentation, and asked the Mondavi siblings to fly to England to do the same thing there. Because Michael had a scheduling conflict, Marcia would have to do it alone. Marcia ended up doing such an excellent job that her father received letters from the presidents of both the London and New York chapters offering "a glowing tribute to what my daughter did there. She's just that articulate."

Marcia's initial plan was to stay in New York for only about a year. But she met and fell in love with a New York–based financier named Thomas Borger, who was the friend of a restaurant owner she had been dating. They married in 1980, at a time when her parents' lives were in flux. Compared to the Medici-like atmosphere in Oakville, Manhattan seemed calm.

On her own turf in Manhattan, Marcia was gracious and dignified. But in Oakville, Marcia found it more difficult to keep her composure while working alongside her brothers and her father, let alone Margrit. In part, she felt hampered by Old World attitudes which dismissed the contribution that women could make to a business, unless it was to adorn the reception desk or lead visitors on tours. Although she was not a vocal feminist, Marcia complained that she felt "totally marginalized" while working at the winery and that her father never listened to her.

Marcia's role in the family may have contributed to her frustration. She was a traditional middle child, trying to smooth tempers and play peacemaker in the family. She often served as a counterbalance to Michael and Timothy, and was a bit of a "daddy's girl"—idolizing her father, despite his faults.

Yet, at least in the early days, she did not feel as if she had real power. As she explained to an interviewer in New York in 1977, she was "the middle body, literally. Michael, my older brother, is executive vice president of the winery; Tim, the youngest, is production manager and a graduate of UC Davis. But do you know something? It would take all three of us to carry on the winery as Dad does. We say it's a democracy— but Dad makes all the decisions." In that respect, her brothers were in the same position she was: essentially powerless relative to their father.

Along with her two brothers, Marcia in later years served on the company's board and made frequent trips between New York and Napa. Following a board meeting where Robert had dismissed one of Marcia's suggestions, her frustration bubbled over. She turned to Cliff Adams to complain about her treatment as an employee. "My father is a chauvinist pig," she told Adams, complaining that Robert wouldn't pay any attention to her and didn't seem to value her opinions on business matters. "You've got to do something," Marcia begged the lawyer. "You've got to make him listen to me!" Marcia's complaints went nowhere, since her father, who had grown up in a household where his mother's place was in the kitchen, was not going to change his attitudes toward women to suit his daughter, no matter how intelligent and persuasive she might be.

And Marcia wasn't the only female employee complaining about Robert's treatment of her. One of Robert's former secretaries, Mimi Brewer, brought a legal claim against her old boss, charging that he'd discriminated against her on the basis of her sex and age. It was an unfortunate and awkward situation. Brewer had been let go in the early 1970s, after working with Robert during the early years of the Robert Mondavi Winery. After she left the company, Mimi brought a complaint to the Equal Employment Opportunity Commission against Robert and the company. Cliff Adams did not take the case lightly, due to Brewer's extensive knowledge of Robert's business, which may have included her boss's rumored sexual dalliances. The dispute was eventually settled out of court with the help of a mediator and Brewer won a modest cash settlement from the winery.

The winery was hit with an even stickier personnel problem a few years later. The married vineyard manager, Charles Williams, began an affair with his assistant, Dorothy Barajas, in early 1982. His wife, Stella Williams, caught wind of the affair and was enraged. She stormed into the winery's executive offices on several occasions to confront Michael, Cliff Adams, Robert, and the winery's female head of human relations, insisting that they put an end to the affair. Stella Williams also called the Mondavi men's wives, hoping to rally their support. The Williamses divorced and Charles Williams then married Barajas. But soon after they married, Adams sat the couple down and explained that Charles would not be permitted to work with his new wife and that Barajas would have to go. In choosing between the two employees, Adams and others at the winery decided to retain the male vineyard manager and fire the female secretary, citing the couple's marriage as the ostensible reason for the dismissal. The company lawyer explained that there were, indeed, two sets of rules at the Robert Mondavi Winery: one that applied to professional staffers and another that applied to Robert, as the winery's founder and majority owner, and his employee Margrit.

Barajas was hurt and infuriated. Like many others who worked for the Mondavis, she considered the company family and felt crushed by the betrayal, as if her own family had thrown her out of the house. Robert himself sought to help Barajas by sending a memorandum to the management council asking if there wasn't a job that could be found for her where she wasn't directly supervised by her husband. "Good employees are not the easiest thing to find," Robert's memo insisted.

But Barajas was terminated anyway, in a letter from Greg Evans. It reiterated an offer by Timothy to give her severance pay equal to seven weeks' salary in exchange for a release of all legal claims against the company, but she didn't take it. Timothy, who initially supported Barajas's efforts to find another job at the company, later turned against her after hearing that some employees felt that she, and not her husband, was running the vineyards unit. Michael, too, felt that Williams and Barajas's relationship had had a damaging effect on employee morale. In later years, Barajas and Williams maintained that the company scapegoated her for doing what Robert and Margrit, as well as others, had also done—engage in an adulterous affair with a fellow employee. Michael, in particular, seemed especially upset by Williams and Barajas's romance, perhaps because it occurred shortly after his father's secret elopement with Margrit. "Michael wouldn't look me in the eye," says Barajas.

Barajas underwent several years of therapy to try to cope with the pain of her dismissal. She also filed a lawsuit against the winery in 1987, alleging employment discrimination, fraud, and intentional infliction of emotional distress. As part of the discussions surrounding that suit, Barajas's attorney had compiled a dossier on Robert's own extramarital affair with Margrit, threatening to publicly expose them. That threat was significant: Not only would it potentially embarrass Robert and Margrit's spouses and children, but it also could undermine Robert's reputation for fair dealing. The company argued that Margrit was not directly supervised by Robert, but by the winery's public relations head, Harvey Posert, and though it conceded it had more than a dozen married couples working for it as well as numerous family members of employees, none of them directly reported to each other. After more than two years of litigation and on the verge of a jury trial, the company settled the case by paying Barajas a cash settlement of around $25,000.

The irony, however, of Barajas's losing her job was not entirely lost on the Mondavi family. After the suit was settled, Barajas visited a gym in Napa that many Mondavi employees use to work out. Barajas had finished her exercise and was slipping into the hot tub when she saw that Timothy was there. They chatted and the conversation turned to the family business where Barajas had found a job. Timothy noted that someone in that company had gotten a job through a relative, who was also employed there. "Isn't that a little bit of nepotism?" Timothy asked her. Barajas flushed deeply and decided not to respond, since Timothy remained her husband's boss.

Although Barajas's dismissal occurred in 1986, long after Gloria Steinem launched *Ms.* magazine and feminists were pushing for ratification of the Equal Rights Amendment, the Robert Mondavi Winery remained a male-dominated company that was not always sensitive to women. It was a period when staffers threw a birthday party for Michael Mondavi and hired a stripper to perform for him in his office—with little thought to how female employees might view such boys-will-be-boys fun. Similarly, there were company events involving scantily clad women, including one party with belly dancers. And sometimes it was the men who took off their clothes. At one party for the sales force in the mid-1980s, Robert stripped off all of his clothes except his white cotton briefs on a dare with a salesman from Florida about jumping into a swimming pool, even though there were female sales staffers present. The attitude, particularly among the sales and marketing force, seemed to be "anything goes."

Likewise, the flirting and suggestive banter by the company's male executives toward female employees were perceived by some women who worked at the winery in the 1970s and 1980s as bordering on harassment. Robert developed a reputation as a man with a voracious sexual appetite and, as the boss, set the tone for the company. On at least one occasion in the 1980s, Michael felt it was necessary to take his father aside and caution him to try to be less obvious in his sexual approaches to women. "Please, use some common sense," Michael asked Robert, "or at least be discreet if you aren't going to use common sense."

Some female staffers, however, just laughed his advances off as part of the Mondavis' macho, Italian-American background. When Robert reached under the table and squeezed the knee of Helen McDermott, the company's female head of human relations, to emphasize a point he wanted to make, McDermott just took Robert's gesture in stride and did not raise a ruckus about it at the meeting or afterward. Through the years, there were rumors in the valley of quiet payoffs to women who worked or came into contact with some of the male employees of the Robert Mondavi Winery. But, like McDermott, the women didn't talk about it either.

CHAPTER NINE

"That Woman," 1978–1980

For Robert, the court decision was more than just a moral vindication: It was the equivalent of the signing of a personal declaration of independence. After working with his family for most of his life, Robert, then sixty-five, set about freeing himself and his family from the final relationship that blocked them from having complete control of their winery: Rainier's ownership stake in the Robert Mondavi Winery. With a loan from the Bank of America, Robert triumphantly bought out his Canadian investors as soon as he could in 1978, assuring that his company would be owned and controlled solely by his family.

Robert was also moving toward declaring another form of independence: ending his decades-long marriage with his high school sweetheart, Marjorie Declusin. In the early years, Marjorie was the epitome of what some people in the valley called a "crush widow"—the winery wife who was frequently left on her own during the long days of harvest season. In Robert's case, he also left Marjorie alone while he crisscrossed the country and the world selling his wines. Although the couple skied together and made a dashing pair on the dance floor at industry events, they began to grow apart as Robert's business trips stretched to weeks at a time.

In the first, chaotic months of the Robert Mondavi Winery, Marjorie had prepared meals in a makeshift kitchen for Robert, Michael, and whoever might be visiting that day. Marjorie hadn't known how to boil water when they were first married, and though she eventually learned to prepare lovely meals of roasts, potatoes, and vegetables, she never became a truly sophisticated cook. By all accounts, Marjorie deeply loved Robert and tried hard to please him. "Marjie's first thought at all times was her husband and her children," recalls Marilouise Kornell, one of Marjorie's closest friends. "They were her life."

But Robert and Marjorie's union was clearly troubled, as Margrit Biever, the Swiss-born tour guide from Krug, assumed a more central place in Robert's life. With her more sophisticated European palate, Margrit took over the cooking at the new winery from Marjorie, preparing lavish spreads of roasted chicken, cured meats, olives, crusty bread, and cheeses. At first, Robert had called and asked her to make a few sandwiches for a lunch meeting. After a few times, she suggested that she make a more elaborate meal for him, drawing on her own upbringing, where lunch had been the most important meal in her family's Swiss home. From that, the idea evolved into picnics on the lawn, and the jazz concerts that quickly became a valley tradition.

What drew Robert and Margrit together was almost certainly more nuanced and deeply felt than Robert's children, his employees, or even many of his old friends could grasp. Robert and Margrit shared the common experience of feeling alone and trapped in marriages they had begun in their twenties. Robert would often show up at the tasting room around closing time, knowing that the tour guides and other staffers liked to end their work day by having a glass of wine together. "May I join you?" he would ask the group. To Margrit, who continued to work as a tour guide and also liked to stay for the after-work drinks, her boss seemed lonely and reluctant to return home. Margrit felt the same way.

Margrit once asked Robert if he'd like to accompany her to the San Francisco Opera, where she had season tickets in the inexpensive section at the very top of the opera house. He leapt at the chance. "We knew right away we were going to end up together," said Margrit, who felt a strong attraction to him almost from the start.

Around this same time, Roman Catholic bishops announced that

Pope Paul VI had ended the automatic excommunication imposed on divorced American Catholics who remarried. Although Robert was not particularly churchgoing, he had been baptized as a Catholic, served as an altar boy, and had married Marjorie in a Catholic ceremony. Even though divorce was becoming more common in the 1970s, many people, and especially Catholics, continued to ostracize divorcés. And although Napa Valley was becoming more worldly and glamorous, as weekending San Francisco socialites made it a fashionable place to own a second home, among locals it remained a conservative rural community.

Faced with the disapproval of Robert's children and the Italian families who had known the Mondavi family for decades, Robert and Margrit tried to keep their affair secret. But the spark between them had been evident even in the Krug days, when Margrit would occasionally slip in to see Robert, entering his and Marjorie's home through the back door. Some members of the family were convinced he had begun an affair with Margrit as early as the mid-1960s. In a small town, their affair was hard to conceal when, for instance, they parked their cars next to each other's in the local motel parking lot.

Margrit liked to say she came from a family of *mangioni*, people who love to eat. She was born in Appenzell, in northern Switzerland, and her family moved nine months later to the green and verdant Ticino canton around Lake Maggiore, just north of the Italian border. Her mother, Greta, like Robert's mother, Rosa, always kept a kitchen garden, and her father, who had trained as a banker just before World War I, later became a practitioner of homeopathic medicine, producing and selling pills out of their home. He also made wine and maintained a modest wine cellar. Her parents embraced the bohemian spirit that swept through Europe in the years between the First and Second World Wars, striking up friendships with artists and attending the opera, even though they were not especially wealthy. Greta, in particular, was a free spirit and a nudist who wore a Californian's golden tan.

Even so, in some respects, Margrit's family was traditional in how it viewed her prospects. Although she expressed interest in her teens in becoming a doctor, her father refused to support her on that path, explaining, "You'll marry." So instead, at twenty, Margrit was attending a finishing school near Lausanne, Switzerland, when she met an American army officer named Philip Biever, who was stationed in Europe after the Second World War. Blond and effervescent, the young Margrit was swept up by a romantic fantasy. So was Philip, who proposed after meeting her only a few times. "I was his little Heidi," Margrit recalls. "It had nothing to do with reality." Buoyed by her mother's belief that life in America would be more promising than in war-torn Europe, where meat and milk were still being rationed, the couple was married on December 5, 1946, in Orselina, Switzerland.

But the realities of life as an army bride were harsher than she had expected. For one thing, not long after she'd become a mother and moved to Germany with her husband and young children, she contracted tuberculosis and spent nine months recovering in a Swiss sanitarium. At one point, Margrit grew so ill the doctors thought one of her lungs might have collapsed. But she was young and eventually fought off the infection.

The Biever family moved fourteen times before finally settling in the Napa Valley in 1962. They lived in Japan, Germany, Puerto Rico, and Igloo, North Dakota, where the Black Hills Army Depot was located, with baking summers and freezing winters. "It was the most unbelievable place in the world," Margrit told an interviewer decades later. "There wasn't a tree for ninety miles. For someone from Switzerland, can you imagine? There were no fresh things—only iceberg lettuce—so I ordered seeds from Sears and planted a garden. It sprouted and I said, 'See, I can do it.' Then one morning, zingo, the locusts ate everything. I decided to have a goldfish pond. Then on August twenty-sixth—I remember the date because I keep a diary—the fish all froze. It went from a hundred degrees in the day to twenty-five at night."

By the early 1960s, the Bievers had two daughters, Annie and Phoebe, and a son, Philip E. Biever, who was nicknamed Babo. After Philip retired from the military, they decided to settle in Napa Valley, which they had once visited briefly on a layover to Asia, struck by the memory of the scented bay trees and brilliant blue skies. Philip first became a physics and math teacher at Napa High School, then got his license as a stockbroker. He invested in real estate in Napa, as well, purchasing small properties as investments when the opportunity arose. Margrit went to work in the tasting room at the Krug Ranch and led tours through the winery. In 1967, she became one of the first Krug employees to follow Robert down the road to his new place, joining as one of three tour guides.

Margrit's interest in wine soon became all-consuming and her family begged her to stop talking about it. At the same time, Philip declined to travel back to Europe with her, so Margrit began taking the three children on her own to visit her family in Switzerland. She also pursued her passions for art and opera. Driving a beige VW bug from her home with Philip in Napa to her job first at Krug and then the Robert Mondavi Winery, Margrit exhibited a touch of her mother's free spirit, ostensibly disdaining the bourgeois pretensions of Napa Valley's unworldly social establishment. Yet she also slowly usurped from Marjorie the role as the winery's de facto hostess.

Looking back on those years, Robert and some of his family members concluded that Marjorie was simply unable to keep up with her husband's tireless pace. As Robert himself wrote, "Throughout some forty years of marriage, Marge did her share and more, but she never loved the wine life as much as I did. Who could? In the end, it wore her out. I wore her out. I did not do this deliberately; I was simply oblivious to her needs and feelings."

But what Robert failed to mention in this account of how his first marriage broke down was Marjorie's struggle with alcohol, which became so overwhelming at times that she required hospitalization. Family members noticed that she started drinking early in the morning and continued into the night, preferring vodka to wine. She was in and out of the St. Helena Sanitarium over the years and her drinking problem was compounded by heavy smoking, which she continued despite her emphysema and gastric problems brought on by drinking iced coffee throughout the day and by poor eating habits. In the early days, friends and acquaintances didn't sense anything unusual when Marjorie drank Bloody Marys during the day by the pool at Wine Institute meetings, since many of the other wives did too. But by the mid-1970s, as her marriage was collapsing and the situation on the ranch grew tenser, her drinking intensified.

Some family members blamed Robert's neglect for Marjorie's heavy drinking, a particularly ironic charge since it was the sales and marketing of an alcoholic beverage that had consumed so much of Robert's attention over the years. Michael, for one, believes his father's behavior, including his relentless criticism and his frequent absences, drove his mother to alcoholism. Yet Robert himself blamed the breakdown of his marriage on Marjorie's drinking, according to Bobbe Serlis Cortese.

During this time, Robert conducted a long and increasingly open love affair with Margrit, who by the early 1970s had expanded her duties beyond being a tour guide to running the retail room and to handling public relations and much of the winery's hospitality programs. Robert and Margrit tried to be discreet, but they were not very successful. They were spotted during those years picnicking together during the work day, relaxing on a blanket laid out in the vineyards. Likewise, sometime in the late 1960s, Robert invited Margrit and her husband for a ski break with him in the Sierras.

On what Margrit says was their first date in 1971, the couple went to Chez Panisse, the restaurant founded by Alice Waters and the epicenter of the movement to create a new American cuisine. Tucked away in a shingled Victorian house in Berkeley—across the Bay from Napa—it seemed like a hideaway where the couple was unlikely to be spotted by people from the valley. But as they walked toward the restaurant's entrance, they saw that two of the winery's newly hired tour guides, Arlene and Michael Bernstein, were seated by the door and clearly saw them. Robert and Margrit turned around quickly, hoping they hadn't been noticed, but Arlene Bernstein leapt up from the table and raced out the door, aiming to convince them to come in.

"Oh, come on you two!" Arlene pleaded. "We know!"

Robert and Margrit quickly became close friends with the Bernsteins, double-dating with them and beginning a new social life apart from the valley community that Robert and his wife had been part of for decades. Many of their new set, like the Bernsteins, were well-educated and sophisticated refugees from the city. In the Bernsteins' case, Michael had been an attorney for the Federal Trade Commission in San Francisco and Arlene was an artist and photographer. They were starting their own "boutique" winery, Mount Veeder, in the valley's eastern hills. But despite the Bernsteins' and other friends' efforts to be discreet, Robert and Margrit's love affair very quickly became fodder for the valley's gossips. "It was a soap opera," Margrit acknowledges.

In 1973, Robert and Margrit continued to appear in public together just as a winery owner and his employee. It was that year they were invited to attend a week-long series of classes and events called the Great Chefs of France, organized by a couple, Michael James and Billy Cross, who had begun looking for a corporate benefactor to sponsor their idea of pairing great chefs and wines. Robert, along with every other vintner James and Cross contacted about getting involved in the program, initially turned them down but accepted an invitation to attend the large and elegant first-night dinner party at an estate in Oakville called High-tree Farm. Robert brought Marjorie, just as Margrit that first evening brought her husband, Philip.

That September evening, forty guests gathered at the Victorian estate that James and Cross had leased for their cooking school. At a time when the main road in Yountville was still a gravel path and walnut groves and prune trees outnumbered grapevines in the southern half of the valley, it was a stunningly elegant scene: James and Cross had set the long table with Limoges china, sterling flatware, and candelabra. For the first course, they served a rolled cheese soufflé in a tarragon cream sauce cooked by the famed French chef Simone Beck, whom James and Cross had flown in for the occasion. Robert and Margrit enjoyed the evening so much that the next day they sent bottles of the winery's best Cabernet Sauvignon reserve to their hosts in appreciation for the evening.

Then they came back later in the week; one night Margrit came on her own, then on another night Robert and Margrit came together. It wasn't long before James and Cross realized that Robert and Margrit's relationship was more than just professional: "Margrit is more than just a colleague to me," Robert told Cross before long.

At Margrit's urging, Robert hungered to bring this kind of experience of the good life—a sumptuous meal paired with fine wines—closer to home. But with the exception of Domaine Chandon's restaurant, which opened in 1977, Napa Valley was a culinary desert. For years, the most popular place for a fancy meal was Jonesy's Famous Steak House at the Napa Valley Airport. So the Robert Mondavi Winery sponsored the Great Chefs program, which aimed to meet the high standards of European aristocracy rather than the plainer ones of rural California farmers. The template, like so many others at the Robert Mondavi Winery, came from France.

The first chef to teach at the program was Jean Troisgros from Roanne, followed by Michel Guérard from Eugénie-les-Bains, and even the famed Paul Bocuse, who, by the time he taught in the program, still presided over his restaurant near Lyon in his chef's coat piped in red and blue, though he hadn't actually cooked for many years. French chefs who had earned three Michelin stars were soon joined by American chefs shining brightly in their own new firmament of American cuisine. Alice Waters once cooked a bouillabaisse outdoors in the vineyards, stirring the seafood stew in a big copper pot set over a fire of vine cuttings. The students' mouths watered as they waited to dip the fire-toasted bread into Alice's mixture of scallops, fish, clams, and crabmeat. Julia Child taught in the program a number of times and once, when a student asked her what she would have done with her life if she hadn't discovered cooking, she replied, in her high-pitched voice, "I would have married a Republican banker and become an alcoholic!"

Starting in the late 1970s, James and Cross would transform the Vineyard Room every night for a week or two each year to host these dinners and the celebrity chefs who cooked them. Overnight, crews would haul in huge, twenty-foot-high mirrors and towering floral arrangements that looked as if they'd come from the foyer of the Metropolitan Museum of Art in New York. Waiters, many of them gay, wore black satin evening suits from the San Francisco clothier Wilkes Bashford. It wasn't unusual to launch a hunt for three hundred stems of rare white orchids just a few hours before the event, sending a staffer with a fistful of cash to buy up as many as he could. And on a beautiful evening, the ceiling would be rolled back to expose a sky full of stars. Robert's support of the Great Chefs program paid dividends: After the chefs spent a week at the winery, many made sure to add Mondavi wines to their lists, even if they were placed in the last paragraph of the final page.

Capable, socially confident Margrit complemented and enabled Robert's dream. She frequently accompanied Robert on his travels, including a three-week trip she organized in 1978 for Robert and the winery's top staffers to visit the great European wine estates—the first of many such company visits to Europe that Robert hosted. The couple stayed in separate single rooms. Yet it was clear they were romantically linked. As well, Margrit played a valuable role in smoothing their way in Europe because of her facility with languages: To varying degrees of fluency, she spoke seven languages, including French, German, Italian, and Japanese. Once, when the group's tour bus broke down in a small town in Germany, Margrit was able to ask for directions in German, translate them into French for their French bus driver, and then explain what was happening to the English-speaking winery executives. On that same trip, Robert, Margrit, and the other staffers ended up in a red-light district of Paris, stumbling into a raunchy motorcycle show in the early hours of the morning, and struggling to stay awake during wine tastings after disco dancing until dawn. More sophisticated than Robert, Margrit understood art, appreciated fine food, and was in touch with European culture in a way that Robert aspired to be, but—having grown up in Lodi as the son of hardworking immigrants—was not.

But Margrit's presence was also an incendiary issue within the winery, particularly among Robert and Marjorie's adult children. None of them understood or were tolerant of their father's affair with a married employee, particularly at the beginning. During the court trial, according to John Martel, tensions between Robert and his offspring were strained by their anger with him over his alliance with Margrit. All three of Robert's children saw their mother as the injured party and blamed their father for the breakdown of the marriage. From their perspective, their father embraced Margrit's gifts—her worldliness, her ability to flawlessly orchestrate a multicourse meal or event, her appreciation of beauty—but he remained, from their perspective, stunningly blind to her faults, which some saw as her determination to marry the boss, regardless of the objections of his children and two long-standing marriages that stood in the way.

To her detractors, Margrit represented the archetype of the scheming "other woman." She was not a great beauty, tending toward feminine roundness rather than the slender, long-legged look then in fashion. Nor was she young: By the mid-1970s, Margrit was already in her fifties. But she was dynamic in a way that Marjorie was not and shared Robert's goal of creating a world-class winery. Unlike Marjorie, who was unwilling or perhaps unable to keep up with the endless string of business functions and travel, Margrit relished being Robert's partner. And more than simply a companion, she was a business asset to him, able to engage a visiting winemaker with intelligent questions about the temperature at which he fermented Sauvignon Blanc grapes or to greet a group of visiting Bordeaux vintners in flawless French.

But Margrit's relaxed sense of style grated on some people in the valley, as well as on Robert's children. Unlike their mother, who dressed conservatively and whose posture was beautifully erect, Margrit favored beads, bright colors, and flowing fabrics. Margrit created a stir at one blessing-of-the-grapes ceremony by wearing a traditional Swiss outfit with a bonnet and broad skirt—a look that staffers dubbed "Little Bo Peep." The kids also belittled her contribution to the winery. When their father would rise from his seat in the Vineyard Room, praising Margrit in front of employees and guests, they cringed. They would exclude her from business meetings that she should have been invited to attend and, in the instances when she did attend, they'd pointedly ignore her, failing to ask her opinion on issues related to hospitality or public relations. They would mimic her thick Swiss accent and question her ideas and their cost.

The Great Chefs program, which Margrit shepherded along, was one of their broadest targets for criticism. Viewing it as her pet project, Robert's children treated the program as a waste of time and money. To some extent, they may have been justified. It didn't help Margrit's credibility or reputation as a manager, for instance, when the program's heads, Billy Cross and Michael James, were unable to locate a whole salmon they needed for a dinner prepared by the famed French chef Jean Troisgros at the Oakville winery and so arranged for one to be purchased at the well-known Swan's Market in San Francisco and delivered by taxi, which charged $165 for the metered journey, at a time when the winery was trying to save money. Margrit, who later would joke about how the "salmon came via taxi, lying in the backseat all by himself," was blamed for this seemingly extravagant expense and other management snafus.

Another criticism of Margrit, and one that would linger for decades, was that she brought too lavish a sensibility to the winery, which was not welcomed by some family members or employees. From a business perspective, charging thousands of dollars per couple to attend a Great Chefs program was criticized by some as elitist and not in the winery's best interests, if it were to continue to appeal to a wide range of customers. Yet Margrit and others rightly countered that the program helped get Mondavi wines onto some of the most exclusive wine lists in the world. And, from the beginning, extravagant flair had been Robert's hallmark. Likewise, through Margrit's efforts, the Robert Mondavi Winery became Napa Valley's community center—a place to hear Dave Brubeck, Harry Belafonte, and the New Orleans Preservation Hall Band on a summer evening. Streams of guests from all over the world flowed through the winery, often welcomed by Robert's warm and effervescent partner.

Still, Robert and Marjorie's oldest and closest friends as a couple were chagrined by the flash and sizzle that accompanied Margrit. It was a far cry from the days when Robert spent his Saturday nights square-dancing at the Lodi Farm Center. While countercultural types in the valley lived together without being married in the late 1970s, the couple did not consider that an option. "Robert Mondavi could not live with me in the Napa Valley without being married [to me] at that time," Margrit recalls. Yet, they found it impossible to keep their affair private for long, since they worked together alongside Robert's children almost every day and lived in a small valley where there were few secrets.

Margrit initially faced the most hostility from Timothy, as it became clear his parents' marriage was breaking up. Robert's youngest and ostensibly most free-spirited child was the most cutting in his remarks to her at first. He did not hold his tongue in letting his father's lover know how he felt about her, confronting her with questions such as "Why are you seeing my father? Don't you realize he's a married man?" Employees who witnessed Timothy's aggressive stance toward Margrit considered his behavior rude and immature, even if they privately shared some of his concerns about their workplace affair.

Michael also expressed his disdain for Margrit. He was convinced she had set her sights on Robert from the beginning, drawn up a plan to ensnare him, and was in the midst of successfully executing it. In one meeting, with lawyers, accountants, and staffers present, he referred to her as "my father's mistress." Robert repeatedly urged his children to be polite in public toward Margrit, at the very least. Margrit, in turn, never doubted Robert's support of her, even when she faced the most intense hostility. His support helped her make it through each day of work, however difficult.

In a similar vein, when Michael suggested the idea of his sister becoming head of public relations, in part to foil what he saw as Margrit's angling for the job, Marcia refused as long as "that woman" stayed at the winery too. Margrit, with her coquettish ways and her habit of cloaking her intelligence under a blond veneer, was abhorrent to Marcia, who sought to remain close to both her parents but sided largely with Marjorie in the breakup. Presenting her father with an ultimatum—choosing his own daughter or Margrit to work at Oakville—Robert chose the woman he loved, even though he knew it would provoke Marcia's wrath. Storming into her father's office, where he was sitting with Harry Serlis, Marcia vented her anger and frustration at Margrit, unleashing a string of invective. Marcia, perhaps because she was female, was the only one of Robert's children who would take Robert on directly.

Robert, who adored Marcia and treated her with a softness that his sons had never known, just absorbed Marcia's outburst. Harry, in turn, sat uncomfortably through Marcia's screed against the interloper Margrit. But although Robert heard out his daughter, he didn't fire Margrit from the winery, nor did he change his relationship with her in any discernible way. He refused to give Margrit up, even though his children clearly despised her. "It was a very, very bitter thing and I don't think I could have done it if my children hated someone as much as they hated her," says Bobbe Cortese. It didn't take long for Marcia to realize that she would be much happier living on the East Coast, far away from her family, helping to represent the winery with restaurants and distributors. So Margrit became the winery's public relations chief instead of Marcia. The women worked three time zones away from each other, which suited them both better.

After a while, the siblings' strategy was to say nothing around her, following the well-worn advice of "If you can't say something nice, then don't say anything at all." Eventually it was Michael who was the first to soften toward Margrit, recognizing that there was little chance of changing his father's mind about her.

The couple did manage to find places of refuge, away from the resentment and hostility and far from the winery. Harry Serlis, the prickly marketing genius who'd served as the Wine Institute's president from 1969 to 1975, offered the guesthouse of his Palm Springs home to the couple as a love nest, offering them cover for their romance. Serlis, who was born in Kansas City to a Jewish family, had become by then one of Robert's closest friends and advisors. In addition to serving on the Mondavi board, Serlis was a "rabbi" or special counselor to the family, helping to teach Michael the ropes in sales early on and proving loyal to Robert in the uncertain months before a settlement was reached. Serlis, who was in his third marriage himself by that time, was certainly sensitive to Robert's fraught personal situation and understood his friend's need to escape Oakville occasionally.

Serlis was highly intelligent and had a talent for quickly grasping the core of an issue. He had entered college at the age of fifteen and, in his early forties, was appointed president of Schenley Distillers, one of the nation's largest wine and liquor companies, with such brands as Roma and Cresta Blanca. Because he had achieved success at such a young age, he grew a mustache to make himself look older. In later years, he became a memorable figure, always wearing impeccably tailored suits and French cuffs that he would flick upward in a nervous habit, as well as a diamond ring on his little finger.

Cliff Adams found himself in the middle of issues that arose between staffers and the couple on whether to report their expenses as business-related or personal. Robert and Margrit always flew first class, for instance, even though the company's rule was that flights under two hours should be economy class. They also stayed at five-star hotels and racked up enormous entertainment bills, in part because Robert would almost without exception order French grand crus at lunches or dinners to compare against his own wines, as he always had. With Adams mediating, some expenses that the couple's assistants felt should be paid by the company were bumped back to Robert and Margrit as personal instead.

In 1978, Robert decided to end his marriage. On the short car ride from their home on the Krug Ranch to a wedding he and Marjorie had been invited to attend in Yountville, Robert delivered his bombshell: He wanted a divorce. The couple arrived at the event, which was being held at Vintage 1870, an old winery transformed into upscale shops, galleries, and restaurants, and joined a table with a group of their closest longtime friends, all of whom they'd known for decades. Marjorie, who normally kept her feelings inside, was distraught and wept silently at her husband's decision. To comfort her, Marjorie's friends gently tried to remind her that Robert had been straying for years.

Robert separated from Marjorie in June and then, eight months later, petitioned the court for divorce, citing irreconcilable differences. The request was granted just two months later, on April 27, 1979, leaving aside for the time being the division of the couple's assets—with the sole exception of Robert's request that the common stock of Robert Mondavi Enterprises, the holding company that held his stock in his own winery and C. Mondavi and Sons, became his separate property. Under California's community property laws, Marjorie probably would have been entitled to 50 percent of the stock in the Robert Mondavi Winery, but Marjorie never insisted on an even split, getting about 30 percent instead. Fighting over money or shares with Robert would have been unseemly. Robert held about 45 percent and their children owned the remainder.

The couple had spent almost all of their married lives living in company housing on the Krug Ranch, so when they went their separate ways, Robert insisted on buying her a lovely, old-fashioned home of her own, providing her with the money to remodel it. The "old crowd" wondered if Robert had bought Marjorie the house to salve his own conscience, noting that he'd ended up with the lion's share of the assets accumulated during the marriage.

Margrit, in turn, was the petitioner to end her long-standing marriage. She separated from Philip on December 20, 1978, six months after Robert had separated from Marjorie. That first Christmas with each other was a wrenching one. Christmas Day, Margrit called Michael James and Billy Cross and asked what they were doing: They invited her and Robert, who was then in his mid-sixties, over to their house, and they ended up staying through dinner, explaining that they had not been welcomed anywhere else, including at their families'. "They had nowhere else to go," recalls Cross. "Michael and I were the first openly gay men in the Napa Valley and we knew what it was like to be ostracized."

Other employees also helped the couple get through that difficult period. The Bernsteins sat on orange crates in the nearly empty house on Spring Mountain that Margrit was camping in after her separation and drank a champagne toast to the couple's new life together. Margrit filed to dissolve her marriage eleven days after Robert's divorce was formalized, in May of 1979, also citing irreconcilable differences with her spouse of thirty-two years. The court granted her petition quickly, but it took several more years for the Bievers to work out their property settlement. In early 1982, after struggling with coronary artery disease for several years, Philip, then sixty-five years old, suffered a heart attack. He died before the couple had completed the division of the property and money accumulated during their long marriage, so Margrit ended up entering into an agreement with her three adult children, the administrators of their father's estate.

In the meantime, Robert and Margrit's affair became public knowledge; Herb Caen, the *San Francisco Chronicle*'s famed gossip columnist, called to ask the couple when the wedding would be, since he wanted to write an item about it for the paper. The Baron Philippe de Rothschild had offered his château in Bordeaux as a place for them to celebrate their wedding. Realizing that such an event would attract attention and upset Marjorie and his children, Robert declined the baron's invitation, explaining they preferred a quiet wedding instead.

But before the couple married, Robert's children insisted that Margrit sign a prenuptial agreement. The financial implication of their father's remarriage was an explosive issue for Michael, Marcia, and Timothy, since it potentially meant that Margrit could have inherited Robert's financial interest in the winery upon his death. To smooth the way for their union, Margrit agreed to several conditions: She waived all rights to any ownership of the winery and agreed to retain her current name, thus never using the honorific "Mrs. Mondavi," which Robert's children felt should be reserved for their mother. At Michael and his other children's insistence, Robert also agreed to put a dollar limit on his gifts to Margrit in any one year—a provision arising out of his children's concerns about such purchases for her as a full-length mink coat, emerald ring, and other luxuries over the years. While it wasn't in the legal agreement, the pair also promised to keep their nuptials low-key, especially since they occurred only two weeks after Margrit's marriage was legally dissolved.

The couple quietly wed, without informing Robert's children, on May 17, 1980, in the tiled living room of the Palm Springs, California, home of their friends Harry and Bobbe Serlis. Margrit was wearing a wraparound silk dress in a shade of deep rose. The ceremony took place in the late morning. A justice of the peace officiated and the Serlises acted as witnesses. When the justice pronounced them man and wife, Robert turned to his new bride and asked, "Okay, Mrs. Mondavi, are you satisfied now?" Bobbe interpreted the remark to mean Robert had been promising to marry Margrit for many years and had finally kept his promise. Margrit looked elated. To celebrate, the two couples sipped champagne and nibbled on caviar. Then Robert and Margrit disappeared into the guesthouse, near the pool.

That evening, the Serlises hosted a dinner party that included Prince Andrej and Princess Eva Marie of Yugoslavia and other glitterati. The Broadway actress Mary Martin was a close friend of the Serlises and had confided her own romantic interest in Robert to Bobbe, telling her friend, "I could really go for that man!" But Robert and Margrit wanted to keep their marriage a secret, at least for a while, so told no one at the party that they had wed earlier that day. Bobbe Serlis told them, "This is your wedding reception but nobody knows it's a reception." Robert was also relatively anonymous as he filed the forms necessary to marry Margrit in Palm Springs. Because of the court case and his winery's growing reputation, Robert by that time was often recognized when he traveled in San Francisco and Napa Valley, but he was still relatively unknown beyond northern California. So when a clerk at the registrar's office in Palm Springs had asked him before the ceremony, "How do you spell Mondavi?" he laughed and spelled it out for him.

The newlywed couple spent several days with the Serlises and then jetted off to Europe for a month-long honeymoon. When they returned to the winery, they picked up their jobs where they'd left off.

But the news of their nuptials soon spread through the valley—although Robert's own children were among the last to know. Indeed, it was only after Michael was invited to a gathering in Robert and Margrit's honor hosted by the grape grower Rene di Rosa that he discovered to his chagrin that they'd eloped. At the party, Michael tried hard to be civil to Margrit, making a point of clearing the air by telling her that while it was no secret the two of them had had a rough relationship, he would promise to support her if she loved and supported his father.

While Michael's promise at the di Rosas' spread helped pave the way for a détente between him and his stepmother, other members of the family remained suspicious. Robert's sister Helen expressed the feelings of other members of the extended family that Margrit had successfully carried out her long-range plan. "I told Marj twelve years ago, 'That woman's going after your husband!'" she fumed to a family friend. The pain and suspicion surrounding Robert's remarriage would haunt his children for many years, as Margrit became the indispensable consort to Napa Valley's king.

CHAPTER TEN

The Baron, 1978–1981

R obert first crossed paths with the colorful baron Philippe de Rothschild in the early 1970s, at a wine distributors' meeting in Hawaii. On the face of it, the men seemed to have very little in common. Robert was a first-generation Italian-American, whose parents had arrived in America with almost nothing. The baron, in turn, was a descendent of a rare-coins trader named Meyer Amschel Rothschild, who worked on Frankfurt's Judengasse, or Jew Street. By assisting the Austrian Empire with its finances during the Napoleonic Wars, Meyer's sons had become hereditary barons by imperial decree in 1822. By the time Philippe was born in 1912, the Rothschilds were one of the richest and most powerful families in the world.

Philippe himself was a colorful, controversial figure—a playboy and bon vivant in the 1920s and '30s who raced cars, wrote poetry, and seduced a long line of beautiful women. He owned a planet named Philippa, sold to him by the astronomer who discovered it, and translated Elizabethan poetry into French for the sheer pleasure of it. His father, a physician who wrote plays under a pen name, had inherited a decrepit, second-tier winery, Château Mouton-Rothschild, that his family had acquired in the nineteenth century. Philippe took over Mouton's management in his twenties and almost immediately began challenging the calcified French wine trade by rallying other leading producers in Bordeaux to begin château-bottling their wines for the first time, rather than shipping them in bulk to wine merchants, who had traditionally stored them during the aging process.

Philippe's proposal directly challenged the powerful role of the wine merchants by offering château producers a way to control more of the process and distinguish their wines from lower-quality ones. Traditionally, France's elite Bordeaux producers had relied on their reputations to sell their wines, shunning marketing. Philippe's proposal encouraged the châteaus to begin marketing their wines themselves, rather than leaving those crucial steps to brokers and merchants. It was "a true Declaration of Independence for Bordeaux winemakers," contends the wine writer William Echikson. "They were no longer mere vassals for the merchants."

As part of this campaign, Philippe rallied his neighboring châteaus in the mid-1920s into a group called "the Association of Five." Consisting of Haut Brion, Latour, Margaux, Lafite, and Mouton, the first get-together took place over dinner at the famed restaurant Chapon Fin in Bordeaux. There, the owners or managers agreed to château-bottling and to help each other in technical and commercial areas. To overcome the proud owners' distaste for publicity, Philippe proposed that they work together to promote the "glamour" of their wines—a more palatable goal.

Philippe himself added glamour to Mouton by associating it with some of the leading artists of the age. For Mouton's first vintage of château-bottled wine, in 1927, Philippe commissioned Jean Carlu, who introduced cubist designs into French advertising, to design the label. Philippe also added his signature to Mouton's labels, which was a novelty in the French wine industry at the time. In later years, he would use eye-catching labels from Jean Cocteau, Salvador Dalí, Andy Warhol, and Pablo Picasso. With such unorthodox marketing techniques, the baron displayed his flair for promotion—or self-promotion, as his critics contended.

But Philippe's progress in reviving Mouton was interrupted by the war. After the Nazis occupied Paris, Philippe made a daring escape from France by foot over the snow-covered Pyrenees, crossing from France into Spain and then on to Portugal and fled to Morocco, where he was imprisoned for eight months. From there, he went to England, where he joined a French army unit poised to support the Allied forces in fighting the Germans. After the war, he learned that his wife, Lili, a French Catholic, had died in a concentration camp. Their daughter, Philippine, was whisked into hiding from the Nazis and saved. When Philippe's father died unexpectedly in 1947, the hereditary title passed to Philippe, his brother, James, and their sister, Nadine. In sorting out their father's estate, Philippe offered to buy his siblings out of Château Mouton-Rothschild, the vineyard they had inherited from their father.

Toward the end of the war, the occupying German army had retreated rapidly, leaving telegraph poles down, wires cut, and guns and concrete pillboxes everywhere. So Philippe faced a task of rebuilding the winery at a time when resources were scarce. As well, the baron found himself at war with those same château owners he had brought together in the mid-1920s. Following a rift with his relatives who owned Lafite-Rothschild, Mouton was unceremoniously dumped by the four first-growth châteaus, who took out an advertisement in the Bordeaux paper declaring, "*Les Quatre Grands, Noblesse Oblige.*"

The baron was infuriated and vowed to fight to protect Mouton's honor. The other four châteaus had used the fact that Mouton had not been ranked as one of France's premier cru, or first-class, makers of red wines, in the system established in 1855. The baron sought to throw out the 1855 classification and replace it with an up-to-date table, appealing to the Syndicat des Crus Classés, an ancient order of winegrowers who were responsible for upholding wine laws in the district. Philippe's challenge to the established system even further inflamed the rift that had begun with Lafite.

The baron was relentless in his efforts. Over more than a decade, he petitioned five successive ministers of agriculture, delivered countless lectures, and wrote many articles as part of his campaign. It was a battle for prestige, and finally, in 1973, the French Ministry of Agriculture passed a decree promoting Mouton to premier cru status. The baron opened a jeroboam of Mouton '24 and all the vineyard workers drank to the future, and their new motto:

Premier je suis, second je fus, Mouton ne change.
(First I am, second I was, Mouton does not change.)

Just as the feud between the Mondavis had garnered Robert's new winery invaluable publicity, the baron's crusade to secure premier-cru status, against the wishes of many in the French wine establishment, did as well. That was one of many experiences that the French aristocrat and the immigrant's son had in common. Both men were highly driven, competitive, and entrepreneurial: Neither could stand to be second-rate. Passionate about marketing rather than numbers, they intuitively grasped the potential of selling an image and a lifestyle around wine. Both also had the fortitude to withstand a long fight. In their famous battles their reputations came under attack. The baron's crusade to elevate Mouton into a premier cru took well over a decade; likewise, Robert's battle to gain his rightful share of the family business stretched out for over ten years.

The baron hit upon the idea of creating a second-tier brand after a disappointing harvest left him with a large quantity of wine that was not up to the quality of previous Mouton vintages. At first, he called this wine Cadet de Mouton, indicating that it was a junior member of the Mouton Rothschild family of wines, but soon changed that to the shorter and more elegant Mouton Cadet. His move had its doubters but the strategy worked and in later years, when he didn't have any of his own wine to spare for it, he produced Mouton Cadet from wines bought and blended from other growers across Bordeaux. It became one of the world's most popular French wine brands, selling about a million cases a year.

Robert's strategy was similar. In 1974, faced with a surplus of everyday wine, he came up with the idea of bottling it in-house rather than selling it to other producers in bulk, apparently coming up with the idea over dinner one night with the cookbook celebrity James Beard. The idea hearkened back to the earliest days of the Mondavis' ownership of Krug, when Robert figured out how to finance the Krug purchase by bottling bulk wine. Michael recalls the origins of the idea a little differently. After a customer balked at accepting delivery of bulk Chardonnay and Cabernet wines from Mondavi, Michael remembers suggesting they sell these commodity wines themselves. To distinguish the wines further, he proposed selling them in 1.5-liter bottles—not as large as jug wines, but twice the size of a regular bottle of wine. As a final touch, he proposed finishing these larger bottles off with a cork, distinguishing it as a higher quality product than twist-top jugs from Italian Swiss Colony and Gallo.

The wines quickly became known as "Bob Red," "Bob White," and "Bob Rose"—the latter being a product Mondavi introduced after the astounding growth of Sutter Home's White Zinfandel. Yet, despite this nickname that referred solely to Robert, the entire family backed the venture, at least at first, and Michael in particular was a strong advocate.

Four years later, as part of the settlement of the legal case with Peter, Robert assumed a lease on a bulk wine facility in rural Acampo, near Woodbridge, and the Mondavis began selling their bulk wines under the Woodbridge brand, since the winery was located on Woodbridge Road, near Lodi, in the San Joaquin Valley. The winery had gone through a series of owners; started just after repeal as a cooperative called the Cherokee Wine Association, by the late 1970s it was known as the Montcalm Winery and had fallen into receivership. C. Mondavi and Sons had leased the facility from Wells Fargo and Company, which in turn had hired Brad Alderson as general manager to turn around the ailing facility.

In 1978, as part of the $10 million in cash, assets, and land that Peter used to buy Robert out of his stake in the family business, Robert assumed that lease and also got the bulk wine inventory stored at Montcalm—some quarter of a million gallons or so—and it, too, became "Bob Red" and "Bob White." In 1979, Robert exercised an option to purchase the winery from Wells Fargo, keeping the highly competent and steady Alderson on to run the operation for him and renaming it Woodbridge. Like Mouton Cadet for the family of Baron Philippe de Rothschild, Woodbridge became a sales juggernaut for the Mondavi family, carrying the risk of becoming too much of a success.

Six years passed between the time the Baron Philippe de Rothschild first summoned Robert to his hotel suite in Hawaii to express interest in working together and 1978, when he approached him again. During those intervening years, Harry Serlis and his wife, Bobbe, had become friendly with the baron and his American wife, Pauline Fairfax Potter, staying with them for several days at Château Mouton-Rothschild during one of the Serlises' many trips to Europe. The couples visited back and forth between each other's homes in France and California. An incorrigible flirt, the baron pinched Bobbe's knee under the table at dinner their first night, causing her to start.

Bobbe's husband, in turn, seldom set aside his business agenda for long. On trips overseas, Serlis would bring California wines as gifts for his hosts and among them was usually a wine from the Robert Mondavi Winery, where he sat on the board and consulted. It was during one of the Serlises' periodic visits to Bordeaux that the baron confided to him that he hoped to ally Mouton-Rothschild with a winery in California, which he had grown to love. Before the war, he'd had a brief fling as a Hollywood movie producer, working under the name Philippe Pascal. After marrying Pauline, he made frequent trips with her to Santa Barbara, where they found the climate to their liking. As well, France's business environment was unstable in the mid-1970s and so the baron sought geographic diversification by investing in California.

So, in reply to Philippe's question about who might make a good partner, Serlis didn't hesitate: "The one person who shares your vision and passion is Robert Mondavi," he said.

Serlis's recommendation led to a call in August 1978 to Robert by the baron's representative, Miklos "Mickey" Dora, who invited Robert to visit the baron at the Château Mouton-Rothschild in Pauillac, a village in France's central Médoc. It was a tempting invitation and Robert very much wanted his children to grasp the elegant world he so admired.

Robert decided to invite Marcia along on a trip that same month to visit the baron in France. It was a rare moment for father and daughter, who had seldom spent much time alone with each other. A few months earlier, Marcia had declined to join the group of winery staffers that her father had shepherded around Europe on a three-week winery tour. "A couple of days on tour with Dad and you need a vacation from the vacation," Marcia explained to *The New York Times*'s wine writer, Frank Prial, that year. But the grueling pace of trips led by Robert was probably not the only reason Marcia declined to join the group. With her father and mother recently separated and Margrit playing a prominent role on the trip, both as a guide and as Robert's consort, the group trip would have been an uncomfortable experience for Robert's austere, all-business daughter.

But a trip just with her father to visit Château Mouton-Rothschild was too tempting for Marcia to pass up. Rolling over the village's cobbled streets in a chauffeur-driven limousine and entering through the grand gates of the château, the Mondavis saw a place that had been transformed in the years after the war. The larger house, known as Grand Mouton, had been a stable block a few decades earlier. At the time Robert and

Marcia visited, its salon was far and away grander than any place that existed in Napa Valley: with Chippendale furniture, paintings by sixteenth-century Florentines, sculptures by Giacometti and Brancusi, all presided over by a nearly life-size Italian Rennaissance figure of a horse, carved in wood and complete with a genuine horsehair tail.

After surprising his fellow vintner with a greeting of "Hiya, Bob!" the baron led his American guests on a tour of the estate, including the grand salon, the newly completed wine museum, and Mouton's chai, its famed wine cellar. Philippe by then was nearly bald, with ethereal wisps of hair on top and wild mutton-chop sideburns to compensate for the lack of hair on his head. Yet, despite his idiosyncratic looks, the baron showed off his wealth to Robert and Marcia in its entire splendor.

That evening, the baron and his guests enjoyed an aperitif of *vin blanc cassis*, made from the estate's own blackcurrants. That was followed by a beautiful dinner of quail roasted on the spit served in the château's library, accompanied by a hundred-year-old Château Mouton-Rothschild. His right-hand man, Philippe Cottin, joined them for the meal, which ended with an ice-cold glass of Yquem. Robert was duly impressed. In the European style, business was not discussed at dinner. But afterward, the baron asked Robert if he and his daughter would mind meeting with him in his private chambers at nine-thirty the next morning, offering the quirky explanation that "ninety percent of all my business is done in my bedroom."

The next morning, after breakfast, they made their way to the baron's bedchamber, where he relaxed in one of his three specially made, extra-large beds—one for his bedroom at Mouton, another for his Paris mansion, and the third for the castle he rented each summer for many years at Hesselager, Denmark. As the biographer Frederic Morton noted in his early biography of the Baron Philippe, "His dynamism is huge—and horizontal. He not only sleeps but eats, presides, instructs, phones, telegraphs, and above all writes, propped up against his pillows."

Diplomatically presenting the proposal of a partnership to Robert as being one of equals, the baron named his Californian partner first. "I would like to have a joint venture in which you have fifty percent and I would have fifty percent. We don't want it big, we want it small, five thousand cases." The baron added, in perfect English honed in boarding schools and through having lived in England in the latter years of World War II, "You will put your name on the label, and I'll put my name on the label." Robert readily agreed, surprised that the baron was willing to go that far, since the Robert Mondavi Winery was clearly the junior partner in terms of age and prestige. They agreed to produce one red wine with a proprietary name. Then the conversation veered into a more delicate area.

"Well, should we have our own vineyard and our own winery?" the baron asked.

"Baron, if we want to excel, the only way to do it is to have our own vineyards and our own winery," Robert replied.

They agreed that Robert would provide the grapes and make the wine for the joint venture until it could do so itself. Then the baron asked, "Bob, I hear you have considerable holdings in Napa Valley. Would you mind selling twenty or twenty-five acres of your land to the joint venture?"

Robert looked the baron in the eye and asked, "Would you like to sell twenty or twenty-five acres of yours?"

"Oh no, no, no!" the baron laughed.

"Well, I don't want to sell it either."

The men agreed to try to locate a piece of property to buy for their joint venture by December of 1981, about two years later. Then they approached another potential sticking point.

"We are six thousand miles apart. Can you think of anyone that could be a go-between for us?"

Robert suggested Harry Serlis.

"Bob, that's the man," agreed the baron.

"But wait a minute," Robert added. "He's a member of my board of directors."

"Oh, that's all right," the baron said. "Don't worry about that. I'm not worried about that. I'll call Harry on the phone and I would like to meet before the end of the year. Since I'm getting along in years, we have to do something now."

Their meeting in the baron's boudoir lasted less than two hours. Yet even more than the Paris Tasting two years earlier, when California beat all of Gaul, the news that the Baron Philippe de Rothschild had entered into a fifty-fifty partnership with Robert Mondavi was a watershed moment for California winemakers. At last, they had arrived on the world wine scene.

Robert returned to Oakville and called his sons into his office, which was then on the first floor of the winery, facing a small patio. He sat behind his small, slightly battered wooden desk, near a table where he displayed wine artifacts he had collected on his travels. Robert then explained the deal to Michael and Timothy, who sat in leather chairs across the desk from him, as well as Adams. "I've got a great idea. I'm going to develop this joint venture," he told them.

Michael's response was not enthusiastic: He had what he considered more pressing issues on his mind, including the rapid sales growth at Woodbridge, and this venture could well have turned out to be another one of his father's follies. Tim, in turn, immediately expressed opposition to the idea, questioning why his family needed the Rothschilds as part-ners in California when they were doing so well on their own. "Oh, no," he told his father. "Why do we want to do business with the people from France? Why do we want to do business with Mouton? We're in a golden era, the wines are getting better all the time. We're being recognized more all the time."

"Well, the association can be a very beneficial one," Robert explained patiently to his younger son, who was then in his late twenties. Although Timothy had been to Europe, he may not have been fully aware at that time of the prestige of the Rothschild name or the elevated social circles that Europe's most powerful banking dynasty had moved in for many generations. Timothy's opposition to the venture pitted him against the more worldly Harry Serlis, who had immediately grasped what a social and business coup it would be for his friend Robert Mondavi to link his name with that of the Rothschilds. So did Margrit, who enthusiastically supported the idea. But with a worldview molded mostly by his experi-ence in California, Timothy didn't initially grasp that it was his family— not the Rothschilds—that would gain most of the luster from such an association, the first between an American winery and a producer of French grand crus.

Robert moved ahead with the deal, despite Timothy's opposition. But before the baron was willing to formally enter into a partnership, he sent his trusted winemaker, Lucien Sionneau, to fly to California and taste the Mondavi wines. If they passed muster, the Rothschilds would then move ahead. Timothy, upon hearing about the French winemaker's visit, looked at his father and asked, "What do we do for this man? What do you want to show him?" Robert's answer: "Show him everything." Timo-thy poured every Cabernet Franc, every Merlot, and every Cabernet Sauvignon they had, as well as showing Sionneau all of the winery's experiments, including the temperature of fermentation, methods of barrel construction, and where its grapes were coming from, with the Frenchman signaling a strong preference for the grapes grown in the To Kalon vineyards. Sionneau, who was not only Mouton's winemaker but also the company's president, returned to Pauillac and gave the venture his blessing. "You know, Baron, we can make good wines in California," he said.

Overall, it took about eighteen months to finalize the details. The transcontinental negotiations took place between Rothschild's managing director Cottin, Serlis, and Adams, and the group decided they would produce a single Bordeaux-style red wine from the 1979 vintage, announcing it in April of 1980. Robert and the baron hosted a press conference in San Francisco, while their progeny—the Baroness Philippine and Michael—fielded questions from reporters in Paris.

The French had agreed to put up all the working capital, while the Robert Mondavi Winery would let the partnership choose from its very best grapes and wines. Mondavi got a disproportionately large share of the profits to compensate it for providing the wine and the venture's sales and marketing. But from the very beginning, the French insisted on teaming their much more experienced winemaker, Sionneau, with Timothy Mondavi to jointly make the wine. In the traditional Mouton manner, the wine would be racked—transferred from one container to another to separate the clear wine from the sediment that has gathered—every three months. As well, it would be aged in new Nevers oak barrels, sent from France by the baron.

One hurdle remained: What to name the new partnership and the wine it produced? Navigating the challenges of the nine-hour time difference between France and California, they brainstormed dozens of ideas, including Duet, Aliage, Alliance, and even Opus, but none seemed to express the venture's high ambitions. Finally, Philippe began searching through various Latin sources and came across what seemed like a promising contender in the horoscope. He telexed his idea to California and organized a conference call a few days later to discuss the idea with his American partner.

The baron called to tell Robert that he had come up with the perfect name. "Gemini," he announced triumphantly, which is the third sign of the zodiac and represented by a set of twins. There was silence. The baron asked his partner what he thought. Robert hesitated, since

Gemini was also the name of a well-known gay magazine in the United States. Once he broke the news to the baron, they had a laugh together and quietly dropped the idea.

The San Francisco–based label designer, Susan Roach Pate, and her husband, Dwight, spent nearly a month with the Rothschilds, traveling between Château Mouton and the baron's mansion in Paris to design a label for the new wine. The search resumed and not long after, the baron and his team returned to the Latin word *opus*, which means "work" and is often used to refer to a work of art or music. As Robert wrote in his autobiography, "the Baron then suggested we make it Opus One, to convey this was the first work of a master composer. That was an essential touch. It was bold and proud, as if our wine were already declaring itself a Premier Grand Cru Classe."

Once the partners had agreed on a name, the next step was to agree on a logo. They turned to Susan Pate, an experienced and talented designer who had made her name working with Moët Hennessy's California venture, Domaine Chandon, in 1982 after trying another, better-known design firm. Pate was also a soignée blonde with more than a passing resemblance to Britain's princess Diana. Knowing that the baron was partial to attractive women, and sensing that Susan Pate's style was very much like the baron's wife Pauline's, Michael and Cliff Adams hoped she could come up with the packaging that would capture the partners' vision, let alone one that Robert and the baron would accept. "We would like you to have an affair with the baron," Michael Mondavi jokingly explained to Pate when he hired her. "A creative affair."

The partners initially agreed to pay Pate $25,000 to design a label, as well as agreeing to foot the bill for her and her husband to make a trip to work with the Rothschilds. Before leaving for France, she read everything she could on the baron and his fabled family. Her stay at the château was just as glamorous as she had expected, with liveried waiters, bells to summon servants, and meal cards embossed with the family's crest for dinner, including the wines that would be served with each course. True to form, Philippe lived up to his reputation as a ladies' man. The eighty-two-year-old could not keep his hands off Pate.

Susan was provided with a small studio on the third floor of the château, next to the room where Britain's queen mother would stay when she visited Mouton-Rothschild. Her day would start with a visit to the baron's bedroom, where he would conduct business in his oversized bed, often with one of his dogs lying nearby. She would present the baron with her ideas and be rebuffed. "No, no no . . . it can't be right!" he would say to her in his perfect, heavily accented English. The baron would later recall that three or four hundred designs had been submitted in total. Finally, she sketched an image based on the Roman god Janus, with two profiles back to back. Robert recalled Michael's coming up with the idea by putting two chess pieces back to back and drawing a rough sketch of the result, while the baron apparently felt the idea was his.

Pate's clearest memory, though, is of months of bickering between the French and the California camps about which man's head should be positioned slightly higher on the label—the baron's or Robert's. The baron eventually won that argument. But whose signature would be first? This time, it was Robert's. They leavened their dispute with humor. Robert would complain, "I don't like my profile," and the baron would respond, "Mine's worse!" Robert also joked, "Who wants a picture of a Jewish nose and an Italian nose?"

Pate sought to capture the dynamic between the two men by merging their profiles, with an expressionistic squiggle uniting them. But finding exactly the right line was not easy, and her various attempts elicited many "*non, non, nons* . . ." from the baron, who explained there were "too many zig-wee-wees," explaining that the fused heads looked drunk to him, with all those lightning bolts through them. Eventually, they decided on a very modest zigzag radiating from their shared pates, and a blue, high-energy squiggle below their profiles. It was a striking, soft-edged design using color that was very different from the conventional, hard-edged, black-and-white wine label of the time. Later on, Pate's label would win widespread praise, although the job ended up taking over two years and costing more than $100,000.

Meanwhile, the 1979 vintage that Sionneau and Timothy produced was not the world-class wine that either side was hoping for. The French winemaker preferred an elegant wine that would go with food; Timothy was a product of the California palate and he advocated a bold, intense wine. They managed to find a compromise but decided to package the 1979 and 1980 wines together for Opus One's first release. Releasing five thousand cases, Opus One recommended a retail price of $50 a bottle— about ten times as much the cost of an everyday bottle of wine.

The press coverage of the new venture in the autumn of 1981 was enthusiastic, but there were a few murmurings in the valley that Robert was overreaching. Some suggested that by "fawning" over a French grand cru producer for the public relations benefit, he seemed to be tacitly acknowledging France's superiority over California. Others wondered how two supremely charming egotists—Robert Mondavi and the Baron Philippe—would ever agree on anything.

Robert and Margrit were also setting a new fast pace with their busy social lives. But while the old crowd of upper Napa Valley vintners looked down on Margrit, in particular, as a social-climbing arriviste, a faster, more sophisticated crowd embraced the new couple. Some of those friends, including the Bernsteins, attended a first-anniversary party hosted for Robert and Margrit by the *San Francisco Examiner*'s society columnist, Pat Montandon. It took place at her mirrored, all-white penthouse apartment, eight hundred feet up in the area of Russian Hill, which her son Sean Wilsey nicknamed "the marble palace."

Montandon's parents were both evangelical Nazarene ministers and she and her six siblings traveled throughout the West from one small town to another during the Depression, with their parents preaching in tents along the way. Born in 1928, Patsy Lou, as she was then known, was a tall, gawky child. But by the time she was sixteen, she was a beauty, with chiseled cheekbones and erect carriage. As a teenager, she got a job modeling at Nieman Marcus and then eventually, in 1960, made her way to San Francisco, where she was hired to run "the Wolf's Den," the gentlemen's formal department at Joseph Magnin, where the salesgirls dressed up like sexy elves at Christmastime. When Montandon racked up the highest seasonal sales in the company's history at the time, she was put in charge of managing Magnin's new store at Lake Tahoe, where she met and dated Frank Sinatra.

When the summer season was over, Magnin's brought her back to San Francisco and Montandon made a few changes. She dyed her hair blond. And, just as Robert had done, she changed the pronunciation of her name from the hick-sounding "Mawntandun" to the more European-sounding "Moan-tan-dawn." She then concentrated on launching a new career as a society hostess, columnist, and author, penning books such as *How to Be a Party Girl*. She married the celebrity trial lawyer Melvin Belli in a Shinto ceremony in Japan in 1966. The marriage lasted just thirty-six

days—a development noted by the rival *San Francisco Chronicle*'s columnist Herb Caen in a tart item headlined "30 Seconds over Tokyo."

After divorcing Belli, Montandon married Al Wilsey, who had made a
fortune in a butter-and-egg business inherited from his father. The couple entertained lavishly, both at their penthouse in San Francisco and at
an estate in the Napa Valley hamlet of Rutherford, where they would
spend weekends. Wilsey was famous for buzzing his private helicopter
above Mike Robbins's gabled Victorian home and his Spring Mountain
Winery, which was the opening shot for the evening soap-opera set in the
Napa Valley, *Falcon Crest*. Trouble was looming in the Montandon-
Wilsey marriage, but Montandon didn't know that on the day she lunched
with Robert, Margrit, and Robert's administrative assistant, Robin Lail—
a daughter of Robert's old friend John Daniel and a member of Napa Valley royalty herself—to discuss raising money for a local hospital.

It was a beautiful, warm afternoon and the foursome ate on a patio
outside the Vineyard Room, with trellised vines and the mountains in the
background. Montandon had an idea she wanted to pitch to Robert, who
by that time was someone with a reputation for making things happen.
Beforehand, Montandon's husband, Wilsey, had warned her that Robert
would ask her for a donation during the lunch, so Montandon settled that
matter straightaway.

"Bob, I'll make a donation to the hospital," she said. "Now there's
something I want to talk to you about. . . ."

Montandon went on to explain her idea of a charity event, which
could be held on the grounds of her Rutherford estate. The group talked
and the idea bubbled up of a charity wine auction similar to the one held
each year by France's Hospice du Beaune. Robert wondered if the Napa
Valley Vintners, the powerful and, even then, fractious trade group made
up of the valley's winery owners, would be able to agree to taking on such
a project. But he also thought he'd be able to recruit Michael Broadbent,
the eminent wine auctioneer from Christie's in London, to take part.

The details fell to Robin Lail, one of many beautiful women who
would work in the Robert Mondavi Winery over the years, who took
charge of organizing the event and rallying support. The vintners signed
on but insisted that the late Louis P. Martini chair it—a more politically
acceptable choice to the group than Robert, who was always on the move
in those days, flying from tastings to appointments to meetings and to
business dinners during his fourteen-hour workdays.

* * *

Volunteers pulled the event together. Molly Chappellet, owner with her husband, Donn, of Chappellet Vineyards, took charge of the auction's "visuals"—the floral arrangements, table coverings, and many other aesthetic decisions. The organizers were forced to quickly shift gears and change the location: By 1981, Pat Montandon was in the throes of a bitter divorce from Al Wilsey, which made it impossible for her to host an event at the Wilsey estate in Rutherford. So the group instead chose a newly revived club called Meadowood, owned by the real estate developer H. William Harlan II and several partners. Molly Chappellet spent many hours at Meadowood, on the flanks of Howell Mountain, studying the trek of the sun across the fairways to plan the best position for the tables in the shade. But despite her best-laid plans, the week before the auction was one of the hottest in memory.

The morning of Saturday, June 12—with only a week to go before the auction—dawned with an unusual, acrid tinge to the air. A fire had erupted in the valley's eastern hills, blackening seven hundred acres and sending smoke so high it could be seen throughout the Bay Area. The conflagration was aided by an unusual heat wave for that time of year, with temperatures hitting more than a hundred degrees and gusts of twenty to twenty-five miles per hour accelerating the flames. The county and state put more than a hundred firefighters on the ground, in trucks, and overhead. Bombers dropped fire retardant on flames to try to quench them. Even crews of prison inmates were used to try to stop the flames from spreading even further.

The day of the auction, Sunday, June 21, thermometers in the valley hit an astonishing 107 degrees. The wines that had sat outside by the pool for the barrel tasting before the live auction had heated up dangerously. By the early evening, the British auctioneer Michael Broadbent had discarded his jacket and stuck his feet in a tub of water to try to cool down from the sweltering temperatures in the tent. There were 590 lots sold in an event that lasted more than seven hours, but there was one clear showstopper: the first case of wine jointly produced by the Rothschilds and Mondavis, which would be released two years later.

The bidding grew heated in the sweltering tent and the prices being offered for the wine—then only known as Napamédoc Cabernet Sauvignon—soared. The owner of a liquor supermarket in Syracuse, New York, Charles Mara, ultimately claimed the lot for $24,000—nearly double of most estimates of what it would sell for and the equivalent of $2,000 per bottle. Mara's winning bid broke almost every record in the history of wine auctions. Although the wine was still aging in French oak and was still a few years away from bottling and release, on that excruciatingly hot afternoon it became the single most expensive case of California wine ever sold at auction.

The Mondavis exulted in their success. For Robert, who was sitting with Margrit in the front row, it was heady vindication of the mantra he'd been repeating over and over for years to anyone who would listen about how Napa Valley wines could be in the company of the world's finest. Robert's doubting son, Timothy, also shared in the triumph of the moment. When approached by a reporter for *The Napa Valley Register* for a comment on the sale, Timothy shed all of his private reservations about the joint venture and credited Robert with the idea. "That's my father's baby," he beamed after the record bid. "That's great. I expected it to take off, but that's above what I thought." Timothy added that he wasn't sure how the wine would be priced when it was released to the market in a few years, "but with that kind of recognition, it won't last long. It will zoom."

By the next day, attention shifted to the fires that were breaking out again. This time, they had been set by an arsonist along the eastern boundary of the valley floor. The fires spread and combined into a violent inferno, scorching hundreds of homes and more than twenty-five thousand acres. Funnels of white smoke began billowing into a brilliant blue sky near the Stags Leap District that Monday afternoon. With the hills parched and temperatures still into the hundreds, the blaze raced through the underbrush and trees, leaping through narrow canyons and folds in the hills. Authorities began evacuating homeowners, and planes began dropping fire retardant over the flames in the area. By the next day, eight hundred firefighters had descended on Napa to try to halt the blaze, but winds continued to fuel it. By Wednesday, the winds had started to quiet and by Thursday, the firefighters had it contained.

But that moment represented a turning point for the valley and for Robert Mondavi and his family. Both publicly and privately, their landscapes had changed unalterably as flames consumed the Atlas Peak home that Margrit had shared with Philip Biever. Gone were the family photos, the European furniture, mementos from the moves she had made as an army wife, and many of the objects that the couple had accumulated during their long marriage. Margrit by then was living with Robert in a small condominium, waiting to move the rest of their furniture and possessions into the home they were building together. It was an apocalyptic sign that Margrit's old life had ended—literally, in ashes—and that her new life with Robert had begun.

CHAPTER ELEVEN

Father and Sons, 1982–1984

Although the fire left Margrit temporarily homeless, her one consolation was that she'd soon move into a new home. During her years as a military wife, Margrit had never felt she'd sunk deep roots in any one place. And although Robert had lived on the Krug Ranch for most of his adult life, the modest house he lived in was owned by the company, not by him personally. So, when the time came for Margrit and Robert to build a home together, they turned to Clifford May, who had designed the winery for Robert in the mid-1960s, for help.

The spot they chose for their new home was the highest hill on the valley floor. With views sweeping from the city of Napa to Mount St. Helena in the north, the land was part of the Oak Knoll Ranch, hundreds of acres of poison-oak-covered, rock-strewn woodlands off the Silverado Trail near Yountville that Robert's old friend, the distributor Chuck Daniels, had helped him purchase in 1969. Rattlesnakes made it their home.

Margrit confided to friends that her dream was to build a small aerie, a tree house perched on the side of a secluded hilltop. But one day, when vineyard manager Charles Williams drove Robert and Cliff May up to the site in his four-wheel-drive truck, May decided the house should command the very top. "Robert, do you want to be queen down here or king of the hill?" May asked him. Robert, naturally, wanted to be king.

So the one-bedroom home Margrit had originally envisioned became much grander, growing to a stunning, sprawling marble palace under Robert's influence. Cliff May initially designed a seventeen-thousand-square-foot home for the couple, dominated by a huge, high-vaulted living area. On the lower level would be an indoor pool with a retractable roof, near the bedroom that Robert and Margrit would share. The upper level would be a lounging area. "I thought of the place as an isolated kingdom where Bob would be king of the mountain, so I suggested they call it Mandalay—though eventually they decided on a name that is more reflective of the valley's history," May said. Instead of naming their new home after the Burmese city immortalized by the Rudyard Kipling poem, Robert and Margrit called it Wappo Hill, after the American Indian tribe who used the site as a lookout.

To critics, the outré design resembled nothing so much as the atrium of a large hotel chain. Others considered it an architectural wonder. As he had done for the Robert Mondavi Winery, May based his design for the home on the Spanish-mission style and it included a campanile reached by a spiral stone staircase, a large kitchen, a wine cellar, and a four-bedroom guesthouse. The design was meant to reflect Robert's expansive lifestyle, which included frequent entertaining for the winery. To no one's surprise, some members of old Napa society dubbed it "Bob's Folly," a put-down similar to the one they'd used to describe his winery in 1966. They saw in the home's grand proportions a reflection of Robert's outsized ego and ambitions.

Because of Michael and Timothy's fraught relations with their stepmother, the job of overseeing the design, construction, and ownership terms of Robert and Margrit's new home fell to Cliff Adams. Michael, in particular, was concerned that if something happened to his father, Margrit and her children would end up owning it. With a value approaching $5 million, it was one of Robert's major assets, and the development of the property was in part financially supported by the company. "We're going to go crazy if in fact she gets the house and all his stuff and our kids get cut out," Robert's offspring told Adams. In response to their concerns, Adams negotiated terms in which Margrit would get the right to live in the home for her life as a "life estate," as long as she did not co-habitate with someone else during that period, meaning that after Robert's death, she could not take a lover and still live there.

The construction itself was nearly as big a challenge as the difficult family politics: The builder balked at May's initial design, which called for slicing off the top of the hill to lay the home's foundation and rebuilding a portion of the hillside to support the cantilevered design. May, who was not a licensed architect, insisted that it could be done, but the builder and Adams concluded it would be prohibitively expensive and potentially unworkable. May quit in protest and Adams brought in a licensed architect to shrink May's design to fit the site. They also ended up importing a stoneworker from Italy to install the extensive marble on the floors and staircases. May eventually rejoined the project, which was scaled back to a nearly twelve-thousand-square-foot home instead.

Their close attention to detail was rewarded in the end: Robert and Margrit's new home was featured in *Architectural Digest* and also filmed from a helicopter for the celebrity television show *Lifestyles of the Rich and Famous*, hosted by the British celebrity-watcher Robin Leach. "The king of the Napa Valley region was the man on whom the hit TV series *Falcon Crest* was based," the show's voice-over intoned. "Mondavi's mansion is a state-of-the-art castle which even has its own tower overlooking the sprawling vineyard." Yet, others noted that they had hidden the house discreetly behind trees, screening it from the valley floor.

In some respects, Robert and his family were re-creating a compound similar to the one they had left at the Krug Ranch. Michael and his wife, Isabel, also lived on the Oak Knoll Ranch, as did Timothy, Dorothy, and their growing family. But unlike the Mondavis' relatively modest lifestyle on the Krug Ranch during the 1950s and 1960s, Robert's branch of the Mondavi family had begun living more lavishly. As one former employee wrote, "the Mondavi style could be best described as Lucullan, with Bob as the Roman general and his family the most privileged Centurions." It didn't go unnoticed that Robert had situated his home higher on the hill than either Michael's or Timothy's.

The comparison to the Krug compound was not exact, however. For one thing, while Robert, Rosa, and later Helen all lived within sight of one another at the ranch, none of the three Mondavis who lived on the Oak Knoll property could see each other from their respective homes, and their drives were mostly separate. Yet, as in the Krug days, there was a blurring of the lines between what belonged to individual family members and what belonged to the company. Robert Mondavi Vineyards, for instance, owned the land that Michael and Isabel built their home on. In 1972, Michael negotiated a fifty-one-year lease for it, paying the modest ground rent of just $176 per year.

Through the 1980s, Robert remained the family's general, showing very few signs of slowing down. A very active septuagenarian, he seemed decades younger than his chronological age, perhaps because of his happy second marriage to Margrit and his heady successes of the past few years. He remained strong and fit, swimming forty laps nearly every day and working on his backhand with a tennis pro at Napa's Silverado Country Club. He never took up golf because it was too leisurely for him. Robert remained so energetic that Michael was known to joke about it. "I run twenty miles every week to stay in shape to keep up with him," Michael said. "He has so much energy because of his search for trying to do something better. If he ever tasted the perfect wine, I think his life would be over. Luckily, he hasn't."

With Margrit's encouragement, Robert also began dressing more stylishly—with a London tailor, shirts from Brioni, and Italian sport coats. He was traveling with Margrit as an ambassador, spending as much as 150 days a year on the road for the winery and California wines. Always a fast driver, Robert drove Oldsmobiles in the early years, explaining that "I make American wine so I drive American cars." Later on, he graduated to Cadillacs. Eventually, because his trips to and from San Francisco for wine tastings became so frequent, and also, some suggested, because his driving became even more speedy as he aged, the winery provided a limousine and chauffeur for him. He left the day-to-day management to Michael, his trusted sales head Gary Ramona, and Cliff Adams. Robert did not curtail his lifelong habit of spending freely and traveling first class, prompting Michael to complain about his father's profligacy.

After reviewing a printout of public relations charges, Michael told a writer for *Town & Country*, "So help me, I think if an Arab sheik asked Bob to conduct a tasting in the middle of the Saudi desert, he and Margrit would catch the next plane. Of course, he'd probably invite along a few wine critics and reporters to assure a story in the morning papers. And on the way back, they'd more than likely stop in Paris, where Bob would take everybody to the Tour d'Argent for dinner and a tasting of our wines against the best in Claude Terrail's cellar," referring to the restaurateur of the French gastronomic landmark.

Just as Robert's activities did not slow down, neither did the sheer volume of his ideas and words, which spilled out faster than he could express them, leaving many of his sentences in fragments and encouraging his habit of repeating certain synonyms and near-synonyms in pairs: "knowledge and know-how," "steeliness and backbone," and "dedication and involvement" were a few favorites. Staffers knew his "speech" by heart, since he'd repeat it over and over again to them, hoping it would sink in. While many of the people who worked for him took his repetitiveness good-naturedly, seeing it as an outgrowth of his passion for the business, it came to grate on Michael. "You don't ever have one conversation with my father. Redundancy is his middle name."

Robert left many sentences unfinished and perhaps, fearing that he hadn't gotten his point across, he'd often start sentences with the phrase "I'd just like to say this. . . ." Bobbe Serlis Cortese recalls interrupting Robert at a dinner party once as he was beginning a new thought with "I'd just like to say this. . . ." When she asked him not to say anything more, her request brought the table up short. Few people were bold enough to interrupt Robert, even though he tended to go on at length. Other friends of Robert's joked that on his tombstone should be the words "I'd just like to say . . ."

Yet, Robert's tirelessness on the part of delivering his message was hugely appreciated by the company's sales and marketing department. Hands down, he was their most effective salesman. His charisma and energy drew glamorous people into the winery's orbit of concerts, dinners, and trips: the movie stars Natalie Wood and Robert Wagner on a sunset cruise in Hawaii, the socialite author Danielle Steel at the Mondavis' new hilltop home, and the glamorous entertainer Ann-Margret in Las Vegas.

His French partners also applauded his indefatigable energy. At a birthday celebration for Robert on June 17, 1983, at the Oakville Winery, the baron's managing director, Philippe Cottin, presented him with the gift of a bottle of Mouton from 1914—the year after Robert's birth, explaining that he hadn't sent the 1913 because it wasn't a very good vintage. In his French-accented English, Cottin told Robert: "You are proof of an adage we have in France: God cannot make great wines and great men in the same year!"

Yet, the social altitude and sheer velocity at which Robert and his family were soaring raised eyebrows among some in the valley. When kings came to the Napa Valley, they visited Mondavi. In the spring of 1984, Sweden's thirty-seven-year-old king Carl Gustaf swung through the valley, touring the Robert Mondavi Winery and tasting the new wine produced by Mondavi's joint venture with the Baron Philippe. When the baron himself came to Oakville to take a vineyard tour, he rode in one of the several dark limousines that wound their way up the hillside, passing Mexican workers in straw hats and viewed from overhead by a turkey vulture wheeling across the dark blue sky. To one observer, the procession of dark cars looked like a Mafia funeral.

Robert and his family's social ascendancy became apparent at public events. Not long after his seventieth birthday, Robert and his sons attended the third annual Napa Valley Wine Auction, which was blessedly cooler than the auction's first year. Lot 34 was an imperial-sized bottle of the forthcoming Opus One. Auctioneer Michael Broadbent started the bidding at $900. It soared to more than five times that amount: $5,200. The Peter Mondavi family, meanwhile, had also contributed three lots of Charles Krug wine to the event. Robert and Peter still weren't speaking to each other after the bitterness of their court battle, and the relationships between the various branches of the Mondavi family were still strained. So when the Krug lots came up for sale, Michael Mondavi refused to lower his paddle until he had won them. Bidding with Timothy, they ended up paying $7,800 for Cabernet Sauvignons made at Krug from 1959 through 1964, when their father was at the winery.

"I've tried every which way to buy those wines Bob made, but my uncle just wouldn't sell them to us," said Michael, in explaining his refusal to drop out of the bidding no matter what it cost. Some observers saw it as a case of not very attractive "familial one-upmanship"—and a way of sending the implicit message to the Peter Mondavi family, which had struggled for years under the debt it had assumed to settle the 1976 court case, that if they wouldn't agree privately to a sale of wines, the Robert Mondavi family would simply buy them. Others interpreted it as a conciliatory gesture by Michael and Timothy, a way of showing respect to the other side of the family, leaving open the possibility that the cousins would someday go into business together. Still, the gesture left a sour taste in some old-timers' mouths, as the Mondavis played out their feud in public one more time.

*   *   *

Just as the relationship between Robert and Peter had not changed in the years since Judge Carter's decision, neither had Robert's character altered much. Some of the same habits and attitudes that had driven a wedge between him and his mother and siblings also caused problems between Robert and his sons. Robert continued to take credit for nearly everything good that happened at the winery, despite the fact that he had turned over the day-to-day operations to other people. He was also highly critical—often in public or semipublic settings—of both his sons. He would criticize Michael for "just moving boxes" rather than emphasizing the educational elements of selling that Robert felt were the most important sales tools. When Michael would suggest pushing Mondavi's lower-priced wines, Robert would say "You're running too fast, you're trying to be a big man." He'd often level these criticisms in front of employees and distributors. Michael would work on plans with his team for weeks and then present them to his father, who'd dismiss them immediately: "I think that's a terrible idea," he would say. "We're not going to do that."

Robert's criticisms emasculated Michael in the eyes of the staffers, underscoring that Robert remained the key decision maker, not his firstborn. Michael, in turn, was hurt by his father's put-downs: "It makes you feel like crap, whether the criticisms were accurate or erroneous. I did quite a bit of running and a lot of exercise to cope."

When asked by a historian in 1984 if he had found it difficult growing up in his father's shadow, Michael revealed some of the pain he felt. "In 1966, when there was my father, myself, and another employee who started up the company, [my father] was the brains, the direction, everything. I was the brawn. As I then gained experience, everything was totally in his shadow. And I think that I helped to pay many of the corporate dividends of Di-Gel, Gelusil, and all those antacid people until about 1973 or 1972. I got to the point where I realized I would never totally please him, but that's good because he always demands perfection, whether it's the wine, or the people, et cetera. If I try to only please him, and only do what he wants, then I won't be happy. I've got to work as hard as I can to do what I think is best and then I have to be able to look back and say, Did I do a good job? Did I do my best?"

Michael seldom received praise from his father, as a boy or as a man, despite his hard work. Michael would typically get up early and work at home from about six-fifteen to seven-thirty A.M. or go for a run in the morning to relieve stress before heading into the office. He packed his schedule with appointments ranging from meeting with the winery's chief financial officer to leading VIP tours for restaurant owners, wholesalers, and retailers. If he hadn't taken a run in the morning, he'd slip out for one in the late afternoon, but not before carrying home extendable folders packed with six or eight inches to read that night, working for a couple of hours after dinner.

Repeatedly describing the wine business as a "sickness," he felt overworked and underappreciated and complained that he went for a period following the start-up of the winery when he had not taken a vacation for years. Even then, when he and Isabel did manage to slip away, they found they couldn't escape the pressures of their famous last name.

"I had not had a vacation in six years—getting the winery started. So I said, 'Come on, we're going on a vacation.'" The couple flew to Las Vegas for a long weekend, hoping to spend some time together, play tennis, and see some shows. In the evening, Michael and Isabel sat down for what they hoped would be a quiet, romantic dinner at one of the clubs, which was a rare occasion for them because of Michael's heavy work schedule. Almost immediately, upon realizing who he was, the wine steward, the maître d', and the captain circled their table and hovered around closely all evening. Michael talked business much of the evening and ended up ordering several bottles of wine for the two of them. As the wine business once again intruded on their personal lives, Isabel ended up in tears.

The pressure and lack of recognition from his father contributed to Michael's explosive temper, which flared up regularly at the winery and elsewhere. Michael's office was down the hall at the Oakville winery from Robert's, and staffers at the time remember doors slamming and shouting between the two men, who were both passionate and opinionated. Michael also erupted over seemingly minor issues. The sales staffer Gary Lipp and his wife and Michael and Isabel were once walking through San Francisco's Union Square after dark when a homeless man said something impolite to one of the women. Michael became infuriated and warned the impoverished man in the harshest possible language to leave them alone. "I'm going to kill you, motherfucker!" Michael shouted that evening, according to Lipp. Although Michael does not recall the incident in Union Square, he says that if someone did threaten his wife or daughter, he'd feel it was his duty to protect them.

Looking back on those years, Michael says he acted out his anger toward his father by venting his rage at unwitting targets. "There were times I would lash out," he acknowledges. "I asked people close to me to let me know when I did that, so I could try not to repeat it."

Sometimes those targets were subordinates in the workplace, either employees or people who did business with the company. Once, in the mid-1980s, the company hired an interior designer to decorate a new administrative office it was opening in downtown Napa. The designer showed rug samples to Michael. But since he didn't express a strong opinion at the time on which rug should be used, the designer ended up making the choice. When he found out about it, Michael began slamming doors, yelling, and screaming. The rest of the staff was befuddled by his outburst.

Michael sought other outlets for his energy during those years. He piloted a Cessna 414 and rode Harley-Davidson motorcycles with a group of young, wealthy winery owners, including Gilliland Nickel, who had inherited a profitable nursery business in Oklahoma, as well as the powerful distribution executive Ted Simpkins, who headed up Southern Wine and Spirits of California. In one small act of defiance against the expectations placed on him as Robert Mondavi's eldest son, he even grew a ponytail.

One of Michael's more humorous ventures was appearing as "the man in the Hathaway shirt," wearing the brand's black patch over his right eye like a charming corporate pirate. Michael, then in his early forties, was strikingly handsome—and by some accounts, better looking than his famous father. His height topped Robert's by four or five inches and, unlike his father, was a polished, though perhaps less passionate, public speaker. He patiently worked through fifty-four takes before the directors got the one they wanted for the sixty-second television ad and another two dozen or so takes for the thirty-second spot. The copy for the print version of the ad read, "Every man has his own management style. Take Michael Mondavi. Proud, persistent, dedicated to a tradition of quality winemaking."

Michael also joined the "Young Presidents' Organization," a networking and peer group for people who were presidents, CEOs, or chairmen of companies before they reached their mid-forties. There he met a group of young and aggressive businessmen from the valley, such as the corporate-executive-turned-grape-grower Andy Beckstoffer and the technology-executive-turned-vintner Garen Staglin. He also got to know many others like himself, who had inherited their wealth and positions in family businesses. The YPO meetings were places to network and to air issues that were unique to second- and third-generation business owners, such as how to deal with difficult family members, how to handle management succession from one generation to the next, and how to minimize inheritance taxes on family-owned businesses when the founding entrepreneur died.

But they also, at times, resembled drunken frat parties: In one instance, a group of YPOers visiting a prominent Napa Valley winery tore around in a golf cart and crashed it, much to the dismay of the winery's management. Members swore to maintain complete confidentiality about matters discussed in the meetings and were obliged to meet one full day per month, except during the summer, as well as attend a mandatory chapter retreat in March for two or three days. The chapters also held a nonmandatory but popular Christmas party each year.

Some staffers felt Michael spent too much time at these off-site networking sessions when he should have been spending more time minding the business. Michael found they helped him think through the issues his family would face in coming years. By the mid-1980s, Michael saw himself as the family's long-term thinker, particularly since he considered Timothy's focus to be on growing grapes and making wine. He also held the title of company president, which allowed him to join the Young Presidents' Organization. Timothy, who didn't hold that title, was thus not eligible. The YPO was another way for Michael to distinguish himself from his younger brother at a time when Timothy sought broader influence at the company and was bridling under the perception that he was just a winemaker.

The Young Presidents' Organization was the type of go-getter group that held no appeal for Timothy, who did not easily fit into the role of a manager or corporate leader. He preferred lower-key outings, such as a fishing trip he took in June of 1989 to a spot near Crater Lake, Oregon. Invited to join his longtime friend Steve Taplin, Steve's brother Bill, and a UC Davis classmate of Bill's named Rich Casias, he took off with Bill and Rich in a rented single-engine Piper and flew to Oregon. There they met Steve Taplin and spent four memorable days of fishing, food, and wine.

On Friday, June 23, Bill Taplin, Casias, and Timothy boarded the plane to fly back to Napa. When the plane took off, it was caught in a downdraft and failed to clear high trees at the end of the runway. Casias, who was piloting the plane, managed a crash landing. The plane caught fire and Casias and Taplin were knocked unconscious. Timothy, seated in the back where he had been reading a book, managed to escape through the rear door and dragged the others out with the help of someone who lived nearby. Moments after pulling them to safety, they watched the plane explode in flames that entirely consumed it. "If I had been knocked out, we would have all gone," said Timothy.

Casias was taken to a burn center in Oregon, where he woke up nine days later and began a slow process of recovery that included extensive skin grafting and physical therapy. Taplin suffered a broken wrist and burns. Timothy was also briefly hospitalized with a cracked rib. When Casias woke up, he was relieved to learn he had suffered the worst injuries, but worried about whether breathing the smoke might have left the younger Mondavi son, who was known for his sensitive palate, with lasting problems.

But to Timothy's colleagues, his behavior at work sometimes seemed less than heroic. His habit of being perpetually late to business discussions, for instance, drove his father and the people who worked for him to distraction. In front of journalists for such influential publications as *Wine Spectator*, Robert would complain about his younger son's tardiness. At a blind tasting of sparkling wines held at the Oakville winery in 1984, for instance, which was attended by two dozen tasters sitting around a twenty-five-foot-long table, Robert began his opening remarks and then looked around the room in puzzlement. "Who knows about these wines we are having?" he asked. "Where's Tim?" Then he'd repeat, "Where's Tim?"

Tim, unusually this time, was already at the meeting and seated at the end of the table. His father just hadn't seen him.

"Tim, you are thirteen minutes late!" his father joked.

At other times, Robert's criticisms would cut his sensitive younger son to the quick. Once, Timothy, the winemaker Zelma Long, Robert, and a few other staffers were tasting wines at a round table in the laboratory. They stuck their noses deeply into the glasses, inhaling the rich scents of the fermented juices. For a short while, they were silent, in appreciation of the poetry of fine winemaking. But not long into the tasting, Robert launched into a criticism of his younger son. As Timothy's eyes filled with tears, the others looked away, in an attempt to ignore the Mondavi patriarch's treatment of his youngest child. But Timothy's humiliation was too blatant to ignore, since it happened in front of his fe-male boss, Long, and other staffers.

Timothy truly loved the artistry of fine winemaking. At the same time, the family politics and heavy expectations placed upon him under-mined his ability to use those talents. Unsurprisingly, Timothy was highly indecisive. A typical example would involve deciding when to pick grapes based on their sugar levels and the weather forecast. Relying on what they knew, a group including the winery's vineyard manager and a grower consultant would agree to hold off on picking over the weekend, in part because it cost more to pay workers for overtime on Saturdays and Sun-days. Timothy would then weigh in at length on the subject; arguing that perhaps they should bring in just ten tons of grapes on Saturday—a small amount, but one that would require nearly as many workers as the typical three hundred tons that they'd bring in during a weekday. In situations such as these, although Timothy cared deeply about choosing the opti-mum picking time, he didn't seem to fully grasp the economic and the business issues underlying a question such as when to harvest the fruit. Timothy brought little urgency to his decision making, preferring lengthy discussion to concrete action.

Robert compounded the problems his sons were having in the business. Not only did he criticize them publicly, but he also seemed to pit Michael against Timothy in subtle ways, leading the brothers in later years to joke with each other about whose turn it was to be in the penalty box with their father. Michael came to believe that Robert engaged in a pattern of keeping his sons in competition with each other as a way of retaining control over them and the company. The Darwinian competition be-tween his sons forced each of them to work harder for the company—and for their father's approval.

This dynamic played out in the lengthy strategic debates that took place in the 1980s over whether to introduce a medium-priced Chardon-nay. Timothy, whose vision was to produce high-end, technically perfect fine wines for connoisseurs, inevitably ended up on the opposite side of this argument from Michael, who pushed for sales growth and who enjoyed deal making and transactions of various sorts. This particular discussion went on for five years as Michael championed the idea of in-troducing a line of Chardonnay that was less expensive than the wines made in Oakville and Timothy adamantly opposed it. The result was that

Robert became the ultimate decision-maker, with both sons and various staffers engaging in behind-the-scenes lobbying of the patriarch to try to sway him to their side.

Fed up with the fighting with his brother and criticism from his father, Michael threatened to quit over the years. Each time, Robert managed to persuade him to stay. "I think it's a mistake. There's plenty of room here for you and Tim," Robert would tell Michael. "If you wish to leave, I'm not going to hold you back. I'll support you a hundred percent, but I think it's a mistake."

Yet, at the same time, Robert showed remarkable sensitivity to the plight of other wine families struggling with some of the same issues he had as a younger man. In 1986, for instance, when the third-generation vintner Sam Sebastiani was fired by his mother from the family winery, Robert dispatched Michael to Sonoma to try to prevent him from making the same mistakes he had made with Rosa and Peter. And later in his life, Robert would take responsibility for the unhappy work environment he'd created. Robert's philosophy had been to speak his mind about the faults and problems he saw around him. At the time, he justified that approach by weighing it against the alternative of backstabbing. But later on, he realized he'd made a serious mistake by being so blunt in group meetings, pointing out faults and upbraiding the person responsible, even if it was one or both of his sons.

"I was unaware, at the time, of what I now call the humiliation factor," Robert wrote in his autobiography, explaining that he didn't realize that if he was going to give one of his employees a dressing-down, he ought to have done it privately. Instead, he humiliated them publicly and made them lose face with their colleagues and staffers. "For many years, I was totally blind to all this. And it caused Mike and Tim enormous pain and anguish, sometimes to the point where they were on the verge of leaving the company."

CHAPTER TWELVE

Thicker Than Water, 1984–1990

Harry Serlis, perhaps better than anyone else outside the family, grasped the troubled dynamic between Robert and his sons. But as his hearing worsened and his health began to fail, Serlis began spending more time at his and Bobbe's estate in Palm Springs, making fewer trips to Oakville. Before Robert's closest confidant left the picture entirely, though, he wanted to convey a final message to the Mondavis concerning the future of the winery. The message he repeated to Robert again and again concerning his sons was "Bob, you've got to think with your head, not with your heart."

To help Robert do this, Serlis supported the decision to hire a Price Waterhouse audit partner named Dale Crandall to study the winery's management. Serlis thought highly of Michael, but he was no fan of Timothy, who he thought lacked maturity and was indecisive. Robert's old friend was convinced that the brothers would come into increasing conflict with each other as Robert began delegating more authority to them. "These kids can't run the business," he warned Robert. Crandall's bland cover story for his assignment was to review and make recommendations about the overall management of the business. To do that, he interviewed Michael, Timothy, and the top nonfamily staffers. By the time the report was completed, Serlis was confined to his bed. To meet with him, Robert, Michael, Timothy, Cliff Adams, Gary Ramona, and Greg Evans, the company's newly appointed chief financial officer, jetted down to Palm Springs in early 1984. They were greeted by Bobbe, who led them to Serlis's sickroom. They pulled chairs around, as Serlis lay propped up by pillows, his complexion a sickly gray and an oxygen tank near his bed. Struggling with emphysema, every so often Serlis would pull the mask to his face and gulp in deep breaths.

Although Robert, Serlis, and Adams had read the Price Waterhouse report beforehand, Robert's sons hadn't. They were in for a shock. At that time, the winery was being run by the "management council," comprised of Michael, Timothy, Adams, Ramona, and Evans. The council met once a week, and it had been conceived at a time when management consultants were praising Japan's group decision-making.

But almost from the beginning, the council was hobbled by the Mondavis' fractious family dynamic. Timothy, if he attended at all, was often late to meetings. When he arrived, he would request that the group start from the beginning for his benefit. Michael, who traveled extensively during this time for sales-related events as well his Young Presidents' activities, wouldn't make every meeting either. But when both brothers did attend, the meetings would frequently bog down in their disagreements, delaying or reversing the committee's decisions.

The Price Waterhouse report recommended that because of the continuing conflict between the brothers, they both be given specific roles, but that overall management of the company pass to Cliff Adams instead. It was a stunning pronouncement and there was silence on the car ride back to the airport.

Robert stayed behind in Palm Springs to spend more time with his old friend, who was weakening by the hour. Michael and Timothy were surprised and upset by the conclusions. When Robert returned to Oakville, they separately asked him to ignore the report's recommendations. Michael reminded Robert of his commitment to keep the management of the winery in the family, while Timothy attempted to strike an emotional chord with his father. Gary Ramona, in turn, made it plain he wouldn't go along with what appeared to be a power grab by Adams: He refused to report to Adams, or to anyone but a Mondavi.

Only four days after that bedside session, Serlis slipped into a coma, and on February 12, 1984, he died at age seventy-two. Although Serlis was born into a Jewish family, his memorial service was held at the Grace Cathedral in San Francisco, an Episcopalian church that was the site of many society weddings and burials. Bobbe had asked Robert to deliver the eulogy, and despite the trying time, both Michael and Timothy attended the packed service.

Robert, in his slightly high-pitched, rapid-fire delivery, began by describing Serlis as one of his closest friends. Perhaps with the Palm Springs meeting on his mind, Robert praised Serlis to the cathedral full of mourners as a wise counselor. "He always seemed to hold court, controlling his audience regardless of his age. . . . Harry took brief but accurate notes on every worthwhile issue. We all realize how firm of mind Harry was, because Harry always did his homework and knew exactly the steps to be taken to be successful. He had little patience with those who did not follow through."

Yet Robert himself failed to follow the advice that Serlis offered him on his deathbed in Palm Springs.

Even before Serlis died, the family realized it needed outside help in grappling with its family problems. Michael and Isabel had begun seeing a psychiatrist named Barry Grundland to help them work through their marital and family difficulties. One of Dr. Grundland's recommendations was that both Michael, who was traveling constantly on winery business and for YPO outings, and Isabel, who was known among the winery's executive ranks as a devoted shopper, spend more time with their two children, Robert Michael Mondavi Jr. (known as Rob) and Dina.

At Michael's suggestion, the company also hired Dr. Grundlund as a consultant, advising the Mondavi family and employees on how to improve their relationships with one another. The bearded psychiatrist, the first of several counselors hired by the family, was a graduate of the University of Minnesota Medical School. He had done postgraduate work in child and adult psychiatry, and became chief of psychiatric services for the U.S. military, eventually ending up as senior psychiatrist for the state of California's Napa State Hospital. He spent only a year in that role before opening a private practice in Napa Valley in 1972. By the 1980s, he was consulting with the Mondavi family and, in special instances, also met with with employees and their families or referred them on to someone who could help them.

Many of his discussions as a consultant to the winery revolved around the painful family dynamics between Robert, Michael, and Timothy, stemming from the years when Robert was always on the road for Charles Krug and leading through his affair with Margrit and eventual divorce from Marjorie. The three men started meeting with Dr. Grundland regularly, with Marcia occasionally joining them.

What became evident through the sessions was that a destructive triangle had arisen among Robert and his two sons. Just as Rosa had intervened to protect Peter, Robert often stepped in to try to defend Timothy in dealing with his older brother, Michael. Yet at the same time, as long as Michael and Timothy continued to fight with each other, Robert could remain the key decision-maker. It was a pattern that other entrepreneurs also struggled with, consciously or unconsciously, as the time came for them to pass control to the next generation: Were they sabotaging their successors in an effort to hold on to the reins a little longer themselves?

To explore these and other issues, the family also went on various family retreats in the 1980s, including a sailboat trip in the San Diego area and to Hawaii. In sessions led by Dr. Grundland, the family examined their painful history and tried to resolve their conflicts. Margrit didn't attend these retreats, but Marjorie did on at least one occasion. Whether it was Grundland's influence or the persuasive powers of their friends, Robert and Peter, who had barely spoken with each other for years and hadn't sat down for a meal together at one of their homes for twenty-five years, finally reached a détente. The brothers participated in a rare tasting of every year's production of Charles Krug and Mondavi wines at a UC Davis fund-raiser, organized by the collectors Barney Rhodes and Tawfiq Khoury. Not long afterward, Peter and Blanche accepted an invitation from Robert and Margrit to join them at their home on Wappo Hill for dinner.

Soon, Dr. Grundland's involvement with the family also extended into their business dealings. It was not unusual for counseling sessions to involve a senior, non-family-member executive. In an expression of the Mondavis' confidence in him, the psychiatrist got extraordinary access to the inner workings of the company. In addition to private counseling sessions, he also attended management-council and board meetings and traveled to the East Coast for sales and marketing strategy sessions. But for some of the winery's staffers, Dr. Grundland's sessions posed a professional minefield; some feared that what they disclosed privately to him might be passed along to the Mondavis. Although there was no evidence of this, some feared the information they shared with him might threaten their careers. In other instances, the counseling was welcomed by non-family staffers. Vice president of production Brad Warner, for instance, attended many sessions over the years in the hope they'd improve his relationship with Timothy. They took place off-site about once a month, at Dr. Grundland's home in the eastern hills of Napa. Robert was very supportive of the sessions, in part perhaps as a way of better understanding the different personalities of his sons.

Unlike Michael, who would get angry and cuss and storm around the office, Timothy's method of dealing with his feelings was the polar opposite of his sibling's: If he was angry about something or disturbed, he would disappear for a few days. To the staffers, Timothy was unusually sensitive, breaking down and crying if the situation got too overwhelming for him.

Michael and Timothy's personality differences hadn't exploded into a punch-up, as the sibling tensions between their father and uncle had in the 1960s. But they were simmering below the surface. With the help of Dr. Grundland, Robert and "the boys" worked out areas of responsibility that essentially kept them far apart from each other. At first, Timothy was assigned to production areas of Woodbridge. Then, in 1985, the family bought Vichon, a struggling winery on nearby Oakville Grade owned by three partners, including a former Mondavi winemaker named George Vierra and the former McKinsey-consultant-turned-Krug-receiver, Douglas Watson. The strategic purpose behind buying Vichon was to expand Mondavi's production of fine wines at a time when there was a surplus of Chardonnay grapes. It was less expensive to buy than it would have been to add capacity at their flagship winery in Oakville. But the acquisition was also perceived by staffers and others as a way to give Timothy an area of responsibility apart from his brother's role at Oakville.

From the start, the situation at Vichon was fraught with potential conflict between the brothers, since the winery's success or failure would depend, in large part, on how hard the Mondavi sales force pushed Vichon wines—an area under Michael's control, working alongside the sales chief Gary Ramona. It was a risky undertaking from the beginning. Vichon was stacked to the ceiling with unsold cases.

Michael fully supported the project, as did his siblings. They all pulled together to invest in the winery, with Michael, Marcia, and Timothy creating a partnership to purchase 60 percent of Vichon, while the company bought the remaining 40 percent. Michael took charge of Oakville and Woodbridge, while Timothy became president of Vichon. Together, Oakville, Woodbridge, and Opus One were producing around two million cases of wine a year in 1985, while Vichon was producing a tiny fraction of that, less than sixty thousand cases a year. Even so, Timothy threw himself into running the newly acquired winery, often forgetting to stop for lunch. His secretary at the time, Sally Knight, would make sure to have a midday meal ready for him, since otherwise he would forget to eat. Vichon represented an opportunity for Timothy to excel on his own, apart from his father and brother. To staffers, he described it as one of the three jewels of fine wines in the family's crown: the Mondavi reserve wines, Opus One, and Vichon.

But when Vichon's sales failed to meet the family's expectations, the stage was set for another conflict between the brothers. Were Vichon's sales poor because the wine that Timothy and his staff were producing wasn't good enough? Or were sales poor because the sales team under Michael and Gary Ramona had made overly optimistic projections and hadn't bothered to push it hard enough, focusing instead on bigger, more promising brands? By 1990, Vichon still accounted for only 4 percent of Mondavi's overall sales. Meetings of the board of Vichon—consisting of Timothy, Michael, Marcia, Cliff Adams, Gary Ramona, and Greg Evans—were rife with finger pointing.

Timothy tried to hold his own in the group but got steamrolled again and again on issues of marketing and brand positioning. At the same time, as well, there was a parade of general managers going in and out of Vichon's doors, reflecting the group's struggle to find the right sales formula. Under pressure from the family to try to fix the problem, Gary Ramona was named general manager of Vichon, further fanning the flames between the brothers, since Ramona was closer to Michael. By the early 1990s, Vichon became the lightning rod for the ongoing debate over whether to introduce a medium-priced wine, costing somewhere between

Woodbridge, at $3 to $7 a bottle, and Robert Mondavi Napa Valley wines, which sold for more than $20 a bottle.

The short of it was that, far from being the "jewel" in the crown of fine, expensive wines that Timothy had wanted it to become, Vichon became a vehicle for Michael's vision of filling a gap in the company's product line. Because of Vichon's poor financial performance and tiny contribution to the company's sales and profits, Timothy lost whatever clout he might have had in the argument.

Not long after, with Michael and Gary Ramona leading the charge, Vichon was reinvented as a $7 to $14 "coastal" wine—which would use less expensive grapes from California's coastal regions, rather than strictly more expensive grapes from Napa. The decision meant that Vichon would sell for slightly more than Woodbridge but a lot less than the best wines being made at Mondavi's Oakville winery. Losing this power struggle with Michael over the direction of Vichon was a bitter blow for Timothy, who, like his father, became convinced that Michael was more interested in boosting case sales than in making fine wines. But he was unable to rally his father or sister to Vichon's defense.

As the Mondavi brothers battled over Vichon's future, Gary Ramona was facing a crisis of his own. As one of Mondavi's longest-serving and most loyal employees, he had entwined his personal and professional life with the Mondavi family's for two decades. The olive-skinned, square-jawed Ramona, whose father was Italian and mother was German, was selling orange juice in southern California when he was spotted by Fred Franzia, the Mondavis' distributor in southern California and an old school friend of Michael's. On Franzia's recommendation, Ramona interviewed for a salesman's job with the Mondavi winery in 1970. Robert and Michael personally guided him on a tour of the Oakville winery, then still a small operation, and Robert felt comfortable enough with him from the very beginning to confide his ambitions to him: "I believe we can do half a million cases—a million!—and still hold quality. But I don't talk to a lot of people about it," he told Gary, "because it scares them off."

Ramona joined Mondavi as a salesman in the important southern California market on January 1, 1971. He worked out of his home, arranging wine tastings and hiring housewives to work in supermarkets explaining which were the best Mondavi wines to serve with various foods. From the very start, Ramona shared Robert and Michael's belief that what they were selling was a vision of the good life—and that a premium winemaker could be large and still produce high quality wines. He not only shared Robert's conviction that Napa Valley wines should take their place with the best in the world and that a bottle of wine belonged on every dinner table, but he was able to translate that message into sales. A tireless worker, he helped the Robert Mondavi family achieve its goal of surpassing Charles Krug, which was still owned by Peter and his family.

Ramona won promotion after promotion, eventually rising to become the company's chief of global sales and marketing. He helped lift the Robert Mondavi Winery into a league of its own with distributors and retailers, in part by the sheer lavishness of its hospitality. One example was a party that took place after the movie *Out of Africa* came out in 1985. The French stylist Axel Fabre and her crew transformed the Vineyard Room into a jungle for the evening. They borrowed a live jaguar, lion, and elephant from nearby Marine World U.S.A., constructed a waterfall, and imported exotic trees to re-create the sounds and smells of Africa. Because the chimps liked to jump on people's laps and would sometimes defecate there, Fabre and her team found a somewhat comical solution to the problem by putting the simians in diapers before the party. About 150 people attended that evening and were served by waiters in pith helmets, khaki shirts, and lace-up boots, and were serenaded by African drummers. Through parties like these, Ramona made Mondavi wines glamorous.

Not only was Ramona well liked by retailers and distributors, but he also had the reputation within the winery of being particularly close to Robert, leading some staffers to call him "the third Mondavi son." After he moved himself and his family from southern California to Napa Valley to work at the company's headquarters, Ramona grew even closer to the Mondavi family. They celebrated birthdays and holidays together, including several trips to Hawaii. Robert took to calling Gary "my adopted son" and Timothy laughingly dubbed him his "stepbrother." The same held true for Ramona's spouse. Although Stephanie Ramona did not share her husband's passion for wine or the entertaining that went along with being a salesman's wife, she became closer over the years to Michael's dark-haired wife, Isabel, and Dorothy, who was married to Timothy. Gary himself was a true believer in the company's mission. "I took the heart and soul of Robert Mondavi . . . and marketed and sold the whole organization around his philosophy."

Yet Ramona was forced to perform a delicate balancing act to avoid angering Robert's sons, particularly Michael, who seemed to resent his father's closeness to the company's sales chief. Barry Grundland met with Ramona several times to talk over these issues. On the face of it, relations between Gary and Robert's sons seemed fine, but Gary privately worried about his fate at the company once Robert retired. He had always felt closest to Robert and had benefited over the years from his special relationship with him. But as Robert began stepping back in an effort to give his sons a freer rein to run the company, Ramona wondered if his status would fade.

By that time, Ramona had fully adopted the opulent style of the Mondavis. Emulating Robert, Ramona embarked on a plan to build his own hillside estate, with a tennis court, pool, and a stable laid out over twenty-eight acres above St. Helena. Other nonfamily members of Mondavi's management council, including Cliff Adams and Greg Evans, also built their own large homes around that time, taking out loans from the company and using their secretaries to help them on construction matters. Timothy, too, built a large, seven-bedroom, seven-bath home for his family in 1985. The Mondavis supported these projects, and Robert's wife, Margrit, even helped the Ramonas by offering them some design suggestions. Because other top executives had done it, Ramona felt justified in taking several hours a day from work to oversee his project, too, viewing it as a management perk. Driving a white Mercedes-Benz, traveling first class, and earning around half a million dollars a year, Ramona enjoyed being one of the stars in the Mondavi firmament.

But to some executives within the company, Ramona seemed to take on Robert's lavish spending habits in other areas as well. One of Ramona's pet projects was the company's Robert Mondavi Wine and Food Center in Costa Mesa, an expensive project the winery opened in 1989 to educate consumers in the L.A. basin about wine and food. Robert had fully supported the project, in part to counter the rising influence of the so-called neoprohibitionists—a term coined by longtime Wine Institute chairman John De Luca to describe antialcohol forces led by such groups as Mothers Against Drunk Driving. But Greg Evans and other executives criticized the center as being poorly managed and conceived, questioning the decision to plunk the winery's Vineyard Room into the middle of a corporate park in southern California and expecting visitors to come.

Ramona was experiencing pressures in other areas of his life. As his responsibilities at the company expanded, his marriage started to collapse. Stephanie began confiding in friends, including Dorothy and Isabel Mondavi, that their daughter Holly had been molested. Although at first Stephanie did not suggest Gary had been the molester, Holly herself then alleged that her father had raped and sexually abused her over a period of years throughout her childhood and adolescence.

The explosive rumors spread like wildfire. Dorothy and Isabel confronted Robert and insisted that their father-in-law oust Ramona from the winery. Shocked by his daughter-in-laws' conviction that his top salesman had committed such a heinous act toward his own daughter, Robert countered that in the twenty years he had known Gary Ramona, he had never lied. He refused to believe the ugly rumors. Michael and Timothy then met with Ramona and let him know that they, too, had heard the talk. With the rumors spread by the Mondavi women to the rest of the family, Ramona was deeply alarmed and vented his anger and dismay to one of his closest friends, the company's national sales director, Larry Graeber.

"I told him it was a goddamn lie," Ramona said. "I didn't know what the hell was going on, but it devastated us."

Despite Ramona's insistence that there was no truth to the whispering campaign, Michael and Timothy took their wives' concerns seriously. No one at the winery ever referred explicitly to the allegations against him, but Ramona and his "personal problems" moved to the center of a variety of issues that he and the Mondavis were grappling with then. Perhaps the most delicate involved the question of who would succeed Robert as the company's ultimate decision-maker. Michael and Timothy both held the equal title of "managing partner" in the early 1990s—with Michael overseeing sales and marketing, while Timothy oversaw production. Although the management council's three non-family-member executives were meant to offset the two Mondavi siblings, they were hamstrung in their decision making by the brothers' disagreements, as Michael and Timothy battled each other for authority and control.

Robert, meanwhile, recognized that the problem between his sons would only stand out in greater relief as the company grew larger. When Ramona first joined the company in 1971, it produced less than a million dollars a year in gross revenue and sold just thirty thousand cases of wine a year. By the end of its 1990 fiscal year, the company's sales had exploded, with $120 million a year in revenues and case sales of three hundred thousand annually. The Robert Mondavi Company, though, was still struggling to shed some of the habits of its days as a small, family-run operation and evolve into the next stage of its corporate life, with clearer lines of command, more sophisticated information systems, and professional management. With those goals in mind, it began recruiting outsiders to the board though even in that respect, the decisions still reflected family relationships. One of the first new recruits was Bartlett R. Rhoades, a Harvard business school graduate and friend of Marcia's who was president of Ag Wave Technologies, a business and consulting firm, at the time he joined Mondavi's board.

The subject of "Gary's problems" repeatedly erupted in the boardroom. To give him time to deal with the family issues that were distracting him from work, the board proposed that Ramona go on a six-month paid leave of absence, returning in January with full power and pay. Robert, deeply torn, believed that his sons were using the leave of absence as an excuse to get rid of Ramona. But having vowed to turn over more control to his sons in the past year, he was reluctant to second-guess them or intervene. On June 10, 1990, the board directed that a leave-of-absence letter be drawn up for Ramona, which would be signed by Michael but delivered by all three Mondavi men.

Eight days later, Ramona drove up the hill to the corporate guesthouse on the Oak Knoll Ranch, near Michael and Isabel's home, to attend a full day of board meetings. The California bungalow, which had been recently redecorated by Margrit in a fresh, country style, was often used by the Mondavis as a private place to conduct business, away from the Oakville winery. The Mondavis and their outside directors had spent all day together in a board meeting. Late in the afternoon, Robert said, "Tim and Michael, I think we should meet with Gary for a few minutes."

"Sure, where do you want to meet?" asked Gary, who hadn't picked up any undercurrent or warnings about what was to come.

"Why don't we just meet outside."

They all strolled out to a nearby picnic table under a tree in the small garden. Robert, Michael, and Timothy sat down and told their top salesman they were putting him on a leave of absence with full pay and giving him a sabbatical to study the wine industry, handing him a two-page letter signed by Michael. "The family has engaged in long and agonizing discussions and are [sic] concerned for you . . ." Gary read, scanning down the letter to the two-step program of his ousting. In their discussions, Robert assured him he was part of the family. As Ramona's head pounded and eyes filled with tears, he heard only snatches of what they said next.

"Are you done?" Ramona asked them.

One of them started to say more.

"Are you done? Ramona choked out.

"Yes."

"Okay, I'll see you." Ramona took the letter and began walking toward his car, but Robert then called out, "Gary, you will be at my birthday party?" Gary said he would.

Stunned, Ramona drove to his mother's house and fumbled to get dressed for the party. Then he drove up the windy road to Wappo Hill, the home he had visited so many times and where Robert had always welcomed him like a son. There were about thirty people at the reception, including Cliff Adams, Greg Evans, Michael, and Timothy. When he arrived, Robert greeted Ramona by hugging him. He stayed for a glass of champagne, but feeling ill, Ramona realized he could not maintain his calm demeanor through the reception and the dinner afterward. He asked Margrit to please remove his name from the seating chart. He wished Robert a happy birthday and left.

CHAPTER THIRTEEN

Heart and Soul, 1990–1992

The banishment wounded Ramona deeply. More than just an employee, he'd felt like a trusted and loved member of an extended family. The Mondavis had generated intense loyalty from their staff over the years through many small kindnesses. Robert, for instance, gave all of his employees a Thanksgiving turkey once a year, and a case of wine quarterly. Timothy made eggnog based on his mother's recipe for the company's annual Christmas parties. Margrit and her daughter Annie Roberts, who'd helped out in the Vineyard Room in the 1970s and eventually became the winery's first executive chef, made ham and cheese croissants for the company's traditional Easter brunch celebration.

The Mondavis paid the highest wages in the industry at the time, generally about 10 percent above average. Partly in an effort to stave off unionization, they were among the first in the valley to develop a benefits plan for seasonal workers and also offered company housing. They'd throw a separate crush party with barbecue and beer for the Spanish-speaking fieldworkers at the company-owned labor camp, a modest single-story cluster of buildings set in the Oak Knoll vineyards, since many felt uncomfortable about joining their white, English-speaking bosses for the other crush party at the Vineyard Room. The workers, whose wives and girlfriends were mostly in Mexico, would dance instead with each other or even a broom. There was a bocce ball court at the Oakville winery and staff would often stay after work to play. At the company's summer picnic each year, Robert was often the first to grab a baseball bat. Willing to poke fun at himself and his passionate family, Robert once wore a T-shirt to a company picnic that said, "Get revenge: Live long enough to be a problem to your children!"

The Mondavi family's caring for employees extended beyond paying good wages and throwing parties. Michael not only attended the funeral of longtime Woodbridge employees, he'd also remember the names of their spouses and children. More than once he'd send Mondavi's finest wines to a friend celebrating a wedding. If an employee was diagnosed with a serious illness or hit a rough patch in his marriage, he might confide his problem to a Mondavi family member. Margrit would offer staffers a shoulder to cry on and was known to boil an egg to comfort a distraught secretary. If a Mondavi employee landed in the hospital, he might get a surprise visit from Michael and Isabel, encouraging him to take time off his job as needed. When Gary Ramona broke down at work and confided to Michael that his wife, Stephanie, wanted a divorce, the eldest Mondavi son gave him a hug and asked, "What can we do?"

But the Mondavis' deep-rooted paternalism started slipping away as the company expanded. That change coincided with a momentous personal event for Robert and his three adult children: the death of Marjorie Mondavi. Through the 1980s, Robert's ex-wife had lived quietly in the Oakville home that Robert had provided for her, which rested on a small knoll near the family's To Kalon vineyards, sheltered by oaks. Frail and suffering from stomach ailments in the years before her death, she focused her waning energy on her children and grandchildren. When she died in October of 1990, at age seventy-five, her death certificate cited gastric hemorrhage as the immediate cause. But some family members maintained that Marjorie had, in fact, died of a broken heart.

The news of her death came as a shock to her ex-husband, who was on a business trip when it happened. Although Marjorie had spent much of her time in her later years in and out of hospitals, often tended by either Timothy or Marcia, the seriousness of her accumulated health problems may not have been apparent to her former husband. Robert, then seventy-seven, flew back to attend her funeral at the Catholic church in St. Helena. As he sat in the front pew, several friends recall Robert openly wept.

Their mother's death was just as traumatic for her three children. Honoring her last wishes for cremation rather than burial, they mixed her ashes with rose petals and arranged for a friend with a small plane to sprinkle them from the sky over the To Kalon vineyards, as the family watched from below. Michael felt Marjorie was the spirit of the winery, particularly in its early years: "My mother was the family magnet. She was the heart and soul of the family. When she passed away, that void was not filled."

After Marjorie's passing, the company's culture took on a harder edge. Margrit persisted in spreading her intimate, personal style in everything she touched, insisting on cooking for large dinner parties at a time when more hostesses in Napa were turning to caterers. But as Mondavi's sales climbed and it began acquiring wineries and vineyards, the genuine, if sometimes disorganized, kindheartedness that was the core of the Mondavi family's relationship to its employees began to be replaced by a more corporate, numbers-driven approach.

That cultural shift grew more pronounced as the company began looking for outside sources of capital. Indeed, Ramona suspected he had been put on leave because Mondavi was preparing to go public and the markets were not likely to look favorably on the news that one of Mondavi's top executives had been accused of incest. His suspicions about a possible public offering were justified. In 1986, the company had hired Goldman Sachs and Company, the top tier New York investment bank, to value the closely held shares as part of Marjorie's gifting of her stake in the company to her three children. By the fall of 1991, as a powerful wave of technology IPOs began breaking across Silicon Valley to the south, both Goldman and a San Francisco–based boutique investment bank called Hambrecht and Quist had approached Mondavi about taking it public.

There were very few precedents of wineries turning to the public markets to raise capital. The Chalone Wine Group Ltd. and what was then known as Canandaigua Wine Company, based in upstate New York, had both done it, but neither had performed spectacularly. Because wineries are capital intensive and subject to the vagaries of weather, pests, and regulation, conventional wisdom held that they tended to operate better as private, long-term investments than as public companies, which would subject them to the quarterly profit pressures of Wall Street.

Mondavi also had unique concerns about opening up its management to the scrutiny of Wall Street analysts and investors. Would investors readily understand or accept the company's odd executive structure—with Mondavi run by committee and brothers sharing the title of managing director? Although the company had created a specially designed space for them to share, named "the partners' office," they were rarely there together. Were the brothers capable of pulling together to present a solid public front when the time came to make the sale to investors?

It seemed inevitable that word of the brothers' feuding would eventually reach Wall Street, since talk of Michael and Timothy's power struggles had already seeped past the Oakville winery's arched entrance and onto the pages of the local newspaper.

Adams and others urged Robert to more seriously grapple with the family management problems. Over the years, Barry Grundland had tried to help the Mondavis change their troubled dynamic, but he'd had little success. After Dr. Grundland himself went through a divorce from his wife of twenty-nine years that alienated some members of the Mondavi family, the company stopped using him as a counselor.

At Michael's urging, the company instead hired Family Business Solutions, a "family transitional advisory team" comprised of Robert Taylor, dean of the College of Business and Public Administration at the University of Louisville; Jerrold Lee Shapiro, a psychiatrist and professor at Santa Clara University; and Michael Diamond, another psychiatrist from southern California. Their specialty was helping family companies make the transition from one generation to the next, using such exercises as having family members write down their aspirations for a year, five years, and twenty years.

One key challenge was convincing Robert to hand over the reins and eventually he agreed to do so, at least on paper. In October 1990, he wrote a memo to the company's directors and the management council announcing in blandly benign language yet another attempt at shaking up the top tiers of the company. Robert began the memo, titled "Transition Plan," by stating: "After several years of thinking, talking with family members, senior management, and outside advisors, I have concluded that we must now end the debate and take the necessary steps to structure the senior management of our company in a way which will position us as a family and a company to make the transition from a small to a large more orderly structured business." He then went on to explain that he had asked Price Waterhouse to do a study and make recommendations about the "appropriate senior management structure." He named Alan Ferguson, his close friend from the Rainier days and still a Mondavi director, as the board's point person on the project. Robert also wrote he would review the plan with the company's investment bankers "to make sure they agree that these changes will position us to raise outside capital."

Price Waterhouse, the firm that had audited Mondavi's books for many years, began digging into the company and delivered a report that was highly critical of Ramona's leadership and management style. It slammed his departments for exceeding their planned expenses by $1.6 million, or 10 percent, in 1990 and it targeted Ramona for doing a poor job, citing "lack of creativity and communication skills and his limited management information system background." It also questioned whether Ramona should keep his job when he returned from his sabbatical.

The report infuriated Mondavi's top salesman. No one at the winery had ever asked him a single question about his daughter's accusations and it seemed that the Price Waterhouse study was a smokescreen to get rid of him, at a time when the company was hoping to raise capital and wanted to limit its exposure to potentially damaging allegations about one of its top staffers. Ramona suspected that Michael and Timothy, with Adams's help, were laying a paper trail to justify firing him. So he decided to counterattack. By addressing the study's points one by one, he sought to lift the veil on Michael and Timothy's management shortcomings, which, in his view, the Price Waterhouse report had entirely ignored.

In a confidential, twenty-three-page, single-spaced memo addressed only to the Price Waterhouse consultants and Robert, he turned the spotlight on his boss, Michael, who he claimed undermined the sales staff's motivation through his inconsistent messages and mixed signals. Ramona also charged that Michael had held up key hiring decisions for weeks by insisting on personally interviewing all final candidates for sales and marketing positions, rather than delegating those decisions. Ramona explained his reluctance to take on the additional jobs of running Vichon and Byron, another winery the company had recently purchased, because he feared getting caught in the crossfire between "the boys." Because of "the differences and sensitivity between RMM (Michael) and TJM (Timothy), it was a no-win situation," he wrote.

Ramona detailed the brothers' battlegrounds, including what he called "family philosophical differences." Ramona blamed the family's inability to agree for the company's three- to four-year delay in introducing its own White Zinfandel—a hot category created by the rival Sutter Home Winery that Michael wanted and Timothy opposed. He noted that the company had been working on a sparkling wine for nearly a decade, but still couldn't come up with agreed-upon packaging or a program. He also wrote that Mondavi's sales force felt intimidated and confused by the family's discussions over introducing a Woodbridge Chardonnay, which Michael had opposed.

"I find it interesting that nowhere in your report did you mention the philosophical differences between RMM [Michael] and TJM [Timothy] and the impact this has had on the day-to-day operation at the Winery, Management Council, and the Sales and Marketing Department," Ramona wrote. "Lack of clear direction and more importantly the opposing philosophies between them make it difficult, at best, to implement short-term plans."

Ramona also raised the uncomfortable issue of nepotism in his memo: referring to Peter Ventura's recent appointment by Michael as the company's marketing director. Ventura, the son of Robert's sister Helen and Michael and Timothy's first cousin, had moved from practicing law in the Central Valley to working for the Robert Mondavi Winery. Outspoken and opinionated, he quickly developed a reputation as a loose cannon, even among Mondavi family members. According to Ramona, he had managed to alienate some nonfamily employees, who found it difficult to work and communicate with him. Ramona cited one example: Ventura's insistence that his office be located on the opposite end of the building from the office of the national sales director, whom he did not get along with, as well as the heads of other departments. Ventura's poor relationships with other staffers "is a highly sensitive issue at the winery and creates a high degree of frustration," Ramona wrote.

Ramona's memo did not stay confidential for long. Michael heard about it and stormed into Ramona's office area, which, although he was on leave, at that point was still staffed by two administrative assistants. He demanded a copy of the memo. They refused to hand it over, but Michael got it from his father over the weekend. The incendiary report further inflamed Michael and Gary's animosity. Ramona threatened a lawsuit alleging unfair dismissal and Adams began negotiating with him to leave quietly.

On December 20, Robert announced he was handing over the day-to-day management of the company to Michael, forty-seven, and Timothy, thirty-nine, who would serve as co-chief-executive officers. "At seventy-seven, the time has come for me to pursue my interests in wine and culture. Having worked with Michael, Tim, Marcia, and our staff for the last twenty-five years, I feel very positive about this transition which limits my direct involvement to serving as chairman of our board of directors," said the carefully worded press release. The memo also noted that Cliff Adams, then forty-six, would be promoted to chief operating officer. Robert, it seems, had chosen to ignore Ramona's warnings in his parting memo about Michael and Timothy's shortcomings as managers.

Unlike the warm, homey atmosphere of the Mondavis' Oakville winery, with its bell tower and canopied wings embracing a green lawn, the symbol of the Mondavi family's surging international ambitions rising across Highway 29 was an imposing and somewhat cold edifice. From an idea conceived in the Baron Philippe de Rothschild's bedroom, the Opus One winery looked out of place in rural Oakville. Its designers were Johnson Fain and Pereira, a Los Angeles–based architecture firm that was known for its futuristic designs of landmark buildings, such as the Transamerica Pyramid in San Francisco. Their design concept in Opus One was to blend California boldness with French formalism, complete with classical columns and a formal, olive-tree-lined avenue leading to the building. When it finally opened in October of 1991, critics were not universally impressed. Some said it looked as if a spaceship, lined in pale yellow Texas limestone, had landed in the middle of a vineyard. Others described it as a modern temple to Bacchus. What everyone could agree on was that it was different from any winery ever before built in Napa Valley.

It also had the distinction of being Napa Valley's most expensive new winery. Construction overruns drove the final cost up to as much as $26 million, vastly more than what the architects had originally estimated. The partners blamed high cost on the fact that the soil below the winery had unexpected warm pockets, due in part to the hot geothermal springs in the area, requiring them to install an expensive cooling system even after burying much of the winery belowground for natural cooling.

The Mondavis and Rothschilds also hit other problems along the way. Despite the publicity generated for their new wine at the first Napa Valley Wine Auction, when a case of it, still unnamed, was presold for a record $26,000, the task of selling such expensive wine proved a challenge. In early 1984, the partners released the first two vintages of what was now called Opus One. They packaged it like a Bordeaux wine, bedding the bottles in oblong wooden boxes. To build excitement, they announced its launch at lavish press events in Paris, New York, Los Angeles, and San Francisco, with the baron's daughter, Philippine, and Michael and Timothy involved.

In San Francisco, Opus One was unveiled like a society debutante to the upper tier of wine lovers. In what was heralded as its first tasting, it was uncorked at a $500-a-plate benefit ball for the San Francisco Symphony. For its coming-out party for the press, the baron and Robert presided over a lunch of salmon mousse at the Fairmont Hotel's chandeliered Gold Room. Philippe, then eighty-four and with his ethereal wisps of hair brushed back from his round face, told the guests in a voice so quiet he could barely be heard, "There were times when Bob might have liked us to move a little faster, but patience is the thing in a great wine." The publicity blitz worked: Although the partners priced Opus One at up to $50 a bottle, making it one of the most expensive American-made wines at the time, it was quickly snapped up.

But within a few years of its initial rollout, sales of Opus One lagged behind production. The result was that the Mondavis and Rothschilds were stuck with too much inventory, particularly between 1985 and 1989. As a solution they came up with the novel idea of offering "Opus One by the glass," charging customers $9 for the pleasure of tasting a wine that otherwise might have been out of their reach. Even more inventive, Opus's general manager, H. Stuart Harrison, adopted a novel marketing idea, pioneered a few years earlier in Napa Valley by the upscale winemaker Joseph Phelps, of asking distributors to presell the wine and provide the winery with a list of their customers, thus creating the impression of a shortage. In time, demand for the wine grew.

The French and the American partners may have agreed on the "Opus One by the glass" program, but they disagreed on much more, ranging from such fundamental issues as whether to ferment wine in French oak tanks or stainless steel tanks, to whether the wine should taste leaner or richer, to such seemingly small matters as the French habit of smoking in the winery, which the Americans objected to on the basis that cigarette smoke blunted the palate. Aesthetic concerns, mainly left to members of the Rothschild and Mondavi families, also were a source of Franco-American tension.

Upon his death in 1988, the baron's role in the partnership passed to his daughter, the Baroness Philippine de Rothschild. The baroness and Robert quickly developed a lively friendship, based in part on sparring with each other. Robert and Philippine first met each other in 1978, where French producers at an event in Los Angeles were pouring a vast quantity of premier cru wines—far more than anyone at the event could ever drink and that had been decanted well before the wines had fully matured. After the event's organizers uncorked the 250th or so bottle, Philippine turned to Robert and asked, "Aren't you shocked by this?" referring to the wastefulness of opening so many unaged bottles of fine wine.

Robert jokingly replied, "In California, we drink much younger wines."

"Well, I don't agree with you," huffed Philippine. She was truly appalled by the extravagance.

Philippine, Robert, and Margrit worked closely together in the following years on the "aesthetics committee," quarreling over such issues as whether to cover the fanlike berms stretching out from the colonnades with wild grasses, as the Californians advocated, or in manicured lawn, favored by the French. The French and Americans also went back and forth on details such as whether its windows should have curtains or roman blinds. The baroness, who had grown up surrounded by priceless art and exquisite furnishings and landscaping, ultimately prevailed on many of the decisions. But Margrit, too, had a good sense of style and would purchase statues and pieces of art on her and Robert's travels, such as a stone Buddha from Asia, then seek approval for them from the baroness and her Paris-based interior designer.

While the Rothschilds and the Mondavis were arguing over aesthetics, a far greater threat to their venture was lurking in the vines. It was a microscopic pest called phylloxera, a voracious form of aphid that hid beneath the soil and quietly sucked on the roots of the vines until they shriveled up and died. The Mondavis first spotted phylloxera in their Q block vineyard in 1988. The French, with their history of the aphids' devastating nearly all of their country's vineyards in the second half of the nineteenth century, immediately understood the danger, but many Napa Valley grape growers, including the Mondavis, were slow to recognize the full threat of the pest.

By the early 1990s, Mondavi acknowledged it had a potential crisis on its hands. About 80 percent of its Napa Valley vineyards—about 750 of its 937 total acres—were infested. Although researchers at the University of California at Davis worked feverishly to try to come up with a pesticide or some other way to tackle the problem, none of the ideas worked. The only solution was to pull out the diseased vines and replant. That's what many growers did, with huge pyres of burning vines pockmarking the land. In early 1993, Mondavi only had 59 percent of its Napa Valley acres still in production. At the same time, the company was forced to write down more than half a million dollars in vineyard assets in the fiscal years from 1990 to 1992. Rumors were ricocheting across the valley that the family was in serious financial trouble.

More alarming than the write-downs, though, was the estimated cost of replanting its vineyards: $20 million or so. That bill was coming due at a time when Mondavi had been aggressively expanding its holdings. After purchasing the Byron Winery in 1990, it had more than a thousand acres in Santa Barbara and San Luis Obispo counties alone, as well as its newly developed vineyard in Carneros, a relatively new growing area to the southwest of Napa. But the buying binge had pushed Mondavi's debt to an alarming level at a time when its longtime financier, the Bank of America, was drastically culling its agricultural lending.

Mondavi also faced another pressing issue: In March 31, 1992, the company had $80.7 million in working capital. A year later, its working capital had plunged to $30.3 million. Heading into harvest, the time of the year that requires the most cash because of the hiring of seasonal workers and purchase of grapes from outside growers, Mondavi was overleveraged and faced a looming deadline: Its line of credit was set to expire on July 31, 1993, and the Bank of America was reluctant to extend it additional credit, beyond its existing line, unless something changed.

With replanting costs of $35,000 to $40,000 per acre, raising money from the public markets suddenly looked more attractive. The plan was to sell off a one-third stake in the business and use the proceeds to pay down bank debt. Because of Mondavi's long history with the Bank of

America, the bank agreed to reclassify its revolving line of credit as long-term debt, allowing it to borrow on more favorable terms. Essentially, the family would swap costly bank financing with shareholder equity.

Not only would the deal improve the company's financial picture, but it would allow individual family members to tap into their wealth. After Marjorie died in 1990, Michael and his siblings became increasingly aware of their father's advancing age and the threat posed by a hefty tax on his estate. Just as the family's worries about the tax implications of Rosa's estate had contributed to the blow-up between Peter and Robert, Robert's children began pondering some of the same questions. How would they pay the tax, which could be up to 50 percent of the value of Robert's property, while keeping the company in the business?

More troubling, how could they handle such a tax at a time when they were already dangerously overstretched? Because their shares were privately held and governed by a buy-sell agreement, they were not easy to turn into cash. That meant the family would probably have to sell off land, vineyards, and other assets to pay the tax, which they were reluctant to do. Another alternative would have been selling a stake in the business to an outside partner to pay the estate taxes, but because of the family's painful experience with Rainier, it resisted that alternative. Finally, both Michael and Timothy had taken out large, no-interest home loans from the company: Michael's balance was $444,000 and Timothy's was $573,000. Eventually, they would have to pay them off.

To Cliff Adams, the company's self-described consigliere, an IPO seemed the best solution. But convincing the family was tough. Timothy and Marcia both feared it would be a change for the worse. *What will happen to our little family winery?* wondered Marcia, who worried that going public would destroy the culture of the winery and potentially exacerbate the troubles between her brothers.

Timothy, on the other hand, was concerned that investors' demands for ever-increasing sales growth would compromise quality. The theme of quality versus quantity ran not only through the Mondavi family's history, with Peter and Robert disagreeing over how fast to grow, but through the industry as a whole. Could a winery truly maintain high quality and become a mass producer? The biggest industry players, such as Gallo, had traditionally been jug wine producers. But in 1980, the industry reached a watershed: Shipments and revenues of premium wine overtook those of jug wines for the first time. They continued to rise as lower-priced wines steadily declined. That in itself was an encouraging trend for the Mondavi family, since even Woodbridge fell into the "popular premium" category wines that were a few notches above those sold in jugs.

Just as worrisome was an onslaught of new competitors, including Kendall-Jackson, Glen Ellen, and new offerings from Gallo, which took direct aim at Woodbridge with their "fighting varietals"—lower-priced wines made from specific varieties of grapes, such as Chardonnay. There were also now hundreds of boutique high-end producers. The most startling indication of the rising competition was the sheer numbers of new wineries being built on the valley floor and on its hillsides. When the Robert Mondavi Winery opened its doors in 1966, there were two dozen or so wineries in operation in Napa Valley. By the early 1990s, there were more than a hundred.

Michael, who was eager to join the ranks of entrepreneurs who had taken their companies public, backed the idea of an IPO. Robert himself was fully behind it, particularly after Goldman and the San Francisco–based investment banking boutique Hambrecht & Quist helped convince him there was a way to retain control and avoid a repeat of the painful showdown he and Michael had experienced with Rainier.

After studying family controlled but publicly traded companies such as Levi Strauss and Company, Coors Brewing Company, The Washington Post Company, and The New York Times Company, the bankers suggested a plan that would create two classes of stock. The Class B shares, owned solely by family members, would have ten times the voting rights of the Class A shares, which would be publicly traded. The public "float" would represent only a tiny fraction of company shares. As an additional assurance of control, the Class B shareholders would have the right to elect 75 percent of the company's directors—effectively making sure they got their way on any decision made by the board, as long as they voted together as a family.

It seemed like an airtight plan for raising capital while assuring family control, and would appear to make a hostile takeover of the company virtually impossible. So, faced with the alternatives of selling a stake to one large investor or offering shares to many small ones, the family chose the second. "Instead of one gorilla, we'd have two thousand monkeys," says Adams, recalling his reasoning at the time.

* * *

But even as Mondavi contemplated selling shares to the "monkeys," the entire jungle was rumbling with change. In 1980, the U.S. Supreme Court had struck down California's Fair Trade Act, which had allowed suppliers to set the wholesale prices at which distributors sold to retailers. The court ruling represented a challenge to one key aspect of the modern liquor-distribution system: the question of who controlled wine and liquor prices.

The country's patchwork system to address this and other questions had grown out of concerns about the mobsters who ran illegal liquor empires during Prohibition. In an effort to try to break the stranglehold that organized crime organizations had on the liquor business following repeal in 1933, many states had adopted a so-called three tier system where alcohol flowed from manufacturer to distributor to retailer. Generally, owners were not allowed to invest in more than one tier, thus defusing control by any single group of industry players. The hodgepodge of various state systems that resulted seemed to work well in its first few decades.

But in removing the artificial price floor set by suppliers, the U.S. Supreme Court's ruling on the California law touched off a flurry of competition among distributors as they began slashing prices to win sales orders from retailers. Consolidation followed. In 1980, when the Fair Trade Act was scrapped, thirty regional companies distributed wine across the state. By the early 1990s, however, that number had shrunk to three statewide distributors and only fifteen local ones. The strongest player to emerge was Southern Wine and Spirits, the privately held and secretive Florida-based distributor owned in large part by Harvey Chaplin, who had gotten his start at Schenley Industries Inc., the New York–based distilling business that Harry Serlis had once run.

Over the years, with its aggressive lobbying tactics and growing political influence, it developed what *The Wall Street Journal* characterized as "a distinctive reputation: suspicions within industry and regulatory circles that Southern has or once had friends in the underworld," a notion that company officials have repeatedly denied. Still, as Southern gained more clout with grocery chains and "big box" retailers such as Costco, Price Club, and Sam's Club, Mondavi, like most other big wine producers, could not take the risk of being excluded from the lineup of wines that it sold—particularly since in some instances Southern became the sole supplier to big customers.

At the same time, these retailers were gaining sway in the marketplace. Price Club was the first warehouse store to open for business in 1976; Costco and Wal-Mart's Sam's Club chain opened in 1980 and 1983 respectively. In 1993, Costco and Price Club merged, attracting even more wine buyers. The grocery chains defended their position as by far the top sellers of wine through the 1990s, in part by deploying such new technologies as store scanner data.

To grapple with these changes, Mondavi started narrowing down its own web of distributors and, at the same time, began hiring some executives from outside the wine industry. One was Cindy Deutsch, who joined in 1989 from a leading market research firm, with the mandate to improve Mondavi's selling to the big box stores and chains. "Can we expect people to make a special stop at a separate store to buy wine? I think not," she told attendees at the 1990 Wine Industry Technical Symposium. "I believe it is more and more likely that people will buy their wine from stores in which they also buy food." As Mondavi began adapting to this fast-changing environment, it was perhaps inevitable hard feelings would arise.

One longtime distributor that lost Mondavi's business was New York–based House of Burgundy, which had taken a chance on distributing Mondavi's California wines in 1972, a time when most fine restaurants in New York favored the French. House of Burgundy's owner, Robert Fairchild, contends that Mondavi changed New York distributors in 1992 because the company was planning to go public and wanted a lot of orders to boost sales for their financial reporting, since a new distributor would place a one-time big order to fill its product pipeline. After two decades of pushing Mondavi wines, which by 1992 represented a quarter of House of Burgundy's business, losing the account stunned the distributor's staffers, who had perhaps grown complacent over the years.

Another instance of Mondavi shedding a longtime distributor involved Robert's old friend Charles Daniels, who ran the northern-California-based House of Daniels with his two sons and sold Mondavi wines to liquor stores, restaurants, and such retailers as Costco and Safeway through its business, Redwood Vintners. The Daniels family had been selling Mondavi wines since the late 1960s, but the relationship had started to deteriorate after 1980, with the U.S. Supreme Court's voiding of California's Fair Trade Act.

To compete against Southern and other large distributors, Redwood

Vintners and many other small outfits began discounting some wines, including Mondavi's. The Danielses believed that their deep-rooted relationship with the Mondavi family would protect their business. That may explain why they felt confident enough to begin the discounting that Mondavi claimed flouted its pricing "guidelines" for distributors—even though Mondavi had already canceled its distribution deal with Ceres, California–based Bronco, headed by Michael's school friend Fred Franzia, because it, too, had refused to adhere to the winery's suggested wholesale prices.

Yet neither Michael nor Cliff Adams nor Robert was inclined to remain lenient indefinitely with what they considered an underperforming distributor, regardless of their families' history together. Around that time, Mondavi was working with more than a hundred distributors across the country—providing them with a rolling, eighteen-month calendar of marketing and promotions, such as one that linked Woodbridge wines with healthy pasta recipes. Yet, at a time when a few big distributors such as Southern were gaining more power, Mondavi's patchwork of mostly small, local distributors looked glaringly inefficient. So they asked Charles Daniels Jr., known as Chuck, and his son Peter to take a ride with them.

In late October 1991, the two Daniels men climbed into the backseat of one of the Robert Mondavi Winery's company limousines for a long trip to San Francisco International Airport. Michael, Robert, and Adams joined them. Michael took the lead in the tough conversation that ensued, remaining businesslike throughout. He explained that the Mondavi winery's objective was to have "price parity" between distributors, especially on prices offered to such powerful customers as the wholesale clubs, and called Redwood Vintners the "instigator" of "low" wholesale prices for Mondavi wines. Michael was incensed that Redwood Vintners was offering to undercut the winery's "suggested prices" to Price Club by $2 a case. Michael then went on to imply he would end Redwood Vintners' lucrative distribution contract with Mondavi, worth some $7 million a year if the Danielses didn't fall into line by ending its deep discounting immediately. "If it were not for our family relationship, you would have been terminated a long time ago," Michael told his father's old friend.

The relationship between the families deteriorated further. In April 1992, the Mondavis fired the Danielses and named Southern Wine and Spirits as their exclusive California distributor. It was a stunning blow to

the elder Mr. Daniels, who had helped Robert in the early days when he
didn't have a penny.

Daniels was so enraged at being terminated that in June of 1992, he
retaliated by filing a lawsuit against the company and Robert Mondavi,
alleging violation of state antitrust law and breach of contract. He sought
$15 million in damages—which would be tripled if Mondavi were found
guilty of violating antitrust laws. At a time when the company already was
heavily burdened with debt and facing huge replanting costs, it was a
threateningly large sum. The Mondavis eventually settled the case by
paying a fraction of what the Danielses had demanded.

CHAPTER FOURTEEN

Going Public, 1992-1993

R obert, by then, had moved on to a more ambitious goal: convincing the world that wine drinking in moderation was not only socially acceptable but downright healthy. With the support of Harvey Posert, the brilliant Tennessee-born public relations man he had hired on Harry Serlis's advice in 1980, he decided to personally launch a campaign against the rising "neoprohibitionist" movement. To run the program, he hired Nina Wemyss, an attractive blond woman who had been raised on the wealthy North Shore of Long Island. By making the case that wine had been a part of civilization for thousands of years and was in itself a civilizing force, he hoped to distance it from problems associated with beer and hard liquor, such as alcoholism and drunk driving.

In what became known inside the company as "the Mission Program," Wemyss and Posert organized a series of symposiums in San Francisco, Philadelphia, London, and Brussels. Part junket and part educational seminar for the wholesalers, hoteliers, restaurateurs, retailers, and the media who were invited, the events drew together influential wine writers as well as campaigning doctors to discuss the risks and benefits of moderate wine consumption. Robert, who himself could polish off a bottle or two of wine a night in those years, sermonized at the start of each symposium that "wine is the temperate, civilized, sacred, romantic mealtime beverage recommended in the Bible, the liquid food praised for centuries. . . ."

Despite some misgivings on chief financial officer Greg Evans's part, Robert staked out a leadership position on the issue and endured a dustup with regulators at the Bureau of Alcohol, Tobacco and Firearms over the precise wording of the mission statement he was determined to put on every bottle of Mondavi wine. The watered-down language for the approved label ended up striking down any direct correlation between drinking wine and health: "Wine in moderation is an integral part of our family's culture, heritage, and the gracious way of life."

The Mondavis hoped that other wineries would adopt such wording, but few, if any, did. Mondavi's mission program was criticized for focusing on the trade instead of the general public—a charge that Marcia tried to answer. "The reason Dad is preaching to the converted is because he wants them to start preaching," she told a reporter. "He wants everyone to be a missionary. He's trying to mass the troops."

He got a big boost on November 11, 1991, when CBS aired a segment by correspondent Morley Safer called "The French Paradox." The story was about a group of medical researchers and doctors who maintained that drinking red wine in moderation could help prevent heart disease. Soon after the broadcast, red wine sales soared. An epidemiologist named R. Curtis Ellison, who had worked at Harvard's School of Public Health, made several trips to Oakville in the early 1990s, staying at the Mondavi guesthouse and lecturing to staffers about the latest findings on wine and health. The research he presented came as welcome news, allaying fears that some Mondavi employees had about the product they made and sold. Around that same time, Mondavi, Gallo, and dozens of other wineries and groups began funding a health study that Dr. Ellison was involved in, tracking the health effects of wine consumption over a five- to six-year period. Mondavi eventually ended its financial support of the study, as did many of the other wineries, over liability concerns.

It was these sorts of concerns, touched off by the CBS segment, that drove the final wedge between Robert and the Wine Institute, the industry lobbying group based in San Francisco. After the episode, some members of the Wine Institute, including Mondavi, felt "The French Paradox" story could be used as a marketing tool. The Wine Institute balked, fearing product liability lawsuits. When the institute decided not to support a small winery that got into a tussle with regulators after mentioning the CBS segment in its newsletter, Robert and Posert were outraged. To protest what they considered the institute's do-nothing stance, Mondavi dropped out of the Wine Institute in the early 1990s, as did a number of other, mostly smaller wineries.

Perhaps because its largest financial backer was Gallo, the Wine Institute preferred to pursue behind-the-scenes lobbying similar to that of the tobacco industry. To its critics, the trade group seemed to adopt the secretive culture of Ernest and Julio's company, which rarely spoke with the press and pushed its message through heavy advertising. In that respect, the Gallos' philosophy was diametrically opposed to the Mondavis', which relied almost entirely on word-of-mouth and lavish entertaining of wine writers and other opinion makers, while spending little on advertising. It was perhaps inevitable that the two cultures would eventually clash.

Meanwhile, Robert uncorked his mission speech at any opportunity. In March of 1993, six-year-old Emma Lipp, the daughter of one of the company's top salesman, had a school project assigned to profile an elderly person. Accompanied by her father, Gary Lipp, Emma visited Robert in his office at Oakville to interview him, asking a series of innocent questions such as "Where and when were you born?" and "What was your school like?" But when Emma asked her final question, "What do you like to do now?" Robert launched into the mission statement, which little Emma dutifully wrote down in pencil in her childish script:

"I like to educate our country that wine is a liquid food which comes from grapes," Robert told the girl. "When consumed in moderation it is part of the good and gracious life. When I was a little boy, three or four years old, my mother served me a little wine with water. If I abused it, it was bad and a disgrace to the family. Never have I seen anyone in my family abuse it. We should be taught the use of wine in our homes, schools, and in our community when we are young. Wine has been with us since the beginning of civilized man, seven thousand years ago. It has been part of our culture, heritage, and religion and will be with us indefinitely. Therefore, we should learn the proper use of it when we are young so we don't abuse it."

Of course, Robert shaded the truth with Emma by claiming he had

never seen anyone in his family abuse alcohol, even though he had witnessed Marjorie's long struggle with drinking. But his determination to
spread the gospel of moderate wine consumption was so intense that he
would not even set it aside during a brief exchange with a first-grader.

Robert's sermons on moderation were ironic, considering the company's
bacchanalian past. On one or two occasions over the years, Robert Mondavi made his entrance as a Marilyn Monroe look-alike, complete with a
blond wig, tight red dress, shaved legs, and dangerously high heels. After
company Halloween parties, Robert, Margrit, and various staffers made
late-night field trips to San Francisco's sexually charged Castro neighborhood to enjoy the scene as tourists. The company also had a history of
holding harvest parties and at some of these, employees got so drunk they
could barely stand, let along drive themselves home.

The Mondavi men's sexual approaches toward female employees
were another example of less-than-moderate behavior. The Mondavi
family's sense of entitlement as the business owners extended to flirting
with their staffers and Robert, in particular, had become audacious in this
habit by the early 1990s after seeing how the baron got away with it.
Robert, too, had trouble keeping his hands to himself and, because of his
position and advancing age, was seldom if ever challenged on it. While
most women saw his attentions as harmless fun, others found them uncomfortable. Adams, as his counselor, did call the problem to his attention, as did Michael, who told his father that some women did not
appreciate his attentions and he shouldn't "push it."

One of Robert's former empoyees claimed she was sexually harassed
by Robert every day, though she never took any formal legal action.
There were other instances of alleged sexual harassment over the years,
all of which were quietly handled by Mondavi's corporate counsel and
never made their way to court. One young journalist, who had admired
Robert during the time she was writing an article about him, was shocked
and upset when Robert, with Margrit out of town, cornered her at a party
one evening in the early 1990s, stroking her body and pushing himself
against her. She attributed his behavior to his advancing age or senility,
figuring that otherwise he wouldn't have shown such poor judgment. She
learned this had happened to other women in the valley, but decided to
drop the matter since the Mondavis, and Margrit in particular, had become so powerful.

Margrit's office at the winery was near Robert's and she joined him on his business trips as often as possible. She also maintained, at least publicly, that his attentions to other women were never serious or lasting. Margrit realized that her husband, at one point, had become infatuated with Nina Wemyss, the wine historian he had hired to run the mission program. In Margrit's view, Nina was fully aware of Robert's affection, but Margrit also realized her husband was not likely to leave her for this other woman. Margrit believed Wemyss was taking advantage of him, and she did not intervene on Wemyss's behalf when the company eventually decided to let her go.

Robert found ways to channel his sensuality. He became famous in the valley for his private massages, having them as many as three or four times a week and, in later years, as much as once or even twice a day. The massages often took place in the carriage house that was about three hundred yards behind Michael and Isabel's home, and were always given to him by women. "Bob always said, 'I never want a man to touch me,'" Margrit recalls. The massages were a source of occasional dismay to Michael on several levels. For one thing, his father would make these trips to the carriage house but seldom, if ever, stopped to see Michael or his grandchildren. The one time that Michael recalls his father visiting his home after one of his sessions was when he couldn't get his car started. "I'm out of gas," Robert told his son. As well, Michael realized that Robert's habit was well-known in the valley.

Robert's penchant for massages also led to some entanglements. A young and particularly beautiful massage therapist suffering from cancer once came to speak with the famous vintner at his office in the Oakville winery, accompanied by her father. Robert ended up paying for the young woman's trip to Mexico, where she sought treatment. When they left, Robert wandered over to Margrit's office and told her, "I've just been had." On other occasions when Robert became involved in the personal affairs of one of his therapists, Margrit felt compelled to intervene. Usually, the women asked for money, as Robert was an easy target for unscrupulous or needy females.

Timothy also developed a reputation for having an eye for a pretty woman. Like his father with Margrit many years before, Timothy by then was having an affair with an employee of the Robert Mondavi Corporation, and the resemblance between Timothy's adulterous path and Robert's was eerie to those who watched it unfold.

In 1985, a highly accomplished chef named Holly Peterson began working for the Robert Mondavi Winery. Then only twenty-five years old, the blond and warmly effusive Peterson traveled around the country for the winery, hosting wine and food events. She was impressively qualified for the job. Not only had she graduated from the University of California at Davis with a degree in enology, but she had gone from there to use her fluent French to earn a Grand Diplôme de Cuisine from the famed La Varenne cooking school in Paris and then spent a year as the first full-time female chef at the Michelin three-starred restaurant Tantris, in Munich. Capping it off, Peterson had an impressive pedigree. She grew up in the valley and came from a family of well-respected wine-makers: Her father, Richard G. Peterson, had been the handpicked successor at Beaulieu Vineyards to the fabled André Tchelistcheff and, after clashing with Beaulieu's new owners, Heublein Corporation, quit and went on to a number of other roles in the industry. Her sister, Heidi Barrett, was also an up-and-coming winemaker.

It's no wonder Holly Peterson caught Timothy's eye: With her green eyes, slender figure, and a relaxed yet lively ability to communicate a passion for food and wine, she was a rising star in the culinary world. Dorothy, on the other hand, had spent the decade and a half since she and Timothy married delivering and raising their five children—Carissa, Chiara, Carlo, Dominic, and Dante. Dorothy wasn't as young, as self-assured, or as glamorous as Holly Peterson, and some members of the extended Mondavi clan, as well as some staffers, wondered unkindly, in an echo of the criticism years earlier of Margrit, whether Peterson had consciously set her sights on marrying Timothy as way of adding the prestige of the Mondavi name to her own.

That view, however, suggests that Timothy was a passive recipient of Peterson's attentions, while in fact Timothy and Holly courted each other at the winery and at industry events. During a trip to Europe in 1989, Timothy, Dorothy, and Holly all went. Timothy and Holly would occasionally dine together without Dorothy, leading employees to wonder if they were having an affair. By the early 1990s, Timothy was making it clear to people at the winery that he was serious about ending his first marriage. As the family members and all of their spouses received legal counsel about their shareholdings in preparation for the IPO, Timothy was insisting that the shares were solely his property and not his wife Dorothy's. Timothy would later maintain that he formally separated from Dorothy on June 1, 1992—more than a year before the company went public—whereas Dorothy maintained the separation took place more than three years later. Holly, meanwhile, recalled that her and Timothy's "committed monogamous relationship" began the same year Timothy said he separated from Dorothy—in 1992.

But the problems in the marriage had begun much earlier and the ongoing tumult in Timothy's private life proved awkward and embarrassing for some Mondavi staffers, just as Robert and Margrit's affair had more than a decade earlier. Unlike Robert and Margrit, who had kept their affair discreet for years, Timothy's open affair with Peterson seemed to some insiders to humiliate his wife. That, in turn, further corroded the respect he commanded at the company, and Robert voiced his criticism of his younger son's behavior toward Dorothy to some of his top executives, as well as to a new psychologist-turned-management-consultant named Alan Schnur, who informally helped counsel some family members for a period. Compounding the situation further, Margrit took Dorothy under her wing and helped arrange for her to work on a volunteer basis at the Oakville winery, serving as its historian. With Dorothy installed at a desk near Timothy's office and Holly Peterson working out of the Vineyard Room across the lawn, the situation resembled a daytime soap opera.

Less than a two hours' drive to the south of Napa Valley, a flood of young executives in Silicon Valley made millionaires on paper by stock options were also breaking the rules of conventional corporate conduct. Most famously, W. J. Sanders III, the chief executive officer of Advanced Micro Devices Inc., threw a twenty-fifth anniversary party attended by eleven thousand employees and family members, California's governor, thirty-six magicians, and the British rocker Rod Stewart. The star of the party was Sanders himself, who grew up poor in Chicago, and found himself hoisted to the stage on a cherry picker amid fireworks, a rendition of "The Star Spangled Banner," and shouts of "Jerreeee, Jerree." It was a period of exuberant optimism, but one that, at least in Silicon Valley, tended to celebrate self-made millionaires, rather than those who inherited their wealth and positions.

The Mondavis, on the other hand, were inheritors. They had gotten their start through Cesare and Rosa Mondavi's hard work. Although Robert was a first-generation American, his offspring had comfortably settled into the right universities, clubs, and paths laid out for progeny of the upper class. By the third generation—Michael, Marcia, and Timothy— their father's wealth and success had turned them into royalty in the small realm of Napa Valley. Robert was genuinely respected for his passion and hard work, but not everyone felt the same regard for his children. Some Mondavi employees, for instance, would call Michael and Timothy members of the "Lucky Sperm" club.

When the opportunity arose for the Mondavis to associate themselves with other members of the international wine crowd through a new organization called Primum Familiae Vini—Latin for "first families of wine"—they were among the earliest members. The idea for the group was hatched by Miguel Torres, of the Spanish family that had been cultivating vineyards since the seventeenth century, and Robert Drouhin of Burgundy, in 1990. The Mondavis, Italy's Antinoris, and Britain's Symington family were the next to sign on when the organization formally got off the ground in 1993. The Mondavis recruited the Baroness Philippine de Rothschild, and eventually membership was limited to a dozen families who positioned their group as an exclusive wine aristocracy.

The Mondavis were the sole American representatives of Primum Familiae Vini. Aside from fabulous black-tie dinners and the opportunity to rub elbows with European aristocrats, the group's stated goal was to help one another with advice on how to successful pass a family business down from one generation to the next. Contrary to the bootstrap mentality of Silicon Valley, the Mondavis were embracing Old World values and seeking guidance on a question that Michael, in particular, had become preoccupied with: How to build a family dynasty?

The logical disconnect between family ownership and Wall Street's short-term demands troubled some Mondavi employees. As the family gathered its Oakville staffers together in the bottling room in the spring of 1993 to explain why it had decided to take the company public, it naturally attempted to spin the news as a positive development in their evolution as a family and a company. Michael took the lead, but Robert, Margrit, Timothy, and even Marcia, who had flown in from the East Coast, were also there. Cliff Adams and Greg Evans also spoke. Their message was that the family would retain control of the company and that not much would change once they'd brought in additional shareholders.

That message rang false to some of the hundred or so employees in the room that day. And staffers couldn't help noticing some other small, but subtle, changes taking place as the family prepared to take the company public. Around that time, Michael cut off the little ponytail that he had been sporting in keeping with his "rebel son" image of the past few years. His "rat's tail" made sense when he was wearing his black leather jacket and roaring through the valley on Highway 29 astride his Harley-Davidson motorcycle with a group of other "RUBS" (rich urban bikers), but that bad boy look was out of step with the solid, reliable image that Wall Street valued. What's more, it didn't fit in with the rarified circles the Mondavis were now traveling in with the Primum Familiae crowd. More practically, he found it difficult to rest his head comfortably on airplanes when his hair was tied back with a rubber band.

For Robert, who had hated Michael's rat's tail all along, the decision to chop it off came none too soon.

Robert's ongoing role in the "Mission" posed a challenge when it came time for the Mondavis to do their road show. The bankers from Hambrecht and Quist, and Goldman, quickly realized that although Robert was by then an iconic pitchman for Napa Valley wines, he also had the unfortunate tendency to stray off script. Their solution was to minimize his role during the two-week trip to sell analysts and investors on the idea of buying shares in the company. In one or two of the cities the group visited, Robert introduced his sons. But generally, the tightly written formula was that Michael emphasized the company's commitment to marketing its wines through education, Timothy discussed its novel winegrowing techniques, and Cliff Adams focused on operating details of the business. The bankers hoped that by keeping Robert's involvement in the road show to a minimum, they would demonstrate that the Mondavi family's succession plan was working and that the patriarch had truly handed off power to his sons.

Michael and Timothy shared the title of co-CEO at the time of the IPO but the investment bankers saw Michael as the more presentable brother in terms of his grasp of business issues and ability to communicate the company's message to investors. As well as being a polished public speaker, Michael also was more comfortable in public settings than the more introverted Timothy. The bankers also tried to control the sales pitch by starting off with a video that opened with a shot of Robert in the vineyards, explaining, "Ever since I was a child I wanted to excel. . . ."

Yet despite the slick multimedia presentation and the coaching they received from the bankers and their own executives, the brothers couldn't entirely conceal their animosity toward each other during the road show. When one would answer a question, the other would get up, walk away, roll his eyes, or yawn. Despite the years of counseling and the attempts on the part of psychiatric consultants and business experts to help them align their goals, they couldn't completely disguise their differing world views. Michael would speak passionately about Mondavi's plans to become a global leader in the wine industry, while Timothy made it clear he preferred slow, steady growth. The analysts and investors who came to hear them talk may or may not have noticed the signs of trouble, but Goldman decided to price the shares toward the lower end of the range that it had originally suggested, perhaps sensing the family discord.

The pricing decision may also have been influenced by a skeptical story in *Forbes* magazine that ran three days before trading in Mondavi stock began. It doubted whether MOND would prove a smart investment: "Tempted to buy a few shares? Here is a better suggestion. Marvin Shanken, publisher of the influential *Wine Spectator* magazine, suggests buying a case or two of Robert Mondavi's Reserve Cabernet Sauvignon 1986 at around $35 a bottle. If California wine prices rise, the bottle's value should keep pace. And if the business goes sour, you'll still have something to cheer yourself up with."

On the morning of Thursday, June 10, 1993, Michael, Robert, Timothy, Marcia, and Cliff Adams converged in lower Manhattan and made their way to Goldman's trading floor to see for themselves the first public sale of their company's stock on NASDAQ, the electronic exchange where Microsoft and Oracle were also traded. The family felt so optimistic that the offering would be a success that it arranged for Mondavi-produced sparkling wine—made in limited quantities and only uncorked for special events—to sit chilled in ice buckets, ready for them to toast their triumph.

They were tense as they stared up at the ticker, waiting for MOND, their stock's symbol, to roll across it for the first time. Priced initially at $13.50 a share at the insistence of Robert, who was optimistic that it would soar even higher, the stock quickly jumped to $14.25, then began falling. Goldman ended up buying much of it to buoy the price and avoid embarrassment. MOND ended the day selling for $13 1/8 a share. Closing below its initial offering price was a bad omen.

As the Mondavis and Adams jetted back from New York to California, they could not ignore the fact that the offering had not gone according to plan. By selling one million Class A shares, the family raised $12.55 million for itself before expenses. The patriarch sold 400,000 Class A shares, raising $5.2 million, while each of his offspring sold 200,000 shares, raising $2.5 million each. The company, in turn, sold 2.7 million Class A shares. Overall, the IPO raised around $37 million for the four Mondavis and the corporate coffers, far less than the bankers' projections of $50 to $60 million.

Yet for the first time the Mondavis could instantly access the wealth that had been locked away in the company for so many years. Each of them instantly became multimillionaires not only on paper, but in reality. On the face of it, it was ideal: They got liquidity and retained what seemed like absolute control. At the time of the IPO, Michael and Timothy each had 18.9 percent of the voting power, Marcia, who had put some shares into a trust for her children, had 20.5 percent.

The family put a good face on a troubling start and got down to the business of celebrating that weekend. The hot ticket at the twelfth annual Napa Valley Wine Auction was the black-tie party hosted jointly by the Mondavis and the Rothschilds at Opus One. Four dozen guests in tuxedoes and long evening gowns ascended the steps of Napa's wine temple, sipped champagne, and sat down to a dinner prepared by the famed and portly New Orleans chef Paul Prudhomme. After the meal, the guests crossed the road to join the more raucous party at the Robert Mondavi Winery, where some of the guests were puffing on expensive Cuban cigars and couples danced to a sixteen-piece band called Steppin' Out. As society columnist L. Pierce Carson reported in *The Napa Valley Register*, "Bob Mondavi and his sons were all smiles, pleased with the near sellout of the 3.7 million shares of stock the company first offered to the public on Thursday."

Carson didn't notice Timothy and Holly Peterson's passionate performance on the dance floor, which raised eyebrows, particularly among valley old-timers who had square-danced with Timothy and Dorothy in the 1970s. The weekend concluded with Robert's annual birthday bash, attended by California governor Pete Wilson. Since Robert could now buy whatever his heart desired, Margrit came up with a novel gift: She presented her husband with a pair of llamas.

Robert's eightieth birthday celebration continued a few weeks later at Vinexpo, the giant annual trade show in Bordeaux for French wine producers, where the Rothschilds and Mondavis were promoting Opus One. The families hosted a five-hour train ride on the Orient Express to Pauillac, where Opus One would accompany a lavish meal. Dorothy and some of their children went on that trip but Timothy chose to spend his time with Peterson, who was there as a Mondavi employee.

Whatever pleasure Timothy derived from openly declaring his involvement with Peterson proved to be relatively short-lived. By humiliating Dorothy at an industry function and displeasing the rest of his family, who remained loyal to her, Timothy would discover that his behavior would cost him much more than just the loss of his family's respect.

PART THREE

EXPANSION

CHAPTER FIFTEEN

Regency's End, 1993–1994

L ater in the summer of 1993, following the IPO, Robert and Margrit joined two other couples for a luxurious, six-day fishing trip to Alaska. Whisked away on a private jet leaving from Napa Airport, the group boarded a seventy-five-foot cruiser outfitted with four state-rooms, a full crew, and a chef. The trip in the company of the frozen-food heir Clarke Swanson, Bill Hall, a music industry veteran, and their wives, was meant to be a joyful commencement to Robert's new life. It turned out to be anything but.

The problem was Mondavi's plunging stock price. After the disappointing first day of trading, it continued to fall. A week after the IPO, it closed at $11.25 a share—17 percent below its original price. Three weeks later, it had sunk by 20 percent. By week five, in mid-July, MOND had hit $9.75. By week nine, it dropped even further to $8.125—a full 40 percent below the IPO price. Between the time that Robert and Margrit climbed aboard the jet and their arrival in Alaska, the stock dipped to a new low of $6.50. More than half the wealth held in the company's stock had simply vanished over the summer and Robert, who got the bad news during a shore visit, experienced a business and personal crisis.

Robert examined his heart, wondering if he might have avoided the problem by handling his sons differently or giving them more control early on. He worried that everything he had worked for—his company and his family's good name—would be lost if the stock plunged further.

Robert spent most of the journey talking about the problem of the plunging share price. But the business issues couldn't be separated from the family dynamics, and that led him to mulling over his own short-comings as a parent. To Bill Hall, he confided his regrets at being away from home so much when his children were young, as well as spending so little time now with his grandchildren. He also pondered his decision to place the operation of the company in Cliff Adams's hands, instead of al-lowing his own sons to run it themselves. Did he lack trust in them or was he simply refusing to fully let go? Michael, in particular, seemed to suffer from "Prince Charles syndrome"; he held an elevated title but had little real operating responsibility, while Adams's role was to run the company for the prince regent.

Robert also had other worries that week. As the struggles between Michael and Timothy escalated, Robert feared a repetition of the family pattern that had led to the breakup of his original family three decades earlier. Between talking, writing page after page in a journal he had along with him on the trip, and drinking good wine each night, Robert turned over in his mind how to handle the problems. His bad luck in the fishing chair mirrored his situation: While Margrit landed a forty-four-pound halibut and Bill Hall's wife, Evelyn, reeled in a seventy-five-pounder, Robert didn't get a single bite.

As Robert was bobbing along in a fishing boat off the coast of Alaska, Michael, Adams, Greg Evans and other executives were grappling with the problem from the company's headquarters in Napa. None of them had imagined they'd suffer such a painful rebuff from investors, and the experience, for them, too, led to some soul searching about whether the investment community knew more about the business's worth than the family did.

One of the problems was that a large majority of the shares were held by institutional investors, rather than by hobbyists and wine lovers who simply owned a share or two of MOND to get discounts on wine purchases. Hedge fund managers and arbitrageurs were different from other financial professionals that Michael or the executive team had encountered before. It didn't take long for them to realize they'd made a key error in assuming that they could woo analysts and investors in the same way they had wooed wine drinkers, critics, and retailers over the years. Mondavi had long relied on wine education and comparative tastings to sell its products. It figured it could approach analysts in the same personal way: leading them on a tour of the vineyards, pouring a crisp Fumé Blanc or an elegant Robert Mondavi Reserve Cabernet, and counting on the romance of the setting to work its magic. It did not occur to them at first that analysts cared more about building an accurate model of next quarter's earnings than discovering whether Mondavi's best Cabernet was as good as a Haut Brion.

Because it enjoyed so much success in public relations under Harvey Posert's direction, the company didn't hire a specialized investor relations manager before the IPO. Instead, it relied on Greg Evans to walk analysts through the numbers and Peter Mattei to field questions on production and vineyards. Evans, in particular, had rapidly assumed more responsibility. He had first joined Mondavi in 1978 as a manager of its bottling and warehouse operation in Oakville and Timothy and Mondavi's then CFO, George Scofield, quickly spotted Evans's talent. Less than a year after joining the company, Evans was admitted to Harvard Business School, and the company offered to pay his tuition if he'd rejoin it after graduating. Evans declined the tuition offer but returned to Oakville in the summer between business school years. After graduating from Harvard with distinction in 1980, he rejoined the company fulltime as a corporate planning officer. Timothy took the bright and detail-oriented Evans under his wing, promoting him to CFO and then COO.

Cautious and circumspect, Evans was a perfect foil to the passionate and occasionally impetuous Mondavi temperament. He was adept at managing his relationship with the family, allowing it to bask in glory while he followed up on details behind the scenes. Unlike Ramona and even, to some extent, Cliff Adams, Evans was skilled at avoiding the crossfire between the brothers. But to some of the people who worked for him, Evans's real genius was not so much in his facility with numbers or his ability to think strategically; it was his political savvy. Perhaps because he had grown up in a family business himself, Evans developed an effective rapport with the volatile Mondavi family. And although he was closest to Timothy for many years, he had earned the trust of Michael and Robert as well.

One way that Evans demonstrated his loyalty to the family was to become the bearer of bad tidings, of which there were plenty in Mondavi's first earnings announcement. Issued on August 2, 1993, the news hardly reassured investors. Net revenues for the fiscal year ending June 30, 1993, were up 15.5 percent to $168.1 million, and earnings for the year climbed 21.9 percent to $8.7 million. But the crucial fourth quarter, generally the strongest quarter in the wine industry, was disappointing; the company's net income dropped 8 percent to $3.2 million. As summer faded into fall and leaves on the vines reddened, heavy rains hit the vineyards. As well, the phylloxera infestation continued to plague the crops.

In the dark days of December, Mondavi was forced to put out an even more troubling news release, announcing that results for the second quarter and six months ending on December 31 would be below financial analysts' projections for the periods. Questions were directed to Greg Evans, as the company's CFO, and the release quoted Cliff Adams, explaining in turgid language that "the economic difficulties California continues to experience are the principal reasons for the expected shortfall to analysts' estimates." The stock dropped further on the news. Adams, for one, felt angry and frustrated that the banks that had been so helpful as the company prepared to go public did not adopt the same approach when it came time to analyze Mondavi's shares.

Neither Michael nor Timothy's name was to be found anywhere in the release announcing the company's missed projections. The family preferred to leave the delivery of bad news to Evans and other staffers. But around the same time, the brothers were pulled into another unfortunate situation they could not avoid.

Enraged by the course that his life had taken, with his wife and daughters turning against him and the Mondavi empire banishing him, Gary Ramona sued his daughter's therapist, psychiatrist, and the medical center that had treated her on the grounds that they had encouraged the recovery of false memories that had damaged him, both in emotional and financial terms. A key element in Ramona's case was his contention that he'd lost his job at Mondavi because of the ugly rumors. That claim spurred on months of discovery, including videotaped depositions of

Michael, Isabel, Timothy, and Dorothy Mondavi, among others. As the trial date approached, the family became aware of another source of disagreement that would soon be aired publicly: Robert had agreed to testify on Ramona's behalf while Michael and Timothy planned to take the stand against him. The case was shaping up as a courtroom drama pitting father against sons and had the potential to publicly expose the internal discord at the highest levels of the Robert Mondavi Corporation.

With a subplot involving Napa's leading family, the lurid incest trial transfixed and rocked the normally sedate valley. Network television crews and reporters from such publications as *People* magazine and *The New York Times* descended on Napa's hundred-year-old white frame courthouse. When the Ramona trial got under way in March of 1994, the courtroom was packed every day. But it was especially well-attended on the day of Robert's testimony.

Limping slightly as he approached the witness stand, Robert reached it and sat down to testify on Gary Ramona's behalf. "My name is Robert Mondavi. M-O-N-D-A-V-I. I'm in the wine business," said the eighty-one-year-old patriarch. Margrit, concerned and composed, sat in the front row of the stands as her husband explained to the judge and jury that Ramona's banishment was "one of the worst things that ever happened in the winery." In answers that were blunt and forthright, Robert explained Ramona's contribution to the company's soaring case sales and told of his decision in the mid-1980s to hand over the reins of power to Michael and Timothy, resulting in an erratic power-sharing arrangement for several years. When asked how he had felt when his sons came to him with the rumors of incest, Robert said he was "shocked," going on to explain "my daughters-in-law were tremendously upset. . . . They didn't want to have anyone who would molest a child working for the company. And I agree with them. But I did not agree that he had molested a child. I know it more so now than ever before!"

The court took a break. Although the company's counsel had advised Robert not to say anything, he paid no heed. Reporters gathered around him as he defended in the court of public opinion the man who had been his third son. "I know the man! He works with his heart and soul. A man of great character. I think that more than ever. I feel he's an adopted son." Margrit, who stood by her husband, resting her hand on his arm, added, "He lost everything, much more than we can ever imagine."

After the break, Robert climbed back onto the stand and told the court how his and Margrit's pleas to avoid prejudging Ramona without proof went unheard. Robert read the June 18 leave-of-absence letter to the jury and Ramona's shoulders heaved with emotion. Robert's strong voice, in turn, came close to breaking when he admitted to the court that he had been powerless to stop Ramona's ouster. His sons "just outvoted me," he said. On cross-examination, he went further in explaining the disagreement between him and his sons over Ramona, particularly following the apparent confirmation of Holly Ramona's charges after she was given sodium amytal, a supposed "truth-serum" drug. Michael and Timothy "thought they did it on business, but I also feel their subconscious mind . . . with this sodium [amytal] idea, and the wives being so concerned, I feel it had an effect on their judgment. . . . They had reasons of their own I didn't agree with."

Robert's cross-examination ended with two quick questions from another lawyer. "Did you raise your sons to always tell the truth? And do they always tell the truth?" the lawyer asked him. Robert answered yes to both questions and stepped down from the witness stand. Then he walked over to Ramona and embraced him.

A week later, Timothy and then Michael took the stand. The brothers' goal was to defend the company's decision to fire Ramona, convincing the jury that it had had nothing to do with the rumors of rape but was purely a business decision related to what they considered Ramona's faltering performance on the job. Although insurers were on the line for the $8 million that Ramona was seeking for the damage to his career, the stakes for the Mondavis were high as well. The family's reputation for fairness was being challenged by Ramona and there was a risk that an even deeper schism could develop between father and sons in the course of the trial. With that in mind, the brothers strove to paint Ramona as a salesman who had failed to keep up with the times. He was a man "limited by his weaknesses," as Timothy put it.

As Robert's youngest son took the stand, the countercultural look of his youth still lingered, despite his title as co-CEO of a publicly listed company. He had a full head and beard of sandy-red hair, which topped a gray double-breasted suit. Slighter and fairer than his brother, Timothy resembled his Irish-American mother's side of the family. "I have always had great regard . . . great affection for Gary. I have admired Gary for his dedication, for his charisma, for his energy. But over time it became evident that his organizational abilities were not as strong as his charisma and dedication," he said. When one of the lawyers asked him, "Were you one of the people responsible for granting Mr. Ramona leave of absence on or about June eighteenth, 1990?" Timothy's mild countenance gave way to a flicker of the anger that lay below the surface.

"Yes, I was."

"Were you also one of the people responsible for Mr. Ramona's termination from the winery?"

"Yes, I was."

Timothy hadn't forgotten the frustration and anger he had felt when Ramona replaced him as Vichon's chief executive, despite the sales chief's earlier apparent disinterest in the small, struggling winery. "In my efforts to get Gary to address Vichon in a timely and organized basis I was ineffective. Based on my ineffectiveness, I think my father effectively asked Gary to take charge of Vichon. I felt it was absolutely inappropriate, given that Gary was overworked and overstressed and unable to basically handle what he had on his plate at that time, in my opinion," Timothy had explained to lawyers in the case before taking the stand. Helping to fire his father's "third son" was, it seemed, in a small way a vindication for Timothy.

Ramona's lawyer probed Timothy's personal animosity toward Ramona. He certainly blamed the sales chief for the failure of his baby, Vichon, to hit its sales targets and for emphasizing quantity over quality. "I think that Gary wanted to discount it more aggressively. I wanted to continue to position it . . . to maintain its reputation in the marketplace for high quality, and I am right in that." The lawyer then went on to ask why, then, Vichon was now sold at the club discount chain Costco. Timothy was forced to admit he'd not only been defeated on the issue—but defeated by his brother, flagging to the jurors and the press in the courtroom that day that the Mondavi front wasn't quite as united as the family had hoped it would appear.

The next day, Michael took the stand. The contrast to his brother's appearance couldn't have been sharper. Wearing his black hair slicked back and a meticulously tailored suit, he looked as hard-edged and sophisticated as Timothy had looked sensitive. Gone was the gawkiness and vulnerability that Michael had displayed in the early days of the winery, when he was just out of college. Now he supported an assertive black mustache and the same craggy features of his father, but without Robert's warmth or apparent humility. The man who had asked Ramona, upon learning of his divorce, what the family could do to help, was gone. In his place was an executive intent on protecting his family and company's reputation.

"A great salesman does not make a great sales manager," said Michael, describing Ramona as an old-time salesman "beyond his skills" in a consolidating marketplace. Like Timothy, Michael denied that the rumors had anything to do with Ramona's termination and invoked spousal privilege when asked about his wife's role in spreading rumors at the winery. He flatly denied that the sales chief was fired for anything but performance-related issues. "Was Gary fired because of his emotional reaction to his divorce?" a lawyer asked him.

"No. Not at all."

"Was he fired because he was spending a lot of time building a house?"

"No."

"Was he fired because he refused to change his role at the winery at a time when the winery needed him to change?"

"Absolutely."

"Did your father agree with you and your brother that Gary Ramona's role . . . needed to change?

"Yes, he did."

But, in cross-examination, Ramona's lawyer suggested that jealousy was a motive for Ramona's firing. "Gary and my father had a wonderful relationship; essentially the adopted son that he was closer to than his blood children," Michael confessed to a stunned courtroom. "That was fine, but Gary felt that he could do what he wanted" whether the sons were supportive or not. "We were a nuisance to him at times. . . . I felt that my father was being taken advantage of. . . ."

The jurors, when asked later about their impressions of the Mondavi brothers' testimony, suspected that jealousy had played a role in Ramona's ouster. He wasn't blood and in the midst of a transfer of power from Robert to Michael and Timothy, Ramona was sacrificed. Even so, although the jurors found that malpractice had occurred, they only awarded Ramona a small fraction of the $8.5 million he had sought: $500,000, roughly a year's pay at Mondavi. Of their award, the jury placed 40 percent of the burden of responsibility on one of Holly Ramona's therapists, Isabella Marche, 10 percent to a consulting psychiatrist, Dr. Richard Rose, 5 percent to the hospital, and another 5 percent to Gary Ramona himself, for failing to get more involved in his daughter's problems.

The remaining 40 percent was assigned to "all other persons." Although the jury was not required to name names publicly, they blamed Ramona's ex-wife, Stephanie, as well as Dorothy and Isabel Mondavi, among others, for spreading the hurtful rumors. They also included in that group Dr. Barry Grundland, the psychiatrist who was battling with his ex-wife over his court-ordered support payments at that time. The jury wasn't asked to decide whether incest had taken place, but its findings suggested the jurors doubted the truth of Holly Ramona's "recovered" memories.

As the brothers were testifying at the Ramona trial, a pitched battle was raging behind closed doors at the Robert Mondavi Corporation. The company was in the final stages of a major business initiative: the introduction of wines made from coastal grapes that would be sold under the Robert Mondavi label. On the face of it, the plan was designed to solve a competitive problem. Although Mondavi was on target to sell more than four million cases of premium wine that year, it had a hole in its portfolio that rivals were rushing in to fill. The company's lowest-priced brand, Woodbridge, was considered a "popular premium" brand, selling for $3 to $7 a bottle. On the other end of the spectrum, its Robert Mondavi Napa Valley and Byron wines were "ultrapremium" brands, selling for $14 to $20 a bottle, and its "super ultrapremium" wines, Robert Mondavi Reserve and Opus One, were selling for generally far more than $20. The gap in Mondavi's portfolio was in the $7 to $14 range, which Vichon had been repositioned to fill.

By 1994, however, the company's rivals had moved purposefully into this fast-growing segment of the market. Probably the most notable newcomer was a San Francisco–based trial lawyer named Jess Jackson, a self-made man who labored as a longshoreman, policeman, and lumberjack in his early years before turning to the law and then becoming a vintner. He began buying land in Sonoma, the less glamorous valley to the west of Napa, in the 1970s and produced his first Chardonnay in 1983, priced at $4.50 a bottle. Accidentally, his winemaker created a slightly sweeter wine that consumers liked.

By the mid-1990s, Kendall-Jackson Vintner's Reserve Chardonnay was priced at $14 a bottle, aiming directly at the ultrapremium segment, the area where Mondavi was weak. From 18,000 cases in the early 1980s, Jackson seemed to have come out of nowhere to sell 1.7 million cases a year by 1994. His success didn't go unnoticed by Southern Wines and Spirits, which by then was the country's largest wine and liquor distributor and had distributed Jackson's wines in California since 1988. Representing both Mondavi and Kendall-Jackson at the time, Southern's California head, Ted Simpkins, privately warned Michael that he needed to quickly come out with a brand to counter K-J. "You're getting hammered," Simpkins told him.

Jackson was hurting Mondavi in other ways as well. Amid his sales success, he was buying up land for vineyards and poaching talented winemakers. He began wooing Mondavi's veteran winemaker, Charles Thomas—the man who made its highly respected Napa Valley Cabernets.

Thomas, for one, had been firmly in Timothy's camp in his doubts about extending the Robert Mondavi name across its various brands. While the marketing and sales side of the company, led by Michael, pushed for brand extension, Timothy voiced doubts, arguing that it could lead to confusion on the part of some consumers about whether they were buying the company's top- or bottom-shelf wines. But just as Timothy had lost the power struggle over Vichon's repositioning, he also lost the fight over Robert Mondavi Coastal wines, which were rolled out against his objections in May 1994.

Timothy was unable to get his point across, in large part because he had undermined his credibility with his family by leaving the mother of his five children for Holly Peterson. Against his father and brother's strongly voiced feelings, Timothy had formally separated from Dorothy by 1994 and was deepening his ties to Holly. Those changes cost Timothy the ability to win his father to his side on business disputes, weakening his power base relative to Michael's.

Robert's younger son would point out the similarity between his and his father's situation to numerous friends and colleagues over the years, but what he overlooked in his argument was the fact that he had been the harshest of Robert's children in condemning his father and Margrit's affair—a fact that few family members could forget. Yet because of the precedent set in the Charlie Williams and Dorothy Barajas affair, Timothy and Holly's relationship drew fire. Arguing that the couple would be violating the company's code of ethics, which prohibited managers at Mondavi from dating or being married to their subordinates, Michael had insisted to Mondavi's board of directors that Holly must resign. After lengthy discussion, director Bartlett Rhoades delivered the painful news and Holly eventually left her job at Mondavi. The fact that Michael had initiated the ouster further estranged the brothers.

Miserable and under intense pressure, Timothy let his guard down for a black-and-white photograph in that year's annual report. Robert, Timothy, and Michael are shot in profile, each holding glasses of red wine, against the vineyards. While Michael and Robert look buoyant, Timothy has got a deeply troubled look on his face as he is positioned between his father and brother.

Timothy's characteristically passionate style of advocacy in business meetings also increasingly seemed at odds with the changing culture of the company. Shortly before it went public, Mondavi realized it needed to bolster its board of directors, which up until then had been made up mostly of family members and longtime friends. In 1992, it recruited the lawyer Frank Farella as Timothy's choice for a director, and investment manager Philip Greer as Michael's choice to join Bartlett Rhoades, Marcia's pick, as the board's three outside directors, although all three had strong ties to the Mondavis.

As well, at Michael's initiative, it decided to hire Alan E. Schnur, a Towers Perrin consultant, to survey employees shortly after the IPO, as Mondavi's stock was plunging. Schnur, an intense man who had earned a Ph.D. in psychology and had consulted for a number of Silicon Valley companies, was hired to assess employee morale and gauge its leadership. Unlike any of the 150 or so previous surveys he had done, he found that the company, and Robert Mondavi in particular, commanded an astonishing level of loyalty. People told Schnur that "they'd lay down in front of a train for 'Mister'"—meaning Mr. Mondavi, as Robert was called.

At the same time, Schnur's survey uncovered deeply felt frustration and concern by employees around the question of the company's leadership and decision making, with these problems originating from the family. Echoing the complaints voiced by Gary Ramona, staffers told Schnur and his team that decision making got bogged down in lengthy meetings and that, if decisions were made, they were often reversed or abandoned.

The Towers Perrin group presented their findings first to the head of human resources and Greg Evans, and then to the family, and eventually spread the message to large groups of employees in the Vineyard Room. Schnur would begin the presentations with the good news of finding an exceptionally high level of commitment among staffers, coupled with the bad news of "extraordinarily high frustration." The study touched a nerve: Staffers were riveted by what he said and some ended up crying during the presentations.

Despite Schnur's troubling message, the accuracy of his diagnosis and his skill in expressing the problem impressed the family enough that they turned to him for guidance. Following the results of the survey, he began helping the three Mondavi men work better with one another, filling to some extent the role left empty by Dr. Grundland's departure. In the meantime, the results of the employee survey, coupled with the low stock price, sent a warning shot to Mondavi's outside directors that they had to do something or they would be neglecting their fiduciary duty to protect shareholders' interests.

Frank Farella, the San Francisco lawyer who grew grapes in Napa and was a close friend of Robert, had advised Timothy that he should consider stepping down from the co-CEO role. Timothy at first refused to take his advice, since it meant playing second fiddle to his brother. But with the stock's dramatic drop, the outside directors realized they might have to force the issue. Farella, Greer, and Rhoades met and concluded that Michael and Timothy's experiment as co-CEOs had failed. With his personal life in turmoil and a lingering habit of tardiness and disorganized work habits, Timothy had lost not only his father and brother's support in the CEO role but also that of the independent directors. Their experiences at other companies and organizations made them less tolerant of his shortcomings.

The outside directors also had concerns about Michael, who did not seem to have a natural interest or aptitude for the nuts-and-bolts duties of a CEO that Cliff Adams and Greg Evans were then performing. Worse, the bickering between the brothers had grown so intense that at times they'd delay board meetings, failing to agree even on an agenda. Problems like these led the directors to brainstorm ideas. Some suggested kicking both brothers upstairs and installing a non-Mondavi as CEO, which was exactly the same recommendation that Price Waterhouse had made fourteen years earlier.

Meanwhile, Farella and Greer continued to work behind the scenes for weeks to try to convince Timothy to step down. Greer focused on Robert, who seemed to feel protective of his younger son. Over breakfast at the company guesthouse, behind Michael's home, Greer sat down with the Mondavi patriarch, hoping try to change his mind. Over several hours, Greer talked, sketched out organizational charts, cajoled, and finally even threatened to quit the board if Robert wouldn't agree to scrap the unworkable arrangement. "Bob, I'm always going to be your friend. But I just can't stay on the board unless we resolve this logjam."

Robert, who'd arrived at the breakfast carrying his own yellow legal pad filled with single-spaced, handwritten notes laying out the reasons why his sons should remain co-CEOS, resisted the idea of removing one or both of them from the job. Since it was then down to a choice between his sons, Greer advised him to choose Michael, who he considered far and away the stronger candidate of the two. Greer believed Michael could do the job but had been repeatedly sabotaged over the years by his brother and father. As the lunch hour approached and they remained at an impasse, Greer set a deadline: If Robert wouldn't make a change, Greer wanted his name removed as a director from the company's proxy—and the SEC document was due at the printer shortly.

Michael quickly learned of Greer's ultimatum, and he and Timothy scrambled to come up with their own compromise to make sure a Mondavi remained in charge of the company. He urged his father to pick between the two of them, vowing that he would accept Timothy as the sole CEO, if necessary.

Despite the recommendation of Farella and the other independent directors, Robert made what, in one respect, might be described as a gently Solomonic decision or, from another perspective, as a milquetoast sop to both his sons: Michael would become sole CEO and Timothy would step down to become managing director and winegrower, in charge of vineyards and production. The informal understanding was that Michael, since he was older, would get first shot at being in charge. Then, in five years or so, Timothy would take his place as sole CEO. The hand-off idea stepped around the potentially explosive matter of Robert's choosing one son over the other.

In the annual report for 1994, published in October, the photograph of Michael that accompanies his letter shows him brimming with what can only be described as joy, his eyebrows arched and wearing an unusually broad grin. Was it any wonder? After working under his father all of his adult life, Michael, at age fifty-one, was finally in charge.

"I am now the President and Chief Executive Officer providing family leadership and management focus on our growth opportunities," as Michael explained the shift to shareholders in the company's annual report. "Clifford S. Adams will continue to be the family's principal advisor and to have the lead oversight role in the financial and operational aspects of our business." What the report left out, of course, was Michael's next plan for consolidating his power. And that involved shedding many of the employees his father had hired, including one of his most trusted advisors.

CHAPTER SIXTEEN

Disinherited, 1994–1996

In the mid-1990s, a moving crew arrived and began hauling Michael and his assistant's boxes and office furniture out of the crowded Oakville winery and loading them onto trucks. The convoy then headed south to an office park on the outskirts of Napa known as Latour Court. The plan was that Michael would join his fast-growing team of marketers and salespeople and work out of the new offices, while Robert, Margrit, and Tim's staffs would stay in Oakville. Though they would work less than a half hour's drive away from one another, Michael's physical separation from the rest of the family echoed a growing philosophical rift about the company's direction.

Following Michael's ascension to sole CEO, the company split into three camps. Some employees remained loyal to Robert, despite the patriarch's waning power. Others supported his eldest son, particularly those on the sales and marketing side. Timothy's backers came mainly from the winemaking and vineyard management staff, including Charles Thomas, who joined Mondavi in 1978 as a "crush slave" and by 1994 had become chief winemaker for the flagship Robert Mondavi wines, the business closest to Timothy's heart.

Timothy's views on growing grapes and making wine had become more nuanced since the days he was a student at UC Davis. Yet his conviction that making high-quality wine should be the company's utmost aim had hardened. Since working with the Rothschild organization in getting Opus One off the ground, he'd adopted a more French attitude toward winegrowing, embracing the notion that terroir, or the place where the grapes were grown, was of utmost importance to the final character of the wine. His new mantra was *"Wine is made in the vineyards."*

Robert's younger son became the guru of quality at Mondavi, often regardless of cost. He insisted on high-density replanting of Mondavi's Cabernet vineyards, which improves the quality of grapes by forcing the plants to compete more vigorously for soil, sun, and water. Typically in Napa, vines are planted in rows that are eight feet apart, wide enough to allow machinery to pass through. In Bordeaux and at Opus One, the rows were typically planted about three feet apart, requiring the use of specialized tractors that cost $150,000 to $200,000 apiece. Although costly, this planting decision helped improve the quality of Mondavi's grapes. At around the same time, Mondavi also got involved in a project with NASA to gauge the spread of the pest phylloxera and other characteristics of the vineyard by using satellite photographs.

Experiments like these bolstered Mondavi's reputation as the "test tube" winery, setting it apart from the flood of new wineries rushing into the valley in the 1990s. But what made Timothy a wine iconoclast was his willingness to discard much of the conventional wisdom he'd acquired at Davis and try new ideas, such as planting twenty different rootstocks and choosing the best from among them. Although neither the board nor his brother saw him as a strong manager, Timothy was passionately committed to making fine wines, and although he wasn't always seen as practical, he kept his team focused on quality.

That's why Timothy's forced abdication was such a blow to his loyalists. The family put the best face possible on the news, but the shake-up removed, at least temporarily, the most vocal champion for fine wines and shifted the balance of power to Michael, who believed that the Robert Mondavi brand could be extended up and down the price scale, in the same way that the German automaker Mercedes-Benz sold some of the world's most expensive cars as well as moderately priced sedans. Each brother had trouble admitting that the other could be right and that brand management was indeed a difficult and delicate balancing act.

The brothers' squabbling was an open secret in the industry, and some rivals sensed opportunity. Jess Jackson, for one, wanted Thomas to join his fast-growing wine business, compelling the soft-spoken and thoughtful winemaker to ask himself whose vision of the wine business he understood more clearly—Timothy's or Michael's? With his love for fine wines, Thomas was more interested in creating fine, artisan wines that reflected their terroir, than everyday wines that were blended from a variety of vineyards with no specific appellation. Thomas decided to accept Jackson's job offer and became one of several talented winemakers Jackson recruited to his new upscale "Artisans and Estates" operation.

The winemaking staff took Thomas's defection hard, as he was one of the few at the company who worked well with Timothy. To some in the Oakville camp, Timothy's enforced absence and Thomas's defection were potent symbols of how the company was moving in the wrong direction under Michael's leadership.

The Balkanization continued as Michael recruited new managers who shared his philosphy. Thomas's last day at the winery turned out to be Alan Schnur's first as a full-time Mondavi executive. So impressed was the family with Schnur's analysis of the company's leadership problems that they had decided to hire him away from the consulting firm as senior vice president in charge of human resources and a member of the management council. Schnur also continued to work individually with Mondavi family members on the psychological and communications issues that hampered their ability to work well with one another.

Yet Schnur almost immediately got off on the wrong foot with some lower-level staffers, most memorably with a contretemps over free, company-provided donuts. On Tuesday mornings for many years, Robert had arranged for the Butter Cream Bakery in downtown Napa to provide donuts for employees. Schnur brought an end to the much-loved tradition in late 1994, with the company explaining it would donate the amount it normally spent per year at the bakery, some $10,000, to local food banks instead.

Michael and Greg Evans had supported the idea of ending the perk, but Schnur took the flack, many Mondavi old-timers interpreting it as a heartless move by the newcomer to slash costs. Another unpopular move by Schnur was cutting the company's "wine of the quarter" program—a paternal tradition of giving workers a case of wine every three months. By axing that, Schnur became an instant pariah at the company.

Schnur was also dispatched to do a delicate job that Michael was not in a position to do himself: soothe Timothy's hurt feelings over having been demoted from the co-CEO job. At the board's insistence, Timothy, who was then forty-three, had agreed to attend a program for advanced management at Harvard for a few months, partly to give Michael breathing room in his new job and also in an effort to help Timothy improve his management skills. But Schnur, serving as Michael's surrogate, was worried that Timothy might instead decide to quit the company, which could further damage morale. So in May of 1995, Schnur flew to Cambridge to check up on him and immediately concluded that Robert's younger son was not taking the expensive executive education program very seriously; he seemed to be skipping classes and putting in a minimum amount of effort.

Schnur's mission was to make sure Timothy returned to work, rather than quitting in a huff and starting his own winery. Over dinner, Schnur deployed a charm offensive, working hard to convince him that the company needed his gifts as a winemaker, viticulture expert, and family representative. Trying to counter Timothy's belief that the only role of value in his father's eyes was CEO, Schnur tried to convince him that he, too, had a crucial role, playing to his ego by proposing that he become the most visible winemaker on the planet, a "winemaking rock star." Schnur's campaign proved effective. Timothy ultimately did return to the family business, but not before making a halfhearted effort to strike out on his own, including scouting out vineyards for sale.

Against the grand scale of Michael's vision for the company, complaints over ending the donut program looked petty. Michael's goal was to turn Mondavi into a leader of the international wine industry, and he began searching for ways to expand the business overseas. Setting his sights far beyond Oakville, he began exploring the idea of setting up an Opus One–style venture in the Old World, this time with a leading Italian wine producer.

His father had become acquainted with the Marchese Piero Antinori decades earlier. Antinori had led a rebirth of the Italian wine industry by introducing Tignanello, produced in 1971 and released in 1974, the first of the so-called "Super Tuscans," a blended red that had been aged in

French oak barrels. Robert and Antinori had a lot in common; willing to experiment, committed to improving quality, and nimble marketers, they had both also had the sometimes frustrating experience of trying to bring their family wineries into the modern era.

Michael, in turn, came to know this noble Florentine family through Primum Familiae Vini, since both the Mondavi and Antinori families were members. But when the Mondavis approached them about a possible partnership, the Antinoris were reluctant to move as fast as their American counterparts wanted. So, the American family instead turned to the Frescobaldis, another wine-producing dynasty whose history in agriculture and wine production in Tuscany stretched back seven hundred years. In the sixteenth century, it sold wine to the English royal family and many other courts. Based in Florence, the family-owned business, incorporated in 1980 as the Marchesi de' Frescobaldi, SpA, faced the same difficult dilemma as the Mondavis: how to grow while maintaining quality.

Back at work in the spring of 1995, Timothy became the family's emissary to the Frescobaldis. During the trip, he developed an easy rapport with his counterpart, Lamberto, the son of Vittorio Frescobaldi, the company's president. Like Timothy, Lamberto, too, had studied at UC Davis, and throughout the visit the Frescobaldis spoke English with their visitor, who had picked up only fragments of the Italian language from his grandmother Rosa. The first day, Lamberto drove his American visitors in his modest Volkswagen station wagon on a tour of family estates, visiting Castello di Pomino, a castle built at the end of the fourteenth century that the family used as its cellar to mature its estate wines, and Castello di Nipozzano, built around the year 1000. The Frescobaldis hosted Timothy at their fifteenth-century palazzo in Florence for an elaborate dinner that evening.

To Lamberto Frescobaldi and his father, Timothy and his technical team from Mondavi seemed serious and straightforward. In their mutual courtship, they assessed each other not just for business compatibility, but also for philosophical kinship. With just a handshake, the two families agreed to enter an equal joint venture to produce wine together in Italy— the first ever such partnership for the Frescobaldis in its nearly seven centuries of winemaking.

The deal was a stunning social coup for Michael and Timothy, whose great-grandparents had been peasant sharecroppers in Marche. To be accepted as equal partners by an aristocratic family that was one of the largest landowners in Tuscany meant that the Mondavis had returned to their homeland in triumph, as the equal partner in a marriage of American upstarts to Italian nobility. There were also a number of parallels between the two families: Timothy and Lamberto were both in charge of production and vineyards. Michael, on the other hand, found more common ground with Leonardo Frescobaldi, Lamberto's uncle, who was vice president of international marketing and sales. Like the Mondavis, the Frescobaldis, too, were believed to be having disagreements among themselves, even having gone so far as to hire a university professor to help them learn how to better communicate with one another, just as the Mondavis had hired Dr. Grundland, Family Business Solutions, and Alan Schnur to help them sort out their differences.

But unlike the Mondavis, the Frescobaldis had installed a seasoned nonfamily member named Giovanni Geddes da Filicaja as its chief operating officer, leaving many of the business decisions to him. The Frescobaldis saw their role as a family as being primarily the owners of the business, rather than the managers, and thus left many day-to-day decisions to Geddes and other professionals. The Mondavis, however, were moving in the opposite direction from this long-lived European wine dynasty by shifting more operational control to Michael, who was not known as being cautious in his decision making.

An early example of Michael's decision-making style occurred shortly after the families announced they'd signed a letter of intent for their fifty-fifty joint venture on July 10, 1995. They had spent the first couple of months writing a business plan for the venture together. But about two months after they inked the letter, a potentially ideal piece of land for the partnership in Montalcino came up for sale. While it was in the heart of Tuscany's most prestigious wine-producing area, it was some of the most expensive agricultural land for sale in Italy at the time. Lamberto couldn't reach Timothy and he was concerned that a rival Swiss bidder might scoop up the property. So he tried Michael on his cell phone, reaching him over the weekend in Alaska, fishing with his son Rob.

Explaining that he could not reach Timothy, Lamberto apologized for disturbing him over the weekend, then launched into the reason for his call.

"Michael, there's a beautiful piece of land. Come over, look, it could be the right place. . . ."

Michael's response was forceful and brief: "If you think it is right, just do it."

The partners tossed aside the business plan they had put together and went ahead with the purchase—in Mondavi's case, sight unseen.

Cliff Adams's power rapidly waned as Michael's power grew. That became apparent on an executive retreat to Tahoe organized by Schnur. On the way up to the Sierras, the group stopped at a gourmet market and Schnur gave them their first exercise: shop together for the food and provisions they'd need for the next three days up in the mountains. Michael, Timothy, Greg Evans, Pete Mattei, and Alan Schnur were all there, as well as Mitchell Clark, the senior vice president of sales, and Martin Johnson, senior vice president of marketing. Cliff Adams decided to drive up separately, thus skipping Schnur's assignment. Schnur hadn't given the group a grocery list for the eight meals they were going to prepare together. The men good-naturedly protested the assignment at first, but they muddled through anyway, ending up with ten pies and a somewhat arbitrary assortment of other foods, and continued up Highway 80. When they arrived, there were three bedrooms with king-sized beds; the rest were bunk beds or singles, some with brightly colored children's sheets on them.

Michael, Timothy, and Cliff Adams got the big beds, while the other executives bunked together. During the day, the men talked over a wide range of issues, and tensions rose between the Mondavi brothers and Adams. Complaints about what was perceived as Adams's top-down management style had been mounting for several years, particularly from Timothy. Adams was dismissive of Robert's younger son, considering him flaky in his work habits and rigid in his thinking. Timothy, for his part, bridled under Adams's leadership, particularly resenting it when he was not consulted on key decisions. But while Adams's problems with Timothy were long-standing, what was new, at least to some of the executives who participated in that Tahoe weekend, was the testiness between Adams and Michael. Perhaps it was inevitable that Michael, in his new role as sole CEO, would insist on asserting his authority over his father's longtime advisor. Michael also had become sensitized, with the help of various counselors, to what he felt was the way Gary Ramona, Adams, and some other executives seemed to play him off his brother in order to increase their sway with Robert.

At the same time, Adams seemed culturally out of place among the new executive recruits. Behind his back, some made fun of him for wearing new jeans that his wife had ironed creases into. Unlike Michael's loyal followers, who kept any skepticism they might have felt to themselves and appeared to participate enthusiastically in Schnur's team building, Adams did not bother to hide his scorn for the exercises and made it clear he thought they were a waste of time. Unlike Greg Evans, who generally raised any concerns or objections with the brothers discreetly behind closed doors, Adams would openly disagree with them. Perhaps most damaging to his career that weekend, Adams spoke his mind on sales and marketing issues, which were areas outside his immediate responsibility, leading some to conclude he was grabbing for power.

Through the late summer and fall of 1995, Mondavi's fortunes were turning: Its secondary stock offering in August had been oversubscribed, raising a total of about $60 million, with $36 million going to the company and $21 million going to the family. Investors were enthusiastic about Mondavi's new flange-top bottle design, which eliminated the need for a metal capsule. Heralded as a packaging revolution, the design boosted Mondavi's sales and was soon widely copied. The stock's rising price—at the time nearly $20 a share—reflected Mondavi's innovativeness, its more stable management team since Michael was named sole CEO, and that team's confidence in the company's opportunities for growth—in spite of risk factors named at length in the prospectus, including phylloxera, an expected grape shortage, and a rush of inexpensive imports from "New World" producers such as Australia and Chile. The company posted record results in 1995, with sales of $200 million and profits close to $18 million. Demand for Mondavi wines exceeded the supply, and most were sold on "allocation."

As Mondavi's stock continued to climb, the family's suddenly accessible wealth heightened tensions between Robert and his children. As the company's principal shareholders, the four members of the Mondavi family could track their rising pile of lucre each day by checking the stock tables of their morning newspaper. Robert's net worth alone, by the late autumn of 1995, was approaching $70 million, and his adult children's were also in the seven-figure range. As the yearly review of his personal finances drew near, James K. Edmunds, his estate planning advisor from Price Waterhouse, and Cliff Adams began discussing with him the tax benefits of setting up a philanthropic organization. Robert and Margrit loved the idea, since it would allow them to focus on the areas they felt passionate about: food, wine, and the arts. The plan would also increase Margrit's sway over how Robert's fortune was doled out—a fortune that she had renounced in their prenuptial agreement. But setting up a foundation would also mean a potentially explosive confrontation with Robert's children. Hoping to initially avoid this, Robert asked his advisors to explain his decision to Michael, Marcia, and Timothy.

On a Friday morning in mid-December, Robert's offspring gathered in the conference room across from his office at the Oakville winery. Adams and Edmunds had met with Robert earlier that morning, and Robert, then eighty-two, did not join his children for the session, hoping his advisors would smooth the waters for him. The hired guns laid out an array of papers with diagrams and explanations of the plan on the conference room table and proceeded to deliver the stunning news to the adult children that their father planned to set up a trust and give away most of his fortune to charitable projects—seemingly disinheriting them.

The news was a bombshell. The way Michael saw it, the new plan—undoubtedly the work of his stepmother—reneged on what he understood to be his father's long-standing estate plan for his shares in the Robert Mondavi Corporation that Robert's fortune would be divided among his children one-third, one-third, and one-third. Under the newly unveiled scheme, almost all of Robert's stock was going to his and Margrit's charitable projects, leaving his three adult children mainly with the stock their mother, Marjorie, had given them before she died.

Robert's eldest son immediately feared the implications: The likelihood of his branch of the family's maintaining control would grow progressively dimmer as the stockholdings were given, in smaller and smaller blocks, to the grandchildren and then the great-grandchildren. He also felt that his father's decision had ignored his sweat equity in the business, working for what he considered the meager pay of $650 a month in his first two years at the winery. Robert's apparent about-face infuriated his eldest son and he flew into a rage, his Mediterranean features darkening and his voice rising. The truth of what Michael was saying, though, was diminished by the childish way he expressed himself.

Timothy and Marcia took the news far more calmly, reasoning that it was their father's money and he had the right to choose what he did with it. As long as the family could still maintain control of the company through its shares, they didn't see a problem. They had been assured by the advisors that their combined stock ownership would have to slip below 15 percent before they lost voting control of the company—a possibility that seemed remote even with their father's giving. And what was left over after the gifts and after Margrit was provided for would still be divided equally among his three children, just as their father had promised. To them, Michael's fury was just one more example of their brother's habit of putting his own interests first, rather than thinking about the larger good of the family or community.

When Michael's temper subsided, the group adjourned the meeting and went to the light-filled Vineyard Room, where Robert joined them for lunch. Michael immediately confronted Robert, while Edmunds and Adams observed the angry scene between father and son, both stubbornly determined to hold their ground. The whole idea was to build a family business that could be passed from one generation to the next, Michael insisted to his father, growing frustrated in his effort to explain to him that by selling out to become a philanthropist, he was imperiling his children's and grandchildren's future ability to control the company through ownership of a large block of their own stock. But Michael failed to win him over. "You children have enough," Robert told him.

During lunch, the patriarch adopted an expression that made it clear he wasn't going to budge: He stubbornly stuck out his chin, as if daring Michael to defy his wishes. Robert felt his children had been well provided for and that he'd given them more than enough opportunity to make good lives for themselves. Michael, in turn, suspected that the philanthropic trust was Margrit's endgame; she had, after all those years, found a way to get around the prenuptial agreement and influence where her husband's fortune went. Although it still wouldn't go to her, at least it wouldn't go to the adult children who had treated her so abysmally over the years.

Margrit had never been present at any of Robert's estate planning sessions, and, following the practice of his father, Cesare, Robert seldom discussed financial matters with his wife. Yet, Robert must have known that he and Margrit could counter their loss of operating control at the company by playing a far more powerful role as benefactor and benefactress. Michael, who sensed that his father and stepmother seemed to enjoy having people come to them and genuflect, felt that he and his siblings "were the happy victims of success."

After lunch, Robert, Adams, and Edmunds walked back to Robert's office. The two advisors were steaming at the verbal abuse they felt they'd taken from Michael. Edmunds, who had advised the Hewlett and Packard families with their estate planning, was particularly incensed by what he considered Michael's unprofessional behavior. He told Robert, "Frankly, I'm not taking this anymore. This is crap. . . ." Adams was also humiliated at having taken the flack for Robert and was deeply upset. He told the Mondavi patriarch that he had no intention of joining Michael or the rest of the family at the company Christmas party that evening, because he refused to subject his wife, Ann, to the experience. Skipping the annual celebration was a slap in the face to the family, but he was tired of Robert's tolerance for Michael's explosive anger.

Adams passed through the arch and drove home. Between Christmas and New Year's, he and his wife disappeared to Mexico on vacation. When he returned home in January, there was a message from Michael on his answering machine, asking if he would meet him at Latour Court on his first day back.

Adams walked into Michael's office, which was a study in contrast to his father's. In place of Robert's battered wood desk and homey wine artifacts collected from around the world, Michael had a black, sleekly modern desk. Michael, Timothy, and Robert were all sitting there when he arrived. It was Michael who delivered the news that he wanted Adams out of the winery. Looking him in the eye, Timothy said, "Mike and I agree." Adams, who had been by Robert's side for nearly two decades, had anticipated the news the moment he walked in the door and saw all three Mondavis sitting there. He also felt relieved. Robert assuranced Adams he wanted to "keep him whole." After leaving the office, Adams called his wife and said, "I'll be home early. I got fired today."

Afterward, Adams suspected that Michael had spent the holidays convincing his father that Adams was a "control freak" and that it was, in fact, Adams's fault that he had lost his temper that day in December. Robert, in looking back, described his long-time advisor Adams as hardworking and no-nonsense, but explained his downfall as the result of his having got caught between himself and his sons: "Cliff loved power and jockeying for more, and that often put him at odds with Mike and Tim." As with Gary Ramona, when it came to choosing between his own blood and a nonfamily executive, Robert chose blood.

But despite the momentary rallying together of the three Mondavi men, Michael's assertion that the Mondavi patriarch had stripped his three children of the bulk of their inheritance was still in the air. Although he and his brother ostensibly remained in charge of the company, the unforeseen risk was that Robert's charitable giving would undermine their family's hold on the company. Killing the messenger Cliff Adams didn't mean that Robert would change his mind.

CHAPTER SEVENTEEN

Michael's Show, 1996–1997

M ichael finally achieved his long-held ambition: to run his own show. Then in his early fifties, Robert's eldest son had apprenticed for three decades under his father and various advisors. In great physical condition from his long-distance running, Michael felt up to the challenge and had plenty of reasons for optimism. Perhaps most encouragingly for Michael, his father's attentions were engaged elsewhere.

Robert had chosen a trash-strewn lot on the wrong side of the tracks for his first big philanthropic project. Situated in the dusty city of Napa, bordered by a tire store and notable mostly for its burned-out barn, the twelve-acre parcel he bought had little going for it except that it was on the banks of the Napa River, which flowed from Mount St. Helena to the San Pablo Bay. At the turn of the century, the river had been beautiful; winding through a dense canopy of willows and cottonwoods, it had once brimmed with Chinook salmon and steelhead trout. But by the mid-1990s, polluted by fertilizer runoff and choked with sediment, the Napa River was an eyesore.

A bend in the river known as the Oxbow was where Robert decided to build his new, as yet unnamed center for wine, food, and the arts. Once again, the Baron Philippe de Rothschild was his inspiration. The baron had spent his final years gathering wine-related artifacts and artwork to display in the new museum he'd built at Mouton. Robert, too, wanted to create his own museum, in keeping with his missionary theme that wine was an integral part of culture spanning back to Biblical days. To fund the project, Robert's advisors set up a $17 million charitable remainder trust, funded by his Robert Mondavi Corporation stock. With that seed money, they solicited contributions from other people in the food and wine world. In February 1996, the company announced that Adams would step down as Robert Mondavi Corporation's executive vice president and instead take on the job as the center's executive vice president.

But his tenure was brief. In late 1996, one of the board members of KQED, the San Francisco Bay Area's public television station, went public with ethical concerns over the funding of a proposed documentary about the Mondavi patriarch's life. What by then was known as the American Center for Wine, Food and the Arts had provided the first and only outside financial support for the project, some $50,000, even though KQED had long been prohibited from accepting money from companies to safeguard its editorial integrity. The allegation made by the KQED board member was that to get around this rule, Mondavi had channeled the money to KQED through the nonprofit American Center. While Adams attempted to defend the gift, suggesting that there was no quid pro quo on the part of the center for a favorable profile, critics nonetheless interpreted it that way, and the Mondavi Corporation indeed planned to use it in its marketing. Amid an embarrassing public outcry, KQED was forced to drop the idea, deepening the schism between Adams and Michael, who had supported the project.

At the same time, Robert realized he needed someone more experienced as a fund-raiser for the job as the American Center's executive director. Using a headhunter, they turned to Peggy Loar, who helped organize Smithsonian traveling exhibitions and was in the final stages of opening the new Wolfsonian Museum and Research Center, a quirky museum devoted to the decorative arts in Miami's Art Deco district. The recruiter called her and asked, "Do you like California?" Loar said, "Sure," and soon she was on her way to Oakville, to meet Robert.

Another in a line of strikingly beautiful women who'd passed through the arches of the Oakville winery over the years, Loar wore a skirt suit and high heels for her first meeting with the by-then famous vintner, not realizing her heels would boost her above the five-foot-eight-inch vintner. Nearly running into Robert in the hallway, she recognized his famous Roman profile from photographs and said, "Mr. Mondavi, I'm Peggy Loar."

Robert, who enjoyed lovely women as much in his eighties as he had in his younger years, tilted his head up and kissed both of Loar's cheeks, European-style.

Loar tried to recover her balance by making a joke: "Does this mean I get the job?"

"It does if I have anything to do with it," replied Robert.

Michael, meanwhile, was on a roll. Investors had pushed Mondavi's stock up from a low of $6.25 a share in August of 1994 to $33 a share in late 1996. Not only was the company well-positioned to benefit from the trend of Americans moving upscale in their tastes from jug wines to premium wines, but at a time when the industry was struggling with a shortage of high-quality grapes, Mondavi seemed well-prepared to ride out that storm. By snapping up land in Central California and the coast, it more than doubled its vineyard holdings in just two years to more than five thousand acres, acting on the belief that owning the land would give it better control of its grape supply.

Mondavi had another advantage as the grape market tightened: its unusually good relations with growers. While many large wine companies viewed the farmers who supplied them grapes as their adversaries and feared that cooperative efforts between them would lead to higher prices, Mondavi, which worked with 150 or so independent growers, approached them as partners and encouraged teamwork. It chose an affable former Peace Corps director named David Lucas as head of grower relations. Hired in 1982 by Timothy, Lucas had managed teams of Peace Corps volunteers in Iran and India and built surfboards for a while before coming to California's Central Valley to work as a fruit and vegetable buyer.

Lucas invited the growers to taste the samples of wine made from their grapes, which were intended to demonstrate the quality differences in fruit grown on different properties. By encouraging them to cooperate and share information with one another, his goal was to raise the overall level of quality from the region by discussing the rootstocks they used, methods of irrigation, and introducing such new techniques as leaf pulling, which promotes air circulation around the grape clusters and reduces diseases and pests.

The growers were willing to cooperate, in large part, because Mondavi paid as much as 100 percent more than other wine producers to ensure it got high-quality grapes. Unlike many wineries, which paid for grapes based on their acid or sugar content, Mondavi came up with incentive-based category pricing that linked price and quality, culling those growers who weren't up to its standards. It also signed seven- to ten-year contracts, offering stability to growers. But almost more important than the higher prices and long-term contracts was the encouragement Mondavi gave them to take pride in the individual expression of place through their grapes. This was a radical notion in the San Joaquin Valley, where most grapes were blended into bulk or lower-priced wines, with little differentiation between vineyards.

Mondavi and Woodbridge were also unique among wine producers in inviting the farmers who sold them grapes to the Woodbridge winery or nearby hospitality room, known as the Apple House, to dine on white tablecloths with six wineglasses lined up in a row—a novelty at the time in Lodi's grape-growing circles. They would also help organize trips to show growers how other regions had improved the quality of their grapes; groups from Lodi went to France and Australia in the mid-1990s. The Mondavi family's hospitality became legendary, yet the business principle behind such events was to elevate the perception of wine as a high-quality product in a region where it was usually sold as a commodity. In admiration, some growers took to calling Woodbridge the "country club" winery.

At a time when "globalization" was the talk of management consultants and business professors, Mondavi decided it would go global as well. It began a series of international forays, sometimes with the intention of sourcing grapes outside the U.S. in the hope of making itself less vulnerable to swings in the prices of domestically grown fruit. That was the reasoning behind the company's first venture into the Languedoc. Only a four-hour drive from Bordeaux, the landscape of this region in the south of France couldn't be more different from France's premier wine-growing region. With its warm, sunny weather, wide-open land, and herb-scented pastures, it resembled California more than Bordeaux's changeable weather and inbred culture. Because of its rugged peaks and broad coastal plains, Languedoc was sometimes described as the Wild West of France.

Woodbridge's manager, Brad Alderson, was looking for such a frontier. Against the backdrop of a poor harvest in 1996, with grape shortages causing prices in California to soar as much as 50 percent from the previous year, he and many other wine producers began searching for alternative sources. He found them in the Languedoc, a region whose role in French winemaking had traditionally been to satisfy the thirst of the French working class. During the past two decades, the European Union had ended up buying much of Languedoc's low-quality juice and turning it into cleaning alcohol.

But Alderson had a more profitable idea in mind for it. He purchased six hundred thousand gallons of some of the better-quality 1995 vintage wine from the region, shipped it in bulk back to the fast-growing Woodbridge winery, bottled it there, and then sold it as Vichon Mediterranean. This initial foray was a success. Not only did the new label represent a promising brand makeover for Timothy's troubled baby, but in the first full year after its launch, Vichon Mediterranean Chardonnay became the number-one French wine sold in the United States. It also made Mondavi one of the first American wine producers to strike a deal with foreign growers for bulk wine bottled in the U.S.

To head its new Vichon Mediterranean unit, Mondavi chose David Pearson, a San Diego native who had studied enology at the University of California and spent a year after graduation working as an intern on French wine estates. Pearson was working as a marketing manager for the Rothschilds in the U.S. when he was contacted by a recruiter for the Robert Mondavi Corporation. He joined the company in August of 1996 and twice helped land the Vichon Mediterranean brand on the industry publication *Impact*'s Hot Wine list. The French-speaking, thirty-nine-year-old Pearson crossed the Atlantic and settled in the Languedoc, just north of the city of Montpellier.

Mondavi hoped to produce both a small amount of high-quality wines from the Languedoc and much larger quantities of more affordable wines, essentially replicating its business model in California. Rather than finding a partner, as it had done with the Frescobaldis in Italy, the company decided to go it alone in France—and there were few, if any, high-quality producers in the Languedoc to partner with, in any case. Mondavi's hope was to elevate the quality of the wines from the region, just as it had done in Napa and Lodi. In the meantime, before it planted vineyards and harvested grapes, it continued to buy locally produced wines for bottling in the U.S.

In 1998, Pearson bought around 440,000 cases to be sold under the Vichon Mediterranean label. But he ran into trouble: Not only did Languedoc's local cooperatives supply him with mediocre wines, but many other producers from the region around that time also began flooding the U.S. market. Forced to sell off much of the French wine at a discount and the rest as bulk wine to custom labels, Mondavi took a $4 million write-down to its 1999 earnings, as well as a $1 million reserve to cover excess inventory it expected to be forced to dump. Overall, it found it had 475,000 gallons of imported wine inventory that was potentially unsalable.

Shifting gears, Pearson came up with a new plan to focus on higher quality, more expensive Languedoc wines. Instead of relabeling wines that had been produced by local cooperatives, he began looking for vineyards and production facilities that Mondavi could control. The goal was to make top-rated—and top dollar—vintages. "The midpriced varietals is Dead Man's Land," Pearson concluded. "In order to survive in Languedoc, you have to move upmarket." Mondavi was convinced that with its experience in choosing the right land for vineyards and the winemaking process—emphasizing low yields and gentle handling of the grapes—it could produce superb bottles of wine from the region selling for $60 or more.

Pearson tasted wines and conducted geological surveys to locate top-quality wine real estate. What frustrated him was the small size of French vineyards. The average Languedoc grower cultivated only a few acres of low-quality grapes that he sold in bulk to be made into wine at a local co-operative. Pearson needed a tract of about 50 hectares, 125 acres, similar to the size of many smaller Bordeaux châteaus, to eventually produce 260,000 bottles a year. Finding the right terroir wasn't easy, but Pearson finally settled on a swath of uncultivated hillside above the two-thousand-person village of Aniane, about fifteen miles northwest of the regional center of Montpellier. For $7.5 million, he leased about 120 acres. The local town council liked the idea of millions of dollars being invested in their village. It also approved of Mondavi's plan to work with the struggling local cooperative to improve and market its output. The co-op would get $400,000 to modernize its equipment. Winegrowers who worked with the Americans would be paid about a 40 percent premium for their crop. And Mondavi would help young growers in the region also install themselves on the mountain site. Naturally, they were delighted, and in July 2000, Aniane's town council voted to grant Mondavi a ninety-nine-year lease on the site.

Seven thousand miles away in Chile, Mondavi embarked on a similar quest: entering a promising wine region characterized by low-quality wines and helping it to produce world-class vintages. Mondavi's interest in the region had begun several years ealier. In 1991, Robert and Margrit met with several of Chile's leading wine-producing families—known as Apellidos Vinosos—during a trip to the country. A fellow Napa Valley vintner, the Franciscan Vineyards owner Agustin Huneeus, arranged for a young scion of one of these families, Eduardo Chadwick, to act as the Mondavi family's tour guide. Chadwick, who was then thirty-one, drove Robert and Margrit in a four-wheel-drive vehicle though the country's stunningly picturesque wine region, which was centered in a valley at the base of the snowcapped Andes. Robert was struck by the climatic similarities between this area of Chile and Napa: morning fog, followed by warm, sunny afternoons, and evenings cooled by breezes from the nearby Pacific. More than once, Robert remarked to his young tour guide that Chile reminded him of the potential he had seen in Napa Valley in the 1960s.

But unlike booming Napa, where new vineyards were being planted every week, the Chilean wine industry had suffered through decades of decline. In the early 1970s, under Marxist president Salvador Allende, most of Chile's vineyards were expropriated and turned over to a National Wine Company, precipitating a steep drop in quality and productivity. When the government of General Augusto Pinochet wrested power away from Allende and returned the vineyards to their original owners, the industry continued to suffer from a lack of investment and know-how. Between 1985 and 1990, nearly two-thirds of the country's vineyards were ripped out to plant more profitable crops such as nectarines and plums. At the same time, Chileans curtailed their wine drinking and prices plummeted. Most of the Chilean industry's sales were exports. As Chadwick explained to Robert and Margrit on their bumpy

Jeep ride, Chileans by then were accustomed to drinking oxidized white wine and few seemed to even realize this quality defect.

But Chile also seemed to offer a promising new land for Mondavi. Phylloxera hadn't decimated Chile's vineyards, as it had Europe's and North America's, and the country's fertile soil and Mediterranean climate provided ideal growing conditions. Chile's labor costs averaged just $2 per hour, one-tenth of those in California. Because it typically took three to five years for newly planted vineyards to begin producing grapes, most of Mondavi's rivals were simply buying bulk wine from Chilean producers and bottling it in the U.S., similarly to what Mondavi itself had done at first in Languedoc. But Mondavi saw an opportunity to make a deeper investment along the lines of its partnership with the Frescobaldis. The company was interested in creating not only a world-class Chilean wine, but also a world-class Chilean winery, as notable as Opus One. Mondavi was not alone in its thinking: Kendall-Jackson, Lafite-Rothschild, Mouton-Rothschild, and Spain's Miguel Torres were planting their flags in Chile.

Throughout the early 1990s, the Mondavi family hoped to form a partnership with one of the country's larger wine companies. So when Chadwick, who'd become president of the family company following his father's death in 1993, approached Mondavi about a possible joint venture, the Californians were not especially receptive, hoping for a more prominent partner. Although Robert saw something of himself in the handsome and well-spoken Chadwick, his family's winery, Viña Errazuriz, was relatively tiny and most of the Chadwick family's interests, such as its Coca-Cola bottling plant, brewery, and mining operations, were outside the wine business.

The Mondavis also saw another warning sign: The Chadwicks' previous joint venture with Napa's Agustin Huneeus had not been successful. Yet the young Eduardo Chadwick's passion to learn more about wine struck a chord with Robert and when the men met again at Vinexpo, the giant industry trade fair in Bordeaux, in 1995, their negotiations with the other potential partner had fallen through. They struck a deal on a handshake, and formalized it in early 1996, calling for a $12 million investment to develop vineyards and build a winery by 1999. In the meantime, it would ship the Caliterra branded wines to the U.S. in bulk and bottle them at Woodbridge. Mondavi would also become the exclusive agent for Viña Errazuriz in the U.S. This time around, Mondavi cast itself in the senior, deep-pocketed role the Rothschilds had assumed nearly two decades earlier with it in California.

Soon after the deal was inked, Michael asked Alan Schnur to propose a list of qualified candidates to head up the new Chilean joint venture. Schnur came up with several possibilities. "You missed a name," Michael told him. Schnur was sure he hadn't. "Have you looked in the mirror?" Michael asked. As the company's senior vice president of human relations, Schnur had grown closer to Michael over the past two years and spoke some Spanish, though not fluently. He also had never worked overseas before.

Despite these potential handicaps, Michael was convinced that Schnur's expertise in human resources would help the company manage the cross-cultural issues that were likely to arise there. Schnur agreed to take on the assignment in addition to his job as head of HR, and quickly came up with a splashy way to build excitement for the new Chilean brand among Mondavi's sales force: He convinced the company to foot the bill for flying the entire sales team of 122 people to Chile for a week, touring Errazuriz's facilities as well as rival Concha y Toro's. While the Mondavi staffers were exposed to Chile's spectacular scenery, few of Errazuriz's staffers spoke English, so the interaction was limited.

That linguistic disconnect hailed other problems ahead. Almost as soon as the first wines from Errazuriz, sold under the Caliterra label, began arriving in the U.S. as a Mondavi import, Schnur, who continued to work at Latour Court in Napa, began fielding complaints from distributors that that the bottles had scuff marks on the labels. He soon realized that the problems were more than superficial: corks had been inserted at different depths, the bottles were filled to different levels, back labels were crooked, and there were mistakes in the translation of the language on the labels from Spanish to English. Schnur called Chile and demanded to know how these mistakes were being made. The answer he got was even more troubling. The Chileans had checked the shipments, knew about the defects, yet released them for export anyway. When Schnur asked why, his Chilean counterpart asked, "Who's going to notice?" It was an inauspicious start for Schnur's first move from a staff to an operating role at Mondavi.

Schnur issued a general recall of the Errazuriz wines, overcoming the Chileans' initial hesitations. He also quickly dispatched several staffers to Chile to investigate the problems, including a bottling manager and a member of Mondavi's accounting staff. Once there, Mondavi's bottling manager discovered that many of the bottles had dust particles in them and others were spoiled by poor-quality cork or oxidation. To tackle these and other problems, Schnur and his team decided to introduce to its Chilean partner Mondavi's thick procedures manual, which ran several hundred pages long. That alone came as a culture shock to Chadwick staffers, who were use to a more intuitive style of problem solving.

Likewise, the vice president of the Chilean venture whom Mondavi had installed, John Adriance, was viewed suspiciously and isolated, not only because he lacked fluency in Spanish but also because he, like the other Mondavi staffers, was insistent on trying to improve quality, which the Chileans viewed as an implicit criticism of the way they did things. He also struggled with the Chadwick family's young heir, Eduardo, as well as the Chadwicks' similarly youthful chief of operations, whose egos, he felt, were bigger than their experience in the wine industry warranted.

The partnership hit a low point after the harvest of 1997. With foreign sales of Chilean wine booming, Errazuriz unexpectedly found itself without enough production capacity to handle the entire harvest that year. Scrambling to find an outside winery that could crush and process the grapes, it was forced to turn to one it had never done business with before for its Merlot Reserve, a superpremium brand in a booming category. By that time most Chilean wineries had converted to stainless steel fermentation tanks, but this particular one used unlined cement vats. To monitor quality, Errazuriz sent a winemaker once a week to test the fermenting wine. One week, the test showed serious contamination, leading the partners to realize that not only did the winery not have a clean facility, but it even lacked enough running water. The Chadwicks and Mondavis had no other option but to dump that year's entire production of Merlot Reserve.

What became known as the "lost Merlot" incident shook Mondavi's confidence in its Chilean partner. Typically, a wine producer would carefully line up the production it needed in advance of harvest, based on detailed forecasts. But that had not happened in this instance. Likewise, there was a great deal of confusion and angst over whether the partnership could properly call certain wines Merlots after discovering that, in fact, the grape that was used to make them was a different varietal called Carmenet. With all of these problems, Schnur, for one, began to doubt whether the ambitious plan to build an Opus One–style winery on a short deadline was realistic. The six-hundred-hectare site the partners chose in 1996 was in the Colchagua Valley, an isolated area about three hours south of Santiago with no access road, electricity, or irrigation. The partners budgeted $6 million for the new winery, to be called La Arboleda, which means "the arbor."

The Mondavis and Rothschilds, on the other hand, had chosen a site for their showcase winery that was along a major highway, with ready access to power and irrigation. Even then, the construction of Opus took longer and cost far more than first estimated. Based on optimistic sales projections, the partners decided to forge ahead with their Opus-like Chilean winery, building roads and infrastructure, constructing homes for the on-site managers, and planting costly, high-density vineyards. This long-term investment seemed to make sense when so many other parts of the Mondavi empire were booming.

But the new pressure from shareholders to grow sales forced Mondavi to look for quick returns from Chile. In one year alone, 1996, when California was experiencing its grape shortage, the venture nearly tripled its sales volume to 620,000 cases, up from 245,000 the previous year. The sales pull came from Mondavi, which became convinced there was a large potential market for Chilean wines in the U.S. But the surging sales strained the partnership, forcing it to rush to fill the production demand at the same time they were struggling to build an entirely new winery from the ground up, with little or no tradition of quality winemaking in Chile to draw upon.

The Mondavi men were in expansive moods. Timothy had convinced a Napa judge to grant him a bifurcated divorce from Dorothy, allowing him to work out the financial details with her after their marriage was legally dissolved. Timothy was in a hurry because he planned to wed Holly Peterson on June 21, 1997, in the beautiful town of Positano, Italy, on the Amalfi coast. In order for the wedding to take place, he needed legal paperwork to show the Italian authorities that both he and Holly were legally single and free to marry. As well, Timothy took a precaution before slipping the wedding ring on Holly's finger: The couple entered into an antenuptial agreement on May 30, 1997, in which Holly, who had never been married before, agreed to waive all claims to Timothy's shares in the Robert Mondavi Corporation.

The wedding was a far grander and more elaborate nuptials celebration than the quiet ceremony that Timothy had had with Dorothy in 1976. The festivities lasted for three days, and the couple arrived for the ceremony in a horse-drawn carriage, clopping through Positano's cobbled streets. Afterward, they were honored at a wedding dinner where five courses of beautiful food were paired with exquisite wines. Costing more than $70,000, it was a fitting celebration for the union of two members of America's wine aristocracy.

Michael, too, was enjoying his life as chief executive of a publicly traded company. Although he'd cut off his ponytail, he continued to ride motorcycles, on one occasion in a group of leather-clad bikers who flew from Sonoma along back roads at high speeds. Another time, Michael and some other biker friends roared up to Opus One on their motorcycles, startling the tourists, who at first didn't realize the group included Mondavi's CEO. In a photo of the group taken after that ride, Michael grinned widely and held a fat stogie in his right hand.

Yet despite these signs of a prolonged adolescence, Michael was serious about being a good parent and he guided his only son, Rob, onto a path very similar to his own. Rob, too, attended Santa Clara University, graduating in 1994 with a degree in English literature. During the summers, he commuted back to Napa to work at the company, as Michael himself had in the late 1950s and 1960s. But Michael was determined not to make the same mistakes with his son that he was convinced his own father had made with him. For one thing, he expressed physical affection toward his son: In front of his colleagues, Michael would tenderly kiss Rob, even when his son was in his twenties.

Unlike Robert, Michael also took time away from his work to spend with his son. One of Rob's happiest memories was of spending the morning of his fifteenth birthday, in October of 1986, duck hunting with his father. "It was five-thirty a.m. Cold. We had a little sip of Scotch from the flask. Then, he lit up a cigar," Rob told a reporter. "I felt bad the rest of the day, but it was such a great memory. And ever since then, we've been smoking cigars. It was a way we communicated."

Michael insisted Rob work elsewhere before formally joining the Robert Mondavi Corporation. With that in mind, he helped arrange for his son to apprentice at Southern Wine and Spirits, under the guidance of his old friend Ted Simpkins. About a year later, Rob headed south to Panama, to spend a year observing the business run by his mother Isabel's family, which were involved in real estate development and restaurants. While he was in Panama, he met people from the Dominican Republic who grew tobacco. That led to Rob's founding the Napa Cigar Company, with some help from his father and Mondavi's human resources head, Alan Schnur, who helped him write a business plan. He also got a line of credit from the bank, but when Michael saw the high interest on the loan, he offered to cosign, helping him to get a lower rate.

The Napa Cigar Company, which he set up in 1996, got off to a fast start, and to some people at Mondavi, Michael's son seemed to grow cocky with his early success. One executive recalled Rob, then in his mid-twenties and not yet employed at Mondavi, popping into his office and telling him, "You know, I like you. I think I'll keep you around." Although Rob almost certainly meant that as a joke, the comment seemed outrageous to the mid-forties executive, who thought to himself at the time, "I'm going to take the kid out back and beat the shit out of him. Somebody's got to do it."

With Mondavi's long record of success, a culture of entitlement had set in. Two-hour lunches where employees lingered over a $50 bottle of wine were not unusual. On Fridays at four P.M., some staffers in the finance department would pour themselves a glass of wine and bring it back to their desks. Underworked by the hard-driving standards of 1990s corporate America, some Mondavi employees did outside consulting using Mondavi resources. With a tone set by Robert and Margrit, Mondavi employees enjoyed company cars and lavish expense accounts; instead of staying at budget motels, where staffers from Gallo stayed, Mondavi employees stayed at the Hilton in La Jolla and other four- or five-star spots.

The Mondavis readily adopted some of the fine trappings of the aristocratic wine families, even though the Robert Mondavi Corporation was now publicly traded. Michael, for one, looked to the Frescobaldis for a model of how a family business dynasty should operate and embraced such status symbols as the use of limousines and private jets. In the early autumn of 1997, the partners threw a lavish party in Italy to launch their new wine, Luce, the first product of the Mondavi and Frescobaldi joint venture. The festivities were no less than a coming-out party for America's first family of wine. The Frescobaldis raised a stream of colorful flags and banners and threw open the doors of their Renaissance villa to Italy's winemaking royalty: the Antinori family and the Folonaris of

Ruffino, as well as Spain's Miguel Torres. Italy's foreign minister was on the guest list as well as other dignitaries. Michael declared to a reporter, "Our objective is to be the preeminent fine wine producer in the world. We don't believe anyone is there yet. It is totally available."

Michael delivered a similar message to the company's shareholders at its 1997 annual meeting, an event that more resembled a social gathering than a sober corporate meeting. Although other wine and brewing companies began courting shareholders with parties and perks around this time, the Mondavi family took the idea and raised it to a whole new level. It introduced its "Partners Circle" in 1996, offering shareholders an array of special events and discounts, including dinner concerts under the stars and special savings on wine purchases.

Under clear blue skies, it began the meeting with café lattes on the Oakville winery's lawn. Some shareholders who'd signed up for the Partners Circle arrived the weekend before it took place, paying to take part in activities the winery helped organize, including croquet at the Meadowood resort, a private luncheon at Thomas Keller's acclaimed French Laundry, and dinner at Opus One. At one point during the festivities, Michael joked to investors, "You're having too much fun—this is business!"

Both the Mondavi family and Mondavi shareholders were in a good mood. The company's stock price hit a new high of $56.75 in October and the company's financial results for the year were strong: Sales jumped 25 percent to just over $300 million, far outpacing the industry's growth, and net income jumped 15 percent to $28 million. Mondavi sold over a million more cases of wine in 1997 than it had in 1996, and was aggressively investing in the second phase of its Woodbridge expansion, as well as other capital projects. During a forty-five-minute slide presentation, Michael highlighted the joint ventures in Italy and Chile and announced that the former Vichon winery on Oakville Grade was being recast as "La Famiglia," devoted to producing wines from Italian varietals. It was Timothy who unveiled a capital-intensive project close to his heart: a $15 to $20 million renovation of the flagship Oakville winery, displaying a three-dimensional model of the To Kalon project.

During the question-and-answer period, when one of the six hundred investors who attended asked if there were any problems on the horizon for the company. Michael thought about the question for a moment and said, "Well, Prohibition would be a disaster." The answer touched off an explosion of laughter and the meeting adjourned for a preluncheon wine tasting, followed by fennel-crusted lamb served with Pinot Noir and a choice of touring Oakville, Opus, or La Famiglia, or listening to a lecture on the history of wine in California.

The one executive missing from that annual meeting was Cliff Adams, who was on the East Coast trying to drum up funds for the American Center with Marcia. When Adams returned from his trip after the annual meeting had ended, he made his way to Robert's office. Their conversation turned to the struggle to raise funds for the center, and Adams explained he'd found it difficult because of the lack of a clearly stated mission. Robert looked past Adams's concern and spoke to the real problem: "I don't think you really have your heart in the project," he said. Adams had to agree. Robert and Adams agreed he should step down from the center and when Robert asked him if he'd like to remain on the company's board, Adams said he'd prefer to leave it as well. After years of juggling the interests of the family members against those of the company as a whole, Robert's loyal counselor had finally had enough.

CHAPTER EIGHTEEN

Waterloo, 1998–2001

I n January 1998, at the peak of summer in the Southern Hemisphere, the Mondavis hosted another blowout. This time, it was to celebrate the release of the Mondavi and Chadwick families' first jointly produced wine, named Seña, which means "distinguishing mark" or "personal signature" in Spanish. To make a splash, they jetted a group of importers, distributors, and wine journalists to Chile, where in sweltering ninety-eight-degree heat, the group boarded air-conditioned buses in Santiago and drove to the Chadwick family's Don Maximiano estate in the foothills of the Andes. Since the construction of La Arboleda was not yet complete, the partners had made their first vintage of Seña there instead. On the estate's formal lawns, bordered by rose gardens, guests nibbled on empanadas and sipped some of the Chadwick family's wines.

At a black tie ball that evening, held at an imposing converted fortress in Santiago called Castillo Hidalgo, Seña made its debut. In a memorable entrance, a parade of waiters carried the distinctive bottles out to the group, amid applause. Priced at around $50 a bottle, the vintage 1995 Seña was one of the most expensive Chilean wines at that time. "It certainly is the best Chilean wine I have ever tasted," wrote the wine journalist Anthony Dias Blue, who joined the festivities. After the wining and dining, the partners presented their guests with small gifts made of lapis lazuli. Not a mention was made in the media coverage of the joint venture's ongoing problems.

The press was far less respectful four months later, when Mondavi unveiled a $10 million plan to develop a wine-themed exhibit in Disney's California Adventure, a new fifty-five-acre park adjacent to the original Disneyland in Anaheim. "Don't expect a Goofy Gewürztraminer or a Pocahantas Pinot," noted the *San Francisco Examiner*. The Associated Press led its story on Mondavi's $10 million Disney project with a light-hearted look at the partnership: "The Happiest Place on Earth may get even happier for adults who want to sip a little Merlot after a dizzying ride on Space Mountain." "Huey, Dewey, Louie and Wine?" was the in-dustry newsletter *Market Watch*'s headline. The *Los Angeles Times* noted that Walt Disney himself strongly opposed serving alcohol at his original park. "I like a drink," Disney had quipped, "but if people want one, they can get it elsewhere."

A few found the very idea of plunking a minivineyard in the middle of a theme park downright offensive: "Here's a promotion I can't help hat-ing: Robert Mondavi will re-create a California wine country experience for Disney's newest theme park. . . . Now you can simply go to Anaheim to experience the rest of the Golden State," wrote Sumi Hahn, a colum-nist for the alternative *Seattle Weekly*. "I guess they deserve it." Almost none questioned whether the tightly controlled corporate culture of Dis-ney, which had $22.9 billion in sales in 1998, would mesh with the much smaller, more loosely controlled culture of Mondavi, which was driven both by the family's passionate interests and a drive for profits.

Disney had first approached Mondavi about supplying wine to its new park, but the talks quickly evolved to forging a deeper partnership. It was Mondavi who pushed to develop and operate the new winery exhibit, and it didn't take long for Michael to become the plan's biggest internal booster, convincing Mondavi's board to support it over the initial hesitations of his family. The business case was compelling enough for the company's out-side directors to accept it: Mondavi would become the sole wine company at Disney's new $1.4 billion theme park. Under the terms of a ten-year contract, it would run and control the exhibit's operations, including a real, twenty-thousand-square-foot working vineyard, a retail room, and an upscale restaurant modeled after the Vineyard Room in Oakville.

Mondavi planned to ride on California Adventure's coattails. With Disney predicting seven to ten million visitors to its new park the first year, Mondavi used Disney's estimates to forecast that it would attract to its strongly branded exhibit roughly a quarter of those, or as many as two and a half million visitors a year. Compared to the roughly three hundred thousand visitors to Mondavi's Oakville winery each year, the company reasoned it was a chance to broaden its exposure, particularly to overseas visitors who might not include a trip through Napa Valley on their U.S. itineraries. Disney representatives traveled to Oakville to explain their marketing plan, which included promoting the new park to those who had never been to California as a way to make a quick swing through the Golden State. It seemed like the perfect platform to achieve Mondavi's larger goal: bringing wine to the masses.

There were also, arguably, some benefits to having two Mondavi centers in southern California, since the Costa Mesa Center for the Food and Arts was located near the park. And the deal appealed to Michael's family pride: Out of hundreds of wine families, Disney had chosen to team up with the Mondavis. "The opportunity to showcase wine as a part of the California experience on this level is the fulfillment of a lifelong dream for my father and our family," enthused Michael when he announced it. The deal seemed to demonstrate his ability to think outside the box: Rather than relying on his father's methods of comparative tastings and word of mouth, the Disney deal showed that Michael was finding novel ways to expose the Mondavi brand to a new generation of customers, just as he was embracing the Internet and sponsoring an IMAX film on California. Michael predicted it would be profitable in its first year.

But the market's confidence in Michael started showing cracks. On January 21, 1998, the company announced its second-quarter results, which were in line with what analysts had expected. But the stock began to tumble after Mondavi announced that it was facing a Chardonnay shortage. The company's shares dropped 16 percent, to $40 a share, and then another 9 percent to $38. Analysts were further spooked by the news that Mondavi had asked retailers such as Costco to reduce the amount of

Woodbridge Chardonnay it was shipping to its stores in order to keep some of the brand on its shelves. They had refused and Michael explained that the stores preferred to sell off their Woodbridge inventory until it ran out.

It was an ominous sign, since it suggested that Mondavi had stumbled in managing the supply of its wines to important retailers. It also indicated that Mondavi had flunked a key test of being a public company: not surprising analysts. Around that same time, more bad news hit. The company was named in a civil complaint against former agriculture secretary Alphonso Michael "Mike" Espy, who was accused of having accepted illegal gifts from such organizations as Tyson Foods, Quaker Oats, and Sun-Diamond Growers of California. The Robert Mondavi Corp. was a bit player in the drama, having given Espy six bottles of wine worth $187 and dinner at a Washington restaurant for him and his girlfriend, worth $207. It also issued Espy a standing invitation to visit the company in Napa and offered the political appointee the use of a guesthouse.

The case drew in Mondavi's head of public affairs, Herb Schmidt—a true Mondavi loyalist who carried three business cards: The first read "Herb Schmidt, Vice President, Public Affairs"; the second, "Herb Schmidt, Industry Gladiator"; and the third, in deference to his employers' Italian roots, "Herb Schmidtavi, Affairs Publici." In July of 1998, Mondavi agreed to pay a $100,000 fine and $20,000 to defray the costs of the investigation in return for dismissing the two-count civil complaint—a mere slap on the wrist compared to the $6 million fine slapped on Tyson Foods. In mid-June 1998, the company threw a big party to celebrate Robert's eighty-fifth birthday. Margrit presented him with a pair of emus and Robert, acting decades younger than his age, donned sunglasses, picked up a guitar, and started jamming with the band. He displayed more confidence than musical talent. But on June 22, the company scheduled an unusual conference call with analysts. Michael warned that Mondavi's fiscal fourth-quarter and full-year 1998 results would be 15 cents below analysts' consensus estimates. The merriment of a few days earlier instantly vanished.

While missing estimates by 15 cents isn't, in itself, unusual or particularly egregious, it was the fact that Mondavi had waited until just eight days before the end of the fourth quarter and fiscal year to alert the market to the shortfall that cratered investors' confidence. As Michael, Greg Evans, and the company's controller, Steve McCarthy, sat around the long glass table in Michael's office at Latour Court, they watched as MOND ticked 15 percent, then 20 percent, then 25 percent down as they were on the conference call with analysts. Officials at NASDAQ ended up halting trading of Mondavi's stock.

As an offering to Wall Street to prove that it was serious about boosting earnings, the company said it would lay off seven executives to get the company down to its "fighting weight." It was a small number of job cuts and analysts who followed the company closely weren't impressed: Many of the people who lost their jobs were close to Robert and Margrit and seemed untouchable in their job security. Alan Schnur told Axel Fabre, who had run the Great Chefs program for more than a decade, and the other terminated executives to immediately clean out their desks. Within five minutes, they were escorted off the premises. Fabre and several others wept as they left.

Wall Street kept punishing Mondavi, pushing its stock down another 14 percent in the days after the news. Although the Chardonnay shortage had begun easing up by the early summer of 1998, another problem loomed: Because Woodbridge Chardonnay was temporarily unavailable, some Mondavi customers began switching their loyalty to other moderately priced wine brands instead. Analysts lowered their investment ratings, explaining they'd lost confidence in Mondavi's management and its ability to fix the slowing trends in Mondavi's crucial Woodbridge brand. From its record high of $56.75 on October 22, 1997, the stock lost nearly a third of its value, tumbling to below $30 a share as the 1998 harvest approached.

Behind the scenes, Mondavi's directors were planning a more radical move. In early August, when the company announced full-year results, it tapped the company's longtime chief financial officer, Greg Evans, to become chief operating officer, taking on some of the duties that had been Michael's. Then forty-nine, Evans had a far better academic pedigree than Michael's and a less volatile personality. While Schnur publicly insisted at the time that the shift didn't mean that Michael or the family was stepping back from Mondavi's management, that's exactly what was happening. The analysts and industry observers who were following the company closely felt the change was overdue.

In his former role as chief financial officer, one of Evans's challenges had been to try to smooth the company's earnings—a task faced by every CFO of a publicly traded company, as he or she sought to avoid surprises.

But that wasn't easy in an agricultural business vulnerable to the vagaries of the harvest and market each year. So one of the first steps Evans and his newly appointed CFO, Steve McCarthy, took after the earnings shock of the summer was to change its method of accounting for its inventory from the LIFO method—which stood for "last in, first out" and helped save on taxes by minimizing earnings—to the more aggressive FIFO method, which meant inventory would be counted "first in, first out" and improved the company's ability to predict and manage earnings.

In explaining the change to investors in the fall of 1998, Mondavi argued that the switch allowed it to better match revenues and expenses of the wines it was selling and would also help it more closely link its executive incentive plans to its financial results. Despite this move, there remained a lingering skepticism toward Mondavi management.

Opus One remained the jewel in the Mondavi family's crown. But despite its success, it was hardly a model for a smooth or easy partnership. Over the years, the bickering between the French and American sides rarely ceased. And the internecine warfare between Michael and Timothy, of course, continued. Finally, the boardroom situation grew so paralyzed that the Rothschilds insisted on having an outsider evaluate the business. The partners hired a local investment banker specializing in the wine business named Vic Motto, overseen by a task force headed by Evans and a Rothschild executive. When Motto took on the assignment in 1998, he discovered a joint venture resembling "a marriage without love."

One of the key strategic issues facing Opus One was its dependence on Mondavi's sales force for sales and distribution. Under Mondavi's watch, the elite brand had occasionally landed on a bargain retailer's shelves. To the dismay of the Rothschilds, wine buyers for a time could even buy it at Costco. Worse, positioning and selling Opus One seemed almost like an afterthought to Mondavi's sales organization, as its pipeline of products swelled with new offerings from France, Italy, and Chile. With Motto's help, the partnership eventually agreed to kick all the owners off the board, including the Mondavi siblings, and work toward giving Opus One more independence from its parent across Highway 29.

Michael suffered no lack of glamorous events to attend, however, as president of Primum Familiae Vini in 1998. During a swing through Asia earlier in the year, with stops in Hong Kong, Taipei, and Singapore, the group marketed itself as being comprised of the world's leading wine dynasties. Even Michael, whom one observer described as set apart from the Old World family representatives by his California accent and feel-good manner, emphasized the dynastic elements of the Mondavi business. When asked indelicately toward the end of the wine-saturated evening, "Do you stand in the shadow of your father?" Michael replied, "I say that when you stand on his shoulders, you can see much further." Using some computer terminology that he'd picked up at executive training seminars and elsewhere, Michael explained how the company aged its reserve wine for eighteen months in French oak barrels, noting that "we want to make it smooth and, to use the computer term, user-friendly." The remark provoked laughter all around.

Michael also explored the possibility of adding another continent to the company's rapidly expanding portfolio. In addition to North America, South America, and Europe, he grew interested in Australia, although Southcorp, Australia's largest wine producer (which also made washing machines, refrigerators, and water heaters) had first approached Mondavi. In 1998, its managing director, Graham Kraehe, made the long journey to Napa to meet with Michael and discuss combining their wine businesses. That evening, Kraehe was invited to dine with Robert, Michael, Evans, and others at Mondavi's guesthouse. Kaehe proudly arranged to serve his hosts his company's finest wine, the $200 Penfolds Grange, an intensely concentrated red. The next day, at a board meeting that included a tasting of many of Southcorp's wines, Robert didn't bother hiding his feelings: "What the hell is this?" he asked, sputtering in outrage that there was no way he was going to enter into any sort of partnership with a company that made what he considered to be such lousy wines.

Robert's visceral dislike of Southcorp and what he saw as its soulless corporate winemaking effectively blocked the possibility of a business combination between the two companies. But Southcorp's courtship piqued the family's interest in finding another way into the booming Australian wine market. They turned to Robert's longtime friend Robert Oatley and his Rosemount Estates, Australia's largest family-owned winery. But over the years, when the Mondavi patriarch had suggested teaming up, Oatley had declined, fearing that he would be the junior member in the partnership. Hoping to change his mind, Michael, Timothy, and

Evans took a trip that year to pay their respects to the family and their privately held company, laying the groundwork for a venture down under.

Soon Mondavi itself was on the radar of rivals looking to expand. Beringer Wine Estates Holdings, the venerable Napa Valley wine producer that had been sold by Nestlé to the Texas Pacific Group in 1996, contacted Philip Greer to explore a possible combination of Beringer and Mondavi. But that idea was abandoned after it became clear in the organizational chart drawn up that Beringer's longtime head, Walter Klenz, would get the chief executive job for the combined companies, not Michael. Then they came up with a second plan. In a stock exchange, Beringer would control Woodbridge, Private Selection, and other lower-priced wine brands, while the Mondavi family would have majority ownership and control of the Oakville winery. After running the numbers, Greer concluded that it not only addressed Timothy and Robert's worries that the company was shifting focus away from its luxury wines, but also satisfied the family's desire for control. To Greer, "it made a hell of a lot of sense."

That idea didn't fly either. Evans claimed "governance issues" were the deal's major stumbling block. But the fact that such a potentially important transaction didn't get a full hearing by the board proved discouraging to some directors. James Barksdale, the former CEO of Internet pioneer Netscape Communications Corporation, quit soon after the demise of the Beringer deal. Since Mondavi's independent directors seemed to have no voice, he didn't see, at a time when he was starting a new company of his own, why he should bother.

Back in Napa Valley, Michael turned more of his attention to his home. He and Isabel arranged for a local fire department to burn it down to make way for a new nine-thousand-square-foot house, including a "mudroom" that was larger than many condominiums, a butler's closet, two fireplaces, an elevator, a pool, a heated spa, and a cabana. They raised eyebrows in Napa by donating the home they'd built in the 1970s to their local fire department for use as a training site—a donation sometimes used by wealthy homeowners to get a tax write-off. Michael and Isabel's home was a particularly welcome gift to the Yountville Fire Department because of its large size and open design. Even before the fire crews moved in, the local SWAT team used the house for an exercise. It took place over four to five days, and Michael periodically stopped by to watch what was going on. When the new house was completed, Michael invited members of the Yountville Fire Department to his new $4 million-plus estate.

Michael still maintained a sharp interest in the Disney venture, and his enthusiasm for the project translated into a full-blown effort to make it a success. The first employee hired for the new venture was Jonathan Smiga, who had an MBA and was a graduate of the Cornell Hotel School. Inspired early on in his career by what he called the "romance of the restaurant business," Smiga wrote his college thesis on how wine and food function as an art form rather than as a craft. His mindset seemed perfect to uphold the Mondavi family's core values of offering quality wines in every price range. Fluent in the management-speak that so many of Michael's new hires seemed to possess, Smiga arrived in February of 1999 as the Disney project's manager.

Before Smiga joined the company, Michael had signed a contract with Disney, obliging it to pay some $10 million in return for the licensing rights to the Golden Vine Winery for a decade. Out of that sum, Disney would build the exhibit, working closely with Mondavi on aesthetic details. The project was very hush-hush: New employees were barred from taking photographs and were issued security passes allowing them to enter and leave the park. Aware that Robert, Margrit, and Timothy were nervous from the start that the populist Disney venture would tarnish Mondavi's upscale image, Smiga and his team paid close attention to aesthetic details and spared no cost.

But Mondavi insisted on cutting corners in another area. When Disney's construction left sharp corners on the mission-style building, the Mondavi team insisted on rounding them off, paying extra to do so. The counters of the seven wine bars were cut from custom-made granite and wrought iron doors were hand-forged. Margrit herself approved the dishes, replications of the famed ceramics from Deruta, Italy, and based on a famous thirteenth-century pattern, as well as the Frette linens in a palette of sienna and terra cotta, and Riedel glassware. Even the glasses at the wine bars, which under Disney regulations could not be real glass, were custom-ordered: Smiga found a Canadian supplier who made an elegantly tapered version out of acrylic for them. The exhibit's seven-minute film,

Seasons of the Vine, cost $1 million to produce—nearly $143,000 per minute. Unlike most Disney exhibits, which were façades, Mondavi's Golden Vine Winery was real, bearing the family's personal touch.

Mondavi also worked hard to make sure its new employees were well-trained, hiring many of them seven months before the opening scheduled for February of 2001. In September, five months beforehand, Mondavi flew some of its key "cast members" to the Oakville winery for a week of rapid education in wine and winemaking. The idea was to transform these workers, some of whom had been recruited from Disneyland in Anaheim, into "Wine Ambassadors" both for Mondavi and the California wine industry. Those who didn't go to Napa were bused to the company's Byron Winery, in southern California's Santa Maria Valley. Mondavi seemed to have done everything right: It located its new Golden Vine Winery not far from a parade route. It also offered four levels of food service, from modestly priced snacks to $50-per-person dinners at the upscale, ninety-seat restaurant called the Vineyard Room. In the days leading up to opening day, the Golden Vine Winery's food operations were packed, perhaps because much of the menu was offered at half-price and the operation hosted many nonpaying guests.

On opening day, the Mondavi family converged on the park, including Michael and his family, Timothy, Marcia, and Robert and Margrit. Smiga and other employees of the venture were nervous. There had been some problems already with the people at Disney, including a last-minute request before a VIP dinner to replace the organic, farm-raised veal on the menu, which the chef had flown in, with chicken. When Smiga explained they didn't have the high-quality chicken they'd need for that evening, the Disney manager asked, "Why can't you just go to the store or defrost some?" The chef eventually managed to find some, and pulled the veal. The expensive delicacies in the Golden Vine Winery's pantry, which included truffle oil and prosciutto di Parma, were outside the experience of Disney's institutional food service operations.

The Mondavis couldn't disguise their sense of superiority on matters of food and wine. On opening day, when the real Robert—not an audio-animatronic one—made an appearance at the park, he took a sip of 1997 Cabernet Sauvignon and declared he felt proud that his family had thrown in its lot with the Magic Kingdom. But his praise was tinged with an awareness that his partners also could learn something from Mondavi about the good life. "Disney is good at certain things, but it doesn't understand wine yet," the patriarch of America's fine-wine industry said.

The Golden Vine Winery's restaurant won good reviews from food writers, but still, opening day was a disappointment. The crowds in the lead-up to the day vanished as soon as the discounts ended. The tables on the patio were empty on a weekend day and Mondavi was soon forced to close some of its seven wine bars due to lack of traffic. Sales failed to cover the project's hefty labor costs, let alone its food costs, overhead, and investment of around $12 million—about $2 million more than it had originally expected. Families on a theme park vacation balked at paying $50 per person for dinner with wine and $14 per child—on top of the park's already hefty admission price. Those who just wanted to pick up a bottle of wine couldn't take it directly back to their hotel with them; it had to be picked up at a package center later in the day. Despite the effort to educate their guests, the most popular purchase was a glass of White Zinfandel wine, which is generally considered a sweet, unsophisticated "starter" wine.

Despite its close attention to aesthetic details, such as placing linens soaked in wine to create the scent of wine in the barrel room where the film was shown, larger problems arose. Although dining al fresco had seemed like a good idea, that spring's unseasonably cold, wet weather forced Mondavi to issue Barbour-style jackets to its wait staff to keep them from shivering in their Disney-issued uniforms. And the vines in the demonstration vineyards kept dying, in part because of a pest called the glassy-winged sharpshooter. Mondavi was forced to replant them at least three times.

Back in St. Helena, the Peter Mondavi family was ripping out nearly half of Charles Krug's 850 acres and replacing them with Cabernet Sauvignon grapes and other Bordeaux varietals. The replanting was long overdue. Hampered by losses for many years, the family finally found the money to replace a hodgepodge of vines dating back to the 1950s and 1960s. They financed the $21.6 million effort privately, having rebuffed potential buyers of their business over the years. And, unlike Robert's family, they had never seriously contemplated taking their winery public. The decades since Krug's court-ordered receivership and the burdensome debt Peter and his family took on to settle the dispute with Robert had been marked mostly by scrimping and making do.

But by the late nineties, the old-fashioned, unionized Krug Winery was turning out wines that were starting to win some good critical reviews. Case sales grew steadily and Peter Mondavi Sr. appeared ready to turn over business to his two sons, Marc and Peter junior. In early 1996, he told his staff he'd relinquish control of daily operations and hand it over to the next generation. But Peter senior—like his brother, Robert—was in fact unable to truly turn over the reins. Then in his mid-eighties, Peter senior continued to work nearly every day in his large office with plate-glass windows, which overlooked the winery's crushing pad, and still sat in on blending sessions with his sons and the winemakers.

Like his brother across the valley, Peter senior also ran into trouble with his offspring. Marc, the older of the two, preferred stalking big game, reeling in steelhead, smoking cigars, and spending time outdoors to sitting inside Krug's drab, 1950s-style offices. Peter junior, the younger brother, took after his father in both his attention to detail and his low-key manner; insiders called him "re-Pete." Like his father, Peter junior was a Stanford grad, with undergraduate and graduate degrees in engineering, as well as an MBA. One of Pete junior's early projects had been to computerize the winery. Marc, in turn, studied viticulture and enology at UC Davis. In a repetition of the family pattern, Marc worked in winemaking and production, while Pete junior oversaw sales and marketing.

Shouting matches sometimes erupted between Peter senior and his older son, usually behind closed doors. Known to wander down from his office past the ancient oaks toward the cellar, Peter senior almost seemed to look for things to criticize Marc for. Deriding his older son in front of some of their employees, he'd ask, "Don't you use more than half your brain?" Marc, who had a fiery temper, would lash back at his diminutive, octogenarian father. "The only reason you come down here is to find fault with things. You don't help, you don't do anything. We're going to bury you out in the vineyard, old man!" More than once, Marc quit his job in a huff.

At one point in 2001, Peter senior and his sons called employees into Marc's office individually to tell them that the company was undergoing a restructuring. Explaining that there was too much overlap between the Charles Krug and the CK Mondavi brands, the family announced that Marc would became head of the popular priced CK Mondavi wines and Pete junior would take over Krug's best wines. Whereas Marc had previously overseen all the production for both brands, suddenly Peter junior—who had no formal winemaking training—was responsible for the company's prestige label, supervising the winemaker and vineyard manager. The transition was abrupt. Even so, Peter senior continued to sign all the checks.

The changes didn't calm the waters, though, particularly on the labor front. On September 5, 2001, during a union lockout, several Krug workers were carrying picket signs on the long driveway of the Krug Ranch, where Marc and his family, along with the rest of the Peter Mondavis, all lived. Driving an olive, open-topped 1954 Jeep, Marc spotted the picketers and grew enraged. He hit the gas pedal and accelerated toward a production worker named Kenneth Drost, who had worked at Krug for twenty years, swerving just in time so that only its right fender brushed against Drost's pants leg. Marc later maintained the worker had stepped in front of his Jeep, blocking his way.

"Get the fuck out of my driveway. Get the fuck off my property," Marc shouted at Drost, who defended his rights to stand there by replying that he was on the public walkway. Marc's face reddened and became contorted with rage. Turning to a female picketer, Emma Martin, he added, "Fuck you!" Before screeching out onto Highway 29, he screamed at the picketers as a group, "You people are ruining my life!"

The French town of Aniane delivered a similar, though more polite, message to the Robert Mondavi Corporation. Although its town council had approved Mondavi's plan to build a hillside vineyard, the vote precipitated a violent backlash. Hunters worried that the wild boar would desert the region as its forest habitat was converted into vineyards. Some environmentalists argued that a virgin forest from the Middle Ages was being razed—an exaggeration that was repeated in the press. The forest, in fact, was not virgin. David Pearson sipped pastis with the hunters and reassured them they and the company could live well together on the site; they would be able to continue hunting and Mondavi would leave much of the land untouched. Instead of planting one large vineyard, the company intended to plant small "islands" of vines inside the forest. This tactic would preserve the natural habitat.

But Mondavi and Pearson couldn't brush off one far-reaching charge—that the invading Anglo-Saxons would destroy the village's social cohesion and subvert traditional winemaking methods, imposing an alien, money-grubbing industrial model. Leading this crusade was a crusty septuagenarian winegrower named Aimé Guibert. In the 1970s, Asian competition drove Guibert's glove factory in central France out of business. He moved south to the hills above Montpellier—right next to Mondavi's site, having done the exact same thing that the American company was proposing—and began making wine. He studied traditional vine stocks, hired famed enologist Émile Peynaud, and planted a new vineyard with mostly Cabernet Sauvignon grapes. He became one of the region's first producers of high-quality wine at his small-scale Daumas Gassac Vineyard in Aniane.

"See that forest? All that is going to be destroyed to satisfy the pride of the Americans and their so-called New World wine," barked Guibert. He claimed he could trace his vine stocks back to the Middle Ages, although most of his vines had been planted since the 1970s, and liked to describe his wine in poetic terms. "The Mondavis will end up destroying our traditional artisans who make wine, just like McDonald's is destroying French gastronomy," he charged. Guibert was aided by José Bové, the militant sheep farmer who became a French hero by wrecking a McDonald's outlet near Aniane in protest of U.S. sanctions on Roquefort cheese, and who came through Aniane just once. Bové went on to interrupt the World Trade Organization's talks in Seattle and was the darling of left-wing antiglobalists the world over. Even the actor Gérard Depardieu got into the act, comparing the villagers' fight with the Gauls' struggle against the Romans. What became known in the French press as "L'Affaire Mondavi" became cited as a key example of French anti-Americanism writ large.

In municipal elections, Aniane's voters threw out the town council and elected an anti-Mondavi communist, Manuel Diaz, mayor. Diaz denounced Mondavi as a menacing multinational similar to British retailer Marks and Spencer, which was in the process of closing down all its shops in France. Robert, the same man who had struck the path-breaking deal with Philippe de Rothschild a generation before, pulled the plug himself. In May 2001, Mondavi canceled the vineyard project and sold off its Vichon brand, amid its own darkening financial picture. Against the backdrop of poor sales and heavy investments, the company's cash reserves sank to $5 million for the year ended June 30, 2001, compared with $32 million in the previous fiscal year.

By mid-2001, Mondavi's financial performance was worrying the board of directors. Over a meal in a Sydney hotel, overlooking the harbor, directors Anthony Greener and Philip Greer broached the subject with Michael of making a management change. His strengths, they told him, were in serving as the company's "Mr. Outside" with the marketplace, not in planning or administration. For the good of the company, he ought to let someone who was better suited to the everyday duties of running a company become CEO.

The discussion continued on the sixteen-hour flight back from Sydney, where Michael and Greener sat in adjoining first-class seats. By then, Robert's hearing had started to deteriorate, making it more difficult for him to participate in board meetings. Greener calmly explained that asking the patriarch to step aside, since he was getting deaf, was simply proper corporate governance. "We need you to become chairman so we can ask your father to retire," he told Michael, soaring miles above the earth. If Robert didn't, they warned him, Mondavi's directors and officers could be held liable if something went wrong. The argument appealed to Michael's long-held desire to be in charge, without interference from Robert.

After about a month of further discussions, Michael agreed to the change. It came at an opportune time. Exactly two weeks before the announcement of Mondavi's withdrawal from France, the company kicked him upstairs as chairman and promoted Greg Evans to chief executive. In doing so, they made Evans the first nonfamily member to assume the role of CEO and it was Evans who became the messenger of the failed venture in France. Robert, in turn, was named chairman emeritus. Timothy was the clear loser in the reshuffling, giving up the title of managing director and becoming vice chairman, a more amorphous, nonmanagement position that gave him little operational control, although he still had some management responsibilities as the company's winegrower. Essentially, the board sidelined the Mondavi men, turning over day-to-day management to professionals. "This new management structure will ensure that our greatest achievements are yet to come," Robert said in a news release announcing the changes.

Within a month, Michael felt he'd made a terrible mistake. With the outside directors' backing, Evans was in charge and Michael had been reduced to a largely ceremonial role, serving as the face of the Mondavi brand to distributors and retailers. Although the directors felt Michael was now in a job where he was highly competent and effective, they had relieved him of responsibility in most other areas. Greer had been so intent on selling him on the benefits of his new role that he hadn't gone into detail on what he would be giving up. Michael, in turn, became convinced he'd fallen prey to a "bait-and-switch game." But if he did not understand how limited his operational control would be after he became chairman, he may simply have not probed deeply enough in the face of Greener and Greer's convincing sales job.

Meanwhile, back in Aniane, the region's worsening wine glut left the village's winegrowers withering on the vine. After Mondavi's Aniane project fell apart, some thirty other village mayors wrote asking the Oakville-based wine producer to invest in their village. It was too late. "For now, we've decided it is too difficult to make wine in France," Pearson said. In September 2001, Pearson became managing director of Byron Vineyards, another Mondavi winery near Santa Barbara. The francophile American left France, in mourning for the failure of a project he had believed in. "I felt like the Cuban boy Elián González, who became a symbol, in a weird, deformed way, of the clash between two worlds," Pearson lamented, just before leaving.

Mondavi's defeat in France wasn't the only blow it suffered. By the summer of 2001, the Disney venture was hemorrhaging about half a million dollars a month, which meant it could lose $6 million in its first full year of operation after investing about $12 million. Mondavi went through two rounds of layoffs and lowered its revenue forecasts to $18 million a year, from $25 million. But the problems were damaging employee morale. Michael flew down to Orange County in the midst of the layoff rounds to rally the troops. In the open-aired Vineyard Room, with a view of Disney's replica of Monterey's famous Cannery Row, he declared, "One thing I can promise you: We will never sell," referring to the Robert Mondavi Corporation, which the family controlled through its dual-class shareholding structure. Smiga, who by then was deeply worried by the problems he saw not only at the Golden Vine Winery but also at Woodbridge and Mondavi's international joint ventures, thought Michael's statement was at best an example of his tireless cheerleading and, at worst, was misleading.

Sure enough, just eight months after opening day, Mondavi and Disney announced the collapse of their venture. Disney would take over management of the Golden Vine Winery from Mondavi, as well as another restaurant in Disney's California Adventure run by the celebrity chef Wolfgang Puck. The attendance problems that had begun almost as soon as the Mondavi-operated attraction opened were compounded by the terrorist attacks on September 11, 2001; instead of attracting about 19,000 visitors to the park a day, it was drawing on average about 4,500. But Mondavi also made mistakes, the most glaring of which was signing a contract that did not protect it or penalize Disney strongly enough if the crowds that were projected didn't show up. In short order, Smiga and the other 150 or so remaining employees of the venture were let go. Some were hired by Disney, while others took Mondavi's generous severance package.

Michael shouldered the burden of communicating that bad news himself and he worked hard to spin the news of the changed relationship with Disney in the most positive way he could, arguing that by becoming the exhibit's sponsor rather than its operator, the company preserved the educational and public relations benefits while eliminating the operating risk. Although he may have believed in the silver lining at the time, Disney quickly erased most traces of Mondavi's involvement in the project, with the exception of a tiny sign hung above the entrance to the "barrel room" theater, noting that the film *Seasons of the Vine* was sponsored by the Robert Mondavi Winery. Upstairs at the Vineyard Room, plates made in China supplemented the dishware picked by Margrit and hard liquor was offered at the restaurant in addition to wine.

At around the same time, Mondavi also quietly decided to sell off the troubled Vichon–La Famiglia winery on Oakville Grade, and shift production of the La Famiglia wines to Oakville and elsewhere. It was another reversal involving a capital-intensive operation, and the last thing Mondavi wanted to do was to draw attention to the failure. The Disney fiasco resulted in a $12.2 million charge to the company's 2002 earnings. It also further eroded Michael's standing as chairman of the board. Although it was neither the biggest problem Michael faced—which was the competitive assault on Woodbridge—nor the most financially burdensome, it became symbolic of Michael's tendency to do too many things at one time. Some came to call the Disney project "Michael's Waterloo."

PART FOUR

DEMOLITION

CHAPTER NINETEEN

Mondaviland, 2001-2003

Just as Michael's Disney project was collapsing, Robert was struggling to get his new center on the Napa River off the ground. He'd begun his fund-raising campaign two years earlier, on an overcast day in March 1999, donning a towering white chef's cap to help raise funds. As a crowd of well-wishers gathered on the undeveloped site in Napa, Robert stood on a platform with a stack of baguettes and urged the group to help "raise the dough" for the project. That day he announced he had given $20 million to get the project up and running and introduced the dynamic couple Garen and Shari Staglin, who were heading the project's capital campaign.

A hot-air balloon floated above the group, lending festivity to the chilly gray day. Yet his dream project still had not yet won as much financial support from other vintners or food people as Robert had hoped it would, in part because some potential supporters were concerned that it would be a showcase for the Robert Mondavi Winery rather than for the wine industry as a whole. That led to a decision to drop the early idea of calling it the Mondavi Center in favor of the more neutral name of

Copia: The American Center for Wine, Food, and the Arts. After the name change, it began to attract a few large backers, including Beringer Vineyards, the Hong Kong–based electronics magnate and dedicated wine-lover M. K. Koo, and Swiss entrepreneur Donald Hess. The center also had an impressive list of "Founding 70" supporters, which included many of Napa Valley's great and good. Marcia and her husband, Thomas Borger, as well as Timothy and Holly supported Robert's new project by making personal donations to it, but Michael and Isabel gave nothing at all—a fact that became a topic of endless dinner party conversations in Napa.

Michael and Isabel were still incensed by Robert's decision to give away the bulk of his fortune to charity. Adding to that sting was the lingering memory of how Robert had refused Michael's request to have the Robert Mondavi Corporation contribute to his effort to build a pediatric intensive care unit at the nearby Queen of the Valley Hospital, where he was a director. Those painful memories had festered over the years and by the time Robert was fund-raising for Copia, Michael withheld his support. "I've already given," he reasoned, since his sweat equity had helped create the wealth his father was now giving away. At the same time, Michael was concerned about how much Robert was committing to his philanthropic projects, and because of the fund-raising shortfalls, Robert was indeed compelled to top up his initial $20 million pledge with another $15 million. Even so, Robert's large gifts combined accounted for just under half the $70 million the project required. "We were in a race to make money faster than he could give it away," Michael recalls.

Nearly as challenging was the center's clash with the blue-collar city of Napa. Some feared the project would transform their working-class town into "Mondaviland"—making it a tourist destination on a par with Disneyland. One particularly vocal critic was the city of Napa's vice mayor Harry Martin, an outspoken publisher who decried it as a vanity project, yet another monument that Napa's most famous vintner was building to himself. "It's cream de la pooh pooh," the politician fumed. "The whole wine culture is about snobbism. It's an artificial society. They are going to hold seminars on how to decorate your table. They want this to be another Carmel, a ticky-tacky town full of little boutiques."

What Martin ignored was that Napa's downtown, the historic heart of the valley, was long overdue for revival. It had been bypassed by Highway 29 and the chic tourist shops and restaurants of St. Helena and

Yountville to the north and by shopping malls east on Highway 80. As a result, Napa's family-owned shops and cafés were slowly dying on the banks of its abandoned and junk-filled river.

No doubt, Robert and Margrit's generosity was slowly changing Napa's character—yet by almost any measure it was changing it for the better. The New York–based Polshek Partnership, the architects who had overseen the renovation of Carnegie Hall and a number of projects for the Smithsonian Institution, came up with a modern, though controversial, design for the center, including plans for a five-hundred-seat outdoor amphitheater, three and a half acres of public gardens that would become a destination in themselves, and an eighty-thousand-square-foot building of glass, ceramic tiles, and polished concrete whose rolling roofline echoed the eastern hills of Napa. When construction crews broke ground for the project in 1999 with a seven-foot-tall purple corkscrew, it was the start of the first world-class complex ever to be built in Napa. Activists and city boosters saw it as the anchor of a dynamic new river city.

Other signs of "Mondaviland" also appeared. Robert helped convince the Oxbow School, a program for high schoolers in the visual arts, to locate their new school directly across the Napa River from the American Center. He donated $4 million to renovate the buildings and $2 million for a tuition endowment program. And less than a mile away, Robert and Margrit were the first and largest backers of a project to renovate an old, shuttered theater with tattered awnings and plywood-covered windows known as the Napa Valley Opera House. The nineteenth-century theater with its Italianate edifice had never, in fact, truly been an opera house: It had been a venue for vaudeville, dance recitals, and political rallies and was only open for thirty-five years, from 1879 to 1914. Gilbert and Sullivan's *HMS Pinafore* was its first performance. In 1905 Jack London read from its stage, and John Philip Sousa's band once performed there. As movies replaced live vaudeville, it remained dark through the following years, and escaped demolition in the 1970s only by being designated as a historic landmark.

But the city of Napa was more notable among locals for the Mervyn's Department Store sited directly across the street from the Opera House and its beloved Butter Cream Bakery on the outskirts of town, with pink-and-white-striped exterior, hot-pink vinyl booths, and sugar-and-fat-loaded comfort food. Situated "downvalley" and just beginning to shed its blue-collar image, it remained a town far less sophisticated than "upvalley," which had become a global status symbol by the 1990s with the arrival of such glamorous new winery owners as the film director Francis Ford Coppola and an influx of Silicon Valley money that was expressing itself in showy vineyards and Tuscan-style megamansions.

Still, the city of Napa was trying to update its image. Prodded by river activists, it won countywide support to partner with the U.S. Army Corps of Engineers to build a model $250 million flood project that its backers hoped would restore the river and inject life back into downtown Napa. Robert and Margrit became the principal patrons of Napa's renaissance following a boat trip that won them over to choosing the Oxbow site for their center. After years of fits and starts to bring Napa's old theater back to life, the Mondavis offered a $2 million challenge grant to encourage other donations. Eventually, to acknowledge their generosity, the group renamed the Opera House's upper-floor theater after Margrit, who posed for photographs on a bulldozer during its ground-breaking ceremonies, wearing her trademark whitish-blond bob and a smile.

With the value of Robert's stockholdings rising, Robert and his wife assumed the mantle of Napa Valley's leading philanthropists, giving generously and attending most of the valley's important fund-raisers. The couple became so ubiquitous at society functions that some of the people who'd known them in earlier decades commented unkindly about their prominence, joking that "they show up for everything—even for the opening of an envelope!" Others marveled at their stamina and boundless civic energy as they moved into their seventh and eighth decades of life. Old friends valued the loyalty that brought them to every private event, however small, if they were in town.

Out of the public eye, the Mondavis' personal style remained relatively modest. They were regularly sighted lunching in small Napa cafés, where Margrit quietly kept up old friendships, in spite of the minute-by-minute scheduling that now drove her and Robert's days. They eschewed a chauffeur for local trips, Margrit usually at the wheel. Instead of hiring an interior designer, Robert asked Margrit to decorate the office whose dark wood furnishings and whitewashed walls were in keeping with the mission-style winery. His workspace was dominated by a large walnut desk, carved with bunches of grapes, and a soft leather couch where he'd occasionally nap. It had a homey feel to it: On his couch, for instance, rested an embroidered cushion with the saying "Age doesn't matter unless you are wine."

* * *

But in the increasingly competitive wine industry, image mattered more than ever. Perhaps the most memorable example of the Mondavi family's and the company's hospitality spending during this period came during the back-to-back parties in March 2001 to celebrate the renovation of the Oakville winery—a project whose budget had ballooned to upward of $26 million, rather than the $15 to $20 million first estimated. The winery hosted two evenings of black-tie parties in the new barrel room, the first for 385 of Napa's mostly upvalley glitterati and the second for 325 members of the wine trade. To make the evening truly special, Margrit commissioned a composer to write an "Ode to To Kalon." The company also published a custom, limited-edition book to mark the occasion, covered in linen and replete with lush color photographs, which it presented as gifts. The Napa Symphony—another recipient of the Mondavis' largesse—performed the "Ode to To Kalon." On both evenings, Robert, elegant in a tuxedo, rose from his seat to conduct the orchestra himself, waving a baton up and down in time to the music. The evening was completed by four courses of splendid food, paired with the company's wines.

Timothy had championed the To Kalon project on the argument that newer production facilities would improve the quality and sales of the company's most prestigious red wines. But some of the decisions made in the course of that renovation were questionable. For instance, instead of using stainless steel fermentation tanks, which were easier to clean and less likely to harbor bacteria, Mondavi chose to install fifty-six handcrafted oak tanks, imported from France, for its red wine fermentation. With a capacity of five thousand gallons and costing $27,500 each, the oak tanks alone cost more than $1.5 million. Rival winemakers and even some of Mondavi's own production staffers wondered if Timothy and others had made that choice for aesthetic more than practical reasons.

There was little doubt that the company was intently focused on the public relations value of the project. Not only were the tours redesigned to show off the new facilities, but the To Kalon project as a whole was designed to present an image of winemaking as a craftsman's art to the hundreds of thousands of visitors who streamed through the Oakville winery each year—suggesting that Mondavi was much smaller and more personal than, in fact, it was. The To Kalon project communicated gentle hand-crafting, whereby the winemakers employed gravity-flow to coddle the incoming grapes instead of pumps and basket presses.

But most of the company's wine was, in fact, made in an unglamorous factory-like setting in the Central Valley. By 2001, Woodbridge alone accounted for 75 percent of Mondavi's case sales, while the Oakville winery's share was just over 5 percent. The reality was that the company was more of a volume producer, with most of its wines selling for less than $10 a bottle. Upscale consumers had become enamored of highly concentrated "cult" wines from tiny, artisan producers—a group of customers that Timothy and Robert identified more closely with. Everyday wine drinkers, in contrast, were moving toward inexpensive foreign imports from Australia and elsewhere, pushed by low-cost retailers such as Costco. For a company that sold wines at both ends of the range and whose capitalization was by then around $600 million, the market's radical polarization touched off a corporate identity crisis.

Family members staked out clashing positions on what kind of company Mondavi should be. Timothy, who described winemaking as "liquid art," felt it should focus on its most elite wines. Michael, as the company's chairman, felt his brother's view was hopelessly naive and out of touch with the realities of running a public company, where investors demanded growth and punished executives who failed to deliver. Conjuring the spirit of Cesare to support his focus on popular, lower-priced, volume wines, Michael frequently told the story of walking in Charles Krug's vineyards with his grandfather, sometime in the 1950s. Explaining to his grandson that Robert and Peter had every right to be proud of their reserve wines, Cesare then warned Michael: "Never forget that most people, most of the time, drink our other wines, and those are the wines they really judge us by."

The brothers seemed locked in an impossible, decades-long argument that neither could win. Sometimes the hostile feelings underlying that argument would erupt in public. In a hardly diplomatic fashion in the months following the To Kalon parties, Michael expressed his disdain for the old way that the company had marketed its wines: "All those black tie events. We were complacent, cocky, and started believing our own press. In the old country, wine was a blue collar beverage, not an elitist, white collar drink."

At the same time, the brothers united in their determination to fend off what they considered the usurpation of the To Kalon name by a neighboring winemaker, Fred Schrader, and vineyard owner, Andy Beckstoffer, who were preparing to release a wine together called "Beckstoffer

Original To Kalon Vineyard" wine. The trademark dispute escalated to a tangle of suits and countersuits, adding an unappealing entrée to the Mondavi brothers' overfilled plates. To Beckstoffer, the dispute was another example of the Mondavis' overexpansiveness—this time in the use of the To Kalon name.

Amid these discussions and distractions, Mondavi's production culture quietly started slipping as Michael and other sales, marketing, and finance executives at Latour Court pushed for growth. In the early years, when Robert was in charge, he would emphasize making the very best wine the company could, despite the cost. But in the years after going public, and as Robert's influence waned, Mondavi began taking quality shortcuts to save money, such as cutting surplus oak tanks in half to reuse as red wine fermenters, sometimes using plastic tanks, not cleaning the tanks as frequently as they had before, and automating the process of filling and emptying the wine without slowing down to taste it and to smell the empty barrels. Even Mondavi's top-end Cabernet was racked four times instead of five. To do an experiment in the cellar, permission was now required from an executive at the Latour Court office as part of an effort to organize a companywide research group. Mondavi also changed the financial incentives for managers, linking their pay to return on capital investments for the first time. That quiet internal act was a very loud statement of a profoundly changed corporate culture.

Mondavi's winemaking style also suffered from the aggressive quest to expand its sales. With Timothy traveling between Tuscany, France, Italy, and Chile throughout the 1990s, the company's chief winemaker was frequently jet-lagged. Compounding the problem, the Oakville facility was bursting at the seams. In the late 1970s, it had produced only about a hundred thousand cases of wine a year.

Meanwhile, the Napa vineyards had became an unmanageable jungle of eight different trellising systems, a mishmash of rootstocks, and wrong varieties planted on the wrong soil. Almost inevitably, the production and winegrowing problems seeped into the bottle.

Wine critics spotted the flaws. Just a few months before Mondavi completed its To Kalon project, it received a devastating blow when wine critic Robert Parker, in his bimonthly newsletter *The Wine Advocate*, blasted Mondavi for producing mediocre wines. In his December 2000 newsletter, Parker reviewed thirty-five Mondavi wines from late 1990s vintages. He awarded most of them meager scores in the 80s, with the exception of the 1997 Cabernet Sauvignon To Kalon Reserve, a $150 bottle of wine which he gave a 94+ score. "In twenty-two years, I have never been more distressed as well as perplexed by evaluations of a particular winery than those that follow," he wrote. "No one in the United States has done more to promote the image of fine wine than Robert Mondavi and his family. They have had a profound positive impact on American culture and we all have benefited from it."

Yet Parker then went on to savage Timothy's wines, calling them "indifferent, innocuous wines that err on the side of intellectual vapidness over the pursuit of wines of heart, soul, and pleasure." In short, the world's most powerful wine critic, a man who could single-handedly make or destroy a winery's reputation, had judged Mondavi's wines "collectively superficial." His verdict sent Mondavi's stock skidding: After it was published, MOND dropped fourteen points.

Parker, whose palate has been called the enological equivalent of Einstein's brain, wasn't the only one who noticed a change for the worse. Just a few months after the To Kalon festivities, the influential critic from *Wine Spectator*, James Laube, also wrote a searing article entitled "A Question of Style of Mondavi," which suggested that Timothy Mondavi had lost his way as a winemaker. "At a time when California's best winemakers are aiming for riper, richer, more expressive wines, Mondavi appears headed in the opposite direction. . . . Call it a matter of preference of style, but the current Mondavi wines leave me wondering if the winery is just in a temporary slump, exacerbated by a pair of challenging vintages in 1998 and 1999, or if it is seriously off-track."

Laube followed up with several more critical articles, including one in October 2003 that argued that the company's rapid overseas expansion and involvement with such ventures as Disney had diverted its focus from its Napa Valley wines. "We're passionate about wine," Laube quoted Marcia in the article, in a not-so-subtle jab at her brothers, "but maybe we're not the best management."

Timothy took the criticisms hard. Although he remained cordial to Laube and Parker in the aftermath of the reviews, their published critiques heightened the tensions between the three Mondavi men. One instance of this took place in the Vineyard Room, when the Mondavis invited Laube to taste some of their new wines in barrel and discuss his views over lunch. As Laube recalls, they started to "politely critique my critique." But almost immediately, they shifted their attention away from the writer and instead started attacking one another. Emotional and frustrated, Robert insisted the problem was that they had taken their eyes off Oakville and failed to get their message across, allowing other winemakers to steal a march on them. Not long after this incident, the company hired the famed Bordeaux-based wine consultant Michel Rolland to help it improve its top wines. Not coincidentally, the wines made by Rolland's clients are some of Robert Parker's favorites.

The bad reviews came at what was already a deeply stressful time in Timothy's life. Always somewhat flirtatious, he hadn't changed his ways even after marrying for a second time. On August 6, 2001, Holly Peterson barred Timothy from returning to the Kortum Canyon home they shared. The rumors in the valley were flying as to why—some believed it was an extramarital episode that had led to his wife's kicking him out of their home. Holly remained publicly discreet about the circumstances of the split, but Timothy acknowledges he'd become involved with other people during his marriage to Holly.

Whatever the cause, it was an ugly breakup. Although the couple underwent marriage counseling for more than a year, their marriage was irreparably torn. Holly filed for divorce on May 8, 2002, and hired a team of advisors, including a forensic accountant, to help her win a large divorce settlement. In court records, it quickly became clear that to finance what Holly described as a "spectacular lifestyle," the couple had been spending far more than Timothy earned.

In 2000, Timothy reported a hefty after-tax income of $438,205, but nearly half of that went to support Dorothy and their children. At the same time, he and Holly spent almost half a million that year—resulting in a deficit of more than a quarter of a million dollars. The pattern continued in 2001, but this time the spending gap climbed to $341,469. To cover the expenditures, Timothy sold off $3.9 million in the company stock, using a large portion of that to pay down a line of credit he'd been using to finance his and Holly's rich lifestyle, which including $6,237 a month to support four horses (two were named Bacchus and Decanter), to buy a new Mercedes and a boat, and to spend $497 a month on maintaining Timothy's aquarium.

Timothy, who was then fifty-one years old, had an estimated net worth of between $20 and $25 million. The judge initially ordered him to pay Holly $12,800 a month for a two-year period representing half the time they were married, which was just over four years. Holly, then forty-three, hadn't worked much since marrying Timothy, instead dedicating her "time, energy, [and] professional expertise completely to Tim, his family, his work, his winery, his travel and events." In her court arguments, she declared she had no substantial income of her own.

Thus began a brutal and prolonged legal battle over the division of the couple's assets. In just over a year, they together racked up $679,552 in attorney and accountants' fees, with Holly spending far more than Timothy. In January of 2003, Richard Peterson stepped in to try to help his daughter and estranged son-in-law reach a settlement. The judge was skeptical of Holly's claim that Timothy "has litigated this case in a fashion reminiscent of Grant through Georgia." To the contrary, the judge found Holly just as much to blame for the protracted fight as her former husband.

They did, however, finally reach a settlement on September 29, 2003. Holly got $1.08 million, including equity in the Kortum Canyon home, Timothy's company retirement benefits, and cash from the sale of a St. Helena property. She also got alimony of $13,000 a month until the fall of 2005. Timothy ultimately won his freedom, but not without a heavy emotional and financial price.

As chairman of Britain's Diageo PLC, the world's largest alcoholic beverages company, one of Anthony Greener's more pleasurable duties was visiting the Napa Valley to review its fine-wine holdings there. On such a trip, the patrician-looking Greener, with graying sideburns, a restrained, no-nonsense manner, and a slightly snaggletoothed smile, was chauffeured to the Oakville winery. Stepping out of the back seat of the limousine, he then strode through the archway and met Michael Mondavi for the first time. Greener, who favored properly British pinstriped suits, had met Robert several years before at VinItaly, the giant trade exposition held in Verona, Italy, each year. Greener considered the Mondavi patriarch a "visionary" and "an absolutely outstanding man." But he'd never met Robert's elder son; Michael was an unknown quantity to him.

Michael and Greener hit it off well. Neither man had excelled in school—Greener never attended university—and both had been born into family businesses. Greener's father had owned a cotton factory in Manchester. Although Greener never joined the family firm, he spent fourteen years at another privately held family business, Dunhill, transforming it from a fusty purveyor of pipes and tobacco to a luxury goods retailer with such brands as Chloé and Lagerfeld. More recently, Greener had helped orchestrate the merger of drinks giants Guinness and Grand Metropolitan. Called "Mr. Nasty" by his detractors after laying off six hundred Guinness workers in Scotland shortly after becoming the beer maker's chairman, he was maligned in the British press as dour, arrogant, and aloof.

Yet he also earned the well-deserved reputation of being a turn-around artist, with the ability to spot and reinvigorate tired brands. Even-tempered and practical, Greener seemed like a perfect fit for Mondavi's board, since he brought international experience, a deep knowledge of brand management, and a cool head for crises. The two men stayed in touch as Michael began recruiting high-powered directors. In the mid-1990s, he brought on James Barksdale, the former CEO of Netscape Communications Corporation, to the board. Barksdale, who was on the board of Federal Express with Greer, had met Michael during a corporate retreat in Napa, but resigned in 2000, not long after Mondavi rebuffed Beringer's approach. To take Barksdale's place, Michael recruited Greener, who by then had retired as Diageo's chairman and had been knighted by the queen of England for his service to British industry.

"Sir Anthony," along with the existing outside directors Frank Farella and Philip Greer, began pushing to further professionalize the board. In 2002, Greer helped recruit John M. Thompson, an executive who'd begun his career as an IBM systems engineer in Canada and ended it, before retiring, as vice chairman of the board of the IBM Corporation, as well as chairman of the Toronto Dominion Bank Ltd. Greener, in turn, helped recruit a Rhodesian-raised executive named Adrian Bellamy, who made his mark running the hugely successful retail operations at London's Heathrow and Gatwick airports and was executive chairman of The Body Shop PLC. The new directors brought a worldliness that Mondavi's board had previously lacked.

But to Greener and the other seasoned newcomers, it quickly became clear that Mondavi's corporate governance was poor and that the company was heading into a full-blown business crisis. This was the result of the company's capital spending spree in the late 1990s, which, to the directors, in retrospect, seemed to have been based on wildly optimistic projections of the sales that would result from the acquisition of new vineyards, the To Kalon renovation, and the Disney project. Greener, for one, felt alarmed not only by the business problems, but by the dysfunctional relations between Robert, Michael, and Timothy, which were demoralizing Mondavi's professional managers.

Michael hoped Greener and Bellamy, in particular, could help the company grapple with managing and protecting its valuable brand name. Robert had sold his name to the company in 1979, well before the IPO, and now the company was struggling with how to fully exploit the Robert Mondavi name without sapping its strength by overusing it on too many different products. One case arose with the Coastal brand, whose sales grew rapidly in the 1990s. But although Coastal became the company's second highest seller after Woodbridge, Mondavi was disappointed that it was not a category leader. So Michael, Evans, and their recently hired team of marketers, supported by Greener, decided to rebrand Coastal as "Robert Mondavi Private Selection," hoping to use the family's name and reputation to spur on sales.

Timothy strongly opposed the move, objecting to the idea of using the Robert Mondavi name prominently on their inexpensive wines. He was acutely aware of the history of Napa Valley's Inglenook brand, which had been widely esteemed as a fine wine but which nosedived into an inexpensive, everyday wine under its new corporate owners. Robert, too, raised questions, and both were concerned about the graphics on Private Selection's label: Michael wanted to incorporate the famous image of the Oakville winery's arch and tower, images associated with its reserve wines.

His brother and father argued passionately against it. Yet Evans and Michael, backed by the board, prevailed by pushing research showing how consumers were confused by the existing low-price labeling. Also working in their favor was Timothy's damaged credibility, a result of the savage reviews of his winemaking and news of his messy divorce. On both the label design and the name change to Private Selection, Michael and Greg Evans triumphed.

Mondavi was facing an onslaught of competition from fast-growing bargain wines. They came from Australia and Chile but also closer to home, from a challenger nicknamed "Two-Buck Chuck." Sold exclusively at the Trader Joe's grocery stores, "Two-Buck Chuck" got this name because it was sold under the Charles Shaw label, which had once been an upscale

Robert as Bacchus, with Margrit.
(Avis Mandel for Pate International)

(From right) Michael,
Marcia, Robert, and
Timothy, in Robert
and Margrit's new
home on Wappo Hill.
(Will Mossgrove for Pate
International)

Isabel and Michael Mondavi at a holiday gathering. (Courtesy of Peter Ventura)

Tim Mondavi, left, with his cousin Peter Ventura and Holly Peterson Mondavi before the couple divorced. (Courtesy of Peter Ventura)

Helen Ventura, left, and her daughter Serena. (Courtesy of Peter Ventura)

Serena Ventura on the slopes in Gstaad in 1971. (Courtesy of Peter Ventura)

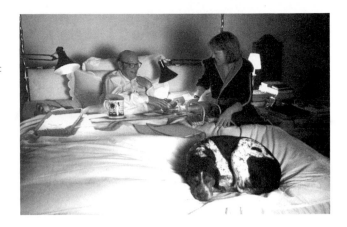

Opus One label designer Susan Pate confers with Baron Philippe de Rothschild, who preferred to conduct most of his business while in bed. (Courtesy of Pate International)

Robert Mondavi, left, with the Baron Philippe de Rothschild and his daughter Philippine, partners in the Opus One winery. (Courtesy of Opus One)

Timothy, Robert, and Michael Mondavi pose with the Baroness Philippine de Rothschild at the Opus One construction site. (Courtesy of Opus One)

Robert Mondavi always loved women. He is pictured with package designer Susan Pate. (Avis Mandel for Pate International)

At the lavish "Out of Africa" party, Robert and Margrit Mondavi, along with Peter Ventura and another guest, pose with an elephant on the winery lawn. (Courtesy of Peter Ventura)

Cliff Adams, left, and Greg Evans,
right, were key non family executives.
(John Casado for Pate International)

John Martel, pictured here in a publicity shot
for his rock music persona "Joe Silverhound,"
returned to the law to help Robert Mondavi
win his court battle against Rosa and Peter.
(Courtesy of John Martel)

Frank Farella, Robert's friend and
legal advisor for more than three
decades, was eventually torn between
his loyalty to the family and his
fiduciary duty as a Mondavi board
member. (Courtesy of Frank Farella)

Mondavi's global sales chief Gary
Ramona, who was close to Robert
and became embroiled in allegations
of child sexual abuse. (Courtesy of the
Napa Valley Register)

Peter Mondavi Jr. (left), with his father Peter Mondavi Sr., and his brother Marc Mondavi. (Courtesy of the Charles Krug Winery)

Helen Ventura, center, with brothers Peter, left, and Robert Mondavi. (Courtesy of Peter Ventura)

Rob Mondavi, Michael and Isabel's son and Robert's eldest grandson. (Courtesy of the Napa Valley Register)

Robert Mondavi and his grandson, Carlo Cesare Mondavi. Carlo's skin care line using grape extracts has run afoul of investors. (Courtesy of Terence Ford)

Ted Hall, a retired McKinsey & Co. partner, was recruited to Mondavi's board and soon replaced Michael Mondavi as chairman in early 2004. (Courtesy of Ted Hall)

Philip Greer joined Mondavi's board in 1992, shortly before the family took the company public. (Courtesy of Philip Greer)

A British executive named Sir Anthony Greener led the board coup at Mondavi. (Courtesy of Sir Anthony Greener)

Richard Sands, chairman of Constellation Brands. (Courtesy of Constellation)

Robert Sands, Richard's younger brother and president and chief operating officer of Constellation Brands. (Courtesy of Constellation)

Robert, left, and Peter Mondavi watch as their lot is auctioned at the 2006 Auction Napa Valley charity event, with Tim, left, and Marc Mondavi looking on in the background. (Courtesy of the Napa Valley Vintners)

After lengthy deliberation, Timothy picked the name "Continuum" for his new Cabernet Sauvignon wine to be released in the spring of 2008. Timothy's partners include his sister Marcia Mondavi Borger (center) and Robert and Margrit Mondavi. His daughter Carissa is project manager. (Terence Ford for Continuum)

Napa brand. Ironically, it was Michael's friend and fellow alumnus from Santa Clara University who had bought the troubled label and turned it into a low-price phenomenon. Fred T. Franzia, like Michael, was the scion of a California winemaking family and related by marriage to the Gallos. But he, his brother, and their cousin were effectively pushed out of the family winery in 1973 by their fathers' decision to sell their stakes in the family company to Coca-Cola Bottling of New York. As part of the deal, they were barred from using the Franzia last name in a winemaking venture—since the name was one of the assets sold. Franzia boxed wines—which are now unconnected to the Franzia family—remain one of the industry's top-selling brands.

Franzia, who was thirty at the time of the sale, tried to convince his father not to sell out. When his father sold anyway, it fueled the Franzias' drive to start again. So in 1974, they began distributing other wineries' products. Their first client: the Robert Mondavi Winery. But Mondavi eventually turned over its distribution to Southern Wine and Spirits and dropped the Franzias as distributors.

Then the Franzias ran into legal trouble. In 1993, Franzia and his company, the Bronco Wine Company, were accused of passing off cheaper grapes, costing $100 to $200 a ton, as more expensive Zinfandel grapes, that sold for as much as ten times that amount. To avoid detection, Franzia scattered Zinfandel leaves as camouflage on top of non-Zinfandel grapes as they lay in bins waiting to be crushed into wine—a step that Franzia called "the blessing of the loads"—a parody of the wine industry's tradition of blessing the grapes at harvest time. Bronco pleaded nolo contendere and paid a $2.5 million fine. Franzia pleaded guilty, paid a $500,000 fine, and was banned for five years from sitting on Bronco's board or holding a position within Bronco that had responsibility for grape purchasing, wine production, or compliance with federal regulations.

However, Fred Franzia and Michael stayed in touch with each other over the years. Together, the Franzias and the Mondavis had a business venture together called Montpellier Investment Partnership LP, which owned some vineyards in the Central Valley and, for a time, a low-cost brand called Montpellier. As members of two California wine families whose roots reached back to Prohibition, they also socialized together. Franzia always invited Michael and his father on the annual "Deer Camp" weekend up in Napa or Sonoma, where members of the Old Italian wine families would gather at the start of deer hunting season each

August. Franzia also invited Michael and Robert to a dinner in 2001 to celebrate the opening of his controversial new bottling plant and winery on the outskirts of Napa.

By then, the disruptive role that Franzias' "extreme value" wines—selling for $2 to $3 a bottle—was playing in the industry could not be ignored. Trader Joe's began selling the Charles Shaw brand in early 2002 and by the fall of that year, the Charles Shaw brand began biting into Mondavi's sales. The following year, "Two-Buck Chuck" became America's fastest-growing wine brand by volume. At the same time, Franzia was embroiled in a protracted legal battle with Napa's wine establishment over the question of whether he could keep selling wine made from grapes grown outside the Napa Valley in bottles with Napa labels—a practice his rivals considered to be cheating. Fred Franzia's rivals, and even some of his friends, considered him the industry's bad boy.

At one point during the candlelit evening in the new Franzia Winery's barrel room in a Napa industrial park, Robert stood up, turned to his son's old friend, and asked a question that was on most Napa wine producers' minds that year: "Fred, I just don't know how you do it. How can you make money selling wines so cheaply?" Franzia deflected the question with a joke and revealed no secrets. But the simple answer was that he was profiting from a dramatic glut in the wine market, buying good-quality wines in bulk from Mondavi itself, as well as Beringer and other well-known producers. Was it possible that Michael hadn't let his father know he was selling Mondavi wines at bargain-basement prices to Franzia? Were Mondavi's profits under so much pressure?

The simple answer was yes. During the booming 1990s, Mondavi could paper over its mistakes as sales soared. But when the market for premium wines started to sour as supply mounted and prices dropped, its problems became more obvious. In 2002, its revenue fell 8 percent to $441.4 million and net income plunged 41 percent to $25.5 million. It was the first time the company's profits had dropped since its IPO. The following year was hardly better; in 2003, the company's net income dropped another 32 percent, to $17.3 million, in part because of charges related to its plan to cut another 103 jobs. The layoffs were the trigger for the almost inevitable collision between Mondavi's management, led by Evans, with Robert and Timothy, who viewed the company's problems with a mixture of pain, fury, and powerlessness.

*   *   *

The company's stock price reflected the strains. It touched an eight-year low of $18.53 in March 2003, tumbling from the low $30s just four months earlier. The low stock price erupted into a personal crisis for Robert, one that threatened to embarrass him personally and destroy his legacy as a philanthropist. The roots of the problem lay in the late 1990s, when Mondavi stock was trading near the top of its range. During those halcyon days, Robert had promised to give the University of California at Davis a stunning $35 million, the largest single private gift ever received by the school and one of the largest ever made to the University of California system.

In keeping with Robert and Margrit's mission to promote wine, food, and the arts, $10 million would support the campus's new performing arts center and $25 million of the gift would go toward a new Robert Mondavi Institute for Wine and Food Science. Margrit played a key role in the $10 million portion of the gift. She'd heard Davis was building a center for the arts and convinced Robert to see the project a week or so later. As the couple walked into Mrak Hall for a lunch on campus, they were greeted with a standing ovation by faculty members and administrators. Robert pushed to sign a preliminary agreement right away, so the Gallos or some other big donors could not trump them. As her husband spoke, Margrit drew Bacchus, the Roman god of wine, on her coaster, and signed that afternoon. The university decided to call it the Robert and Margrit Mondavi Center for the Performing Arts. It became by far the largest gift to have Margrit's name on it—and the first to drop the Biever name entirely. The final paperwork sealing the gift was completed just after September 11, 2001.

The university had held a muted ceremony in Davis on September 19 to honor Robert and Margrit for their generosity. Robert, beautifully turned out in a crisply tailored dark suit, stood by Margrit, who was wearing a chartreuse pashmina shawl and matching hat. Explaining that he had used Davis professor Maynard Amerine's textbook on winemaking as "his bible," Robert credited much of his success to Davis's teaching and research. "I learned to make wine only because I followed that book so religiously. I succeeded because of that. . . ." The ceremony was attended by California governor Gray Davis and Timothy, but not by Michael, and it was just as much Margrit's moment as Robert's. The large gift to Davis was backed by his stock in the Robert Mondavi Corporation. Soon it began causing him and his advisors anxiety, particularly as the shares plummeted. When the stock dropped below $20 a share, Robert was underwater—the dollar value of his shares couldn't cover his many philanthropic commitments, which by then had swelled to include not only Copia and UC Davis, but also Stanford University's Cantor Arts Center, which had named a gallery after him, and a host of smaller bequests. The few people around Robert who understood his situation were deeply worried that he would not be able to keep his promises.

The knot that Robert's philanthropy had tied around him was seemingly intractable. He was in a dire financial situation and faced insolvency if the stock continued to decline. Timothy and Marcia pushed Robert's lawyer, Frank Farella, to try to renegotiate the terms of Robert's gift to Davis. By convincing the university to lengthen the term of his father's payments, they hoped Davis would relieve some of the financial pressure on Robert. Farella gently broached the idea of whether the project at Davis might be delayed but got nowhere. The university had already set aside the site, drawn up the building plans, and included Robert's contribution in its financial plans, which had wound their way through the state legislature. The university also planned to drop the Mondavi name from the Institute if Robert reneged on his pledge. Keenly aware of the bad publicity that could ensue, Robert and his advisors were stuck.

The deadline for funding the gift to Davis was January 2006—still almost three years away. The real stress during that period came from Robert's pledge to Copia, which was secured by his shares. When the price of the shares dropped below $20, Robert came perilously close to breaching the coverage of the escrow deposit required by the insurance company, entitling them to foreclose on the escrow shares. Farella succeeded in convincing the insurer to reduce the ratio from 1:15 of the value of the shares to 1:1. As well, Robert borrowed fifty thousand shares from all three of his children as security in case the shares dropped even further, though he never ended up having to use these shares and eventually returned them. Robert's deadline for meeting his full $23 million commitment to Copia was also January 2006, and his advisors had put a stock-selling program into effect. Thus, it was in his and his advisors' strong interest to boost the share price.

Robert's forceful personality wasn't enough to solve the problem. Approaching his ninth decade, hard of hearing, and serving in a largely ceremonial post, he relied on his advisors to write out their thoughts for him, since he could barely hear them. In meetings, he was constantly twiddling with his hearing aids, hoping that by adjusting them he might capture conversation more easily. He was no longer capable of doing what he'd long told his sons and other employees to do when encountering a problem, which was to "just fix it." For years, he'd lay out his ideas for Michael and Timothy in an attempt to communicate with them more clearly, sometimes rising from his warm bed in the middle of the night to scrawl down his thoughts on yellow legal pads, occasionally asking Margrit for spelling help. But by 2003, with his coordination failing, he could no longer reach them that way.

Robert turned to an instrument of power that had long been his friend. In the six months leading up to his ninetieth-birthday celebrations that June, Robert gave several press interviews where he lashed out at his sons. "We could have promoted our high-end wine, but, no, we were too busy looking at dollars and cents and not realizing we were losing the image," the elder Mr. Mondavi told *The St. Helena Star.* He told the reporter that he talked to his sons constantly but "they weren't hearing. Basically, they were making money." To the *Los Angeles Times,* he took direct aim at his elder son and Greg Evans, declaring that "when you have to make money in a corporate environment, you begin to cut a few corners," referring perhaps to the production shortcuts that had begun in the 1990s. The once-powerful patriarch had slashed back at his sons and Mondavi's management in public, as the palpable measure of his triumphs and accomplishments seemed to be slipping away.

CHAPTER TWENTY

The Board Coup, 2003-2004

Timothy's mounting rage began to focus on Greg Evans. From his perspective, the quiet, numbers-focused executive had ushered in a "reign of terror" at Mondavi. Timothy empathized with employees who were girding themselves for the edicts concerning cost-saving and job cuts coming out of Evans's Latour Court office. The prospect of even more layoffs hung over Mondavi like a layer of smog on a warm California day. Timothy sensed the paralysis settling into some of his longtime friends and colleagues: Few employees seemed willing to speak out, lest they be marked in Evans's next round of firings.

It was during a planning meeting in the spring of 2003 that Timothy finally took his stand. Evans had summoned Mondavi's vice presidents and managers to what he called a "Come to Jesus" gathering, hoping to shake up his lieutenants and force them to confront the severity of Mondavi's problems. In the midst of intense competition and falling profits, he wanted them to start thinking more radically about ways to save the business. He did not invite Michael, Timothy, or even Robert, reasoning that since none of them held day-to-day operational roles anymore, it wasn't their place to participate in these planning meetings. Yet Evans also admitted to himself he was worried they might try to undermine his efforts. As the business situation worsened, the Mondavi family had become a burden for him.

Among the two dozen or so executives gathered in the Carneros Room of the Latour Court offices were Clay Gregory, the general manager of Mondavi's Oakville winery; Valerie Dietrich, the new head of human relations who had replaced the controversial Alan Schnur; and Brad Alderson, who was in charge of Woodbridge. To Evans's consternation, Timothy had also turned up—tipped off by a family loyalist that the session was taking place. Battle lines were drawn between Latour Court, which had been directing the job cuts, and Oakville, which was at the receiving end of many of them. Timothy and some of the staffers who'd worked for the family for years felt Oakville had been disproportionately targeted during the layoffs, while the Latour group thought that spending at those operations had been out of control for years.

The tension in the room was palpable. Evans, who lacked Robert's charisma and Michael's speaking skills, possessed an equanimity that the passionate Mondavis lacked. Although he sought to engage his executives, many sat uncomfortably mute in their chairs. Evans tossed out ideas meant to provoke his team, including one that Timothy agreed with. He turned to Alderson. "Brad," Evans suddenly asked, "what if you decided Woodbridge wines didn't need barrel aging in the future? Would that allow us to cut costs?" The question met with stunned silence. The very idea was sacrilege to executives brought up believing that Woodbridge had been the quality leader in its category precisely because of its barrel aging. However the company's recent marketing research had shown that some former Woodbridge drinkers were turning to fruitier wines not aged in barrels, including some from Australia. Timothy, too, had suggested to Alderson and Evans that Woodbridge move away from a heavy use of oak to a fresher taste. Alderson, a conservative man who had worked with the Mondavi family for more than three decades, said almost nothing, since to his mind Evans was proposing a complete about-face in Woodbridge's wine style.

Timothy then asked the question of why Gallo, a name long associated with bottom-shelf wines, was doing so well in the marketplace. Evans suggested that Gallo's large size gave it a cost advantage—a suggestion that provoked Timothy, who believed Gallo's resurgence had more to do with its new strategy of brand differentiation. He was dismayed by what he considered Evans's superficial understanding of the market. Evans, whom he had helped promote to CEO, seemed to him to have blinders on. Shaking with anger, he retorted to Evans, "You've got to be kidding me. It's not just about scale!" His face reddening as he spoke, Timothy asked how truly innovative Mondavi was being in its sales and marketing, an area outside his expertise. "Let's get creative," Timothy implored, making a heartfelt pitch for launching new, fresher wines from the coastal regions, including a shelved red wine he'd championed a few years earlier called Red Square. To Alderson, Timothy's proposal was futile: Other wineries had already jumped on the opportunity that Mondavi had missed with Red Square.

In the midst of his outpouring, Timothy felt like the sole brave knight willing to battle for what was right. From his perspective, Evans had created an environment of fear at the company that suffocated dialogue. Evans, in turn, felt Timothy's pitch for his pet project came at a time when Mondavi was in a crisis caused, in large part, by the company's and the family's mistake of trying to do too many things all at once.

As the meeting broke up, Evans confronted Timothy in the hallway outside the conference room. His bald pate was glistening and his face was flushed. His eyes flashed behind his wire-rimmed glasses. Furious, he drew closer to his former mentor. "That was out of bounds. Totally unacceptable," Evans sputtered, a few inches from Timothy's face.

"Well, that's your opinion and I have mine," spit back Timothy.

That night, at around dinnertime, Evans called Timothy on his cell phone from outside his home, so he wouldn't disturb his wife. He'd already prepared a short memo to Mondavi's directors about Timothy's behavior at the meeting, laying out what had happened and telling the board that Timothy had been disruptive and undercut his authority. The memo was certain to undermine Timothy's already wobbly standing among the outside directors. Greener, in particular, was certain to grasp how wrong it had been for Timothy, as a business owner and shareholder, to tell off the CEO of a publicly traded company in front of his own troops. The political damage to Timothy's career was likely to be irreparable once Greener and the other directors heard about it.

But Evans didn't tell Timothy he was planning to send the memo: instead, he spoke his mind about Timothy's crusade to protect the company's high-end wines. "Tim, you are a one-note fanatic," he told him.

Timothy, who was also pacing outside his home on his cell phone during the call, replied furiously, "I'm going to get you."

It was no secret that Timothy was under tremendous strain that spring. He was struggling through the final stages of his divorce from Holly. The business was in trouble. As Mondavi's stock sank, his paper wealth was shrinking every day. To complicate matters, his father had taken a bad fall. Shortly before the planning meeting, Robert had risen from his bed at his Wappo Hill home in the night and slipped, bumping his head. Margrit got him back into bed, but the next morning, he had seemed confused and suffered from vertigo. Fearing he may have suffered a stroke, she arranged for Robert to check into a local hospital, where he underwent a battery of tests.

Robert's mental confusion also alarmed Michael, who wondered if it was due strictly to his hearing loss, or if he was exhibiting early signs of dementia. Around the time of the fall, he suggested to his father that he fly to the Mayo Clinic and get a full workup on both his body and his mind. Robert spent four days at the clinic without getting a clear diagnosis of his problem. Margrit then took him to a neurologist at the University of California at San Francisco, who eventually put him on Namenda, a drug prescribed for the treatment of moderate to severe dementia associated with Alzheimer's disease. He had days when he was mostly lucid and others when he seemed confused. Robert's health problems meant that Timothy effectively lost an ally for championing quality at the company.

Amid these problems, Evans pounced. After Timothy threatened to "get" him, he e-mailed his memo to Mondavi's directors. The next day, he arranged a conference call with Michael, Greer, and Greener. The two outside directors were members of the board's "transition committee," which had been formed after Evans became CEO to mediate any problems that might arise between the Mondavi family and its first nonfamily chief executive. On the call, Evans complained that Timothy's behavior had been out of line. By contradicting him and becoming emotional, he had disrupted the meeting and made it dysfunctional. Threatening to quit unless Timothy took a sabbatical, he asked Greener, "Am I running the place or not?"

Marcia, who was also a director, then heard from Greener of what by then was being characterized as Timothy's emotional outburst, and called the human relations head, Valerie Dietrich, to get her version of events.

Dietrich relayed her concerns that Timothy had been deeply upset at the meeting and that he had been shaking as he spoke and his fair skin had flushed with emotion. Dietrich painted a picture of a man on the verge of an emotional breakdown. With Robert temporarily out of the picture, Marcia and Michael decided to talk with their brother themselves, hoping to convince him to take a six-month sabbatical that would help him regain his balance.

As they rode together in the back of one of the company's limousines on their way to meet with the psychologist Jerry Shapiro at a hotel near the San Francisco Airport, Michael and Marcia confronted their younger brother. In the two-hour car ride, they said they were worried about him. Marcia, in particular, poured out her concerns. Her younger brother seemed to be under a tremendous amount of stress and she was alarmed. Michael reminded Timothy that he hadn't taken a vacation in two years. They suggested he might need a rest.

They reached the hotel and met with Shapiro. By the end of their session, Timothy had agreed to take a six-month sabbatical and had been effectively ousted from the company by his own family, at least temporarily, for the second time in his career. The long drive back to Napa Valley was excruciatingly painful for Timothy as he mulled over the similarities between his own forced exile at the hands of his siblings and Robert's forced exile from Charles Krug in 1965. Both he and his father were in their mid-fifties when they'd gotten the boot.

About two months later, Timothy boarded a jet and flew to the Hawaiian island of Kauai for an extended vacation with his family. They stayed on the island's North Shore, known for its hippie colony and wild rainstorms. His son Dominic, then in his early twenties, urged his father to "live a little" by changing the way he looked. Taking his son's advice and striking a blow for unconventionality, Timothy shaved his head during his stay on the islands, as did Dominic. When he returned to the mainland to attend, out of a sense of obligation, his father's ninetieth birthday celebration in June, his shorn head startled the rest of his family, particularly his conservative sister Marcia. He toured Sonoma vineyard properties with the idea of quitting the family business and starting over on his own. But with his finances strained by his divorces and five children in various stages of schooling, he decided to return to his job at Mondavi, still hairless on top.

Evans imposed strict conditions on his continued employment:

Timothy had to agree to start reliably showing up for scheduled appointments and adhere to a set of performance goals, just like other Mondavi executives. Timothy agreed to the conditions but fully intended to follow up on his threat to "get" Evans.

The outside directors grew alarmed not only by Timothy's erratic behavior but also by Robert's philanthropic bind. Farella had quietly alerted Mondavi's other directors about the situation and the news increased their urgency to find a way to lift the company's stock price. There remained several potential ways out, including Robert's backing out of his pledges or Marcia's stepping in to help, but if Mondavi's stock kept dropping Robert could be in dire financial straits. Boosting the stock price seemed the best course of action, but to make a dramatic change by selling off a division or merging with another company, they'd have to break the tight grip the Mondavi family held on the company through its supervoting shares. To shift the balance more in their favor, the outside directors decided to bring on one more of their own.

"I know this chap Ted, and he'd be great," suggested Adrian Bellamy, referring to a recently retired McKinsey and Company partner named Ted Hall, who seemed to fit the bill perfectly. Not only was he an expert in fixing broken companies from his days as a management consultant, but he was also a Napa Valley vintner who owned the 650-acre Long Meadow Ranch where he, his wife, Laddie, and their son, Christopher, grew organic grapes and raised grass-fed cattle in the Mayacamas Mountains, eight hundred feet above the valley floor. To look him over, the Mondavi family invited Hall to lunch on a patio outside the Vineyard Room in the fall of 2003. Robert, Michael, Timothy, Marcia, and Frank Farella were there and the conversation ranged from vineyard management to brand building, and Hall impressed his hosts with his knowledge of both farming and business.

"What do you think are the biggest challenges facing the company?" Timothy asked. Hall spoke knowledgeably about the problems, but when he touched on Mondavi's confused brand identity, Timothy perked up. At the end of the meal, Marcia and Robert's younger son felt they'd found a champion on the board, someone who cared about improving the quality of Mondavi wines and would be strong enough to stand up to Evans.

A few days later, Timothy took up Hall's invitation to visit Long Meadow Ranch. Hall showed him around in an open-sided Land Rover, and took obvious pride in the land and displayed a deep knowledge of organic farming—principles Timothy embraced and, in fact, was pushing for at the Oakville winery. Hall's winery, designed by the architect William Turnbull and built of the earth excavated from the ranch, impressed Timothy in its simplicity. Hall knew every head of cattle by name and spoke eloquently about the geology of the area, as well as the ranch's nineteenth-century history. Timothy believed that he'd found not only a powerful ally in Hall but someone who shared his values and sensibilities.

The rest of the board was also impressed with Hall and they invited him to observe the September meeting at the Oakville winery, even though he was not yet officially a director. By then, Hall knew about Robert's brush with insolvency earlier that year. It was there, in the course of a normal five-year business review, that Hall made a critical comment when Greg Evans and his team finished their presentation. He summarized it as a "do more better" plan—meaning that, if only Mondavi could manage to sell more wine, it would work its way out of its problems. But the problem with this sort of plan, Hall explained to the group, was that no matter how much you "do more better," it wouldn't solve the basic structural problems Mondavi faced, including the post–9/11 decline in luxury goods consumption and rapid consolidation of distributors. Mondavi's management was only taking baby steps. He implied their plan wasn't radical enough to fix the problems.

The outside directors quickly grasped Hall's larger point: Another round of layoffs or another spate of restructurings wouldn't reverse the company's slide. It needed a more radical shake-up—an idea that Timothy embraced, particularly if it meant defying his brother and Evans. Michael, in turn, seemed to lay the blame for Mondavi's problems on Evans and the other professional managers, telling the outsiders "everything would be perfectly all right if management had only done what I told them to do." Regretting that he'd ever given up the title of CEO, Michael even suggested he take back the job from Evans. Yet, to Hall and Greener, the heart of the problem was not Evans or his team: It was the quarter of a billion dollars or so of virtually unproductive capital investments made under Michael's watch during the late 1990s and early 2000s. And they weren't about to give the helm to Michael or to any other Mondavi.

One small pebble in that mountain of unproductive assets was the company's guesthouse, which sat on 2.7 acres of land adjacent to Michael and Isabel's new home. Michael wanted to buy the property for his son, Rob, and his daughter-in-law, Lydia, and, earlier that year, had pitched the sale to the board as a way of chipping away at that mountain. But what should have been a relatively simple matter dragged on for months and became increasingly adversarial. Greer, who was the chairman of Mondavi's audit committee, as well as Frank Farella got involved in what, in monetary terms, was a minor business transaction. If all had gone according to plan, the sale would have ended up happening quietly and been buried in a footnote in one of the company's SEC filings.

To make sure there was no hint of a sweetheart deal, the company hired three independent appraisers to submit estimates of the property's value. But even with these appraisals, Michael and the two directors ended up haggling over the price, including Michael's insistence that he should get a discount because his father used it as a massage parlor. Exasperated by the amount of time and energy he had wasted at a time when Mondavi was in trouble, Greer finally ended up giving Michael an ultimatum: "Take it or leave it: This is the appraised value and this is the value we're going to use. If you and Rob don't want to buy it: fine. We'll sell it to someone else," he warned. "It's not preordained that we sell it to a family member." Greer was fed up with the issue: "We've talked about this ad nauseam," he said. Michael finally agreed to a price of $2.1 million—$100,000 more than averaged appraisals, less adjustments for needed repairs in the amount of $100,000—resulting in a price of $2.0 million. He bought the property from the company in September 2003.

At a time when the company was faced with far more pressing problems, Michael's actions burned up some of his goodwill with the board. But before that, his standing with the outside directors had begun to erode as a result of his long campaign to promote Rob at Mondavi. His efforts began in the late 1990s, after Rob's Napa Cigar Company began losing money and was sold to a rival. "Rob, I need you to come join us," Michael told him. Rob started at the troubled La Famiglia Winery, scrubbing tanks and hauling hoses. On his last day of work there, toward the end of harvest, some of his fellow cellar-workers asked him to climb into a large fermenting tank and give it a scrub. Rob did what he was told. His colleagues shut the door behind him and stuck a two-inch hose into the tank, spraying the Mondavi heir with the "lees"—the sludgy residue of dead yeast and sediment left behind after fermentation. When they let him out, they told him "You're now blessed as a true winemaker."

Well-liked by employees, Rob soon moved to Atlanta to work as a Mondavi sales representative handling its Chilean and Italian imports. But in June of 2000, to the surprise of some Mondavi executives, who had heard Michael talk about the importance of Rob proving himself in various low-level jobs before moving up the corporate ladder, Michael's son was named to the newly created job of director of marketing for the Robert Mondavi Winery. Based in Oakville, the job was a marketer's dream—representing the company's crucially important halo brand—and heading up hospitality and public relations for the winery.

Rob worked hard in his new position, but even so, to give that job to anyone without any substantial corporate marketing experience or a graduate degree was foolhardy, at best—even if his last name was Mondavi. At worst, it was another instance of the company's corrosive nepotism. The creation of that new job for Rob was the result of hard negotiating on Michael's part, stopping into Evans's office and calling him on the phone repeatedly over a period of months to insist that Rob come back from Atlanta and land in a high-level post. Evans finally told Michael he felt it wasn't appropriate for him to act as his son's ombudsman. Michael, in turn, worried that Rob might become a sacrificial lamb; that Rob's career might suffer because of his own increasingly fractious run-ins with Evans and the board.

Once Evans gave in, he and Michael finally settled on a job title and salary for Rob. Michael's aggressive lobbying on his son's behalf extended to his company-reimbursed moving expenses. Around the time he moved to Atlanta, Rob had bought a modest home in the hills north of Napa's Atlas Peak for around $800,000. Three years later, and a year after he moved back to Napa, he sold it for $1.5 million, almost twice as much as he had paid for it. Rob asked the company to reimburse him for some of the costs relating to the sale of the home. To Evans, the transaction looked murky and didn't fit within the company's reimbursement policy, so he balked at approving the request.

On the face of it, Rob, with his father's support, seemed to be trying to "game" Mondavi's policy. And considering the Mondavi family's wealth, the amount of money involved was a relatively meager $30,000. Nonetheless, Evans refused to agree to the reimbursement. Evans and the outside directors that fall were growing increasingly sensitive to the new, tougher corporate governance rules imposed on publicly traded companies under the Sarbanes-Oxley Act of 2002. These new standards were signed into federal law after the scandals involving Enron, Tyco International, and other companies. Requiring much fuller disclosure of executive pay and insider transactions, one of the act's goals was to prevent self-dealing on the part of corporate insiders.

Michael's actions seemed that of a chairman who was more concerned about his son than about the company or its shareholders. They were consistent with his desire to groom Rob as the fourth-generation leader of the Mondavi business and provide him with all the dynastic privileges. Michael's aggressive pursuit of his and Rob's interests didn't sit well with Evans or the outside directors. And within the Mondavi family, both Michael and his son were increasingly at odds with Robert and Margrit.

One source of tension was the carriage house. Robert had long enjoyed using it for his massages, but when Michael purchased the property for Rob and Lydia, it became a divisive issue. Rob wrote a letter to his grandfather in the late spring of 2004 offering him the opportunity to continue using the carriage house, but insisting they would have to come to some financial arrangement if Robert wished to do so. Years before Rob and Lydia moved onto the property, Robert had spent tens of thousands of dollars to refurbish it, adding a bathroom, deck, and a massage table. But Rob thought his grandfather should pay the utility bills for the carriage house if he wanted to keep using it as, what Rob called, "his massage parlor," rather than having them in what he describes as his grandfather's own "colossal" home. Dismayed by the ungrateful tone of the letter, Robert showed it to Ted Hall, who empathized with the old man's anguish. Michael and Rob's seemingly arrogant handling of the issues surrounding the purchase of the guesthouse property also dismayed and angered their fellow family shareholders.

Rob's behavior on the job was another flashpoint. One weekend during his short tenure at Oakville, Rob had decided that it would be a good idea to freshen up the winery's Mission Room, an odd, rhomboid-shaped office on the ground floor that had been his grandfather's original office, hoping to make it into a more businesslike venue for VIP guests to taste wine. Margrit had commissioned the Italian-born muralist Carlo Marchiori to paint it. Marchiori charged $180 to $250 per square foot for his playful and classically inspired work. When Margrit discovered that Rob had ordered the room to be whitewashed, painting over the expansive mural without discussing it with her first, she was shocked and dismayed.

Rather than risk a blow-up if she spoke to Rob about it in person, she wrote him a note expressing her unhappiness over it. She couldn't understand why Rob wouldn't have checked with her first, rather than just going ahead and destroying the mural. "Just because it's a little gray, you don't paint over Leonardo da Vinci's *Last Supper*," she maintained. Rob's reply, as she recalls, was brief and flippant. He felt he was doing what was best for the business. As well, the hospitality center hadn't been profitable for many years and Rob considered certain aspects of its style, such as the muraled Mission Room, "antiquated." The incident festered and Margrit shared her anger with Robert. "He needs to learn humility," Margrit recalls her husband saying about his grandson.

Rob, in turn, felt that he was one of the few people willing to challenge the powerful Margrit. He questioned the business logic of *Annie and Margrit*, a cookbook by Margrit and her daughter, Annie Roberts, published in 2003, which was originally funded largely by the winery. As well, just three months or so into his new job at Oakville, Rob decided that expenses were out of control at the winery's kitchen, and began interviewing candidates for a new executive chef position above Roberts. "Everywhere I turned, I just kept stepping in things," says Rob.

Michael, meanwhile, had become convinced that Evans and the outside directors had adopted toward him and his son an aggressively "ABM" stance: "Anyone But Mondavi." From his perspective, he and his family had been forced to abide by even stricter rules than other executives and suffer financial penalties as a result, citing the $30,000 in relocation expenses that the company refused to reimburse Rob for. To Michael, it became a matter of principle.

Greener mulled over the September board meeting during a ten-hour flight from San Francisco to London. Seated in the first-class cabin, he jotted down his thoughts on a pad of paper. At various times over the past few months, Greener, Greer, and Farella had helped mediate an array of minor issues involving Michael, and they had begun losing confidence that he was the right person to serve as Mondavi's chairman. Greener, especially, became convinced that Michael was simply not up to the task of steering the company through the storm. He felt that the only thing that would save Mondavi's stock from sinking lower was strong intervention on the part of the board. That meant that Michael had to go.

Upon his return to Britain, Greener shared his thoughts with Adrian Bellamy, who agreed that they needed to oust Michael as chairman. During a late evening meeting in December after a shareholder meeting in a Yountville motel room, Greener and Bellamy won the other outside directors to their side. The next morning, Greener brought up the subject with Marcia, who was on the board and was the company's single largest shareholder by that time. Marcia agreed with Greener but did not relish her role in her brother's firing. She felt that her family and the company were facing a desperate situation and after years of watching the battles between her brothers from the relatively safe distance of New York, Marcia threw her weight in with the outsiders, rather than try once again to play peacemaker with her family. Keenly aware of the possible humiliation facing her father if he was forced to renege on his philanthropic promises, she decided Hall was more likely to resolve the problem than her older brother, who was starting petty fights motivated by self-interest rather than focusing on the greater good of the company or the family. But even though she'd lost confidence in Michael's leadership, she still hoped he'd stay on at the company in an ambassadorial role.

The outside directors chose not to tell Timothy of the decision, a reflection of how much respect Robert's younger son had lost in their eyes since the showdown with Evans. They felt he was too emotional and did not trust him to keep the information to himself. In the meantime, Hall agreed to become chairman. Not only did he live in Napa Valley, but since retiring from McKinsey he had the time to take on the job. With the holidays approaching, the outside directors decided to wait until early in the New Year to break the news to Michael.

On Tuesday, January 6, after taking a break over the New Year's holiday, Farella and Greer drove up the two-laned Oakville Grade Road to Marcia's home. Sitting in her sunny breakfast nook, the men and Marcia were joined by Robert, who was still glowing from his trip over the New Year's holiday to the Big Island of Hawaii with Margrit, Timothy, and Timothy's children. Because Robert was having trouble hearing what was said, Farella wrote down the news for him on paper: Michael was being removed that day as chairman. Robert wasn't happy to learn that the directors were about to fire his son, but he did not try to stop them.

Although Marcia had known over the holidays what was about to happen to her brother, she later explained to Timothy that she didn't call because she was reluctant to upset them on their vacation. In fact, the outside directors had warned Marcia to keep the decision a secret from them.

Michael also returned to work on January 6 after the holiday break. Sitting in his Latour Court office that morning, he got a call at about ten-thirty A.M. from Timothy, who himself had just heard the news from Frank Farella. Setting aside decades of differences, Timothy decided to pick up the phone and give Michael a warning beforehand.

"Heads up," Timothy told him. "You're about to get your ass handed to you in a sling."

Michael was scheduled to have lunch that day with Philip Greer and Frank Farella at the Oakville winery. Before Timothy's phone call, he had hoped to use that meeting to lobby Greer and Farella to rein in Evans as CEO. But his bravado faded as he passed through the winery's arch and made his way at around eleven-thirty to the Cliff May Room, which was tucked on the ground floor behind the Vineyard Room. Feeling an ache in his chest, he sat down, facing Greer and Farella. A hospitality staffer waited on them, filling their wineglasses with the company's finest Fumé Blanc, then a Pinot Noir. After some small talk, they told him that they thought it best if he'd step aside into the role of vice chairman, allowing Ted Hall to take his place. Michael asked them what his job would be as vice chairman and then raised the subject of his compensation. "We'll figure it out," they told him.

Michael picked at his chicken breast, which normally he would have consumed with gusto. He was being fired from the only company where he'd ever worked. In the space of an hour-long lunch, the legacy he'd spent a lifetime building for his children and grandchildren had crumbled. Waves of anguish and disbelief washed over him. He grew pale from the shock.

Farella, too, felt pained by the news he had to deliver to Robert's namesake, however long overdue it might have been. And for Greer, whose friendship with Michael had lasted for nearly two decades and whose wife, Nancy Greer, was friendly with Isabel Mondavi, the luncheon was agonizing. Over the holidays, Nancy Greer had urged her husband to quit Mondavi's board. But as much as he'd have preferred to avoid delivering this crushing blow to their friends, Greer felt he had a responsibility to see it through. Still, in the weeks leading up to that lunch date, Greer had found himself dreading it.

Both Farella and Greer were gentle, choosing their words carefully so as to inflict the least damage. One of the most delicate pieces of information they conveyed was that Marcia had thrown her support behind his ouster. Marcia's betrayal was one of the most disappointing events of Michael's life. Finding it impossible to stomach the idea of staying for dessert and espresso, he left.

Michael went home rather than returning to the office. His siblings and father, meanwhile, had cut across the valley on the Oakville Grade Road to an impromptu gathering at Marcia's house to talk with Ted Hall. Sitting on a stone wall bordering Marcia's drive, the avuncular former McKinsey man laid out his plans in a reassuring tone, explaining how he would look out for the best interests of the company and its shareholders. He used an analogy he had used many times before, describing his role as that of an emergency room doctor who'd dealt with all sorts of corporate traumas over the years. Although Hall had joined the board by that point and been offered as a candidate to replace Michael, he had not yet formally been voted in as chairman. Winning the confidence of these family members, who together controlled the largest bloc of voting shares, was crucial to Hall's appointment and he did so handily that afternoon. Faced with Robert's philanthropic problem, they hoped Hall could reverse the stock slide and avert potential embarrassment, if not disaster.

Michael returned to Latour Court early the next morning. By midday, word of the event had spread quickly through the Mondavi empire. That day, Michael had an uncomfortable meeting with Hall, followed by a videotaped message to employees from Michael, Timothy, and Hall. The rumor mill was whirring: Some staffers reported that Michael had stormed around Latour Court that afternoon, furious at what had happened. Michael recalls feeling depressed and embarrassed; how, he wondered, would he tell people he'd worked with for decades that he'd been fired? Timothy, meanwhile, made a last-minute attempt to install his sister, rather than Hall, as chairman. His gambit failed, though, and two days later, on January 9, Hall's appointment as chairman was formally announced. Timothy, worried about how Michael was coping, felt protective toward him. Reverting to the pattern that stretched back to the Krug days, Timothy suggested during another family meeting at Marcia's that Michael take a sabbatical.

That spring, Mondavi once again retained McKinsey and Company to help it better understand its branding issues and distribution challenges. It also hired a prominent New York–based public relations firm best known for its mergers and acquisition work, Kekst and Company; the Wall Street law firm Davis, Polk & Wardwell; and investment bankers from Citibank. The hiring of such a large team of advisors in itself suggested a breakup might be in the works.

Another recurring pattern was the expulsion of the erring family member: Michael was ousted by his own family, just as Robert had been in the 1960s. Yet, now there was no member of the Mondavi family at the company. At Charles Krug, Peter junior had assumed the position of head of the family business. But Timothy, whose credibility with the board had continued to erode, had no realistic hope of convincing the board to give him additional responsibility, particularly as the company's financial performance worsened.

And it did. Less than two weeks after Michael's ouster, on January 22, Mondavi downgraded its second-quarter earnings guidance. Despite the Mondavi's splashy black-tie fete in Santiago, its Chilean wine had failed to make a lasting impression in the crowded export market. The company announced it would sell its disappointing Chilean Caliterra brand and assets to its partner Viña Errazuriz, taking a $3.9 million charge. Meanwhile, Michael's school friend, Fred Franzia, picked up the phone and gave him a call.

"How ya doing?" Franzia asked.

"Been better," Michael replied, "considering I've never been fired before."

"Ah, hell," said Franzia. "Don't let the bastards get you down."

CHAPTER TWENTY-ONE

Brothers, 2004

Twenty-seven hundred miles away, at the opposite end of the country, the upheaval at Mondavi caught the attention of another pair of brothers who were on the prowl for acquisitions. Richard and Robert Sands were, respectively, the chairman and president of Constellation Brands Inc. They worked out of a modest office park in the Finger Lakes region of upper New York State. Known for their ferocious deal making rather than the quality of their wines, they were carrying on a family reputation in the wine business that was as far from Robert Mondavi's as possible—the Sandses got their start with rotgut wines. Yet, the Sandses, like the Mondavis, could also rightly claim to have wine running in their veins.

Their grandfather, Mordecai E. "Mack" Sands, was rumored to have been a bootlegger during Prohibition, running alcoholic beverages over the U.S. border from Canada. Shortly after repeal, Mack joined a partner in a small Long Island winery, Geffen Industries, which turned out millions of gallons of poor-quality wine. Federal wine regulations are said to have been put in place to curb Geffen Industries' production of cheap wine. When his partner retired, Mack bought an old sauerkraut factory in Canandaigua, the heart of New York State's wine region. He turned it into a distillery and put his son Marvin in charge. Recently decommissioned as an ensign in the navy following the end of World War II, Marvin followed his father into a rough and unglamorous business that was still suffering from the lean years of Prohibition.

Marvin Sands expanded the business, called Canandaigua Industries, by making wines in bulk for eastern bottlers—a business similar to what Sunny St. Helena and Charles Krug were doing at the time. But profits were slim and competition was fierce. His father, Mack, meantime, in 1951 opened Richard's Wine Cellars in Petersburg, Virginia, a winery that he named after his infant grandson. It quickly became the biggest winery in the state. Three years later, in an effort to move Canandaigua out of the bulk business by developing brands of their own, Marvin invented the sweet, fortified dessert wine Richard's Wild Irish Rose.

Made from local Labrusca grapes, which have a pinkish tint, Wild Irish Rose was the Sandses' flagship brand through the 1960s and 1970s, a time when most wines consumed in the U.S. were still dessert wines. Canandaigua also produced the fortified wine Cisco, syrupy hooch that has been described as tasting like fruit-flavored Robitussin mixed with liquid Jell-O and two-hundred-proof vodka. Cisco is sold in bottles with bright, fruit-colored labels and its critics decry it as a "skid row" wine designed to produce an inexpensive high. The company also bought other bottom-shelf brands such as Manischewitz, made from Concord grapes. In 1973, Marvin took the company public on NASDAQ. Although neither of his sons had yet joined the business, he used a two-class stock structure to ensure his family stayed in control, similar to the structure that the Mondavis later used.

The Sands family, unlike the Mondavis, had a clear succession plan. Marvin's elder son, Richard, who earned a Ph.D. in social psychology from the University of North Carolina at Chapel Hill, briefly flirted with the idea of becoming an academic. Instead, he joined the family business in 1979, initially working on the production side. As the pace of the company's acquisitions picked up, Richard discovered that his understanding of organizational psychology, as well as his agility with math and numbers, served him well in business.

His talents took root quickly. As sales of Wild Irish Rose began to decline in the mid-1980s, Marvin considered selling the whole business.

Richard suggested they move instead into the booming market for "wine coolers," prepackaged cocktails made from wine and fruit juice popular with young drinkers. The result was the Sun Country line, which, when the company rolled it out in 1984, became an immediate hit, selling a million cases within the first six months. The brand helped Canandaigua double its sales to $173 million by 1986. Following that success, Marvin promoted Richard to president in May 1986.

A month after Richard's promotion, his brother quit his job at a Rochester, New York, law firm and joined Canandaigua Industries as general counsel. Robert had graduated Phi Beta Kappa from Skidmore College, earned a law degree from Pace University, and worked briefly as an associate at a law firm in Rochester. Like Timothy Mondavi, Robert Sands was eight years younger than his brother and relatively unproven when he first arrived to work in the family business. In 1999, the Sands moved their company's listing to the New York Stock Exchange.

By all appearances, the Sands were a closely knit family. They spent their summers together at a cluster of homes on Canandaigua Lake. The clan's matriarch, Richard and Robert's mother, Marilyn, nicknamed "Mickey," migrated north from Florida as the weather in the Finger Lakes grew warmer to spend time near her sons and their families. When Marilyn's husband, Marvin, died in 1999, Richard assumed the company's chairmanship from his father.

The Sands brothers worked closely together and their offices re-flected their outside passions. Richard's was working with wood. On the property of his home in Rochester, he had a large workshop where he built the intricate "zebra wood" coffee table that sat in his office as well as towering modern wood sculptures. Robert, who wore heavy gold jewelry around his wrist and favored sharply tailored suits, enjoyed collecting modern art. He displayed in his office both a Helmut Newton photo-graph and a brightly colored Harlequin painting by the local artist Mar-tine Lepore.

Although there were some signs of disagreements between the Sands brothers, they shared a common vision for the company, building it pre-dominantly through acquisitions. Their timing was good: Their deal mak-ing coincided with the explosion of the corporate takeover wars in the mid-1980s. Not only was the wine industry poised for consolidation, but their agility with numbers and clear focus on the bottom line played to the brothers' strengths as strategists. Together, they transformed their family-controlled business, which they renamed Constellation in 2000, into an industry powerhouse.

The Sandses also gained a reputation for smoothly rolling the wineries they acquired into their operations, showing particular sensitivity to some of the psychological needs of the families who sold out to them. One such example was with Napa's Franciscan Estates, where the Sandses agreed to hire Agustin Huneeus Jr., whose father had built Chile's largest winery and also Napa's Franciscan Winery, as head of its burgeoning fine wine division for a period, despite the talk of nepotism that accompanied this decision. At a time when strife-torn Mondavi was struggling to balance its lower-priced volume brands with its higher-priced elite wines, the Sandses were steadily buying their way into the fine-wine business; with the 1999 Franciscan deal an example of that.

The smoothness and relative calm of the Sandses came as a relief for some of the troubled wine companies they bought. They brought a professionalism and clear focus on generating profits that some of their targets had not had before. There was also a powerful momentum to the Sands organization. After buying Australia's top wine producer, BRL Hardy, in 2003, Constellation overtook Gallo as the world's biggest wine producer, logging $1.7 billion in wine sales as well as another $1.5 billion in liquor and beer sales, giving it immense distribution clout. Mondavi, in contrast, was slipping down the rankings, with just $452.7 million in sales for the year ending June 2003, inching up only 3 percent over the previous year.

The Sandses could never claim to be the vintners the Mondavis were: Neither Richard nor Robert knew how to make wine or took deep interest in the subtleties of what took place in the cellars they owned. But they were solid businessmen who could fulfill contracts, expand sales, and keep their promises. After all that the House of Mondavi had been through, it badly needed professionalism and direction. So, at a time when the Mondavi brothers were battling over branding issues, the Sandses were patrolling industry waters, scenting blood.

On Kekst and Company's advice, Mondavi kept a low profile that spring as Hall began working intensely with Evans and a small group of top executives to explore ways to regain Wall Street's confidence. Meanwhile, Michael sent a voice mail to employees on Friday, the thirteenth of February explaining his sabbatical. When the company's newly hired press relations vice president, Hilary Martin, fielded questions about why Michael had left, she put a positive spin on it, explaining he planned to tour Italy with Isabel and take cooking classes.

But it soon became clear that he had other intentions—laying the groundwork for a new company and starting to produce his branch of the family's own wine that fall. There were also signs that Timothy was becoming even further marginalized. The forced sabbatical had stripped him of most his power and when he returned he found his views commanded little sway with Greg Evans or the board. Although he held the exalted title of vice chairman, in truth he'd been almost entirely sidelined, with little operating or strategic control.

The one lever Timothy hoped to pull was his relationship with Hall, who had initially seemed to sympathize with his views about brand confusion. At a board meeting that spring, Timothy tried to focus the outside director's attention on the problem by laying out an array of Inglenook wines: some from the 1960s—when Robert's old friend John Daniel was focused on quality—and Inglenook's current jug wine. He gave each director a bottle of one of these fine library wines as a reminder. Yet Timothy failed to make his case, even though there was some truth in what he was saying. The problem was that Woodbridge and Private Selection were Mondavi's moneymakers, not its Napa Valley reserve wines. It had already invested heavily in Oakville through its To Kalon project, without an adequate payoff. His argument revealed a superficial grasp of Mondavi's business problems.

Behind the scenes, Timothy placed the blame for Mondavi's brand problems squarely on Michael and Greg Evans. He lobbied hard through the spring for Greg Evans to be fired. Not only did he make his case to Hall during their long conversations at Long Meadow Ranch, but he also boarded a plane for the fifteen-hour flight to Scotland, where Sir Anthony had a second home. Greener, whose practical temperament was poles apart from Timothy's artistic approach, was not receptive. Timothy also trekked to Adrian Bellamy's home in the San Francisco suburb of Hillsborough and made his pitch over dinner with Philip Greer and Frank Farella at Allegro Romano, a neighborhood restaurant near Greer's home on San Francisco's Russian Hill. They listened politely to Robert's son but did not offer him any encouragement. Evans, who was working twelve- and fourteen-hour days at Latour Court, grappling with Mondavi's business problems, was unaware of Timothy's efforts to sabotage him.

But Timothy's maneuvers backfired. Instead of eroding Evans's support, his efforts fueled the directors' growing conviction that Robert's younger son was a loose cannon and perhaps even mentally unstable. His campaign was a failure; Timothy was pointedly not invited to join the management group studying various alternatives, and directors became less willing to spend hours in discussion with Robert's long-winded and emotional son.

After the board stripped away the last vestiges of their operational control, Michael and Timothy converted some of their Class B shares, each carrying ten votes, into regular voting Class A stock and began selling their shares. In February of 2004 alone, Timothy sold shares valued at $2.7 million; people close to the family and some company watchers realized that the sales were linked to his divorce settlement with Holly. Michael, meanwhile, sold about $2 million after he left on his sabbatical in February of that year to pay down the mortgage on his new home. The insider sales raised questions about whether the Mondavi brothers were bailing out.

In New York on June 8 and 9, at the Rihga Royal on West Fifty-fourth Street in Manhattan, Wall Street's demands were about to collide with the Mondavi family's dynastic dreams. Board meetings were held in one of the conference rooms of the Art Deco–style hotel. First, Greg Evans and his team presented a strategic plan laying out various options that focused on continuing to operate Mondavi as a single business. Then a group of bankers from Citigroup, which had been hired by Mondavi to explore its options that spring and which was led by a seasoned mergers-and-acquisitions pro named Leon Kalvaria, presented the results of its own analysis. They laid out such possibilities as selling the company, taking it private again, or breaking it up.

Since the moves laid out by the investment bankers would achieve higher values for the business, the board felt compelled to vote down management's plan and explore these more radical courses of action. Marcia sat in the conference room, tense and visibly unhappy. Marcia and Michael managed to make small talk, but Marcia did not apologize to her brother, even though his crossed arms and glares made it clear that he remained furious at her support of his dismissal. Adding to the sour smell of stress in the air, Michael, Hall, and Greener would slip out after board presentations for private discussions with Michael, including how much and what size bottles he'd get to take with him from Mondavi's decades-old wine library.

The board, including the three Mondavi siblings, who remained directors, unanimously agreed to explore the more radical options. But before it could do that, it had to grapple with the dual-class shareholding structure, which effectively locked up control with the B shareholders. As the meeting wound down, it became clear to Ted Hall and the outside directors that they needed to do more: They needed to finally crack the Mondavis' hold on the company. Effectively, by bringing in investment bankers to lay out the options to increase shareholder value, the outside directors had put Mondavi into play.

Sensing that he was being trapped in an impossible position by his dual roles as Robert's proxy as well as an independent director, Farella fired off an e-mail to Hall, offering to resign. A charming man with a thatch of silver hair and a triangular nose that made him look a bit like the cartoon character Mister Magoo, Farella felt impossibly conflicted by his deep friendship and admiration for Robert and his fiduciary duty to represent the interests of all shareholders. Hall, however, insisted that Farella's primary role as a director was to all shareholders, not just Robert, and that boosting Mondavi's stock price would serve both interests. Hall convinced him to stay, thus averting what could have been a public fissure in the board.

Timothy, too, by then realized that the kind of changes he was hoping for under Hall's leadership weren't likely to happen. It also began to dawn on him that his first impression of Hall as a sensitive organic farmer who shared his view on branding issues wasn't right. That insight came to him at a lunch that took place during the June board meeting. The group had traveled eight blocks north from their hotel to eat at "21," the glamorous night spot that had been a watering hole for Hemingway, Bogie, and Bacall in the 1950s. The multicourse lunch, to Timothy's palate, was ponderously rich, drenched in cream, and symbolic of the heavy-handed proceedings.

Events had spun out of the Mondavis' control in the New York meeting, but the real showdown between the family and the outside directors took place in St. Helena over a two-day meeting on August 9 and 10. The board held its meeting at the Harvest Inn, notable, in a valley filled with overblown architectural follies, for its slightly eccentric Old World charm. Built in a Tudor style, with exposed exterior beams painted black against a white stuccoed exterior, and with brick columns twirled in a playful design, the inn was built in the 1980s by the scion of a famous San Francisco family. The board met in a lofty upstairs conference room with views of vineyards out the window. Ted Hall presided, occupying the center seat, and corporate counsel Michael Byers took notes.

Mondavi's chairman entered the meeting leaning heavily on a pair of crutches. A week after the June board meeting in New York, Hall had been walking at Long Meadow Ranch when he slipped on a cow patty. He fell and fractured his shinbone, but continued to walk on it for about a week before realizing he had broken the bone. Through his long career with McKinsey, Hall had learned to cloak his feelings and to keep secrets. But he couldn't entirely hide his physical discomfort during the meeting or his full understanding of what the board's actions were likely to mean to Robert and his family.

Hall wasn't the only one in pain at that meeting. The stress of the past few months was apparent in Timothy's tottering frame. He arrived at the meeting leaning on a cane, with a lumbar support pillow under one arm. To try to alleviate some of the muscle spasms he'd been suffering for several weeks prior to the meeting, Timothy had been given a cortisone shot. For a time, he'd been forced to lie flat on his back, unable to walk.

As the family sat around the U-shaped table, the outside directors, led by Greener and Greer, presented a recapitalization plan that would get rid of Mondavi's two classes of shares. The plan had been carefully explained to them in the preceeding weeks, but nonetheless, the family listened in horror, and the full implication of it hit them: The outside directors wanted them to surrender control by handing over their votes. In return, they'd get a 15 percent premium for converting their B into A shares, worth a total of about $30 million at the time to them as a group, which would dramatically ease Robert's financial crisis. But to get that premium and that chance, they would have to sign a voting agreement, relinquishing their control of the company. They knew that Hall and his team were looking at a wide variety of options for the company, including a possible breakup. Once they signed the documents, their power as a voting bloc would vanish.

Timothy and Marcia balked. "Where did you get these ideas?" Marcia angrily asked, interrupting the presentations. "How did you come up with these numbers?" Marcia and Timothy were figuratively in one corner of the ring, while Michael was in the other. One or another of the siblings angrily stomped out of the room several times. But challenging Hall's advisors had little effect, especially after the outside directors then wielded their final and most powerful weapon: They told them they would quit en masse unless the Mondavis overhauled the company's governance by signing the voting agreement and agreeing to the plan to get rid of their supervoting shares. The outside directors threatened the Mondavis with the possibility of a public boardroom walkout.

It was what Greener and other directors called "the nuclear option." If the family had defied the outside directors, who then would have resigned in protest, the news almost certainly would have sent Mondavi's shares plunging even further, increasing the chance that Robert would face insolvency because of his exuberant philanthropy.

By then, Evans and Hall had come to believe it was a mistake to view the Mondavis as a family, since they did not act in unison or vote together as a group. They saw them as four distinct shareholders with four distinct personalities. That knowledge became a source of leverage for them.

Indicative of the divide between the Mondavis, Michael had by then channeled his sense of betrayal into a focused desire to sell his shares in the company for as much as he could. He had already negotiated his severance package and was well into making plans for his new company. To keep his energy up and reduce the stress he was feeling, Michael exercised and ate voraciously during that time, pumping the StairMaster at his home gym. Michael supported the recapitalization plan from the beginning, hoping it would put more money in his pocket as he set off on his own.

Timothy and Marcia, on the other hand, initially opposed the plan for what were at root emotional reasons: It threatened to wipe out their birthright. Their responses were layered with feelings that stretched back to their childhoods at Charles Krug, where discussions of wine and the family business dominated every family meal. By stripping away their control, Ted Hall and the outside directors threatened not only their identity as America's first family of wine but also the emotional core of what had long held them together.

Nonetheless, fearing lawsuits and hoping to save their father from further financial strain, they concluded they had no choice but to sign. "We felt the directors were holding a gun to our father's head and asked us to pull the trigger," says Timothy. "I could not run the risk of his bankruptcy, even if he would have."

Robert and Margrit had been in Italy at the time of the Harvest Inn meetings. Upon their return, they met with Timothy and Marcia on Wappo Hill to talk through their options. Unlike other publicly traded family businesses, the Mondavis had never adopted a structure that would allow them to vote as a bloc. Why they didn't do this is unclear. But with the outlook grim, they clung to the hope that they might be able to start again, by buying the Oakville winery or, if not, at least some of Mondavi's historic To Kalon vineyards.

On Tuesday, the tenth of August, Robert's three children signed the agreement that effectively put an end to their reign at the Robert Mondavi Corporation. Afterward, they gathered for lunch at Marjorie's old home off the Oakville Grade Road, which was now owned by Marcia and her family. Marcia and Timothy were deeply depressed, Michael was emotional, and Robert struggled to maintain a stiff upper lip. The family sat around the patio table, surrounded by To Kalon vineyards. The winery's catering staff had arranged a light meal for them of pasta salad, grilled salmon, and Mondavi's Carneros Chardonnay. "Well, it's over," one of them said. The finality of that moment brought tears to their eyes.

Four days later, Robert rode in the back of a chauffer-driven car up the narrow, winding road to Long Meadow Ranch, where Hall and Farella would further explain the recapitalization to him. The three men met at the thick wood conference table in Hall's office above the winery. With flat-weave kilim carpets on the floor and a longhorn cattle skull mounted above the fireplace, they could have been in Montana rather than Napa. On Hall's bookshelf was *Blood and Wine*, a saga of the Gallo family's tragic problems over the years.

In their course of their conversation that Saturday morning, Hall was struck by Robert's practical acceptance of the situation as well as the Mondavi patriarch's sad admission that his own sons weren't capable of running the business. Regardless of his deep empathy for the old king's anguish, Hall believed that going along with the plan was Robert's best hope of escaping the embarrassing possibility of defaulting on his pledges. "I never thought I'd have to be making these kinds of decisions at age ninety-one," Robert said.

Farella, who had known Robert for decades, couldn't fail to sense his old friend's sadness, but was also struck by Robert's enduring optimism. Having one of his more alert days, Robert was convinced that somehow the situation would work out, and perhaps his offspring would find a way to buy back the Oakville winery. About halfway through the meeting, Farella left, leaving Robert and Hall alone to talk privately. At the end of the morning, Robert left Hall's office and hobbled toward his car to head back down the windy road to Wappo Hill. Soon afterward, he, too, signed the voting agreement.

The directors turned to the next order of business: the restructuring plan. On August 20, after reconvening the meeting at the Harvest Inn, the board directed Evans and his team to come up with a plan to break the company into two separate operating units: with one focused on "lifestyle" brands selling for less than $15 a bottle, and the company's moneymaker, focused on more costly "luxury brands." Timothy did not leave the second-floor conference room immediately because he was searching for his cane, which he'd misplaced. After the other directors were gone, he made his way toward the door, his back pain forcing him to walk slowly. Down below, he heard the management group, led by Evans, erupt into a cheer when they learned that the board had given them the go-ahead to no longer view the business as a whole. Timothy overheard Evans, whom he had hired, say, "Now we're in the lifestyle business. Hurray!" He felt deeply betrayed.

Late in the afternoon of Friday, August 20, 2004, Mondavi announced its recapitalization, including a brief mention of the crucial voting agreement that put control in the hands of the outside directors. The market applauded the changes, sensing they were a precursor to a takeover. Mondavi's shares surged 9.4 percent to $40.69 on the news. But the Mondavi family loyalists were incensed by how the board had seized power from the family. They started calling the group of outside directors "the Raiders."

The truth of their tenuous position as shareholders who'd signed away control was cloaked from the wider public as the leaves on grapevines faded that fall. But the news that Napa Valley's first family had been deposed quickly spread among the family's inner circle. Margrit, for one, alluded to a betrayal of the family by the board of directors, but it wasn't clear precisely what had happened behind the Harvest Inn's heavy wood doors. The precariousness of Robert's financial situation remained a closely guarded secret, known only to his advisors, family, and perhaps one or two top UC Davis officials. Timothy and Marcia remained mum, harboring the hope that with the extra money they'd receive by exchanging their supervoting shares, they'd be able to buy back Oakville and some of the surrounding vineyards. Farella had written a memo to the siblings in August, counseling them that they would have to act quickly if they had any hope of buying back the winery. He not only urged them to move swiftly, but also laid out an organizational plan for how to proceed with a bid. To explore this possibility, Timothy and Marcia retained a lawyer of their own, rather than Farella, to represent them and spoke with an investment banker. Michael hired his own advisors as well.

But as the weeks passed and there was little sign that Timothy and Marcia were preparing a bid, one of the other directors grew alarmed. On a hot afternoon in the early autumn, Greer and Farella were attending the wedding of former Mondavi director Bartlett Rhoades at his home in the western hills between Napa and Yountville. Before the ceremony began, Greer took Farella aside. "Frank, you've got to go to the family. You're the only person who can pull them together to bid for the winery before this whole thing gets away from them." Farella assured him that he'd already tried and explained that the family couldn't even agree to the extent of setting up a joint fund of a few hundred thousand dollars for expenses related to a possible bid. "Try harder," Greer urged him.

The board reconvened in September, once again at the Rihga Royal in New York. For the most part, the Mondavi family knew much of what was coming: The company would reincorporate in Delaware, which had regulations that favored shareholders more than California's rules did. The voting power held by the Class B shareholders would drop from 84.9 percent to 39.5 percent, and the company would pay a 1.165 premium to Robert, Michael, Marcia, and Timothy for those shares.

The final element of the plan was to spin off "luxury" assets—including the holy shrines of the Oakville winery and Opus One—and focus instead on its "lifestyle" wines, mainly Woodbridge and Private Selection. To retain the use of the Robert Mondavi name, it would arrange a licensing agreement with the purchaser of the Robert Mondavi Winery in Oakville. While their plan seemed to be a complete and dramatic repudiation of everything the Robert Mondavi name had originally stood for, it was a key element of the board's larger plan to offer the opportunity for members of the Mondavi family to bid for some assets. Hall and Evans assumed that the buyer of Oakville would be a wealthy private individual who would see it as a trophy property. If all went according to the plan, the Mondavi family themselves would win the prize.

On September 20, Mondavi CEO Greg Evans strode confidently into an investor conference organized by Bank of America Securities in San Francisco. Standing at a podium, with a screen flickering with a PowerPoint presentation behind him, Evans revealed even more to the market about Mondavi's planned restructuring than he had a month earlier. He told the conference room of analysts and money managers that Michael Mondavi was leaving the company, though would remain on the board. He said that the changes would bear a whopping pretax price cost of $200 million or so. But the real kicker was Evan's confident pronouncement that the asset sales would generate $400 to $500 million in after-tax proceeds, implying a total valuation for Robert Mondavi Corporation of $749 to $929 million within a year. At those values, the shares should hit $41 to $51, assuming all went according to plan.

Analysts were skeptical; Mondavi's projections seemed overly optimistic. One particularly harsh voice came from Timothy S. Ramey, an analyst with D. A. Davidson and Company, based in Lake Oswego, Oregon. A wine producer himself who had first begun covering Mondavi more than a decade earlier as an analyst at a Wall Street firm and was known as a friend of Michael's, Ramey declared it "bizarre" that the company would have set its expectations so high for what it would reap from the asset sales. Ramey's own estimate was closer to $320 million. Other analysts were similarly wary and later voiced surprise at the level of detail provided. Evans had unintentionally put a price tag on the company.

With the stock trading at the time around $38 a share, Evans's forecast was indeed the equivalent of dumping a bucket of chum to a ravenous shark. Soon, an investment banking team at Merrill Lynch retained by Constellation to investigate a possible Mondavi deal began ramping up its efforts. Although the company's own management seemed to be inviting suitors, Hall and Evans had no intention of selling the whole thing. Their plan, after all, was to keep Woodbridge and Private Selection, while readying the company for a peaceful, negotiated sale of Oakville and other assets. Hall says he hoped to avoid setting it into play. But what Evans did was to put a price tag on the whole enterprise—a risky decision that he says he realized could draw suitors. To Constellation's bankers, it felt as if the stars, moon, and the sun all suddenly lined up.

The Mondavis were powerless to stop the unfolding events, and Michael was outraged. Not only had the board decided to remove him from the company's management, but his son, Rob, was fired during a wave of layoffs around that same time, adding salt to his wounds. As director of marketing for the Robert Mondavi Winery at Oakville, Rob had suffered through painful digestive problems as Mondavi employees he'd known all his life lost their jobs. The stress of this time "ripped through my stomach," he recalls, requiring him to take medications. When his supervisor finally called Rob into his office and offered him either an entry-level sales job or a severance package, Michael's son was not surprised. "Let's not beat around the bush," Rob replied. "You've got my Dad out—obviously you want me out, too." Rob's sacking ended Michael's dreams of his branch of the family ascending to the chairmanship of the Robert Mondavi Corporation. Rob took the news hard. Yet having signed over his votes like the rest of the family, Michael's hands were effectively tied.

After mulling over what to do and consulting with his attorney, Michael gave a *Los Angeles Times* reporter an exclusive interview. In the story, headlined "Winemaker Is Hoping for a High-end Harvest," Michael said that family members had voiced objections to the breakup, believing it was a mistake to sever high-end businesses, including the Oakville winery, from the rest of the company. Although the siblings opposed the plan, Michael, Marcia, and Timothy had not voted against it, but, in fact, abstained from voting. At the same time, Michael confirmed what the industry by then suspected: The Mondavi siblings hoped to buy Oakville and some surrounding vineyards themselves. In the interview, Michael suggested that the high price Hall and Evans expected to receive for it might chase other buyers away. "This is one harvest you won't be able to do again," Michael said.

The story ran on the front page of the *Times*'s business section on September 27, 2004. When Hall and the outside directors saw it, they were incensed by Michael's open flouting of the tight control of information that Hall had imposed on the board and company since joining. The board's nominating and governance committee, made up of Anthony Greener, Philip Greer, Adrian Bellamy, and John Thompson, wrote to Michael on October 1, expressing their view that his public airing of what had taken place behind closed doors "violated the confidentiality of board discussions and undermines the board's effort to conduct a fair process for the disposition of company assets." Worse, in the eyes of some directors, was Michael's poor judgment in talking down the value of the stock.

Michael shot back an e-mail to Hall that read, "Because I strongly believe that the strategic plan recently adopted by the board is contrary to the best interests of the company and all of its shareholders, I do not feel comfortable serving on the company's board of directors at this time." In effect, Michael refused to accept that he'd been fired from the board: He'd quit instead. Adding insult to injury, Michael's lawyer made sure the missives were released publicly. It was open warfare between Michael and the board. Ultimately, Michael's view prevailed; the company's proxy reported that he resigned from the board on October 4.

CHAPTER TWENTY-TWO

The Takeover, October to November, 2004

itting behind his modern green desk in Fairport, New York, Richard Sands monitored the Mondavi news as it arrived on his flat-panel screen. A burly, genial man who swept his curly gray hair back from his domed forehead, Sands had first begun closely tracking Mondavi about three years earlier when its stock dropped sharply, probably shortly after the disappointing second quarter of 2001. At that time, Sands had picked up the phone and called Michael. "Look, you know if we can be of some help, we'd be glad to"—suggesting that the family might want to focus on the fine-wine business, while Constellation would be interested in buying Woodbridge and possibly its Coastal brand. Michael had been cordial during the phone call but never called Sands back.

The news in January that Mondavi's board had forced Michael out as chairman drew the Sandses' attention again. The first thing they did was assign Constellation staffers to develop a detailed financial, strategic, and operational portrait of what the companies would look like combined. When Mondavi's recap hit the news in August, the speculation was that the board meant to sell Woodbridge.

The Sandses, meanwhile, had deeper sources in Napa than many others in the industry. Their top man, a talented and blunt-spoken executive named Jon Moramarco, had recently replaced Agustin Huneeus Jr. as head of the company's fine-wine division. Ahead of the rest of the industry, the Sands brothers learned that Mondavi's board planned to sell its fine-wine business.

The only way, the Sandses reasoned, that the Mondavis would have agreed to such a plan was if there was an understanding in place that they'd be allowed to bid for the fine-wine assets. But as Robert Sands, with his legal background, pointed out, "you cannot prewire a deal" under SEC rules: Any auction would have to be conducted as an arm's-length transaction.

By then, the Sandses also understood the nature of the Class B shareholders' "voting agreement" with the board: While much of the industry believed that the Mondavis still wielded significant voting power, the Sandses saw that the opposite was true. By signing the agreement that turned over their votes to the outside directors, the family shareholders had given up the power to block any board initiative. It was Ted Hall and the outside directors—not the Mondavis—who were calling the shots.

The Sandses also knew that even if they had been able to act as a voting bloc, the Mondavi family was fighting itself. Some of the Sandses' advisors joked that the Mondavis were a real-life *Falcon Crest*, referring to the 1980s prime-time soap opera about the scheming and bickering of wealthy wine families in northern California.

The way the Sandses and their advisors saw it, Michael felt he had never been given proper credit for increasing the size and the profitability of the company. They figured that Timothy was more interested in making fine wines than profits and that Marcia was more intent on preserving the original family estate than in maximizing shareholder value. Robert, for his part, just wanted his children to get along and apparently worried about the younger children, Timothy and Marcia. But they sensed that Robert was less concerned about Michael, perhaps because he felt his eldest son could take care of himself.

More intriguing to the Sandses and their advisors was that Michael, unlike his siblings, seemed to be signaling the market that he, for one, hoped to cash out at the highest price possible. His interview with the *Los Angeles Times* could be interpreted that way, since it highlighted the fact that the assets were for sale. But an even clearer signal came from Michael's investment banker at Perseus Group, who reached out to the Sandses and a wide variety of other potential buyers through back channels, intending to drum up interest in a sale. True to the Mondavi history of palace intrigues, Michael's action came at a time when his brother and sister were desperately hoping to buy back the Oakville winery.

Was this Michael's method of exacting payback for Marcia's betrayal of him? Whether his back-channel approach to Constellation was motivated by his desire for reprisal or simply an effort to drum up a higher sales price, Michael's communication had its desired effect. The Sandses realized that the Mondavis had turned against one another, and, better still, they seemed to have found an ally in Michael.

The "war room" at Constellation was windowless and buried deep in the interior of the building. Oil paintings of two generations of Sandses decorated its walls—"Mack," wearing thick black eyeglasses, a red tie, and a plain tan suit, and, hanging near him, his son Marvin, wearing a dove-gray suit, framed by a pair of velvet curtains, and with a glass of red wine nearby. Canandaigua Lake, painted in classic Italianate Renaissance style, provided the backdrop for Marvin's portrait, as if the Sandses were the Medicis of the Finger Lakes region. Outside, on the wall leading to the Sandses' executive conference room, was an oil portrait of Robert, wearing a dark suit less grand than his father's, but not quite as austere as Mack's. Richard's portrait had not been painted yet.

Richard's passion for wood infused the war room, which in more peaceful times was used as a boardroom. Its long conference table was a deeply polished dark wood bordered by fine inlay. A large video-conference screen dominated one end, and against another wall was a display of ornate crystal wineglasses, some delicately etched, others tinted in the hue of bloodred.

By October, the Sandses were meeting every day with a large team of advisors. They had retained Merrill Lynch's investment banking team, which was headed by William Rifkin, a veteran of many hostile deals and buyouts during the 1980s. They also brought on the most famous takeover lawyer in the U.S.: Martin Lipton, a partner of the New York law firm Wachtell, Lipton, Rosen and Katz, who is widely credited with inventing the so-called poison-pill takeover defense in 1982. At a time when there were fewer takeovers taking place than in the past, it was Robert, with his background in law, who sensed that Constellation's pursuit of Mondavi might turn hostile.

The Sandses' first approach was neither hostile nor friendly. On October 12, Richard Sands called Ted Hall, laying out Constellation's offer to pay $53 for Mondavi's Class A shares—a 37 percent premium over the price that the stock was trading in the days before the call. They were employing a tactic known in the investment banking world as a "bear hug"—a strong embrace that Constellation hoped would be too compelling for Mondavi's board to refuse. But Hall's response was not what Sands had hoped for. "We're not for sale," Mondavi's chairman told him. Hall suspected that by calling him at his office on the Columbus Day holiday, Sands was trying to ambush him. Politely noncommittal until he could relay the approach to Mondavi's directors, Hall hung up as soon as he could, avoiding what he sensed was a trap to draw him into discussions.

The Sands brothers and their advisors quickly reconvened in the war room to discuss their next move. They decided to send Hall a letter that same day, reiterating Constellation's offer and suggesting that the two companies' talks remain confidential. The letter, signed by Richard Sands, contained a veiled threat: "We believe your stockholders would be surprised that you were so dismissive of our proposal as they would regard our proposal as just such a superior alternative and would strongly prefer our plan to the proposed recapitalization and restructuring."

In not very subtle terms, the missive implied that Ted Hall, who had developed an expertise in corporate governance during his years at McKinsey and Company, was failing to uphold his own fiduciary duties by rejecting the offer so quickly. It also hinted that if Hall did not share the information of Constellation's offer with the entire Mondavi board, the Sandses would escalate their private parry into a public duel.

Constellation's advisors had put some thought into the psychological aspects of the deal. They'd investigated Hall's background and arrived at a series of assumptions about the personal motives of Mondavi's gruff chairman, who had retired from McKinsey in his fifties. For one thing, they learned that he had some expensive hobbies: including ocean sailing, running a sprawling ranch in Napa, and the costly business of launching his Long Meadow Ranch wines in a crowded and competitive market.

Recalling the old saying in the wine business that to make a small fortune, you need to start with a large one, the Sandses' advisors reasoned that Hall preferred to keep his lucrative and prestigious position as Mondavi's chairman, since it paid him a $50,000 monthly retainer fee plus cash bonus of at least $400,000 a year. They figured he did not want to lose that position.

They also believed that Hall's loyalty lay with Robert, rather than his children. By that time, the Sandses and their advisors had some understanding of the financial bind that Robert's philanthropic giving had put him in. So they reasoned that while Hall personally might have preferred to remain in his job as Mondavi's chairman, Hall knew enough about corporate governance and was sufficiently concerned about preserving Robert's reputation that he must eventually take their offer seriously.

Coached by the New York public relations man Gershon Kekst, another veteran of the takeover wars of the 1980s, Hall countered with two letters of his own, acknowledging receipt of the offer and promising to convene a board meeting to discuss it. Two days passed with no word. So Richard Sands sent another letter, this time turning up the volume by a few notches. Sands warned Hall that if Mondavi pursued its restructuring plan or began selling off assets, that would "adversely affect the premium we can make available to your shareholders," adding the kicker that "we believe that any such action would be contrary to your fiduciary duties while our offer is pending."

Hall refused to be bullied by the Sandses into haste. A leisurely four days later, on October 18, Mondavi's board finally held a meeting by conference call to discuss Constellation's offer. Hall pulled in his investment bankers from Citicorp and they advised that Mondavi begin shopping itself around to other potential buyers. Then, in a move intended to preempt the possibility that Constellation would go public with its offer, Hall released the scantest details of an offer to the press, emphasizing that the company had not rejected it but would continue to look at all of its options. Somewhat unusually, Hall refused to reveal the name of the suitor or the price it was offering.

That was interpreted by the Sands team as a move that amounted to Mondavi's hoisting a For Sale sign above its headquarters and soliciting bids. From Hall's perspective, it was a key move in his effort to wring the highest possible price from Constellation. The very next day, on

October 19, Constellation went public with its $970 million offer for Mondavi. In a sign that investors took it seriously, Mondavi's stock soared 30 percent, to $52.18, on the news.

In a conference call with analysts to discuss Constellation's bid, Sands delivered a diatribe that was sure to be picked up in the next day's papers: "We are very concerned about the Mondavi business being torn apart. I mean, you basically have to crush grapes to make good wine, but you don't have to crush a wine company to make shareholder value." Following the morale-gutting layoffs at Mondavi, the Sandses hoped to position themselves as a white knight—rescuing the company from the hands of Ted Hall and Greg Evans.

A week later, Hall boarded a jet to New York. He was on his way to London to meet with the British drinks giant Diageo to discuss whether it might be interested in buying all or parts of Mondavi. He agreed to stop in New York on the way, where he and Greg Evans would meet the Sands brothers, accompanied by their investment banker, William Rifkin, and Mondavi's banker, Leon Kalvaria. The opposing sides met at the Harmonie Club on East Sixtieth Street, a building designed by the Gilded Age architect Stanford White and across the street from Manhattan's famed Metropolitan Club.

Founded in 1852 by wealthy Jews who were not welcomed at other clubs, the Harmonie Club had become a locus of a group that became known as "Our Crowd"—New York's German Jewish establishment. With a covered awning leading to a discreet entry, the club's entrance gallery was richly furnished in dark woods and marble. Pale stems of phalaenopsis orchids brightened the dark space and Hall and Evans walked past a list of members engraved in brass: The names included Federal Reserve chairman Alan Greenspan, Citibank's Sanford Weill, assorted Solomons, Strauses, and Rothschilds, and Leon Kalvaria, the party's host for the evening. If the Sandses, who were also Jewish, hoped that Hall and Evans would realize they were no longer on their home turf, the Harmonie Club conveyed that message powerfully.

Hall was no country bumpkin, despite the scuffed leather boots he wore at the ranch. During the course of his twenty-seven-year career at McKinsey, he had wrestled with boards and bankers representing some of the world's most powerful companies. As the worldwide head of McKinsey's finance practice in the 1980s, he was involved in some big deals, including the $11.6 billion takeover of First Interstate Bancorp by Wells Fargo and Company in 1996, the largest U.S. bank merger in history at the time.

Evans, on the other hand, gave the impression to the other side that he was somewhat intimidated by the company and his surroundings. The group adjourned to a private dining room at around eight P.M., and Evans said very little over the course of the two- to three-hour dinner. He sat tensely as the Sandses made their pitch.

Throughout the meal, which was held at a round table, Richard Sands remained businesslike and made a point of emphasizing the positive aspects of the way Evans had run the business, being careful not to imply that Constellation would jettison him as CEO if it succeeded in taking Mondavi over. Sands also promised to keep the business intact, which he suspected was what Evans may have privately preferred.

But what the Sandses really wanted from that meeting was to convince Hall to give them forty-eight hours to conduct due diligence before continuing to beat the bushes for counterbids. They knew Hall was shopping the company around and they wanted a chance to prowl through Mondavi's operations before raising their offer. Hall, in turn, spent the evening laying out the rationale for the company's overhaul, including its recapitalization and the move to Delaware. The two sides ended the evening at an impasse.

A few days later, the Sandses' investment bankers let Mondavi's advisors know that Constellation planned to file documents with the SEC, which would lay groundwork for a proxy battle, a contest for control of a company in which rival groups seek support from a company's shareholders through proxies to back a takeover attempt. The bankers warned that unless they immediately began negotiating a merger agreement, the Sandses would use that hardball tactic to get arguably the most famous brand name in America's burgeoning fine-wine business. Not only would capturing Mondavi help Constellation grow its upscale operation, but the deal would resonate with symbolism—vaulting the Sandses from makers of gutter wines to the owners of a company named after the industry's most visible leader.

Hall, for one, did not take the threat of launching a proxy fight seriously, since the voting agreement that the Mondavis had signed in August handed over effective control of the majority of shares to the oustide directors. In the following days, the pressure mounted on Mondavi's chairman.

Curt, intensely focused, and demanding, Hall kept his secretary and Mondavi staffers working late into the night without notice. He didn't cave in to Constellation's pressure tactics that evening at the Harmonie Club, but agreed soon after following further discussions of the terms. Acting on the advice of Mondavi's legal team, he insisted on building a back door into the contract: If a better offer came along, he wanted the freedom to accept it. Hall also put pressure on Constellation and its advisors to move quickly by actively cutting other potential buyers. At Constellation, as many as thirty advisors huddled in the Sandses' war room, working late into the night crafting their strategy for the next day's negotiations with Hall and Mondavi.

On Sunday, October 31—Halloween—Constellation and Mondavi inked a confidentiality agreement with limited standstill provisions. The deal was nearly done. Knowing that gossip in Napa Valley spread quickly, the group from Merrill visited Latour Court and Oakville over the weekend, hoping not to draw too much attention or alert other potential buyers. In a ghoulish way, it probably helped their cause when Napa was shaken by a grisly double murder in the early hours following Halloween night. The front page of *The Napa Valley Register* was dominated by the stabbings of two young women. The team from Merrill managed to slip out of town quietly.

Before his troops had even begun their due diligence at Mondavi, Sands cranked the pressure up another notch. He raised his company's offer to $55.00 a share for the Class A stock and $64.08 a share for the Class B—16.5 percent higher than the existing premium paid to Robert, Michael, Marcia, Timothy, and the other Class B shareholders under Hall's plan. Constellation had made its offer before Hall's plan to swap the Class B for the Class A shares could take place. At the same time, Sands warned Mondavi's board he would launch a proxy fight in just two days, by the morning of November 3, unless it agreed to a deal.

This time, Hall didn't delay in organizing a conference call with Mondavi's directors. Not only was the higher price going to be hard to refuse, but the company's efforts to drum up a counterbid had failed. Although it meant that his carefully laid plan to break up the company and permit the Mondavis to bid for some parts of it had failed, Hall faced a clear-cut obligation to get the highest price he could for shareholders.

By nine A.M. Pacific time, he had updated all of the directors, including Timothy and Marcia, about Constellation's sweetened offer. Citicorp also briefed the group on how its efforts to beat the bushes for other buyers had fared. Potential purchasers such as Pernod Ricard, Diageo, and Kendall-Jackson all took a pass on bidding for parts or all of the company. Several concluded they couldn't top Constellation's offer. Although Timothy and Marcia had hired Deutsche Bank as their investment banker, the Mondavi siblings' bid never got off the ground.

With the Mondavis out of the picture, the best countermove, in Citicorp's view, was to push for a higher price with Constellation in hopes of buying more time to drum up interest. So after Mondavi's directors disconnected from the conference call, Citicorp, Hall, and Evans contacted Constellation. Sensing victory, the Sandses agreed to raise their offer once again, this time to $56.50 a share for the Class A shares and $65.82 for the Class B. One of the conditions of the offer, though, was that Robert, Timothy, and Marcia sign papers compelling them to support the deal, which would squash any later actions they might take if they experienced sellers' regret. Since Michael was no longer a Mondavi director, he and his lawyer were separately communicating with Constellation. From the perspective of the Sandses' advisors, Michael clearly supported the deal.

Meanwhile, Mondavi's outside directors instructed Hall and Evans to find out whether Constellation still planned to announce its proxy battle the next morning: When they reconvened by telephone at seven-fifteen P.M. that night, the Citicorp bankers told them that the Sands brothers would hold their fire, as the companies were close to finalizing a definitive merger. Sitting in his underwear in a hotel room, Hall participated in the call from London, where it was the middle of the night. Working with much of the negotiating taking place between lawyers and bankers in New York, the two sides hammered out the agreement.

At nine A.M. the next morning, Mondavi's tired board once again convened by telephone. Morgan Stanley stamped the deal with a "fairness opinion" and the 16 percent premium for the Class B shares won approval from outside consultants. Timothy, Marcia, and Robert all agreed to sign the "support agreement," although once again the Mondavi siblings expressed their unhappiness with the takeover by abstaining from the board's otherwise unanimous vote to accept Constellation's offer.

The deal meant an enormous payday for Robert's children. Michael's stock was worth roughly $85 million. With the value of his options and other bonuses added in, Michael's take was worth more than $100 million, while Timothy's somewhat less than $59 million and Marcia's the highest at about $107 million. Robert himself would net around $70 million—most of which was already committed to his various philanthropies. Under Ted Hall's chairmanship, Mondavi's stock had soared from $38.32 a share when he arrived to $65.82 for the B shares from Constellation's offer.

Yet even so, Timothy and Marcia, along with many Mondavi employees, were in tears as the family legacy was sold off to the highest bidder. Their vision of dynastic continuity had collided brutally with the unbridled goals of the free market and they felt betrayed by the board of directors.

On November 4, George W. Bush's victory in the presidential election dominated the headlines of three of the four newspapers on sale on the covered porch of the 123-year-old Oakville Grocery. But the fourth paper, *The Napa Valley Register*, chose to run a banner headline that declared, "Mondavi Agrees to $1.35 Billion Buyout Bid." On that gray, overcast morning, the Mondavi news sent chills through the valley.

The parking lot in front of the Robert Mondavi Winery was nearly empty that morning and the hospitality staffers at the elegant To Kalon tasting room were all alone. Over the mantel of the fireplace hung a photo of Robert with his arms slung over his parents' shoulders, beaming with pride on the day he graduated from Stanford. Another photo showed Rosa and Cesare on their wedding day in Sassoferrato, Italy.

With a gas fire burning, an Oriental rug on the floor, and a dining table set as if the Mondavi family were about to appear any minute for dinner, the To Kalon was the utmost expression of the personal history and style the Mondavi family brought to their business. To visit the tasting room felt as if one were visiting the Mondavi family's home.

The previous day, Jean-Michel Valette, the chairman of the Oakville winery, had called together its employees in the Vineyard Room to tell them the news of the takeover. One of the first questions was whether the Sandses planned to halt the ongoing layoffs that were planned for the operation. Would Constellation rescue them and stop the bloodletting? Valette delivered the bad news that the cuts would continue and that the Sandses were likely to slash Oakville's production to less than half its current case sales.

The takeover shattered any remaining hopes that some Mondavi family members would buy back Oakville and restore it to its glory. The early talk from Timothy and Marcia proved empty: They never submitted to the board a formal proposal to purchase Oakville. In addition to Frank Farella's memo, the siblings also had a list of potential bankers and advisors provided to them early on in the process to help them make a bid.

Among employees, Greg Evans became the most obvious scapegoat for the company's fall. Some took perverse pleasure in the likelihood that Evans would be one of the hundreds of staffers who would lose their jobs because of the deal. The company's headcount had shrunk dramatically in the last year that Evans was in charge, with about eleven hundred employees in early 2004 dropping to some three hundred or so about a year later. That morning, a longtime Mondavi employee huddled at her desk. She had quietly wept for the end of an era. "The amount of waste is incredible. Look at all the empty cubicles upstairs," she said. "We've all been such a family."

Timothy, too, suffered as the days darkened and the grapevines lost their leaves. The back problem that had forced him to hobble into the Harvest Inn in August lingered on. The uncertainty weighed on him heavily. It was not clear whether he would have a job at the company when Constellation took over. Could he rebuild a career on his own in his early fifties? Could he and the rest of the family somehow find a way to save face from the board's humiliatingly public lack of confidence in himself and Michael? Timothy clung to the idea that he and perhaps his sister and father could pool some of their money to start over again, this time on a smaller, more manageable scale. They hoped to buy 240 acres of the To Kalon vineyard from Constellation, particularly "Marjorie's Vineyard," where their mother's ashes had been scattered.

Timothy and Robert confided to friends and family members that they wished they'd never taken the company public in the first place. But they couldn't help taking some pleasure in the entrepreneurial energy of the next generation of Mondavis. At an afternoon barbecue at Timothy's home on Wappo Hill around harvest time that fall, Timothy's son Carlo brought his grandfather a ten-page draft of a plan he'd written for a luxury skin care line based on grape pomace. Named after his great-grandfather and grandfather, Carlo Cesare Robert Mondavi wanted to test out the idea against Robert's marketing instincts. Carlo knew that a company in France was successfully selling a skin care line based on pomace, which is the remaining skin, seeds, and stems of grapes after the fruit is crushed to make wine. He also knew that the women in his family seemed to be buying antiaging products.

Sitting on his father's terrace, overlooking an orchard, Carlo wanted to show his grandfather his plan. "Nonno, I want you to take a look at this. What do you think?" Carlo said. Robert took a look and grew excited by the opportunity. Not only did it make use of a by-product of winemaking, but Robert knew that his friends in the Lauder family were flourishing. "Carlo, you have to do this," Robert said. "It would be a shame if you didn't."

Michael and Rob, meanwhile, were moving ahead toward the first release of their own wine, made from their family's Atlas Peak vineyard. As a surprise for his mother, who had developed a taste for dry French roses, Rob decided to use juice from crushed Cabernet grapes. It turned out so well, they decided to release it under a new brand, I'M. (Constellation would own the Robert Mondavi name once the sale was completed.) They made it at the Napa Wine Company at Oakville Cross, a custom crushing company kitty-corner from the Oakville Grocery on Highway 29 and not far from the Robert Mondavi Winery. In a small valley where people talked, the news of their venture quickly leaked out. At the same time, Michael was setting up Folio, an import company. Rumor had it that he was hiring some of Mondavi's salesman and, in the wake of the Constellation takeover, was planning to approach Italy's Frescobaldi about representing their wines in the U.S. market.

Although Michael maintained a tougher exterior than his brother did, he suffered as much as, or more than, anyone else in the family from the board coup that had ripped the company away from the Mondavi family's control. Always the hard-charging sales executive who could close the deal through sheer force of will and self-confidence, this time Michael was unable to stop what was happening and instead chose to try to make the most of it. Although he immediately threw himself into new ventures, he was infusing the accumulated years of anger and sense of betrayal into his decision. Much of his pain grew out of his complex feelings toward Robert, who had always been his boss but could not be his father when he needed him most. He now realized he would never please his perfectionist father. With the help of a new therapist whom he starting seeing after his ouster, he came to believe he'd been Robert's victim and spent as little time with his father as possible. Michael was determined to break the cycle and avoid making the same mistakes with his own children.

The effect on Robert was shocking to those who hadn't seen him recently. Nine months earlier, Robert, by then a nonagenarian, was still exhibiting the physical strength and joie de vivre of a man two decades younger. During a trip in March of 2004, for instance, he and Margrit had been joined by Peggy Loar, the director of the American Center for Wine and Food, and her fiancé, on a two-week trip to Southeast Asia. Since Robert had had both knees replaced, the others asked him, "Bob, do you want to wait in the car?" "Nope," he replied, and proceeded to eagerly climb a steep flight of steps to visit an ancient temple in Cambodia.

But by late 2004, Robert had gone dramatically downhill and seemed to reach his true physical age almost overnight. He was now relying heavily on Margrit to help him understand what was being said, to gently take his arm to guide him to where he was going, to organize their still-busy social life, and to make sure he was always turned out in his legendary dapper style. Robert now shuffled slowly, more than ever isolated by his deafness. Some of their friends confided to Margrit that they were convinced Robert's decline was hastened by the psychological effects the company's sale had had on him. Some wondered whether his worsening deafness was in part psychosomatic: his mind's way of shutting out the painful realities.

Ted Hall tried to reach out to Robert during that time, arranging a lunch with him and Margrit in the Cliff May Room, a small, cloistered room with a low, slanted ceiling where hospitality staffers would sometimes retreat during the summer months to escape the heat. The lunch took place on Wednesday, November 24, the day before Thanksgiving, and Hall hoped to buoy their spirits. Looking out onto the lawn and vineyards though a window with wooden bars on it, the threesome discussed their holiday plans: Hall was hosting a family reunion at Long Meadow Ranch, while Robert and Margrit would spend the day with Margrit's daughter, Annie, and her family. According to Hall, Robert had just learned to their dismay through a secretary that Timothy had gone to Hawaii and thus would not be joining them. For years, as well, Michael and his family had not shared holidays with Robert and Margrit. Hall recalls thinking at the time, "He was a man without a family."

Margrit, who had had gum surgery that morning and was still numb from novocaine during the lunch, felt a heavy sadness. Earlier that day, Robert, accompanied by Frank Farella, had signed some papers related to the sale of his stock holdings. Margrit still hoped the family would pull together somehow, asking during the lunch, "Can't anyone salvage something here?" Hall turned the conversation to what Robert would be able to do after the deal was finalized, including fulfill his philanthropic commitments and continue his role as spokesperson for the winery. Margrit, who recalls that Hall tried to cheer them up by suggesting they could fly first class or go on cruises, sat silently, thinking to herself how little Hall understood what motivated her husband, which was never money, and ruing that the family had ever left matters to people who operated more like calculating machines than passionate human beings.

CHAPTER TWENTY-THREE

Damage Control, December 2004 to April 2005

The legal endgame played out with cold dispassion in a Napa courtroom a few days before Christmas. The Mondavi loyalists clung to one last hope: a court challenge to block the takeover. On Monday, December 20, a group of plaintiffs' attorneys, representing Connecticut-based Bamboo Partners and other Class A shareholders in Mondavi Corporation, sought an injunction to halt the sale, which was set to be finalized two days later. The plaintiffs' attorneys huddled together outside Courtroom E of the courthouse of Napa Superior Court, a modern cube of a building that activists decried for blocking views of the Napa River.

Frank Gregorek, Bamboo's tightly wound general counsel, led the lawyers who sought to block the sale. Their opponents were a group of highly paid attorneys from some of the nation's leading law firms, charged with defending Mondavi's corporate officers and Constellation and allowing the sale to go through.

The two sides had plenty of time to look each other over. Although the hearing was scheduled for nine A.M., the Honorable W. Scott

Snowden, the presiding judge of the Napa Superior Court, kept the two sides waiting outside the courtroom for nearly an hour and a half because of a crowded calendar. Dark-suited lawyers whose billing rates hovered at $500 an hour or more paced the floor outside a courtroom that was normally used to hear cases involving burglaries, car theft, drug offences, and spousal abuse.

In the weeks leading up to this hearing, the plaintiffs' attorneys had jetted between New York, San Francisco, Toronto, and Napa, deposing Mondavi's directors. Their goal was to gather enough evidence to support their contention that the interests of the small shareholders in the Robert Mondavi Corporation had been ignored by the directors, who instead had sold out on terms favorable to the Class B shareholders of the Mondavi family.

For Napa Valley, which had never before experienced a billion-dollar-plus takeover, the stakes were enormous. If the judge granted the injunction that the plaintiffs were asking for, it was unclear what would happen next. The deal could be scuttled, sinking Mondavi's stock. By halting or preventing the takeover, its opponents could save, at least temporarily, several hundred jobs that were slated to be eliminated under Constellation's ownership. And if the plaintiffs were able to present convincing evidence the board had indeed acted unfairly toward Mondavi's minority shareholders, it was likely that Hall, Greer, and other board members might be drawn into a lengthy court brawl—something that they hoped to avoid.

Judge Snowden finally called the combatants into his courtroom. Jeff Westerman, representing Bamboo Partners, wasted no time. Mondavi's sale to Constellation, he argued, was a "self-dealing transaction" on the part of the board in which "no one was looking out for the interests of the A shareholders." He then suggested a less draconian option: allowing the sale to proceed, but putting the $50 million difference in the price paid to the A and B shareholders into a trust.

Frank Gregorek, from Wolf Haldenstein Adler Freeman and Herz LLP, then followed up, reading to the judge Philip Greer's deposition, taken on Friday morning in San Francisco, just three days before the hearing. When asked whether he was looking out for the interests of the minority shareholders, Greer had answered, "I personally never thought, 'I'm a representative of the A's here and I want to get as much as I can for the A's.'" Greer said, "I just wanted to do a deal."

If this was intended to be the "smoking gun" that the plaintiffs' attorneys had hoped for, it was not an effective one. Likewise, Gregorek also argued that the board and the bankers on the deal were riddled with conflict of interest. Specifically, he mentioned Ted Hall's scheduled bonus of $2.5 million if the deal closed, suggesting that Hall was motivated by the prospect of personal financial gain. Judge Snowden, who had a skeptical look on his face, was not swayed.

After a short break, Amelia Starr rose to argue Robert Mondavi Corporation and Constellation's case. A partner with the prestigious firm of Davis, Polk and Wardwell, Starr rapidly focused on the realpolitiks of the situation. She said Mondavi's proxy solicitation firm had informed her that as of two-thirty Eastern Time that afternoon, the vast majority of the Class A shareholders who had already voted were in favor of the deal—with only about fifty thousand shares, or one-half a percentage of the total shares outstanding, voting against it.

She also delivered what might have been read as a veiled threat: If there were a material event, such as an injunction, blocking the sale, Constellation could walk away from the deal: Neither the A nor the B shareholders would get their premium. Not only that, she continued, but the price of Mondavi stock might tank on the news of the court's decision. And, in a final, understated tone, she managed to undercut the credibility of the lead plaintiff in the case, referring to Bamboo Partners as "professional plaintiffs" with just one hundred shares of Mondavi stock, and which had sued companies fifteen times in the past year. Constellation's lawyer weighed in, too, noting that the New York–based company was "ready, willing, and able to write a check for the 99.999 percent of the shares of Mondavi not represented in this courtroom. We are ready to do that this week. And as Ms. Starr has pointed out, an auction has been conducted . . . and the vote is running a hundred to one in favor of the transaction."

Judge Snowden called a short break. Upon returning to the courtroom he delivered the news to the lawyers, executives, and journalists who had gathered there: He would not block the deal. But the judge refused to throw out all the claims, which meant that the case would still hang over the deal and consume time and resources.

Less than forty-eight hours later, as thick mist swirled through the canyons of San Francisco's financial district, small groups of people headed for the last annual meeting of the Robert Mondavi Corporation. Since it was December 22, just three days before Christmas, many office workers had taken the week off. But the decision to hold the gathering at the Omni Hotel—fifty-eight miles away from Oakville—at eight-thirty A.M., was a deliberate choice on the part of Ted Hall to mini-mize attendance after the company received several threats. The strategy worked: Only a fraction of the company's shareholders turned up to wit-ness the last hours of the Robert Mondavi Corporation as an indepen-dent company.

The meeting was held in a large, cheerless ballroom. Not a single member of the Mondavi family came. Between shareholders, advisors, and company executives, perhaps fifty people gathered in a room that had been set up to accommodate three hundred. Armed security guards were posted at the front of the room. Two artificial Christmas trees were mournfully tucked into the back corners of the room. The Mondavi family had shunned the meeting because they abhorred the very thought of being in the same room as Hall and Evans. Greer, who attended, felt as if he were at a funeral.

Promptly at eight-thirty A.M., Evans rose to the podium set at the front of the ballroom and, reading from a script, laid out the meeting's agenda. His clipped presentation lasted less than fifteen minutes. Toward the end, looking uncomfortably around the room, he asked the small group of shareholders if there were any questions. One asked Greg Evans to comment on reports of further layoffs among winery workers and asked whether some of the longtime employees who had been let go might be hired back. Evans declined to comment.

The rest of the meeting's agenda was completed and Evans an-nounced that more than 80 percent of the votes cast by the Class A share-holders and 94 percent of the votes cast by the Class B shareholders favored the sale of the company to Constellation. With that cold tally, the battle that had gripped Napa Valley and the wine world for the past four months came to an end.

As he stood in front of the ornate entrance of the Omni Hotel, Evans cut a solitary figure. For most of his working life, he and his family had woven their lives into the fabric of the valley, as well as into the extended Mondavi family. For him, the meeting meant the end of a long career with California's most famous wine producer. When he returned home that day to Napa Valley, he knew he was being blamed by some members of the Mondavi family and some Mondavi alumni for what they considered a hostile takeover. Not only had Evans lost his job as CEO of the most famous company in the valley; he and his wife, Anne, a local writer, also faced the prospect of continuing to live in a place where he would be shadowed for his role in the takeover.

Unlike Hall, who had been awarded a $2.5 million bonus for his work as non-executive chairman in 2004, Evans's even heftier payoff helped compensate him for the painful months and years of grappling with Michael and Timothy. He received a salary of some $562,000 and a bonus of less than one-tenth of what Ted Hall had received—getting a relatively meager $156,000 for his efforts in 2004. But unlike Hall, Evans had built up a sizable stock holding in the company over the years. His 218,709 shares, which included options, were worth $12.35 million before subtracting out the options' strike price. As Evans waited on the sidewalk for his car to be retrieved by the valet, Ted Hall's had been returned—a Mercedes 550 sedan with the license plate LMR WINE—short for "Long Meadow Ranch Wine." Ted Hall flew down California Street in his snazzy sedan as Greg Evans stared pensively down at his overnight case on rollers.

The rainy season in early 2005 was unusually long, with days of unceasing gray. Even the bright, regenerative bloom of yellow mustard, normally such a welcome sight between the bare vines in February and March, seemed damply muted. The energy and creativity that had infused the Robert Mondavi Winery for so many years was seeping away as Constellation laid off hundreds of longtime Mondavi employees. Those who remained girded themselves for the next round of cuts.

A debate had begun over whether Highway 29, the artery that sliced the valley lengthwise from south to north, should be dedicated to the Robert Mondavi Winery. For advocates of the idea such as state senator Wesley Chesbro, supported by Robert's longtime lobbyist Herb Schmidt, the idea backfired in the worst possible way. Not only did several wine trade groups give it the cold shoulder, but the proposal sparked angry letters and editorials, most notably one from Michael Dunsford, Calistoga City Council member, in *The St. Helena Star*, explaining why the council unanimously voted down the idea.

"Calistogans have great admiration for Bob Mondavi," wrote Dunsford. "However, we must not forget that Robert Mondavi now represents big business and is now a corporate icon. His winery recently sold for $1.3 billion. That's billion with a *B*. . . . It is the small family wineries that are now the treasures of the Napa Valley and they should not be overshadowed. God Bless Bob Mondavi, but let's not Disneyfy the Napa Valley and turn it into Mondaviland."

Dunsford's prickly comments came on top of an even more searing public criticism of Robert Mondavi and the wine empire he'd built. The film director Jonathan Nossiter, whose other credits were *Signs and Wonders* and *Sunday*, had decided to explore the subject of globalization through the lens of the wine industry in a film called *Mondovino*. In part because of Mondavi's well-publicized retreat from Languedoc, he cast the Robert Mondavi Corporation as one of the primary villains, portraying it as a corporate imperialist, intent on spreading mediocre wine around the world.

In the poorly lit interview with Michael, shot in the newly refurbished To Kalon barrel room, Michael jokes about expanding Mondavi's sales not only around the globe but into outer space, in comments that reinforce the film's point of view about the superficiality and commercialism of corporate wine producers. "Ten, fifteen generations from now it would be great to see our heirs producing some wine on some other planets," Michael chuckles to the filmmaker while he's being filmed. "That could be kind of cool. Beam me up, Scotty, send me some wine from Mars or something."

Margrit and Robert had long felt pleasure on passing through the archway of the Oakville winery. But in recent months, that feeling had been replaced by a sense of edginess and dread. They rode an elevator up a floor and made their way into the thickly carpeted executive wing of the Oakville winery, passing one empty cubicle after another until they reached their side-by-side offices, guarded by secretaries who had survived the corporate putsch. They were stepping onto hostile turf from which so many of their old friends and employees had been banished.

The winery's head, Jean-Michel Valette, continued to occupy his nearby office under Constellation's ownership. Tia Butts, a Mondavi employee who had handled public relations for the Woodbridge brand and won a significant promotion in the aftermath of the layoffs, had been moved a few doors away. Chief among her many responsibilities was minding Robert and Margrit.

The couple had signed employment contracts with Constellation specifying that they would continue serving as ambassadors for the Robert Mondavi brand. That meant they would appear at public functions and hospitality events at the winery. But there was no doubt on either side that the arrangement was an uncomfortable one.

To make matters worse, it was growing increasingly difficult for Robert to play the ambassadorial role he had performed so masterfully for so many years. His hearing had deteriorated, and by March, some longtime friends had begun to realize his mental acuity was slipping even further. On bad days, he was having trouble expressing complex thoughts and seemed unable to follow the thread of a conversation. Timothy suspected his father had suffered a series of small strokes. Margrit worked hard to draw her husband out of the isolation imposed by his hearing problem, particularly in front of Butts and other Constellation representatives. But following a painful and ultimately unsuccessful attempt at an interview with a journalist, Margrit realized that the time had come to limit his public appearances to situations where he was only obliged to shake hands and say a few words.

Despite these concerns, Robert's grandson Carlo brought a group of Asian visitors to meet his grandfather on February 19, 2004. A few months earlier, Carlo had detailed his wine family lineage on a private offering memorandum to raise money for the luxury skin-care company he had founded, Davi Skin Inc. Issued on November 1, 2004, just days before Constellation entered into an agreement to acquire the Robert Mondavi Corporation, the memorandum sought to raise $10 million. One of the selling points for the stock was that Robert, Timothy, and Michael were all listed on the company's executive advisory board, assisting Carlo, who was then just twenty-four years old, and the company's other officers to make "certain high level planning decisions."

A strapping six-foot-two snowboard champ, Carlo had founded the company in 2003. His partner in the company was his friend Josh LeVine, a fellow snowboarder who, like Carlo, had also gone pro for a time. Together, Carlo, LeVine, and the CEO they hired merged Davi Skin with a publicly traded Nevada shell company called MW Medical, in June 2004. Davi Skin became a penny stock.

Based in an office suite in Beverly Hills and incorporated in Nevada, the company had no products and its chairman, Carlo, had no experience in manufacturing or selling skin-care products. Nor did he have a college degree. But Carlo did have one big advantage: the Mondavi name. Although the company had yet to sell a single product, it did have a beautifully constructed Web site, with soft music, burgundy tones, and a crest, suggesting Carlo Cesare Mondavi's place as a member of America's leading wine dynasty. The site also featured a black-and-white photo of Carlo sitting next to Robert, both holding glasses of red wine, that had been taken a year earlier at Opus One. Extolling the Mondavi family's long history in winemaking, the site included both Robert's and his grandson's signatures.

So when Carlo brought a group of potential investors to the Napa Valley that February, they had every reason to expect to meet Carlo's family. And they did, enjoying a private dinner with Robert and Margrit at their Wappo Hill home, as well as a tour of the Robert Mondavi Winery and Opus One, which Carlo seemed to imply the family still owned and operated, which, of course, it didn't. Timothy joined his son and the group for a meal at the expensive restaurant Auberge du Soleil, perched on a hillside in Rutherford. During that grand tour, one of the potential investors, Takahiro Tashio, allegedly came to understand that Carlo had promised him that he could become a distributor for Opus One wines in Japan and also that Timothy and Robert were investing significant amounts of money in Carlo's business. Tashio, who speaks no English, relied on others in the group to translate for him. But he ended up investing about $965,000 in Davi Skin stock, apparently believing that the company had signed contracts for the rights to use the pomace from the Robert Mondavi Winery and Opus One. As a parting gift, Carlo offered the investors bottles of wine signed by Mondavi family members.

Some members of the Mondavi family, as well as Greg Evans and Mondavi's general counsel Michael K. Byers, had grown alarmed by Carlo's expansive business plans well before that visit. Byers warned Carlo several times and Ted Hall and the rest of the board were briefed on Carlo's plans, as well as the steps that had been taken to rein him in. Although his charisma, good looks, and entrepreneurial energy resembled those of Robert in his younger days, Carlo was also naive. Timothy warned him about using Robert's name in promoting his company, particularly because the Robert Mondavi brand name had belonged to Constellation since December 2004. What also bothered Timothy was that at least one of Carlo's business ideas, a Robert Mondavi–branded line of stemware, seemed the kind of overuse of the Robert Mondavi name he'd fought so hard against over the years.

Other members of the family were even more worried. Marcia warned Margrit, "If Carlo asks you to invest, don't do it!" Neither Robert nor Timothy invested in Davi Skin. Michael didn't, either, and he later told his nephew he did not want to serve as a figurehead on Davi Skin's executive advisory board, especially since they hadn't talked to each other in over a year. Michael thought highly of his nephew, but also felt that his naïveté made him vulnerable to unscrupulous people who would suck him dry.

The bleakness of that time was finally relieved by a week-long showering of awards and praise on Robert in April. By this time, workers had mowed the mustard in anticipation of bud break—the first sign of life from the bare vines. The Mondavis' own resurgence kicked off with a trip to New York, where Robert was one of six Americans honored by the Statue of Liberty–Ellis Island Foundation as a distinguished descendant of immigrants. Having made it on that trip was in itself a bit of a triumph. A few weeks earlier, he'd been hospitalized briefly for mild pneumonia. Timothy had been worried and called Michael, urging him to come visit his father in the hospital. Michael didn't go, since he was traveling. And before that, he'd had a mishap during a session with his personal trainer. He'd accidentally gone into the swimming pool at his home while wearing his hearing aids. The result was that these tiny yet crucial electronic devices shorted out.

While a seemingly minor inconvenience, the loaner hearing aids he tolerated for some weeks severely limited his ability to communicate with almost anyone except Margrit. To everyone's relief, by the time of the Ellis Island event, his own hearing aids had been fixed and returned to him. With Timothy and four of his children looking on, as well as Marcia, and longtime friend Warren Winiarski, Robert was presented with a framed copy of the original ship's passenger manifest, documenting the arrival of his father in New York aboard the *Vaderland*. Some sense of the stature this winemaker had reached could be measured in the other honorees that day: General Colin Powell, Astronaut Scott Parazynski, and Nobel Prize–winning physicist Murray Gell-Mann.

A few days later, the French ambassador to the U.S. gave Robert one

of the most coveted honors in the world: the medal of the Légion d'honneur. Established in 1802 by Napoléon Bonaparte, the French government has conferred the medal on only a few U.S. honorees, including the
late president Ronald Reagan, Colin Powell, and David Rockefeller.
Robert's ceremony took place closer to home, so that many more of the
Mondavi family's friends could attend. Those lucky enough to be invited
to the Sunday afternoon event at Opus One had received an invitation
with one of Margrit's watercolors, featuring a playful cherub waving an
American flag in one hand and a French flag in the other. Jointly hosted
by the French embassy and the Franco-Californian winery, the ceremony
and reception were to have been held outside on Opus One's grassy outer
forecourt, ringed by mature olive trees.

The overcast weather didn't cooperate, so the event was moved to a
utilitarian mezzanine, with cinder block walls and a resin-based floor.
Two soaring arrangements of red roses, white snowbells, and blue del-
phinium, set against a dramatic spray of magnolia leaves, provided relief
from the room's industrial feel, as did the U.S., California, French, and
EU flags hanging on the walls. A pair of sliding doors, large enough for
equipment and pallets of grapes to pass through once they'd been hoisted
up to the mezzanine floor, opened to a view of Opus One's Cabernet
vines, which were just beginning to sprout tiny green leaves, flecked delicately with pink at their tips. In front of the view, facing the rows of
seated guests, sat a pair of eighteenth-century French theater chairs.
They twinkled with their recent regilting and were upholstered in a
French drawing-room fabric; they looked like nothing less than thrones.

Most guests had arrived by three P.M. when Robert arrived, arm in
arm with Marcia. Slightly hunched over and walking unsteadily, he
looked shockingly small as he leaned against her for support. A glow of
good spirits infused him, and Robert's dapper pink silk tie suggested a
man who, despite his age, was meticulously cared for. Over the past difficult months, Robert had come to rely on Margrit even more heavily. Yet,
Marcia made the crucial entrance with her father, quickly guiding him to
his seat at the front of the room, with his back to the open doorway and
the mountains.

After making sure he was comfortably seated, Marcia then began to
work the crowd. Looking businesslike in an understated dark pantsuit
with a large pink flower in her lapel, her dark hair cut casually in a becoming style that brushed her jawline, she reached over to clasp the

hands of friends who were seated already and beamed at others who were too far to touch. She was assuming the role that Michael had long played as polished ambassador for the family and the winery.

Ten minutes passed and the guests started to grow restless, whispering to one another over what could have caused the delay. Timothy and the French delegation still hadn't arrived. Timothy's first wife, Dorothy, waited patiently in a seat on the aisle, about halfway back, and most of their five children were there to witness the honor to be bestowed on their grandfather. Carlo, in particular, stayed close to Robert. While the room quietly buzzed, it was difficult to ignore the empty front rows. They had been reserved for the French guests, as simultaneous-translation earphones rested on the seats. A few more minutes ticked by and Marcia made her way to the back and engaged the PR representatives in intense conversation, not hiding her exasperation.

Finally, about twenty minutes late, Timothy and the French delegation arrived. After their lunch in the Vineyard Room, the younger Mondavi son had led the delegation on a tour of the winery. They settled into their seats and David Pearson, Opus's CEO, rose to address the room at the podium. He thanked the French for coming and announced the honored guests—the French ambassador, the French consul general in San Francisco, five members of the French Senate, and members of the Mondavi family.

Then he noted who wasn't there—most conspicuously, the Baroness Philippine de Rothschild, who he reported was "distraught" at not being able to attend the event because of a previous commitment. Ironically, that commitment, he revealed, was a meeting of the Primum Familiae Vini, the "first families of wine," which was taking place in Moscow that weekend. Robert's old friend Piero Antinori had also declined the invitation for the same reason. Sadly, the Mondavis had been forced to resign from Primum Familiae Vini once they sold out to Constellation. If Robert had understood the nature of the baronness's other commitment, it surely would have been a bittersweet reminder of what his family had lost by selling out.

Timothy, wearing dark-framed tinted glasses and a sleekly tailored gray suit, rose to speak. Reading from prepared remarks in a high, slightly nasal voice, he stumbled over a quote from the wine writer Hugh Johnson. Unlike David Pearson's, Timothy's presentation was less fluid. But his sincerity was evident and his remarks heartfelt. His emergence from

Michael's shadow was welcomed that day by Robert and Margrit's friends, who'd watched Michael in the role of the heir apparent for many years. On this, one of the peak moments in Robert's life, Timothy was there to support his father.

The French ambassador, in turn, spoke in heavily accented English and praised Robert and his role in this French-Californian joint venture. He referred to Thomas Jefferson's penchant for French wine and expressed gratitude for Robert's efforts, including "the use of French oak wine barrels. Thank you!" he said, as the crowd chuckled. "We are appreciative of this smart move." Several times, he remarked that President Jacques Chirac himself had been intent on making sure that Robert should receive this honor. Then, amid all this goodwill, the ambassador made a faux pas that raised eyebrows. "We are deeply appreciative to your family—to your son and daughter and most particularly to your wife, Margrit Biever Mondavi."

Unintentionally, the ambassador had erased Michael from the Mondavi family in his remarks. During the cocktail chatter at the reception afterward, many guests quietly noted that Michael was absent from the ceremony that had conferred international recognition and great honor upon his father. The official explanation was that Michael was unable to attend because of a scheduling conflict. But the truth was that Michael didn't feel like putting himself through the potentially humiliating exercise of making small talk with his father and Margrit's friends as if nothing had happened. The Peter Mondavi family had also been invited and they, too, had chosen not to come.

Margrit took the seat of honor next to Robert where Marcia had been sitting. Robert stood up and took a few steps toward the center. With Timothy standing alongside him, the French ambassador pinned the gold medal, hung on red ribbon, to the left side of Robert's chest, just above his heart. Margrit captured the moment with a small camera. Robert then moved to the podium and said, "God bless all of you. . . . Very emotional. It's a wonderful thing for two countries such as France and America to work in harmony with each other."

Momentarily confused, Robert looked around and asked, "Where are you?"—searching for the ambassador, who was to his left.

"Oh, there you are," he said, when he caught sight of him.

It was a lighthearted moment and the guests smiled. Robert continued reading and then slowed for a moment. Timothy pointed to the

medal on his chest as a way to jog his memory that the subject at hand
was the medal, and Robert continued, noting that he felt optimistic, particularly "to work in harmony, for a change, instead of fight."

The crowd rose and began to applaud. The cinder block walls and
hard floor amplified the clapping. Then, a five-piece woodwind group
began playing the U.S. national anthem, followed by the French national
anthem, which elicited another round of applause. Waiters emerged with
trays of Riedel Vinum stemware, containing dark red pools of Opus One,
as well as more of the champagne. Tray after tray of delicacies appeared:
pan-seared wild salmon brushed with white truffle oil, Ahi tuna on lotus
root chips, Maine lobster salad served on purple Peruvian potatoes, and
duck confit with essence of thyme baked in puff pastry.

Forgoing the appetizers and the alcohol, Richard Sands, the chairman of Constellation Brands, left as soon as he could. That Sunday, he
was in the thick of negotiating his company's next possible deal—a joint
effort by Constellation and several partners to top a $14 billion acquisi-
tion of the British drinks giant Allied Domecq. Waiting for his car to take
him back to the airport, he clutched a phone to his ear. To make sure
none of the other guests waiting for the valets to deliver his car could
overhear him, he retreated down a dirt row, between trellised vines. His
young nephew waited on the curb. Staying to mingle was not his top pri-
ority that day.

Two days later, Robert Mondavi arrived at the imposing Victorian mansion occupied by the Culinary Institute of America in St. Helena, where
many of the valley's most powerful vintners would gather to pay tribute
that evening to his six extraordinary decades in Napa Valley.

With his bright red Légion d'honneur medal pinned to his chest,
Robert arrived shortly before five-thirty P.M. and hobbled into the small
elevator up to the second floor. On the floor above him, facing down into
the stairwell, a squat gentleman with an Old World face played the theme
from *The Godfather* on his accordion.

Its effect was to deepen the pathos of the moment. By having sold
out, Robert Mondavi was no longer, strictly speaking, a vintner—a
change that the Peter Mondavi side of the family were not averse to mentioning publicly on more than one occasion. Under the vintners' group's
rules, he was no longer eligible to be a member, though in recognition of
his many years of service, the group named him a "member emeritus."

Still, Robert was painfully aware that for the first time in more than six decades, he was not making wine. With his failing health, the vintners were aware this could be the last time they would see their old friend.

Robert entered the dark, echoing reception room, where the vintners had held their banquets and meetings for many years. Votive candles on round tables provided flickering light. The wooden-beamed ceiling and stone walls conveyed an atmosphere of intimacy, despite the hall's capacity to hold hundreds of people. Only winery owners were welcome, not their employees. Each had been asked to contribute a magnum of wine to the evening and some wonderful wines did indeed appear—such as an older vintage from the famed Martha's Vineyard. The Mondavis also contributed two magnums of 1994 Fumé Blanc Reserve. Since all members were invited, Ted Hall and his wife, Laddie, were on the list, whether the Mondavis wanted them there or not.

One of the first to arrive was Robert's younger brother, Peter Mondavi. Upright and far more mobile than his older sibling, Peter, like Cesare before him, was a short-statured, unassuming man. He stayed to the sides of the room, lifting the small, elegant bowls of Thai crab soup to his lips and gulping it all at one time, as if he were drinking a shot of espresso. Meanwhile, Robert had made his way to the front of the room, where a long sofa had been placed on a low platform, with a backdrop of draped peach curtains in the background, softening the scene, which had been framed on either side by towering arrangements of white flowers. The gathering seemed mournful, as if all the life had been drawn out of it. Two hundred vintners were expected but far fewer actually showed up, leaving delicate fans of escarole leaves uneaten and dozens of bottles of rare wines unopened.

Robert sat as vintners slowly made their way up to grasp his hand and say hello. As his nephew Peter Ventura approached to pay his respects to his uncle, he said, "Hey, Bob, do we kiss your ring now? Should we be kneeling and kissing your ring?" Robert didn't seem to comprehend his nephew's barbed comment, the result of decades of resentment and bitterness stemming from the 1976 trial.

When it came time for the current president of the Napa Valley Vintners to make a brief speech and presentation, Margrit guided her husband to the sofa. None of the organizers even bothered offering an explanation for Michael's absence. Peter Mondavi left soon after the president of the vintners had made his speech and the family photographs were taken.

H. William Harlan made a late appearance, missing the presentation but arriving in time to pay his respects to Robert and Margrit before leaving. In recent years, Harlan had quietly hired many of the talented employees who had been discarded by Michael's regime at the winery: The label designer Susan Pate had designed all of the classic, banknote-style etched labels on Harlan's wines; the wine historian Nina Wemyss helped conduct classes for one of his ventures; Robin Daniel Lail even worked for Harlan for some time. As one of the contenders to inherit Robert's role in the valley, Harlan had come to pay his respects to its fading king. He'd been pondering the question of family dynasties for many years and had watched carefully as Robert Mondavi's dream of passing his wine empire to his children unraveled.

CHAPTER TWENTY-FOUR

Billionaire's Ball, June 2005

The Napa Valley Wine Auction celebrated its twenty-fifth anniversary the same weekend the grapevines bloomed. Inconspicuous greenish-white sprays delicately encircled the vines' tendrils, producing a shimmering fragrance that could be caught for just a moment before floating away. From Highway 29, big bidders riding in limousines couldn't see the flowers tucked discreetly beneath the vines' dark-green foliage. This vital transformation of bud to bloom took place largely out of sight. Not so the violent changes in the Mondavis' lives. Six months after Napa's first family sold out of their namesake winery, the weekend was a chance to set aside their differences and present a united front.

An exception to this was Michael. On paper, he was one of the auction's twenty-four cochairs. But in reality, he did not attend any of the planning meetings and had no intention of attending the auction itself, almost certainly because his stepmother and father were so prominently involved. Relieved to be free of the family obligations that had yoked him for years, Michael had dropped out of the public eye. He planned to spend the auction weekend ensconced with his campmates at the Bohemian Grove, a private, 2,700-acre forest sixty miles north of San Francisco.

But through the intervention of his old friend Fred Franzia, Michael had quietly begun to make peace with his father. "For Christ's sake, he's your dad," Franzia had scolded him at their annual Deer Camp gathering the previous August. "You just got to make a move. You only got one father. He may not live that long. When you look back on it, in a few months or a few years, it won't mean a damn thing." For the first time in many years, Robert had not made it up to Deer Camp that year. But Rob did, and Franzia also said the same thing to Michael's son. "You of all guys shouldn't carry any grudge against your grandpa," Franzia told him.

As the months passed and his health worsened, Robert grew anxious to try to reconcile with Michael. He appealed for help to Franzia, who called Michael that spring with an important message: "Your dad wants to see you and tell you he loves you." Michael made his way up the long, windy road to his father's home on Wappo Hill. He'd made sure to come at a time when he knew Margrit wouldn't be there. Sitting inside, next to the indoor pool, father and son made small talk and discussed Michael's new business. When it came time to leave, Robert thanked Michael for coming and they gave each other a hug. "I love you," Robert told him. "I love you too," his son replied.

Despite these loving words, their estrangement continued. Michael withdrew from most public events involving the winery and Timothy slipped comfortably into the role of Robert's fair-haired son. He was solicitous of Robert, helping him into and out of his seat, adjusting his clothing for him, helping explain what was going on. His son Carlo was also at his grandfather's side during this time. At *Wine Spectator*'s annual wine auction kickoff party at the famed valley watering hole Tra Vigne, on Wednesday night, June 1, Timothy spotted Michael from across the room and approached him, pointing out that their father was also there. He urged his brother to say hello to Robert. Michael approached his father, who was sitting in a wheelchair, briefly said hello, then quickly returned to the party.

Behind the scenes, Timothy proved willing to go along with a plan to restore his family's reputation, volunteering as the Robert Mondavi family's face for a public reconciliation with the Peter Mondavi family. Built around the first barrel of wine to be jointly produced by the families in forty years, it was an event staged to coincide with the Napa Valley Vintners' charity wine auction in June. The recent push for a family reconciliation came from Serena Ventura, another cousin. After the death of her mother, Helen Ventura, in 2003 and of her aunt Mary Westbrook in 2004, Serena actively sought to bring her extended family back together. Having just completed a master of fine arts degree in writing at the University of San Francisco, Ventura had retained a literary agent who was actively pitching her memoir of the Mondavis, based on her UCSF dissertation, to publishers in New York.

The news became a public relations coup for the Mondavis. When veteran *New York Times* wine columnist Frank Prial wrote the first article in January of 2005 about the plan for the Robert and Peter Mondavi families to jointly produce a barrel of wine, it attracted a rush of media attention. National Public Radio, the Associated Press, and a host of local publications followed the *Times*'s story. But people close to the respective Mondavi families were guarded as to how genuine the reconciliation really was. Margrit detected a hint of Schadenfreude in Peter and his family's sudden change of heart toward reconciling after the Robert Mondavi family's setbacks. It did not go unnoticed that Peter, after a lifetime in Robert's shadow, had succeeded where his brother had failed: in holding together Charles Krug as a family-owned operation. Yet Peter's family also had its difficulties.

Since the stinging judgment against Peter from Judge Carter in 1976, Charles Krug had periodically struggled financially, with the bulk of its revenues coming from low-priced wines. The fractious dynamic between Peter senior, Marc, and Peter junior sometimes delayed decision making; the makeshift sign at the front of Charles Krug wasn't replaced quickly and vineyard replanting was overdue. Similarly, Marc and Peter junior had moved off the Krug Ranch, where they'd lived for decades. The family tattle was that they moved because Blanche wouldn't tether her dog to keep him from frightening Marc's four daughters, but Marc says it was time to move from a 2,300-square-foot house on the ranch to a more spacious place of their own.

The previous attempt to reconcile Peter senior and Robert two decades earlier, orchestrated over a dinner at a luxurious hillside resort in Rutherford, never really took hold. The jet-setting Robert Mon-dah-vi family, it seemed, moved in a different world from the stay-at-home Peter Mon-day-vee family. But by the early nineties, the Peter Mondavi side of the family, too, began pronouncing its surname in the European fashion. At least the linguistic rift had ended.

Over the years, Michael had suggested that the two families produce wine together, but Peter senior was reluctant to partner with a publicly traded company. Once Robert's side of the family sold out, however, Peter senior's objections vanished. This time, the reconciliation was not only a way for Robert's side of the family to regain face and for Peter's side to get attention as it began to focus on its higher-end Charles Krug wines. It was also a marketing boon to the Napa Valley auction, as the event had been renamed that year. In the catalog, the jointly produced barrel of 2004 Cabernet Sauvignon was presented as a sign that "their brotherly bond is strong again," signaling "the dedication and commitment that the entire family of four generations shares in making and keeping Napa Valley paramount among wine growing regions."

Robert's longtime PR man, Harvey Posert, who handled the publicity for the lot, wrote a press release that called it "a joyful chapter in the history of the Mondavis of Napa Valley." Named "Ancora Una Volta," Italian for "one more time," the lot included sixty numbered, etched magnums and three social events with the Mondavi families to taste the wine as it developed. It was widely expected to command the highest price of any lot at the vintners' live auction on June 4.

The Napa Valley Vintners, in turn, embraced the publicity stunt. It had been looking for a way to add sizzle to an event that had been suffering a malaise over the past few years. Founded in 1981, the vintners' auction had long been a key event on the social calendar, where moneyed oenophiles, celebrity chefs, and Hollywood stars descended on California's most famous wine region for three or four days in June. The success of Napa's event, long the grande dame of charity wine auctions, had inspired hundreds of similar auctions all around the country, from fundraisers for preschools to black-tie balls.

But over the past two years, Napa's event had been upstaged by a rival charity auction in Naples, Florida—a city built partly on reclaimed swamp in a state not known for its viticulture. In 2004, the Naples Winter Wine Festival had trumpeted itself as the world's biggest charity wine auction after raising more money than Napa's auction for the first time: $7.67 million, compared with Napa's $5.3 million. The following year, Naples held the single most successful charity wine auction in history, raising $11.1 million from a relatively small group of 312 bidders, with each lot averaging over $160,000.

Recapturing its rightful role as the preeminent charity wine auction in America was a key goal for the Napa Valley Vintners. In addition to raising money for charity, the group's unapologetic mission for the auction was for it to help market the valley as a wine lover's Eden. It had long been a prestigious social event, costing $2,500 per couple to attend and drawing international media attention and celebrity bidders.

Taking a cue from Naples, Napa's Vintners recast their entire auction—tossing out a Friday-night black-tie ball before the live auction, focusing instead on more intimate soirees that allowed bidders to mingle with vintners, even changing the name to Auction Napa Valley. They slashed the number of lots and radically truncated the live auction, which in the past had run more than six hours. And, in a risky gamble, they nearly tripled the admission price to $7,500 per couple.

The Napa organizers also hoped to regain their events' sparkle by including glamorous lots. Not only was there the barrel jointly produced by the Mondavi families, but also four three-liter bottles of wine from Colgin Cellars accompanied by a dinner for eight prepared by the French Laundry's Thomas Keller, and a bit part in the television show *Desperate Housewives*, which accompanied a lot from Frank Family Vineyards. By tripling the price tag of the main event and making the live portion more elite, Napa's vintners aimed to lavish attention on the high rollers. In the past, everyone—including the billionaires—had lined up for buses at a winery on the valley floor to make the short trip to Meadowood. This year, chauffeur-driven sedans and limousines whizzed the big bidders from one event to another.

But fearing that the live auction would become strictly a "billionaire's ball," Napa's organizers also opened up the less costly barrel auction to the wider public, complete with live entertainment and a ring toss for bottles of wine. Despite all the changes, ticket sales for the full weekend of events, including the live auction that raised most of the funds, were sluggish, forcing the vintners to cancel some events.

The hospitality event hosted by Mondavi on Thursday night had a lighthearted theme: an eighties party intended to capture the mood of the time when the first Napa Valley Auction had taken place. The Vineyard

Room was transformed into a glitzy discotheque, with mirrored balls on the ceiling and tablecloths of metallic foil, like a glittering shagged carpet. The event was sparsely attended by bidders, who preferred instead to attend hospitality events hosted by cult wineries, such as Colgin Cellars and Harlan Estate. To save face, the winery at the last moment had invited employees and many nonbidding trade guests to fill out the numbers.

But the biggest difference at the Robert Mondavi Winery's event was the commercialism that pervaded the evening. Booths had been erected on the patio outside the Vineyard Room to display the showy platinum and diamond creations of Beverly Hills jeweler Martin Katz. An array of sports cars, including an Aston Martin Vanquish S priced at $255,000, sat on the lawn. It was the first time the winery had entered into a sponsorship deal for its auction hospitality event, an idea hatched by the winery's marketing team, many of whom had lost their jobs by the time of the party. Its partner was the Robb Report, a media company devoted to luxury goods and the lifestyles of the very rich. The winery had also paid to fly in a large funk band from North Carolina named Liquid Pleasure. Dressed in shiny red jumpsuits, the band kicked off their performance by leading the guests in a conga line around the Vineyard Room.

For old-timers, the weekend was a time to reflect on how much the valley and the wine auction had changed. The very first auction was a low-key and almost entirely local affair. Unlike the four-day extravaganza with a cast of thousands it has since become, the first event involved a bucolic al fresco luncheon with round tables tucked discreetly along the edge of the golf green, shaded by tall trees. Each tablecloth was a variation on the hues of the vineyards—with purples, greens, and whites—and lunch was served in baskets woven by volunteers out of grapevines and filled with local cheeses, pâtés, crusty breads, and salads. Purple balloons were bunched together to resemble clusters of grapes.

In each succeeding year, the event itself ballooned and the amounts raised for charity swelled. In 2000, just as the dot-com bubble burst, the bidding during the live auction reached hard-to-believe levels, even for Napa, raising a record-breaking $9.5 million—nearly double the previous year's $5.5 million total. The top bid of the day for a single lot came from B. A. Adams of Patterson, Louisiana, who'd made his fortune in the oil and gas business. He bought ten one-and-a-half-liter bottles of Harlan Estate wine for $700,000, pricing out at about $7,000 per glass. Perhaps even more astonishing was tech executive Chase Bailey's $500,000 bid for one six-liter bottle of 1992 Screaming Eagle Cabernet Sauvignon—the most expensive bottle of wine ever purchased in any charity wine auction.

Outsiders may have missed it, but hundreds of Napans knew the history they were witnessing at the barrel auction on Friday as two very old, warring brothers sat together, holding each other's hand. To stoke interest in the barrel of wine jointly produced by the Robert and Peter Mondavi families, the public relations staff of the Vintners had arranged a photo opportunity with the two elderly siblings, among the last of their generation still alive. The two men sat on a raised platform, surrounded by photographs of themselves. Some were black-and-white photos from their youth; others were more contemporary photos of them holding wineglasses. In one of the photographs, the boys—perhaps seven and eight years old at the time—wear shorts, knee socks, overcoats, and ties. Their hair is slicked back and precisely parted down the middle. Cesare stands between them. There's a similar photo of the Mondavi sons with Rosa, taken in their late high school or early college years. Robert in this one wears a striped three-piece suit and tie; Peter, dressed more informally, has rolled up his shirtsleeves and is jacketless.

On this day, the brothers, both in their early nineties, sat patiently together. Photographers snapped pictures of them as the crowds attending the barrel auction milled past. Many people stopped to gaze in wonder at the scene and their responses ranged from those who were touched by the sight to others who felt it was a cynical ploy to stir interest in the lot. A few rival vintners questioned how dignified the public reconciliation really was. It appeared that the two men were being put on display simply to raise money. Robert, for his part, seemed to have little understanding of the events. Although some of the visitors tried to talk to him, they generally didn't get very far. When a reporter asked Robert what had changed to bring the brothers back together, he answered with a single word: "Time." For the most part, Robert sat on the podium and smiled. Peter, on the other hand, had all his wits about him and said more than a few words at that event. Truly it may have been one of the first times in their lives that Peter, as the younger brother, got the final word.

* * *

Saturday night's live auction began with Jay Leno, the host of *The Tonight Show*, delivering rapid-fire jokes to warm up the crowd. "This is a performer's dream," he said early on. "Rich people who've been drinking." Of the thousand people in the tent, only about three hundred were bidders. The rest were vintners, press, and guests. To first-timers, the seating arrangements in the big top might have seemed casual or even a bit chaotic. Officially, there were few reserved tables. But within the social order of the Napa Valley, the tables were as precisely choreographed as the dance steps at an eighteenth-century ball. The leading families of Napa—the Mondavis, the Davieses, the Martinis, and the Trincheros—all had tables staked out beforehand by stand-ins well before the other guests had arrived.

As well, the Napa Valley Vintners, the powerful winemakers group that organized the event, always made sure that the top bidders from the previous year had their choice of seats. Some preferred the back, which gave them a broader view of the action, while others preferred the front, closer to the auctioneers.

Robert and Margrit sat front and center, flanked on either side by family members. A longtime arts, wine, and society reporter for *The Napa Valley Register*, Pierce Carson, sat at the table in the front row next to the left Mondavis, while Peter Mondavi senior and his younger son, Peter junior, sat at the table immediately to the right. The Peter Mondavis were joined by H. William Harlan, an original partner in Meadowood who was now better known as the man behind Harlan Estate, the producer of expensive, small-production "cult" wines, and his wife, Deborah.

Margrit had made sure to get her husband settled in his seat early, before the crowd descended. She also made sure he had a large glass of red wine within easy reach throughout. A longtime Mondavi employee served as the sommelier and waiter to the two brothers' tables, making sure that their trays of olives, prosciutto, Parmesan cheese, and crackers remained filled.

Timothy and his companion, the Argentinian-born winemaker Delia Viader, a cult winemaker in her own right, sat with Robert and Margrit, as did one of Tim's daughters. As the clock ticked toward the opening bid, the high bidders were slipping into their seats. There was a frisson—a kind of force field of excitement—that formed around them. The auctioneers knew who they were, as did many of the leading vintners.

Toward the back was a table headed by Koo Ming-kown, founder of a Hong Kong–based company, Nam Tai Electronics Inc., a maker of calculators, cordless telephones, and other gadgets. Born in Shanghai and with operations in Hong Kong and British Columbia, Koo, sixty, had developed a taste for expensive wine. Over the years, he had regularly flown a group of Chinese friends into Napa for the long auction weekend. One of the auction's consistently high bidders, Koo had, a year earlier, made a $100 million donation to the Hong Kong Baptist University—the single largest personal donation the university had ever received. The Vintners hoped he would be in a giving mood this year.

Another big bidder was Gary Rieschel, a Silicon Valley venture capitalist who had teamed up with Masayoshi Son and Ron Fisher at Soft-Bank Holdings, the powerful Tokyo software company, early in the Internet boom. As head of SoftBank's Palo Alto–based venture capital affiliate, he'd made some early and smart bets on Internet winners like VeriSign and GeoCities Inc. Now renamed Mobius Venture Capital, his firm had some $2 billion under management as the auction began. The forty-nine-year-old Rieschel, too, had become an avid wine collector—and had cumulatively spent, by his estimate, $1.5 to $1.8 million at the Napa Valley auction in the eight years he'd attended. Rieschel had been wooed earlier that year by the Naples Winter Wine Festival. Assigned paddle number 1 in honor of his bidding record, he had remained loyal to Napa's event, at least for now.

The bidding got off to a fast start, with a surprise entry of a replica of a custom-made cork jacket that Robert had worn at the first wine auction, in 1981. "Tonight we are going to auction off this jacket," said Leno. "If you wanted to make one yourself it'd probably cost you twenty dollars." The bidding jumped from $70,000 to $85,000. Settling at $95,000, the lot went to Koerner Rombauer, a burly vintner whose great aunt was the author of *The Joy of Cooking*. With an American flag shirt stretched across his sizable girth, Rombauer made his way to Robert's table at the very front, leaned over, and kissed the nanogenarian on top of his head. Robert's lower lip seemed to quiver, perhaps involuntarily, after he took off the jacket and passed it over to Rombauer, who then put it on. Timothy, sitting behind his father, had his hand laid gently on his father's shoulder. Leno had literally sold the jacket off Robert's back.

Another few lots rolled past, including the package from Frank Family Vineyards, which included an appearance on the hit ABC television series

Desperate Housewives. To hawk the lot, actress Teri Hatcher, one of the stars of the series, climbed the podium to stir up interest. "Jay knows there's a lot I will do for more money," joked Hatcher, in a form-fitting dress and high heels. The bidding was so lively that Rich Frank, a top Disney executive and a vintner, and Hatcher decided to offer it to both the top and the second bidder, raising $580,000 in total.

Then came Lot 414, which the Vintners had billed as the sentimental favorite of the evening. "The biggest lot of the night should be for the wine of these two gentlemen," said Leno, who ended up staying onstage well past his monologue in order to help out with the sale. The auction-eer was Ursula Hermancinski, a striking woman who was once dubbed "the goddess of the gavel" by *Food & Wine* magazine. She quipped that the brothers had engaged in "the most famous fistfight" in wine industry history, but now they were coming back together again. Hermancinski, who had worked as an auctioneer at Christie's wine department in New York before diving into the world of dot-com auctions in 1998, was known for her sassy delivery and her delight in egging on bidders.

This time, Timothy pulled a face when she referred to the fistfight between his father and uncle. He mouthed a long "Oooh." But the crowd loved it.

The bidding quickly soared to $130,000. Jay Leno, with his soufflé of gray hair and square jaw, looked slightly confused as it settled at $200,000 and paused. Clearly, he had expected it to go a lot higher. "Barbara Stan-wyck is not in *The Big Valley* any longer. Hess is gone. These are the only two men left in *The Big Valley*," he joked as he tried to urge bidders higher. It moved up to $225,000. Hermancinski teased Gary Rieschel, the big bidder who was sitting in the middle of the tent, to push it higher, referring to his family's recent move to China. The price jumped to $300,000, and then even further to $360,000. Peter senior raised his arms in victory—stretching all of his five feet, six inches or so to full height. Unlike his older brother, whom Margrit had dressed elegantly for the evening, including pinning Robert's Légion d'honneur medal to his dress shirt, Peter was dressed like the farmer he had been for six decades: in a plain, open-collared cotton shirt, ironed cotton trousers, and sensible tan shoes.

Jay Leno jumped in once again. "This is the most historically impor-tant barrel of wine to be made since 1966, when these guys used to be friends," he said, eliciting even more guffaws. However corny, Leno's prodding worked. A new bidder had suddenly leapt into the fray. A woman raised her paddle just as the bids seemed to languish. No one knew her. She was a first-time attendee at this or any other wine auction and she hadn't really planned on bidding for the Mondavi family's lot before she'd arrived. But she'd been moved by the brothers' reuniting.

Heads turned toward her table, in a section set on risers toward the rear. Strikingly dressed in an orange silk skirt and beaded turquoise shawl, she kept her paddle raised. Goaded on by Leno, she moved the bid up, and up again, to $401,000. She had bought the Mondavi barrel. Leno couldn't resist throwing in one final wisecrack about the lot before he ended his appearance for the night: "Hang on," he warned. "The two brothers have started punching each other again!" Robert, who was trying to listen with the fierce intensity of the hard of hearing, hardly changed throughout, while Peter seemed to relish the attention. He made sure to get in a few words to the television reporter who was interviewing Pete junior and Timothy. Robert, in contrast, for once remained out of the media spotlight.

"It may sound kind of hokey," said the winning bidder, Joy Craft, in a slow South Carolina drawl. "But it is as if I had an opportunity to sit with Albert Einstein or Ben Franklin. I saw it as a once-in-a-lifetime chance to sit with two innovators," said Craft. "Divine intervention took over" and urged her to share this special moment for another family.

Craft, who had moved to Woodside, California, and ran a family foundation, said she knew very little about the history of the brothers' feud or about the fistfight that was joked about during the bidding. But she had made her first visit to a winery when she stopped at Charles Krug as a twenty-one-year-old who came from a family of teetotallers. Craft recalled that she had made her first trip to Napa Valley in the driving rain. She approached Krug and on an impulse decided to turn in. She remembered feeling lucky the winery's visitors' center was still open and brought a signed bottle of wine home with her. The bottle smashed in her suitcase. The way she saw it, she was "coming full circle" in again buying the jointly produced barrel from the Mondavis.

As the excitement surrounding the Mondavis died down, a parade of California's most prominent vintners came to pay their respects to Robert and Peter. Francis Ford Coppola, who had used some of the fortune he'd made from his *Godfather* films to buy and restore the old Niebaum-Inglenook Estate, moved toward the old man and, like Rombauer, kissed him on the head. The billionaire vintner Jess Jackson likewise made his way to the Mondavi brothers' tables. Always, they were especially courteous to Margrit, kissing her on one or both cheeks. Blanche, Peter's wife, was absent that evening. For several years, she had been in poor health. Peter junior accompanied his father, wearing an elegant gold signet ring.

The final lot involving the Mondavis came toward the very end of the evening. Lot number 455, it was billed as a "Musical Summer Weekend for 10" and included a private dinner at Robert and Margrit's hilltop home. "Ladies and gentlemen, I want to make a toast," hailed the evening's other auctioneer, Fritz Hatton. "I hope you all share this sentiment. To Margrit Mondavi: This is a sentimental wish to express to you. We raise our glass to your long-standing contributions. . . . Margrit, you are a treasure!" Hatton went on to dedicate the lot to Margrit, who had spent much of the auction up until then with a pen in hand, noting down the amounts of the winning bids and keeping a running tally of the total raised. She was nervous throughout the event, worried that the auction would fail to bring in a respectable amount of money after all the efforts to revamp it.

Dressed in a lace skirt embroidered with tiny pastel flowers, and wrapped throughout the evening in a pink pashmina shawl, Margrit lifted her head from her tally and beamed at the applause and attention. The bidding for the lot started at $100,000 and rapidly moved up to $120,000, $150,000, and then $190,000. Ron and Teri Kuhn, who had become close friends of the Mondavis over the years, made the winning bid at $200,000. Margrit, accompanied by Timothy and Delia, made their way to the Kuhns' table to thank them.

Neither of the Mondavi lots was the highest of the night. That title went to Lot 454, the one just before the Robert Mondavi Winery's entry, which fetched $650,000 for four three-liter bottles from Colgin Cellars. The winning bidders, John and Tamra Gorman of Austin, Texas, shattered Napa's previous record for the highest amount ever paid for a single lot. Then, Joy Craft became the night's highest bidder by offering $550,000 for a lot that would allow her and nine friends to raid the cellars of some of the valley's best-known wineries: Cakebread, Château Montelena, Joseph Phelps, Schramsberg, and Silver Oak. Her spending totaled

$951,000 that evening. To end the auction, the vintners shot off confetti cannons over the crowd and truly had something to celebrate. They'd nearly doubled their take from the previous year.

Margrit was elated. The aucton's malaise had been lifted; although Naples had held on to its bragging rights as the world's biggest charity wine auction, Napa had nearly doubled the amount it had raised for charity in a year and was nipping at the Florida crowd's heels. If the auction was a measure of where the Mondavis stood after a year of chaotic change, they had endured it with grace and aplomb and Margrit, in particular, had come into her own as the powerhouse behind her ailing husband.

Robert sat stony-faced through most of the hoopla. When the auction ended, Margrit and Timothy took his arms and helped him make his way slowly out toward the smaller tent, where they would host a post-auction dinner for bidders and guests. Although the reconciliation he had long sought with his brother had finally taken place, it had only happened after Robert had lost his company, giving Peter's side of the family the distinction of being the only remaining Mondavi to own a winery.

EPILOGUE

Robert Mondavi will turn ninety-three on June 14, 2007. He is confined to a wheelchair but still lives on Wappo Hill with Margrit. He and his wife are partners in a new wine venture, named Continuum, with Timothy and Marcia and their families.

Margrit Biever Mondavi remains active in a wide variety of philanthropic and community activities. She is the only member of the extended Mondavi family who still works at the Constellation-owned Robert Mondavi Winery.

Michael Mondavi works with his son, Rob, and his daughter, Dina, at Folio Fine Wine Partners, a wine distributor, and recently purchased a winery and vineyard. Folio is distributing wine from Italy's Frescobaldi family. His business card reads "founder/coach."

Marcia Borger Mondavi lives in New York but is a frequent visitor to Napa Valley. She is extensively remodeling her mother Marjorie's old home.

Timothy Mondavi is making wine and has, with his sister, father, and stepmother, made offers to buy some of the To Kalon vineyards from Constellation. He is working with his daughter Carissa and has not remarried.

Carlo Mondavi has been named as a defendant in two shareholder lawsuits alleging he engaged in fraud and misrepresentation in connection with his company Davi Skin Inc. The lawsuits were pending in early 2007. He launched his skin care line at Bergdorf Goodman in October 2006.

Peter Mondavi Jr. is transforming the Charles Krug brand into a maker of fine, Bordeaux-style red wines. Its wines have won some high ratings from *Wine Enthusiast* in recent years.

Peter Mondavi Sr. continues to come to work every day and is in good health.

Marc Mondavi has steered clear of the labor disputes between Krug and the United Farm Workers Union.

Helen Mondavi Ventura died peacefully at her home in Napa Valley in 2003 of natural causes. Her sister, Mary, died in 2004.

Greg Evans is building a vineyard estate with his wife in Sonoma Valley.

Ted Hall's Long Meadow Ranch lost most of its wine inventory in a fire in 2005. He continues to make wine, raise cattle, and produce organic olive oil.

Sir Anthony Greener remains a director of several publicly traded companies.

Philip Greer remains a director of Federal Express and is chairman of Tulane University's board of trustees. He seldom visits the Napa Valley anymore.

Frank Farella remains Robert Mondavi's legal counsel and continues to sell grapes to the Robert Mondavi Winery.

John Martel is the author of four novels and he continues to practice law at Farella, Braun and Martel.

Joseph L. Alioto died of prostate cancer in 1998. He remained married to his second wife, Kathleen Sullivan, until his death.

Fred Franzia and his family are now believed to be the single largest owners of vineyard acreage in California.

Gary Ramona works for Fred Franzia.

Cliff Adams is an advisory board member of Rodney Strong Vineyards, a privately held family winery in Sonoma, California, and is CEO and chairman of Congdon Orchards Inc., in Yakima, Washington.

Harvey Posert now advises Fred Franzia, the Robert Mondavi Winery, and members of the Mondavi family on public relations. He is helping to organize Robert Mondavi alumni reunions, as well as putting together a directory of former RM employees. The alumni group could approach three hundred to four hundred people.

Opus One is now a fifty-fifty joint venture owned by Constellation Brands Inc. and Baron Philippe de Rothschild SA.

The Sands brothers now run the world's largest wine producer.

ACKNOWLEDGMENTS

I wish to thank my teachers and friends from the Squaw Valley Community of Writers, particularly Moira Johnston Block, Michael Carlisle of Inkwell Management, and Frances Dinkelspiel, whom I first met as a sixteen-year-old and, through Squaw, rekindled our friendship many years later. At Gotham Books, I am indebted to Bill Shinker, Patrick Mulligan, Brett Valley, and Brendan Cahill. I am also grateful to my friends and colleagues at *The Wall Street Journal*: Don Clark, who first suggested the idea of writing about the Mondavis; Mike Miller and Matthew Rose, who urged me to dig deeper; Steve Yoder, who supported me in so many ways; Dan Hertzberg, who found a way for me to stay at the paper; Rob Guth, who not only read the entire manuscript but hand-delivered his edited copy to my home; George Anders and Susan Warren, both of whom kindly read portions of the book and offered their wise counsel; Jim Carlton, who opened up a new avenue of reporting for me; and Carrie Dolan, Marilyn Chase, and Peter Waldman, who generously lent me their ears. My former *Business Week* colleague Bill Echikson, who now writes about wine for *The Wall Street Journal Europe*, not only provided reporting from the Languedoc but reviewed the chapter of the book on the Baron Philippe de Rothschild for accuracy. I'd also like to thank the group of writers from Nth 24th who saw this project through from the very beginning, including Allison Hoover Bartlett, Leslie Crawford, Sharon Epel, Susan Freinkel, Katherine Ellison, Katherine Neilan, Lisa Wallgren Okuhn, and Jill Storey, as well as to my dear and greatly admired friend Christina for bringing her great sensitivity and intelligence to this story. For our friends who time and time again helped out in a pinch while I was writing this book, I'd also like to thank Liz Epstein, Marian Mancini, Tanya Rauzi, and Caroll Yandell, and especially my mother, Roberta Grant Flynn, who read the manuscript twice, offered wise comments, and never hesitated to help out with her grandsons. Most of all, I'd like to thank my husband, Charlie Siler, and our boys, Cody and Andrew, for their bottomless patience, humor, and love.

NOTES

PROLOGUE
2   **a front-page story:** Julia Flynn, "Grapes of Wrath: Inside a Napa Valley Empire, a Family Struggles with Itself," *Wall Street Journal*, June 3, 2004, p. 1.

PART ONE: FOUNDATION

Chapter One: The Valley, 1906–1952
9   **aboard . . . the *Vaderland*:** "List or Manifest of Alien Passengers for the U.S. Immigration Officer at Port of Arrival," SS *Vaderland*, arrival date March 7, 1906 (New York: Ellis Island Foundation), list 39.
9   **Cesare Mondavi's first job:** Joseph Maganini, interview with the author.
10   **to learn to write his name:** Angelo M. Pellegrini, *Americans by Choice* (New York: The Macmillan Company, 1965), p. 135.
10   **"what an ugly joke":** Serena Mondavi Ventura, "Crush: A Memoir of My Mother, the Mondavis, and Me" (Thesis, M.F.A.—Writing, University of San Francisco, 2005), p. 20.
11   **"He never entered my house again.":** Pellegrini, *Americans by Choice*, p. 145.
13   **before the day was over:** Pellegrini, *Americans by Choice*, p. 128.
14   **"good as gold":** Robert Mondavi, *Harvests of Joy: My Passion for Excellence: How the Good Life Became Great Business* (New York: Harcourt Brace and Company, 1998), p. 131.

15   **declaring himself the world champion:** Robert Mondavi, *Harvests of Joy*, p. 131.

15   **home winemakers and others:** Ruth Teiser and Catherine Harroun, *Winemaking in California* (New York: McGraw-Hill, 1983), p. 178.

16   **when he was about seventeen:** Ventura, "Crush . . . ," p. 12.

17   **before the "noble experiment":** Charles Sullivan, *Napa Wine: A History from Mission Days to the Present* (San Francisco: The Wine Appreciation Guild, 1994), p. 182.

25   ***"Grazie, e te amo":*** Ventura, "Crush . . . ," p. 72. In English, the sentence means, "Thank you and I love you."

Chapter Two: France, 1943–1963

30   **a Chinese laborer:** Louis Stralla, who lived on the property before the Mondavis arrived, said: "I remember when I first moved there [to the ranch] I asked what it was. They said, 'That's a grave for one of the Krug daughters.' But nobody ever dug [the body] up and nobody ever found it. . . . I think they ought to go out there and see if there are some bones down there. I mean it seriously. . . . There are things that you just don't hear about." Louis Stralla, interview by Jim Beard (St. Helena: Napa Valley Wine Library Association, 1979), transcript p. 28.

30   **its final rest:** Marc Mondavi, interview with the author.

30   **his resentment began to build:** Deposition of Peter Mondavi in *Robert Mondavi v. C. Mondavi and Sons*, consolidated cases 29917 and 30122, Superior Court of California in the County of Napa (hereinafter referred to as *Robert Mondavi v. C. Mondavi and Sons*).

30   **ignoring Peter:** article referred to in *Bottles & Bins*, Charles Krug's newsletter, January 1964.

30   **a higher salary:** Peter Ventura, interview with the author.

30   **the United Kingdom:** Peter Ventura, interview with the author.

31   **"anything anymore":** Peter Mondavi Sr., "Advances in Technology and Production at Charles Krug Winery, 1946–1988," 1988 interview by Ruth Teiser (Berkeley: Regional Oral History Office, Bancroft Library, University of California, c 1990.), p. 18.

31   **"wear a grape stake down":** Serena Mondavi Ventura, "Crush . . . ," p. 12.

31   **"writing a book?":** Serena Ventura, "Crush . . . ," p. 70.

31   **in New York on business:** Marc Mondavi, interview with the author; Peter Mondavi Jr., interview with the author; Peter Ventura, interview with the author.

31   **uncomfortable with physical contact:** The wine historian William F. Heintz, who interviewed the brothers separately over the years and was hired to work on a history of Charles Krug, noted in an interview that "Robert likes to rub shoulders with people and the personal contact of the business, while Peter goes out of his way to avoid it." William F. Heintz, interview with the author.

31   **once he made up his mind:** Peter Mondavi Jr., interview with the author.

32   **rise too high:** Peter Mondavi Sr., "Advances in Technology . . . ," p. 10.

32   **warned Robert not to buy all those grapes:** Peter Mondavi Sr., interview with the author.

32   **got the go-ahead from him:** Decision, August 12, 1976, *Robert Mondavi v. C. Mondavi and Sons.*

32   **financial disaster:** Ibid.

32   **for years afterward:** According to Cliff Adams, Peter brought up this blunder in the 1970s during litigation as a justification for why Robert had been removed by the family in his role as general manager of Krug. Cliff Adams, interview with the author.

33   **permission from the bank:** Cliff Adams, interview with the author; Peter Ventura, interview with the author.

33   **"set us back ten to fifteen years":** Peter Mondavi Sr., interview with the author.

33   **"fire him":** Peter Ventura, interview with the author.

33   **around the country:** Decision, August 12, 1976, *Robert Mondavi v. C. Mondavi and Sons.*

34   **an elderly female pedestrian:** Serena Ventura, "Crush . . . ," p. 44. Michael Mondavi confirmed that Cesare was in an accident of some sort, though he couldn't relate the details; Michael Mondavi, interview with the author. Peter Ventura recalled that his grandfather had killed two women, not one, in the incident; Peter Ventura, interview with the author.

35   **strawberries in red wine:** Serena Ventura, "Crush . . . ," p. 74.

35   **crying and wailing:** Joseph Maganini, interview with the author.

36   **"nobody to take care of it":** Peter Ventura, interview with the author.

36   **his request was ignored:** Anthony Cook, "Brother Against Brother: The Wine Feud That Split the Mondavi Family," *New West*, November 8, 1976, p. 23.

36   **at company expense:** Cliff Adams, interview with the author.

36   **France's most famous cooks:** Jancis Robinson, "La Pyramide, Vienne—a Culinary Landmark," http://www.jancisrobinson.com/articles/nl205, July 3, 2003.

36   **"floating in butter":** Robert Mondavi, interview by Robert Benson; *Great Winemakers of California: Conversations with Robert Benson* (Santa Barbara: Capra Press, 1977), p. 203.

37   **fresh local ingredients:** Paul Lukacs, *American Vintage: The Rise of American Wine* (Boston: Houghton Mifflin, 2000), pp. 209–302.

38   **a shock to the wine world:** Frank J. Prial, "Wine Talk," *New York Times*, March 14, 1990, p. C-10.

38   **"He was uncontrollable!":** Anthony Cook, "Brother Against Brother," p. 24.

38   **"He always criticized.":** Peter Mondavi Sr., interview with the author.

39   **world-class wines:** Robert Mondavi, *Harvests of Joy*, p. 11.

39   **"good for everyone":** William Bonetti, "A Life of Winemaking at Wineries of Gallo, Schenley, Charles Krug, Château Souverain, and Sonoma-Cutrer," 1997 interview by Carole Hicke (Berkeley: Regional Oral History Office, Bancroft Library, University of California, c. 1998), p. 53.

39   **nicknamed "Stalin":** Robert Mondavi, 1997 interview by William Heintz (St. Helena: Napa Valley Wine Library), audio recording.

39   **"further the cause of winemaking":** Robert Mondavi, "Creativity in the California Wine Industry," 1984 interview by Ruth Teiser (Berkeley: Regional Oral History Office, Bancroft Library, University of California, c. 1985), p. 27.

40   **the surging demand:** Krug even advertised that fact. In late 1965 in *Wines & Vines* and other magazines, the winery ran an ad apologizing to its customers: "There's a drought at Charles Krug. To put it simply, we don't have enough of certain types of Charles Krug wines to go around." William F. Heintz, *California's Napa Valley: One Hundred Sixty Years of Winemaking* (San Francisco : Scottwall Associates, c. 1999), p. 321.

40   **"Bob Mondavi was there":** Bonetti, "A Life of Winemaking . . . ," p. 56.

41   **"Mondavi's Miscarriage":** Peter Ventura, interview with the author.

41   **the winery's popularity:** Heintz, *California's Napa Valley. . .* , p. 321.

42   **an order for 125 barrels:** "Robert Mondavi Biography," press release from the Robert Mondavi Winery (St. Helena: Napa Valley Wine Library), p. 3.

42   **in French oak:** George M. Taber, *Judgment of Paris: California vs. France and the Historic 1976 Paris Tasting That Revolutionized Wine* (New York: Scribner, 2005), p. 102.

Chapter Three: East of Eden, 1963–1965

44   **in the company of such notables . . . :** "How Not to Take It Easy," *Time*, January 24, 1964.

44   **a family furor:** Michael Mondavi, interview with the author.

45   **crickets and bullfrogs:** Marc Mondavi, interview with the author.

45   **mostly an immigrant occupation:** Michael Mondavi, interview with the author.

45   **serve it as a side dish with bacon and onions:** Serena Ventura, "Crush . . . ," p. 166.

46   **"everyone was speaking Italian":** Peter Mondavi Jr. is referring to the mid-1970s, when he first began driving his grandmother shopping. Even then, St. Helena's shopkeepers spoke Italian. Peter Mondavi Jr., interview with the author.

47   **"Stop shooting the house, boys":** Peter Ventura, interview with the author.

47   **"Blacka Jacka!":** Serena Ventura, "Crush . . . ," p. 53.

47   **the monthly dinner dance:** Serena Ventura, "Meet Signora Rosa Mondavi," *California Living*, February 15, 1976, p. 14.

47   **from a family that was well off:** William Morrisroe, interview by Catherine Thorpe.

47   **an obscure snatch of poetry:** Charles Perotti, interview by Catherine Thorpe.

48   **"I didn't think you had it in you":** This comment is solely from Michael's recollection of the event. Because of his health problems after this comment was made to the author, Robert Mondavi was not available to confirm or respond to it. Michael Mondavi, interview with the author.

48   **"if I came home and complained":** Michael Mondavi, interview by William F. Heintz, February 23, 1984 (St. Helena: Napa Valley Wine Library Association).

49   **something other than business:** Charles Burress, "Helen Mondavi Ventura—Sister of Vintners," obituary, *San Francisco Chronicle*, June 18, 2003, p. A-23.

49   **on the nine that they did:** Peter Ventura, interview with the author.

49   **followed with criticisms:** Robert Mondavi, *Harvests of Joy*, p. 324.

49   **". . . could have used more salt":** Peter Ventura, interview with the author.

49   **criticism for twenty minutes:** Robert Mondavi, *Harvests of Joy*, p. 324.

50   **Robert's wife was an alcoholic:** Douglas Watson, interviews with the author; William F. Heintz, interview with the author.

50   **a thickly braided blond pigtail:** Description based on James Conaway, *Napa* (Boston: Houghton Mifflin, 1990), p. 34. Confirmed with Margrit Biever Mondavi, interview with author.

50   **as her marriage began to unravel:** Peter Ventura, Joe Maganini, and Elsa Maganini, interviews with author.

51   **to talk with Peter:** Decision, August 12, 1976, *Robert Mondavi v. C. Mondavi and Sons*, p. 27.

51   **Robert swung:** Based on Robert Mondavi, *Harvests of Joy*, p. 16; as well as Peter Mondavi Sr., interview with the author, and Michael Mondavi, interview with the author. Peter Mondavi Sr. later recalled to Paul Chutkow, who coauthored *Harvests of Joy*, that Robert had hit him only once; Paul Chutkow, "The Fall of the House of Mondavi," *San Francisco*, November 2005, p. 195.

51   **purple marks on his throat:** Anthony Cook, "Brother Against Brother: The Wine Feud That Split the Mondavi Family," *New West*, November 8, 1976, p. 24. Michael Mondavi's recollection is that the bruises on Peter's neck came from a blow from Robert, and that the brothers never rolled around on the ground, though Michael was not a witness to the fight; Michael Mondavi, interview with the author.

51   **Peter insisted he didn't know:** Chutkow, "The Fall of the House of Mondavi," p. 195.

51–52 **he had run into a door:** Conaway, *Napa*, p. 23.

52   **Alioto had joined the board:** Bancroft, p. 37.

53   **McKinsey concluded that the winery:** Bancroft, p. 36, and Judge's decision, *Robert Mondavi v. C. Mondavi and Sons*, page 29.

53   **to fire Robert:** Decision, August 12, 1976, *Robert Mondavi v. C. Mondavi and Sons*, p. 29.

54   **table that could seat twenty:** Serena Ventura, "Meet Signora Rosa Mondavi," p. 14.

54   **Michael would not be working for the Family business:** Robert Mondavi, *Harvests of Joy*, p. 18.

54   **her husband died:** Deposition of Rosa Mondavi, December 4, 1973, *Robert Mondavi v. C. Mondavi and Sons*, cases 29917 and 30122, Superior Court of California in the County of Napa.

55   **she would weep in her bed:** Serena Ventura, "Crush . . . ," pp. 94, 96.

56   **"I'm going to build a winery":** Robert Mondavi, "Creativity . . . ," pp. 37–38.

Chapter Four: To Kalon, 1963–1966

57   **he'd carry a folding card table. . . :** Robert Mondavi, *Harvests of Joy: My Passion for Excellence: How the Good Life Became Great Business* (New York: Harcourt Brace and Company, 1998), pp. 18–20.

58   **left him dispirited:** Robert Mondavi, *Harvests of Joy*, pp. 18–19.

58   **"Be a good boy—then we'll see":** Decision, August 12, 1976, *Robert Mondavi v. C. Mondavi and Sons*, p. 29.

58   **no longer be part of the business:** Decision, August 12, 1976, *Robert Mondavi v. C. Mondavi and Sons*, p. 30.

58   **Robert would almost exclusively talk business:** Michael Mondavi, interview by William F. Heintz, February 22, 1984 (St. Helena: Napa Valley Wine Library).

58   **"Every meal . . . had wine involved":** Michael Mondavi, Heintz interview.

58   **working at the Charles Krug Winery:** Michael's background and early plans are related in his first-person section of *Harvests of Joy*, pp. 321–322.

59   **unless they really wanted to:** Michael Mondavi, Heintz interview.

59   **Had the eminent professor somehow discovered . . . ?:** Michael Mondavi, interview with the author.

59   **the business school:** Michael Mondavi, interview with the author; James Conaway, *Napa* (New York: Avon Books, 1990), p. 166.

60   **they were willing to make sacrifices:** Robert Mondavi, "Creativity in the California wine industry," 1984 interview by Ruth Teiser (Berkeley: Regional Oral History Office, Bancroft Library, University of California, c. 1985), pp. 40–41.

61   **". . . a form of nonvoting shares":** Peter Ventura, interview with the author.

61   **Rosa flatly turned him down.:** Decision, August 12, 1976, *Robert Mondavi v. C. Mondavi and Sons*, p. 32.

61   **smarting, silent rebuke from his mother:** Serena Mondavi Ventura, "Crush: A Memoir of My Mother, the Mondavis, and Me" (Thesis, M.F.A.—Writing, University of San Francisco, 2005), pp. 112–113.

62   **Kern County oil:** William F. Heintz, *California's Napa Valley: One Hundred Sixty Years of Winemaking* (San Francisco : Scottwall Associates, c. 1999), p. 335.

62   **". . . we will resolve our differences":** Robert Mondavi, interview by Ina Hart and T. E. Wilde, December 29, 1978 (St. Helena: Napa Valley Wine Library Association).

62   **retained 50 percent of its equity:** Bancroft Robert Mondavi, "Creativity . . . ," p. 44.

62   **"most beautiful":** Charles Sullivan, *Napa Wine: A History from Mission Days to Present* (San Francisco: The Wine Appreciation Guild, 1994), p. 43.

62   **... a wide variety of grapes. . . :** Robert Mondavi, *Harvests of Joy*, p. 59.

63   **"the boss vineyard":** Sullivan, *Napa Wine*, p. 88.

63   **$1.35 million:** "Charles Krug Buys 500 Acre Napa Valley Vineyard," *Wines & Vines*, February 1962 (St. Helena, Calif.: Napa Valley Wine Library Association).

63   **The Mondavis held the property . . . :** Various sources on the To Kalon purchase, all with contradictory dates. I've used the date cited in a 2003 Robert Mondavi Winery media information sheet on "To Kalon Vineyard History." See also Sullivan, *Napa Wine*, p. 254, and Robert Mondavi, *Harvests of Joy*, p. 58, for different takes on the event.

64   **this was the place:** Robert Mondavi, *Harvests of Joy*, p. 63.

64   **Alexis Lichine at his Château Lascombes:** Hugh Johnson, *Hugh Johnson's Wine Companion: The Encyclopedia of Wines, Vineyards, and Winemakers* (London: Mitchell Beazley, 2003), p. 180.

64   **... to collect artifacts:** Charles Daniels Sr., interview with the author.

64   **". . . at three o'clock in the morning!":** Robert Mondavi, *Harvests of Joy*, p. 64.

65   **". . . you will pay me then":** Robert Mondavi, interview by Hart and Wilde.

65   **a sixth-generation Californian:** Cyril Ray, *Robert Mondavi of the Napa Valley* (Novato, CA: Presidio Press, 1984), p. 97.

66   **to take over the winery when he was gone:** Sullivan, *Napa Wine*, p. 276.

66   **"I wanted to get started that first year":** Robert Mondavi, interview by Hart Wilde.

66   **approval from the county:** Robert Mondavi, *Harvests of Joy*, pp. 69–70.

67   **to conclude he had been an American spy:** Michael Mondavi, interviews with the author. Mr. Alcantara is deceased.

67   **occupied through November with training:** "Mondavi Winery Celebrates First Season's Harvest" *St. Helena Star*, September 8, 1966.

68   **"Bobby, don't do this":** Robert Mondavi, *Harvests of Joy*, p. 70.

69   **Alioto graduated magna cum laude. . . :** Lance Williams and Larry D. Hatfield, "Joseph Alioto, 1916–1998," *San Francisco Examiner*, January 30, 1998, p. A-1.

69   **... the California Cooperative Wineries:** Bancroft of oral history of Joseph L. Alioto, pp. 24–27, 37–42.

70   **"So we don't steal you blind":** Joseph Maganini, interview with the author; John Martel, interview with the author, April 19, 2005; Robert Mondavi, *Harvests of Joy*, p. 18.

70   **a temporary cease-fire:** Bancroft of oral history of Joseph L. Alioto, p. 80.

70   **"exiled" for six months from the business:** Bancroft oral history of Joseph L. Alioto, p. 79.

70   **"even though she paid him his wages":** Bancroft oral history of Joseph L. Alioto, p. 81.

71   **a searing letter:** Letter from John Alioto to Robert Mondavi dated August 4, 1966, marked as Exhibit A, *Robert Mondavi v. C. Mondavi and Sons*, cases 29917 and 30122, Superior Court of California in the County of Napa.

71   **excoriated him for starting a new winery:** In fact, with this letter, Alioto was cagily laying the groundwork for the litigation that he correctly predicted lay ahead for the family. That letter was a piece of evidence he would later introduce to support his contention that Robert had been justifiably exiled from Krug because he was setting himself up as a rival to the family enterprise. Surely Alioto must also have known that Robert was at the same time receiving substantial sup-

port from Krug's in starting his own winery—down to Krug's even crushing grapes for him that year. The letter was patently disingenuous. Sensing this, Robert ignored it.

71 **"I couldn't sleep for three months . . .":** Robert Mondavi, "Creativity . . . ," p. 39.
72 **without staying to eat with them:** Anthony Cook, "Brother Against Brother: The Wine Feud That Split the Mondavi Family," *New West*, November 8, 1976, p. 26.

PART TWO: CONSTRUCTION

Chapter Five: Crush, 1966-1972

76 **"the Robert Mondavi Winery was meant to reach out":** Warren Winiarski, interview with the author.
76 **to borrow equipment and chemicals:** Warren Winiarski, interview with the author; Warren Winiarski, "Creating Classic Wines in the Napa Valley," 1991 and 1993 interviews by Ruth Teiser (Berkeley: Regional Oral History Office, Bancroft Library, University of California, c. 1994), p. 29.
76 **he never performed any consulting services:** Decision, August 12, 1976, *Robert Mondavi v. C. Mondavi and Sons*, p. 34.
76 **"we wanted to see him make a success . . .":** Ibid.
76 **poplar trees:** Cyril Ray, *Robert Mondavi of the Napa Valley* (Novato: Presidio Press, 1984), p. 100.
77 **even as Warren Winiarski made the wine:** Robert Mondavi, "Creativity in the California wine industry," 1984 interview by Ruth Teiser (Berkeley: Regional Oral History Office, Bancroft Library, University of California, c. 1985), p. 42.
77 **Father Levinus of the nearby Carmelite monastery:** "Mondavi Winery Celebrates First Season's Harvest," *St. Helena Star*, September 8, 1966.
77 **in English sprinkled with Latin words:** Based on recollections of Warren Winiarski; Warren Winiarski, interview with the author.
78 **that support would infuriate Peter:** Memorandum in Support of Joint Motion of Cross-Defendants Robert Mondavi et. al. for Partial Summary Judgment, March 26, 1976, *Robert Mondavi v. C. Mondavi and Sons*, cases 29917 and 30122, Superior Court of California in the County of Napa, p. 44.
78 **"a little bit mindful of destruction":** Warren Winiarski, interview with the author.
78 **barely three dozen bonded wineries:** William F. Heintz, *California's Napa Valley: One Hundred Sixty Years of Winemaking* (San Francisco: Scottwall Associates, c. 1999), p. 336.
79 **"and American wine in particular":** Paul Lukacs, *American Vintage: The Rise of American Wine* (New York: W. W. Norton, 2005), p. 133.
79 **"Robert's folly":** Brian R. Golden, Henry W. Lane, David T. A. Wesley, "Mondavi: Caliterra" (case study, Richard Ivey School of Business, University of Western Ontario, 1999), p. 2.
79 **mostly looked the other way:** Warren Winiarski, "Creating Classic Wines," p. 30.
79 **to Europeanize his last name:** Charles Daniels Sr., interview with the author.
79 **Robert's linguistic coup:** There are numerous sources for this, including Peter Mondavi Jr. in interview with the author and James Conaway, *Napa* (Boston: Houghton Mifflin, 1990), pp. 163–164.
80 **such perks as weekly wine tastings:** Robert Mondavi, "Creativity . . . ," p. 56.

80   **"I'm Michael Mondavi. Would you like a tour?":** Michael Mondavi, interview with the author.

80   **"Nepotism can be a good thing":** Gary Lipp and Michael Mondavi, interviews with the author. Lipp recalls Michael saying, "nepotism has always been good to me."

81   **inadvertently exposing the wine to air:** Michael Mondavi recalls taking the lids off the tank but says he did this because they fitted poorly. He attempted to replace them with something else to prevent oxidation. Michael Mondavi, interview with the author.

81   **to start a vineyard of his own:** George M. Taber, *Judgment of Paris: California vs. France and the Historic 1976 Paris Tasting That Revolutionized Wine* (New York: Scribner, 2005), pp. 95–105.

81   **"It was their material":** Warren Winiarski, interview with the author.

82   **"my son Michael, who is very young":** Miljenko Grgich, interview with the author.

82   **"a little Andre Tchelistcheff!":** Ibid.

82   **other methods he had learned at Beaulieu:** Miljenko Grgich, "A Croatian-American Winemaker in the Napa Valley," 1992 interview by Ruth Teiser (Berkeley: Regional Oral History Office, Bancroft Library, University of California, 1992), p. 19.

83   **"the test-tube winery":** Golden, Lane, and Wesley, "Mondavi: Caliterra," p. 2.

83   **ten times as much:** Miljenko Grgich, interview with the author.

83   **"I want to have total control and perfect wines":** Ibid.

83   **"it was always the family member":** Zelma Long, interview with the author.

84   **"one of Burgundy's finest products":** Taber, *Judgment of Paris*, p. 3.

85   **California wines were not considered good enough:** John L. Alioto, interview with the author.

85   **the first of many such marketing coups:** Based on accounts in Lukacs, *American Vintage*, p. 157; Robert Mondavi, "Creativity . . . ," p. 54; and Robert Mondavi, *Harvests of Joy: My Passion for Excellence: How the Good Life Became Great Business* (New York: Harcourt Brace and Company, 1998), p. 75.

86   **a judge dismissed related criminal charges:** Lance Williams and Larry D. Hatfield, "Joseph Alioto, 1916–1998," *San Francisco Examiner,* January 30, 1998, p. A-1.

86   **drained the energy from the administration:** John De Luca, interview with the author, May 16, 2005.

86   **"I fly by the seat of my pants":** Charles Williams, interview with the author.

87   **approaching an astonishing 100,000:** Declaration of R. Michael Mondavi, March 18, 1976, *Robert Mondavi v. C. Mondavi and Sons,* cases 29917 and 30122, Superior Court of California in the County of Napa, p. 2.

87   **look for an outside investor:** Robert Mondavi, "Creativity . . . ," p. 44.

87   **$12.5 million in cash to invest:** Charles Daniels Sr., interview with the author.

88   **wanted to compete with his brother:** Ibid.

88   **"being the best, not the biggest":** Decision, August 12, 1976, *Robert Mondavi v. C. Mondavi and Sons,* p. 74.

88   **shared his drive to excel:** Robert Mondavi, "Creativity . . . ," p. 44.

88   **he was determined:** Robert Mondavi, *Harvests of Joy,* p. 154.

88   **they gave equal say:** Cliff Adams, interview with the author.

89   **he could help pave the way:** Robert Mondavi, *Harvests of Joy,* pp. 151–154.

89   **"suede shoe boys":** Charles Williams, interview with the author.

90   **the real discussions:** Peter Ventura, interview with the author.

90   **refusing to allow him to ask questions:** Cliff Adams, interview with the author.

90   **any visible détente in the boardroom:** Ibid.

90   **a life of their own:** Op cit.

91   ***"an estate for them and their children":*** Decision, August 12, 1976, *Robert Mondavi v. C. Mondavi and Sons*, p. 9. Emphasis added by the judge.

92   **Share allocation table:** *Robert Mondavi v. C. Mondavi and Sons*, p. 15.

92   **a family member who wanted to sell out:** *Robert Mondavi v. C. Mondavi and Sons.*

93   **"bulldoze Mother":** Memorandum in Support of Joint Motion of Cross-Defendants Robert Mondavi et al for Partial Summary Judgment, March 26, 1976, *Robert Mondavi v. C. Mondavi and Sons*, p. 83.

93   **take over Krug, and destroy their winery:** Decision, August 12, 1976, *Robert Mondavi v. C. Mondavi and Sons*, pp. 76–78.

93   **Krug was simply too big and too expensive:** *Robert Mondavi v. C. Mondavi and Sons*, pp. 76–78.

93   **"with you as the controlling factor":** *Robert Mondavi v. C. Mondavi and Sons*, p. 41.

94   **pay the inheritance tax:** *Robert Mondavi v. C. Mondavi and Sons*, p. 47.

94   **"marriage between the Mondavi and the Schlitz":** Letter to Joseph Alioto dated April 3, 1972, contained in Decision, August 12, 1976, *Robert Mondavi v. C. Mondavi and Sons*, p. 46.

95   **"driving her crazy":** Bancroft oral history of Joseph L. Alioto, pp. 81–82.

Chapter Six: Gunslingers, 1972–1975

98   ***"no payment to be made for goodwill":*** Decision, August 12, 1976, *Robert Mondavi v. C. Mondavi and Sons*, p. 51. Emphasis added by the judge.

99   **asked his son John:** Exhibits of the minutes of C. Mondavi and Sons board meetings, *Robert Mondavi v. C. Mondavi and Sons.*

99   **"Your job is to vote":** John Alioto, interview with author.

100   **"He knew it was going to result in litigation":** Ibid.

100   **the flamboyant court veteran:** Cliff Adams, interview with the author, May 23, 2005.

100   **leaving Rosa alone in that role:** Trial Brief Submitted on Behalf of C. Mondavi and Sons, et al., April 1, 1976, *Robert Mondavi v. C. Mondavi and Sons*, cases 29917 and 30122, Superior Court of California in the County of Napa, p. 7.

101   **leaving Adams at sea:** John Martel, interview with the author. Cliff Adams doesn't recall whether the judge and Alioto spoke Italian together.

101   **drop bombs on cows and rice paddies:** John Martel, interview with the author.

102   **"somewhere between a shambles and a shipwreck":** Ibid.

104   **more than ten times as much:** Pretrial Statement and Trial Brief of Plaintiff, April 1, 1976, *Robert Mondavi v. C. Mondavi and Sons*, cases 29917 and 30122, Superior Court of California in the County of Napa, p. 18.

104   **"subsidize a competitor":** Pretrial statement and brief of defendant, *Robert Mondavi v. C. Mondavi and Sons*, p. 14. Decision, August 12, 1976, *Robert Mondavi v. C. Mondavi and Sons*, pp. 36–37.

105   **"presently experiencing serious financial difficulties":** Ibid., footnote 19 of page 33 of the trial brief.

105   **Americans would be drinking far more wine:** William F. Heintz, *California's Napa Valley: One Hundred Sixty Years of Winemaking* (San Francisco: Scottwall Associates, c. 1999), pp. 337–347.

105   **found him exhausting:** Ted Simpkins, interview with the author, November 16, 2005.

106   **summoning Robert to Seattle:** Michael Mondavi, interview with the author. Cliff Adams recalls that the meeting was in Toronto.

106   **poor recording-keeping and accounting:** Robert Mondavi, *Harvests of Joy: My Passion for Excellence: How the Good Life Became Great Business* (New York: Harcourt Brace and Company, 1998), pp. 170–171.

106   **Robert would later blame . . . an accountant:** Ibid.

106   **his own unchecked spending:** Background interview with the author.

106   **Charles Daniels's friendship:** Charles Daniels, interview with the author.

107   **"as long as it means dealing with Peter":** Letter to Robert Mondavi Winery dated September 8, 1975, labeled as Exhibit A, attached to Reply Memorandum in Support of Motion for Partial Summary Judgment, May 6, 1976, *Robert Mondavi v. C. Mondavi and Sons*, cases 29917 and 30122, Superior Court of California in the County of Napa, p. 1.

107   **a man of integrity:** Decision, August 12, 1976, *Robert Mondavi v. C. Mondavi and Sons*, p. 149.

109   **"Wait! She hasn't finished her answer!":** Bruce MacLeod, interview with the author.

110   **"a god-damned thing":** In the transcript from Peter Mondavi's deposition as part of the *Robert Mondavi v. C. Mondavi and Sons* case, this is recorded as "GD."

Chapter Seven: Judgment, 1975–1976

115   **in Napa County history:** Anthony Cook, "Brother Against Brother: The Wine Feud that Split the Mondavi Family," *New West*, November 8, 1976, p. 26.

115   **Robert's supporters sat on one side:** Cliff Adams, interview with the author.

115   **a "cotillion intermission":** Ibid.

115   **"One has longer legs and is a devil":** James Conaway, *Napa* (New York: Avon Books, 1990), p. 171.

116   **"a cerebro-vascular" accident:** Certificate of Death, Rosa Mondavi, County of Napa.

116   **"to the very best of one's ability":** Editorial, *St. Helena Star,* July 8, 1976.

117   **"at the family mausoleum":** Cook, "Brother Against Brother," p. 21.

117   **There were separate receptions:** Joseph and Elsa Maganini, interview with the author.

117   **Peter "dominated and controlled":** Helen Ventura, Answers to First Set of Interrogatories Propounded to Helen Ventura in *Robert Mondavi v. C. Mondavi & Sons*, cases 29917 and 30122, Superior Court of California in the County of Napa.

118   **returned at her family's request:** Peter Ventura, interview with the author

118   **a "legal interrogation":** *Robert Mondavi v. C. Mondavi and Sons*, cases 29917 and 30122, Superior Court of California in the County of Napa.

119   **another emotional collapse:** Elsa and Joseph Maganini, interview with the author.

119   **"nothing that money wouldn't cure":** Joseph Maganini, interview with the author.

119   **Martel would wake up:** Bruce MacLeod, interview with the author.

121   **"the God Almighty in the wine industry":** Memorandum in Support of Joint Motion of Cross-Defendants Robert Mondavi et al. for partial summary judgment, March 26, 1976, *Robert Mondavi v. C. Mondavi and Sons*, p. 23.

122   **mainly a semantic argument on Martel's part:** In an e-mail dated January 11, 2007, and sent by Peter Mondavi Jr., Peter Mondavi Sr. strongly objected to Mr. Martel's characterization of this moment during cross-examination. He wrote: "The opposing attorney (Mr. Martel) used semantics to portray wine that was of

lesser quality to mean poor quality or not wine at all. We all know that winemakers 'complain about quality' but that does not mean it was not acceptable by industry standards and it absolutely didn't mean it was inferior. It only meant that it does not meet the quality standards I expected. It is unfair to recount 30+ years after the fact that a wine was not wine or was unacceptable quality.

122   **blow for the defense:** John Martel and Bruce MacLeod, interviews with the author. Despite numerous efforts to track down the transcription service and individual transcribers, the trial transcript could not be located.

122   **it was not even usable:** Decision, August 12, 1976, *Robert Mondavi v. C. Mondavi and Sons*, p. 59.

122   **"He had basically collapsed":** Bruce MacLeod, interview with the author.

123   **"It doesn't look good":** Joseph Maganini recalled Peter Ventura telling him this. Joseph Maganini, interview with the author.

123   **the thirty-five-year-old Kathleen Sullivan:** Lance Williams and Larry D. Hatfield, "Joseph Alioto, 1916–1998," *San Francisco Examiner*, January 30, 1998, p. A-1.

123   **the judge found them guilty:** Decision, August 12, 1976, *Robert Mondavi v. C. Mondavi and Sons*, p. 128.

123   **Krug's "majority" directors:** Ibid.

124   **"totally lacking of evidentiary support":** Decision, August 12, 1976, *Robert Mondavi v. C. Mondavi and Sons*, p. 77.

Chapter Eight: The Heirs, 1976–1978

125   **in a sink at night instead:** Michael Mondavi, interview with the author.

125   **borrowing money . . . to buy groceries:** Cliff Adams, interview with the author; Zelma Long, interview with the author. Michael Mondavi says this is an exaggeration and doubts his father ever borrowed money for groceries, but does say the company was extremely cash-strapped in those days; Michael Mondavi, interview with the author.

125   **"You're going to have to give me a receipt":** Brad Warner, interview with the author. Elaine Clerici is deceased.

126   **agreed to a reduced rate:** Robert Mondavi, Declaration in Support of Motion for Award of Attorneys' Fees and Reimbursement of Out-of-Pocket Expenses, October 2, 1976, *Robert Mondavi v. C. Mondavi and Sons*, cases 29917 and 30122, Superior Court of California in the County of Napa, p. 2.

126   **lost the winery:** Timothy Mondavi, interview with the author.

126   **$46 million:** Decision, August 12, 1976, *Robert Mondavi v. C. Mondavi and Sons*, p. 15.

126   **one of the worst experiences:** Robert Mondavi, *Harvests of Joy*, p. 189.

126   **"retelling an age-old conflict":** John Norton, "Mondavi—A Dynasty Torn and a Family Divided," *Napa Valley Register*, August 13, 1976, pp. 2.

127   **"One man can force you . . .":** Cook, "Brother Against Brother," p. 27.

127   **Rosa's gifts to Peter's sons:** Peter Ventura, interview with the author; Cliff Adams, interview with the author.

128   **eleven times as much:** Max Gutierrez, Declaration in Support of Request for Fees for Extraordinary Services, filed in June 1983, exhibit in Rosa Mondavi Probate case.

128   **her partnership interest:** Decision, August 12, 1976, *Robert Mondavi v. C. Mondavi and Sons*, pp. 68–69.

128   **to Mary's sons:** Rosa Mondavi, "Last Will and Testament of Rose Mondavi," signed November 28, 1976, contained in Rose Mondavi Probate file at Napa County Courthouse.

129   **"betrayed them at trial"**: Peter Ventura, Declaration dated June 15, 1977, Appendices to Memorandum of Points and Authorities, *Peter Mondavi and Mary Westbrook v. Superior Court of Napa County*, Civil Case 41502, Court of Appeal of the State of California, First Appellate District, Division Two, p. 1.

129   **they should earn more**: Minutes of the Meeting of Board of Directors, C. Mondavi and Sons, November 13, 1977.

129   **"refused to pay unreasonable prices"**: Minutes of the Meeting of Board of Directors, C. Mondavi and Sons, November 13, 1977.

131   **for decades afterward**: Peter Ventura elaborated, "My mother had attempted to commit suicide over [the family breakup] one or two times. She was traumatized beyond a level that I don't think either of the brothers was able to appreciate. Ten, twenty years later, she would wake up screaming and it would be from the family issues. She was never able to exorcise those demons." Peter Ventura, interview with the author.

131   **they felt shunned**: Peter Ventura, interview with the author.

132   **remedial work costing more than $125,000**: Douglas Watson, Declaration, June 10, 1977, Appendices to Memorandum of Points and Authorities, *Peter Mondavi and Mary Westbrook v. Superior Court of Napa County*, Civil Case 41502, Court of Appeal of the State of California, First Appellate District, Division Two, p. 3.

133   **Blanche was furious**: Doug Watson, interview with the author.

134   **"too sincere, too earnest, too truthful"**: Henry Miller, *Big Sur and the Oranges of Hieronymous Bosch* (New York: New Directions Publishing Corporation, 1957), pp. 61–62.

134   **ready to loosen up**: Charles and Lili Thomas, interview with the author; Brad Warner, interviews with the author.

134   **"Tim, the poet . . ."**: Based on the recollection of Arlene Bernstein, who attended the same party; interview with the author. Mini is deceased.

135   **far more mature**: Based on a photo in the *Redwood Rancher: The Magazine of Redwood Empire Agriculture*, September 1971, p. 7.

135   **"And you can go on and on"**: Robert Mondavi, "Creativity in the California Wine Industry," 1984 interview by Ruth Teiser (Berkeley: Regional Oral History Office, Bancroft Library, University of California, c. 1985), pp. 80–81.

136   **"there's always going to be turmoil"**: Robert Mondavi, *Harvests of Joy*, p. 170.

136   **he would good-humouredly help**: Zelma Long, interview with the author, March 28, 2005.

136   **the episode could have been tragic**: The accident anecdote was related second-hand by retired UC Davis Professor Cornelius S. Ough, who visited Stellenbosch shortly after the accident; interview with Aleta George, August 29, 2005. Timothy Mondavi confirmed the accident occurred; interview with the author, December 15, 2005.

136   **the kind of sibling squabbling**: "I was planning a different career," recalled Timothy later. "Growing up, with all the family strife at Krug, I had decided that a family business was something you don't want to be in. There was a lot of pride, but little joy." Robert Mondavi, *Harvests of Joy*, p. 169.

137   **fighting with his own brother**: Timothy Mondavi, interview with the author.

137   **he partied a lot**: Former Mondavi vineyard manager Charlie Williams, interview with the author.

137   **Timothy married**: Marriage certificate, Timothy Mondavi and Dorothy Reed, County of Napa, July 30, 1976.

137   **"a little time to play"**: "Wine—It Is a Way of Life," *San Francisco Chronicle*, reprinted from *Women's Wear Daily*, January 3, 1977, p. 23.

137   **the "Santa Clara man's image":** *The Redwood* (Santa Clara, Calif.: Santa Clara College, 1965), p. 62.

138   **half her class was female:** "Enrollment spirals," *The Santa Clara*, September 27, 1962, p. 1.

138   **"for the purpose of mate selection":** Dr. Witold Krassowski, "Krasowski: Co-eds Assist Mate Choices," *The Santa Clara*, May 16, 1963, p. 4.

138   **stormed the university's cafeteria:** *The Redwood* (Santa Clara, Calif.: Santa Clara College, 1969), p. 106.

138   **Students also staged a sit-down:** *The Redwood* (Santa Clara, Calif.: Santa Clara College, 1969), p. 108.

138   **The couple separated:** Petition to dissolve marriage, Superior Court of California, County of Napa, *Marcia Anne Morey v. Michael Warren Morey*. March 5, 1973, case 29870.

139   **hesitance about the terms:** "Marcia's somebody of great integrity: She was not about to sign something that was not true," says Cliff Adams, who handled the dissolution for her. Cliff Adams, interview with the author.

139   **Marcia successfully petitioned the judge:** Petition to dissolve marriage, Superior Court of California, County of Napa, *Marcia Anne Morey v. Michael Warren Morey*. March 5, 1973, case 29870.

139   **"I'm a slow mover":** "Wine—It Is a Way of Life," *San Francisco Chronicle*, reprinted from *Women's Wear Daily*, January 3, 1977, p. 23.

140   **aggressively courted New York restaurants:** Robert Fairchild, interview by Catherine Thorpe, May 23, 2006.

140   **her job was to educate:** Robert Mondavi, *Harvests of Joy*, pp. 168–169.

140   **"She's just that articulate":** Robert Mondavi, "Creativity . . . ," pp. 79–80.

141   **her father never listened to her:** Louisa Thomas Hargrave, conversation with the author.

141   **"daddy's girl":** Frank Farella, interview with the author.

141   **"Dad makes all the decisions":** "Wine—It Is a Way of Life," *San Francisco Chronicle*, reprinted from *Women's Wear Daily*, January 3, 1977, p. 23.

141   **"You've got to make him listen to me!":** Cliff Adams, interview with the author, February 22, 2005.

141   **alleging that he had discriminated:** The northern California office of the EEOC says complaints are purged after a year.

142   **modest cash settlement:** Cliff Adams, interview with the author.

142   **ostensible reason for the dismissal:** Dorothy Barajas-Williams and Charles Williams, interview with author. Cliff Adams, interview with the author.

142   **crushed by the betrayal, as if her own family:** Dorothy Barajas-Williams, interview with the author.

142   **"Good employees are not the easiest":** Memo from Robert Mondavi to Management Council dated May 23, 1986, submitted as Exhibit F, *Dorothy Barajas-Williams v. Robert Mondavi Winery*, et al., case 5385, Superior Court of California in the County of Napa, p. 1.

142   **severance pay equal to seven weeks' salary:** Memo from Greg Evans to Dorothy Barajas-Williams dated May 23, 1986, submitted as Exhibit G, *Dorothy Barajas-Williams v. Robert Mondavi Winery*, et al., case 5385, Superior Court of California in the County of Napa, p. 1.

143   **she, and not her husband:** Timothy Mondavi, interview with the author.

143   **a damaging effect on employee morale:** Michael Mondavi, interview with the author.

143   **not directly supervised:** Declaration of Clifford S. Adams in Support of

Summary Judgment, *Dorothy Barajas-Williams v. Robert Mondavi Winery*, et al., case 5385, Superior Court of California in the County of Napa, September 11, 1989, p. 5.

143   **Timothy remained her husband's boss:** Dorothy Barajas-Williams, interview with the author.

144   **boys-will-be-boys fun:** Brad Warner, interview with the author; Michael Mondavi, interview with the author.

144   **there were female staffers present:** Michelle Oltman, interview with the author.

144   **Robert developed a reputation:** Harvey Posert, interview with the author.

144   **"or at least be discreet":** Michael Mondavi, interview with the author.

144   **took Robert's gesture in stride:** Charles Williams and Dorothy Barajas-Williams, interview with the author. McDermott declined to be interviewed.

144   **the women didn't talk about it either:** Background conversation with a prominent litigator in Napa Valley.

Chapter Nine: "That Woman," 1978–1980

146   **Robert's business trips:** Michael Mondavi, interview with the author, July 1, 2006.

146   **hadn't known how to boil water:** Robert Mondavi, *Harvests of Joy*, p. 72.

146   **picnics on the lawn, and the jazz concerts:** Margrit Biever Mondavi, Annie Roberts, Laurie Smith, and Victoria Wise, *Annie and Margrit: Recipes and Stories from the Robert Mondavi Kitchen* (Berkeley: Ten Speed Press, 2003), preface, p.xiii.

147   **divorced American Catholics who remarried:** *Chronicle of America* (Mount Kisco, NY: Chronicle Publications 1992), p. 856. Author was a contributor to this book.

148   **served as an altar boy:** Opening remarks by Robert Mondavi at the mission program, October 1990. Transcipts of the Robert Mondavi Mission Programs, 1988–1990, courtesy of Harvey Posert.

148   **in a Catholic ceremony:** Divorce records of Robert G. Mondavi and Majorie E. Mondavi, 1979, case 39362, Superior Court of California in the County of Napa.

148   **as early as the mid-1960s:** Michael Mondavi, interview with the author.

148   **they parked their cars:** Michael Mondavi, interview with the author; Margrit Biever Mondavi, interview with the author.

148   **a modest wine cellar:** Margrit Biever Mondavi, interview with author.

148   **"I was his little Heidi":** Margrit Biever Mondavi, interview with the author.

148   **"twenty-five at night":** Blake Green, "A Charmed Life in the Napa Valley," *San Francisco Chronicle*, September 22, 1981, People section, p. 19.

149   **"oblivious to her needs and feelings":** Robert Mondavi, *Harvests of Joy*, p. 245–246.

149   **she required hospitalization:** Joe and Elsa Maganini, interview with the author.

149   **preferring vodka to wine:** Peter Ventura, interview with the author; Serena Ventura, "Crush . . . ," p. 78.

149   **smoking . . . despite her emphysema:** Michael Mondavi, interview with the author.

149   **blamed Robert's neglect:** Ibid. Additionally, Brad Warner described the Mondavi children's blaming of their father for their mother's drinking problem; interview with the author.

149   **his father's behavior:** Michael Mondavi, interview with the author; Fred Franzia, interview with the author, May 16, 2006. Franzia shared Michael's view after traveling with Robert and Marjorie to Europe in the early 1970s.

149   **Yet Robert himself . . . :** Bobbe Serlis Cortese, interview with the author.

150   **a ski break:** Michael Mondavi, interview with the author.

150   **"Oh, come on, you two":** Arlene Bernstein, interview with the author.

151   **"more than just a colleague":** Billy Cross, interview with the author.

151   **Jonesy's Famous Steak House:** Ibid. Jonesy's is listed in the top tier of restaurants in a guidebook of the era; Michael Topolos, Betty Dopson, and Jeffrey Caldewey, *Napa Valley Wine Tour* (St. Helena: Vintage Image, 1977), p. 43.

152   **The students' mouths watered:** Drawn from a speech delivered by Margrit Biever Mondavi on the occasion of the thirtieth reunion of the Great Chefs program, July 14, 2006.

152   **"married a Republican banker . . .":** Ibid.

152   **the last paragraph of the final page:** Drawn from a speech delivered by Margrit Biever Mondavi on the occasion of the thirtieth reunion of the Great Chefs program, July 14, 2006.

152–53 **after disco dancing until dawn:** Zelma Long, interview with the author.

153   **"Little Bo Peep":** Charles Williams and Dorothy Barajas-Williams, interview with the author.

154   **they cringed:** Brad Warner, interview with the author.

154   **failing to ask her opinion:** Axel Fabre, interview with the author.

154   **"in the backseat, all by himself":** Drawn from a speech delivered by Margrit Biever Mondavi on the occasion of the thirtieth reunion of the Great Chefs program, July 14, 2006.

155   **successfully executing it:** Michael Mondavi, interview with the author.

155   **"my father's mistress":** Billy Cross, interview with the author. Michael Mondavi, interview with author.

155   **polite in public . . . at the very least:** Brad Warner, interview with the author.

155   **"that woman":** Cliff Adams, interview with the author; James Conaway, *Napa* (New York: Avon Books, 1990), p. 165.

155   **a string of invective:** Bobbe Serlis Cortese, interview with the author. Michael Mondavi also said he "wouldn't be surprised if Marcia got upset and stormed into Dad's office and called him a lot of names"; interview with the author. Marcia Mondavi Borger declined to comment.

156   **three time zones away:** Cliff Adams, interview with the author.

156   **cover for their romance:** Harvey Posert, interview with the author.

157   **Robert held about 45 percent . . . :** Cliff Adams, interview with the author.

158   **providing her with money to remodel it:** Cliff Adams, interview with the author.

158   **"we knew what it was like to be ostracized":** Billy Cross, interview with the author.

158   **toast to the couple's new life together:** Arlene Bernstein, interview with the author; the event is also described in a letter from the Bernsteins to Robert Mondavi on the occasion of his ninetieth birthday.

158   **insisted that Margrit sign a prenuptial agreement:** Cliff Adams, interview with the author. Michael Mondavi says he does not recall whether his father and Margrit had a prenuptial agreement, nor does he remember insisting that they sign one; interview with the author.

159   **She waived all rights:** Cliff Adams, interview with the author. Adams drew up the prenuptial agreement. Michael Mondavi did not recall that his father and Margrit had had a prenuptial agreement; interview with the author.

159   **reserved for their mother:** Cliff Adams, interview with the author.

159   **a provision arising out of his children's concerns:** Background interview; this limit in the prenuptial agreement was confirmed with Cliff Adams in an interview with the author.

159 **two weeks after Margrit's marriage was legally dissolved:** Final Judgment of Dissolution, May 2, 1979, *Margrit Biever v. Philip Biever,* case C39749, Superior Court of California in the County of Napa.

160 **he laughed and spelled it out for him:** Margrit Biever Mondavi, interview with the author.

160 **if she loved and supported his father:** Michael Mondavi, interview with the author.

Chapter Ten: The Baron, 1978–1981

161 **one of the richest and most powerful families:** Baron Philippe himself described his family in this way, as recounted in Joan Littlewood, *Baron Philippe: The Very Candid Autobiography of Baron Philippe de Rothschild* (New York: Crown Publishers, 1984), p. 1.

161 **He owned a planet named Philippa:** Littlewood, *Baron Philippe,* p. 286.

162 **"no longer mere vassals for the merchants":** William Echikson, *Noble Rot: A Bordeaux Wine Revolution* (New York: W. W. Norton and Company, 2004), p. 79.

163 **. . . and concrete pillboxes everywhere:** Littlewood, *Baron Philippe,* p. 258.

163 **"Les Quatre Grands, Noblesse Oblige":** Ibid, p. 299

163 **"Premier je suis, second je fus, Mouton ne change":** Op. cit., p. 324.

164 **about a million cases a year:** Echikson, *Noble Rot,* p. 81.

164 **with the cookbook celebrity James Beard:** Brad Alderson, interview with the author.

164 **they sell these commodity wines themselves:** Michael Mondavi, interview with the author.

165 **the baron pinched Bobbe's knee:** Bobbe Serlis Cortese, interview with the author.

166 **the baron sought geographic diversification:** Ibid., as well as Frank Prial, "2½ Decades Later, a Very Good Year," *New York Times,* August 24, 1994, p. B-1 (national), C-1 (local).

166 **austere, all-business daughter:** Cyril Ray cites the Baron Philippe de Rothschild's describing Marcia as "very austere, very severe and businesslike, even more than her father." Cyril Ray, *Robert Mondavi of the Napa Valley* (Novato: Presidio Press, 1984), p. 20.

167 **its salon was far and away grander:** Based on a description by Cyril Ray. Cyril Ray, *Mouton-Rothschild: The Wine, the Family, the Museum* (London: Christie's Wine Publications, 1977), p. 120.

167 **"Hiya, Bob!":** Cyril Ray, *Robert Mondavi of the Napa Valley* (Novato: Presidio Press, 1984), p. 114.

167 **"my business is done in my bedroom":** Robert Mondavi, "Creativity . . . ," p. 83.

167 **"propped up against his pillows":** Frederic Morton, *The Rothschilds: A Family Portrait* (New York: Atheneum, 1962), p. 287.

169 **"I'm going to develop this joint venture":** Timothy Mondavi, speech to the San Francisco Wine and Food Society, May 18, 1985, transcript p. 17.

169 **"We're being recognized more all the time":** Ibid.

171 **well-known gay magazine in United States:** Robert Mondavi, *Harvests of Joy,* p. 220. Susan Pate, who was on the conference call in question, also related the story; interview with the author.

171 **"A creative affair":** Susan and Dwight Pate, interview with the author.

171 **could not keep his hands off:** Susan and Dwight Pate, interview with the author.

172 **with one of his dogs lying nearby:** Tati is the name of the dog that Susan Pate recalls.

172   **three or four hundred designs:** Ray, *Robert Mondavi of the Napa Valley*, p. 123.

172   **"a Jewish nose and an Italian nose?":** Harvey Posert, interview with the author, September 9, 2005.

173   **Others wondered how two supremely charming egotists:** Bruce David Colen, "Master Vintner: Robert Mondavi," *Town & Country*, December 1983, p. 312.

173   **"the marble palace":** Sean Wilsey, *Oh the Glory of It All* (New York: The Penguin Press, 2005), p. 72.

174   **"30 Seconds Over Tokyo":** Herb Caen, *The World of Herb Caen: San Francisco 1938–1997* (San Francisco: Chronicle Books, 1997), p. 73.

174   **a reputation for making things happen:** Pat Montandon, interview with the author.

175   **A fire had erupted:** Account based on articles in *The St. Helena Star* the week of June 12–22, 1981.

175–76 **nearly double of most estimates:** James Laube, "Two Days That Changed Napa Valley," WineSpectator.com, June 3, 2005, http://www.winespectator.com/Wine/Features/0,1197,2732,00.html.

176   **it was heady vindication:** Moira Johnston, "A Magnificent Obsession," *New West*, August 1981, p. 67.

176   **"It will zoom":** Stan Vaughan, "A Classic Wine Region," *Napa Valley Register*, June 22, 1981, p. 1.

176   **had it contained:** Ibid.

Chapter Eleven: Father and Sons, 1982–1984

180   **"Queen down here or king of the hill?":** Charles Williams, interview with the author, November 10, 2005.

180   **"more reflective of the valley's history":** Bruce David Colen, "View from Wappo Hill: Robert and Margrit Mondavi's Napa Valley Vineyard," *Architectural Digest* 46, no. 5 (May 1989), pp. 279–281.

180   **financially supported by the company:** Cliff Adams, interview with the author, October 6, 2005. Adams was referring to the company's financing of road construction through the property.

180   **"We're going to go crazy":** Cliff Adams, interview with the author, September 1, 2005.

181   **a nearly twelve-thousand-square-foot home:** Robert and Margrit's main house is 11,830 square feet. Napa County Assessor, record for parcel 039-040-042-000.

181   **"a state-of-the-art castle":** *Lifestyles of the Rich and Famous*, episode 97126.

181   **"Lucullan, with Bob as the Roman general":** Jay Stuller and Glen Martin, *Through the Grapevine* (New York: Wynwood Press, 1989), p. 244.

182   **the modest ground rent of just $176 per year:** Prospectus, Class A Common Stock, Robert Mondavi Corporation June 9, 1993, p. 45.

182   **"I run twenty miles every week . . .":** James Suckling, "Robert Mondavi: Man of the Year," *Wine Spectator*, May 1, 1984, p. 1.

182   **"Bob would take everyone to the Tour d'Argent":** Bruce David Colen, "Master Vintner: Robert Mondavi," *Town & Country*, December 1983, p. 317.

183   **"Redundancy is his middle name":** Deposition of R. Michael Mondavi, April 17, 1992, *Gary Ramona v. Stephanie Ramona, Marche Isabella, et al.*, case C61898, Superior Court of California in the County of Napa, p. 31.

183   **"I'd just like to say . . .":** Ray, *Robert Mondavi of the Napa Valley*, p. 56.

183   **His charisma and energy drew glamorous people:** Moira Johnston, *Spectral Evidence: The Ramona Case : Incest, Memory, and Truth on Trial in Napa Valley* (Boston: Houghton Mifflin, 1997), p. 54.

183   **"great wines and great men in the same year!":** Bruce David Colen, "Master Vintner: Robert Mondavi," *Town & Country*, December 1983, p. 224.

184   **king Carl Gustaf:** The Swedish king's visit was reported in *The Napa Valley Register*. "Sweden's King Gustaf in Visit to Napa Valley," *Napa Valley Register*, March 12, 1984.

184   **looked like a Mafia funeral:** Moira Johnston, "A Marriage Made in Napa," *California Living* magazine, April 22, 1984, p. 18.

185   **"I think that's a terrible idea":** Cliff Adams, interview with the author.

185   **"It makes you feel like crap":** Michael Mondavi, interview with the author.

185   **"Did I do a good job? Did I do my best?":** Interview of Michael Mondavi by wine historian William F. Heintz, February 22, 1984.

186   **"I'm going to kill you, motherfucker!":** Gary Lipp, interview with the author.

187   **"I could try not to repeat it":** Michael Mondavi, interview with the author.

187   **Michael began slamming doors:** Cliff Adams, interview with the author.

187   **He patiently worked through fifty-four takes:** Ibid.

187   **"Every man has his own management style":** Original print advertisement from archives of the Wine Institute.

188   **tore around in a golf cart and crashed it:** Background anecdote from CEO of a prominent Napa Valley winery, after hosting a YPO event in the late 1980s.

188   **to maintain complete confidentiality:** Andrea Cunningham, interview by Catherine Thorpe.

188   **Young Presidents' Organization:** Andrea Cunningham, interview by Catherine Thorpe.

188   **Michael spent too much time:** Cliff Adams, interview with the author.

188   **bridling under the perception:** Deposition of Gary Ramona, March 23, 1993, *Gary Ramona v. Stephanie Ramona, Marche Isabella, et al.*, case C61898, Superior Court of California in the County of Napa, p. 1002.

188   **a fishing trip he took in June of 1989:** The account of the trip that follows is based on three sources: Brief of Accident/Probable Cause, SEA89FA117, National Transportation Safety Board, approved June 22, 1992, pp. 1–2; Factual Report SEA89FA117, National Transportation Safety Board, pp. 2–4; and Pilot Rich Casias, interview by Catherine Thorpe.

189   **"we would have all gone":** Timothy Mondavi, interview with the author.

189   **"Tim, you are thirteen minutes late!":** James Suckling, "Robert Mondavi: Man of the Year," *Wine Spectator*, May 1–15, 1984, p. 12.

189–90 **Timothy's humiliation was too blatant to ignore:** Zelma Long, interview with the author. Timothy acknowledged his father would make him cry in meetings. Timothy Mondavi, interview with the author.

190   **preferring lengthy discussion:** Brad Warner, interview with the author.

191   **"There's plenty of room here for you and Tim":** Deposition of Gary Ramona, March 23, 1993, *Gary Ramona v. Stephanie Ramona, Marche Isabella, et al.*, p. 1023.

191   **Robert dispatched Michael to Sonoma:** Sam Sebastiani, interview with the author.

191   **"what I now call the humiliation factor":** Robert Mondavi, *Harvests of Joy*, p. 266.

Chapter Twelve: Thicker Than Water, 1984–1990

193   **"These kids can't run the business":** Cliff Adams, interview with the author.

194   **the overall management of the business:** Dale Crandall, interview with the author.

194   **Serlis would pull the mask to his face:** Greg Evans, interview with the author.

194   **frequently bog down in their disagreements:** Ibid. Cliff Adams, interviews with the author.

195   **"He always seemed to hold court":** Robert Mondavi, draft of eulogy for Harry Serlis, Wine Institute archives, February, 1984.

195   **One of Dr. Grundland's recommendations:** Deposition of Gary Ramona, January 28, 1992, Volume IV, page 826, in *Gary Ramona v. Stephanie Romona, Marche Isabella, et al.*, case 61898, Superior Court of California in the County of Napa.

195   **He spent only a year in that role:** Deposition of Barry Grundland, July 2, 1991, *Holly Ramona v. Gary Ramona et al.*, case 621124, Superior Court of California in the County of Napa, pp. 3–4.

196   **also met with employees and their families:** Deposition of Barry Grundland, July 2, 1991, *Holly Ramona v. Gary Ramona, et al.*, p. 23.

196   **Peter and Blanche accepted an invitation:** James Laube, *Wine Spectator,* July 16, 1985.

196   **for counseling sessions to involve . . . :** Brad Warner, interview with the author; Deposition of Barry Grundland, June 11, 1992, *Gary Ramona v. Stephanie Ramona, Marche Isabella, et al.*, case C61898, Superior Court of California in the County of Napa, pp. 10–11.

197   **attended management-council and board meetings:** Moira Johnston, *Spectral Evidence: The Ramona Case: Incest, Memory, and Truth on Trial in Napa Valley* (Boston: Houghton Mifflin, 1997), pp. 63–64.

197   **crying if the situation got too overwhelming:** Brad Warner, interview with author. Zelma Long, interview with the author.

197   **the acquisition was also perceived:** Deposition of Gary Ramona, March 23, 1993, *Gary Ramona v. Stephanie Ramona, Marche Isabella, et al.*, p. 1019; Michael Weis, interview with the author.

198   **"stacked to the ceiling":** Robert Fairchild, interview by Catherine Thorpe.

198   **two million cases . . . in 1985:** Extrapolated from a chart of case sales by brand for 1988, 1989, and 1990; Prospectus, Robert Mondavi Corporation, June 9, 1993, p. 16.

198   **"he would forget to eat":** Michael Weis, interview with the author.

198   **the sales team . . . had made overoptimistic projections:** Deposition of Timothy Mondavi, May 22, 1992, *Gary Ramona v. Stephanie Ramona, Marche Isabella, et al.*, case C61898, Superior Court of California in the County of Napa, p. 17.

198   **further fanning the flames:** Memorandum from Gary Ramona to Dennis Blanc, dated October 25, 1990, pp. 3–4; marked as Exhibit KK attached to Deposition of Gary Ramona, January 27, 1992, *Gary Ramona v. Stephanie Ramona, Marche Isabella, et al.*, case C61898, Superior Court of California in the County of Napa.

199   **"scares them off."** Moira Johnston, *Spectral Evidence: The Ramona Case: Incest, Memory, and Truth on Trial in Napa Valley* (Boston: Houghton Mifflin, 1997), p. 41.

200   **goal of surpassing Charles Krug.** Deposition of Gary Ramona, March 23, 1993, *Gary Ramona v. Stephanie Ramona, Marche Isabella, et al.*, p. 503.

200   **simians in diapers:** Axel Fabre, interview with the author. Peter Ventura, interview with the author. Ted Simpkins, interview with the author.

200   **birthdays and holidays together:** Deposition of Gary Ramona, March 23, 1993, *Gary Ramona v. Stephanie Ramona, Marche Isabella, et al.*, p. 717.

200   **his "stepbrother":** Deposition of Gary Ramona, January 27, 1992, *Gary Ramona v. Stephanie Ramona, Marche Isabella, et al.*, p. 479.

200   **"heart and soul of Robert Mondavi":** Johnston, *Spectral Evidence*, p. 44.

201   **seven-bedroom, seven-bath home:** Napa County assessor, record for parcel 039-040-045.

201   **half a million dollars a year:** Deposition of Gary Ramona, January 8, 1992, *Holly*

Ramona v. Gary Ramona, et al., case 621124, Superior Court of California in the County of Napa, p. 158.

201   **"neoprohibitionists":** In his interview as part of the University of California at Berkeley's Bancroft series of local oral histories, John De Luca claims to have coined the word "neoprohibitionist" though some dispute that claim.

201   **expecting visitors to come:** Deposition of Gary Ramona, March 23, 1993, *Gary Ramona v. Stephanie Ramona, Marche Isabella, et al.*, pp. 135–136.

202   **"I told him it was a goddamn lie":** Deposition of Gary Ramona, January 27, 1992, *Gary Ramona v. Stephanie Ramona, Marche Isabella, et al.*, pp. 469–470.

202   **hamstrung in their decision making:** Deposition of Gary Ramona, January 27, 1992, *Gary Ramona v. Stephanie Ramona, Marche Isabella, et al.*, p. 502.

202–03 **the company's sales had exploded:** Deposition of Gary Ramona, March 23, 1993, *Gary Ramona v. Stephanie Ramona, Marche Isabella, et al.*, p. 948.

203   **"The family has engaged":** Letter to Gary Ramona dated June 18, 1990, marked as Exhibit 1 to Deposition of R. Michael Mondavi, April 17, 1992, *Gary Ramona v. Stephanie Ramona, Marche Isabella, et al.*, p. 1.

204   **"Gary, will you be at my birthday party?":** Deposition of Gary Ramona, March 23, 1993, *Gary Ramona v. Stephanie Ramona, Marche Isabella, et al.*, pp. 939–944.

204   **wished Robert a happy birthday and left.** Johnston, *Spectral Evidence*, pp. 138–140.

Chapter Thirteen: Heart and Soul, 1990–1992

205   **the winery's first executive chef:** Margrit Biever Mondavi, Annie Roberts, Laurie Smith, and Victoria Wise, *Annie and Margrit: Recipes and Stories from the Robert Mondavi Kitchen* (Berkeley:Ten Speed Press, 2003), p. ix.

206   **set in the Oak Knoll vineyards:** The Mondavi labor camp was on the Oak Knoll Ranch, the same property where Robert, Michael, and Timothy built their homes. Author research.

206   **would dance instead with each other or perhaps a broom:** Charles Williams and Dorothy Barajas-Williams, interview with the author, November 15, 2005.

206   **"Get revenge":** Glenn Carnahan, interview with the author.

206   **"What can we do?":** Johnston, *Spectral Evidence*, p. 111.

206   **gastric hemorrhage:** Death certificate of Marjorie Ellen Mondavi, registered October 23, 1990, County of Napa.

206   **died of a broken heart:** Elsa and Joe Maganini, interviews with the author.

207   **they mixed her ashes with rose petals:** Michael Mondavi, interview with the author.

207   **"She was the heart and soul of the family":** Michael Mondavi, interview with the author.

208   **"partners' office":** Cliff Adams, interview with the author.

208   **a divorce:** Barry Grundland filed for a dissolution of marriage from his wife, Nan Grundland, on March 14, 1988. The court record shows more than a decade-long history of Dr. Grundland having trouble keeping up with his spousal support payments. *Barry Grundland v. Nan Grundland*, case C55487, Superior Court of California in the County of Napa.

208   **the company stopped using him:** Michael Mondavi, interview with the author. Efforts to reach Dr. Barry Grundland for comment were unsuccessful.

208   **aspirations for a year, five years, and twenty years:** Ellen Hawkes, "Mondavi Family Values," *Success*, December 1998.

209   **"to make sure they agree":** Memorandum dated October 9, 1990 from Robert Mondavi to RMW board of directors and management council, marked as Exhibit

EE and attached to Deposition of Gary Ramona, January 27, 1992, *Gary Ramona v. Stephanie Ramona, Marche Isabella, et al.*, p. 1.

209   **whether Ramona should keep his job:** "Analysis of Sales and Marketing Department Financial and Administrative Systems; Report to Management Council" dated October 12, 1991 by Price Waterhouse, marked as Exhibit HH and attached to Deposition of Gary Ramona, January 27, 1992, *Gary Ramona v. Stephanie Ramona, Marche Isabella, et al.*, p. 6.

209   **Ramona also charged:** Deposition of Gary Ramona, March 23, 1993, *Gary Ramona v. Stephanie Ramona, Marche Isabella, et al.*, p. 1005.

210   **"no-win situation":** Memorandum from Gary Ramona to Dennis Blanc dated October 25, 1990, marked as Exhibit KK and attached to Deposition of Gary Ramona, January 27, 1992, *Gary Ramona v. Stephanie Ramona, Marche Isabella, et al.*, p. 3.

210   **Michael wanted and Timothy opposed:** Deposition of Timothy Mondavi, May 22, 1992, *Gary Ramona v. Stephanie Ramona, Marche Isabella, et al.*, p. 43.

210   **"difficult, at best, to implement":** Op. cit.

210   **a reputation as a loose cannon:** Deposition of Timothy Mondavi, May 22, 1992, *Gary Ramona v. Stephanie Ramona, Marche Isabella, et al.*, p. 33. Ventura was described similarly by Cliff Adams, Harvey Posert, and George Sheppler in interviews with the author.

210   **Michael got it from his father:** Deposition of Gary Ramona, January 27, 1992, *Gary Ramona v. Stephanie Ramona, Marche Isabella, et al.*, p. 452.

211   **"At seventy-seven, the time has come . . .":** "Robert Mondavi announces transfer of executive responsibilities at the Robert Mondavi Winery to his sons," press release, Robert Mondavi Winery (Business Wire), December 20, 1990.

211   **vastly more than:** In interviews with the author, H. Stuart Harrison said the original architect's estimate was $4.5 million, while Cliff Adams recalled it was $12–$15 million.

211   **an expensive cooling system:** Opus One winemaker Michael Silacci, interview with the author.

212   **"patience is the thing":** Moira Johnston, "A Marriage Made in Heaven," *California Living*, April 22, 1984, p. 17.

213   **"Well, I don't agree with you":** Baroness Philippine de Rothschild, interview with the author, September 22, 2005.

213   **her Paris-based interior designer:** Ibid. Margrit Biever Mondavi, interview with the author.

213   **The Mondavis first spotted phylloxera:** Prospectus, Robert Mondavi Corporation, June 9, 1993, p. 6.

214   **slow to recognize the full threat of the pest:** Phil Freese and Greg Evans, interviews with the author.

214   **serious financial trouble:** *Wine Business Insider,* April 23, 1993. Robert also wrote of having "serious problems on our hands" in *Harvests of Joy: My Passion for Excellence: How the Good Life Became Great Business* (New York: Harcourt Brace and Company, 1998), p. 272.

214   **plunged to $30.3 million:** Op. cit., p. 24 of the RMC prospectus.

214   **Bank of America was reluctant to extend it additional credit:** Greg Evans, interview with the author.

216   **there were more than a hundred:** The Napa Valley Vintners had 103 members in 1993, according to the trade organization.

217   **The hodgepodge of various state systems:** See Alix M. Freedman and John R. Emshwiller, "Vintage System: Big Liquor Wholesaler Finds Change Stalking Its

Very Private World—Southern Wine & Spirits Is a Mandated Middleman Under Increasing Attack," *Wall Street Journal*, October 4, 1994, p. A-1.

217   **"friends in the underworld":** Ibid.

218   **"people will buy their wine":** Cindy Deutsch, interview with the author; Cindy Deutsch, "The Scan What Am, Supermarket Style (Evaluating Grocery Story Scanner Data for Wines)," *Wines & Vines*, September 1991.

218   **a one-time big order:** The Mondavi prospectus may offer some support of Fairchild's contention, stating that "a portion of this volume growth [in gross revenues] is related to the growth in distributor inventories in the same period." Prospectus, Robert Mondavi Corporation, June 9, 1993, p. 20.

218   **grown complacent over the years:** Robert Fairchild, interview by Catherine Thorpe.

219   **a rolling, eighteen-month calendar:** Prospectus, Robert Mondavi Corporation, June 9, 1993, p. 31.

219   **some $7 million a year:** The Daniels suit claims the contract was worth $15 million a year, a figure that includes loss of business opportunities related to being Mondavi's distributor. In the third cause of action, a figure of $9.75 million is cited by the plaintiff for loss of investments, out-of-pocket damages, and diminution of value of ownership of House of Daniels, Inc.

219   **"our family relationship":** Complaint for Damages, June 11, 1992, *House of Daniels v. Robert Mondavi et al.*, p. 15.

220   **when he didn't have a penny:** Charles Daniels Sr., interview with the author. Complaint for Damages, June 11, 1992, *House of Daniels v. Robert Mondavi et al.*, case CGC-92-943622, Superior Court of California in the County of San Francisco, p. 5.

220   **paying a fraction:** Author interview with Victor J. Haydel III, the Farella, Braun attorney who settled the case; Charles Daniels, interview with the author, May 15, 2005. This pattern of distributor consolidation continued through the 1990s. In 2000, Paradise Wines, a Hawaiian distributor, claimed that Mondavi severed its contract unfairly, after a twenty-year relationship that weathered the recession of the early 1990s. But this suit, too, was eventually settled out of court.

Chapter Fourteen: Going Public, 1992–1993

222   **"the liquid food praised for centuries":** Robert Mondavi, opening remarks, Robert Mondavi Mission Symposium, San Francisco. Transcripts of the Robert Mondavi Mission Programs, 1988–1990 provided courtesy of Harvey Posert.

222   **a dustup with regulators:** "Dear friends . . . ," press release, Robert Mondavi Winery (Healdsburg, CA: Sonoma County Wine Library collection), August 22, 1991.

222   **"He wants everyone to be a missionary":** Anitra S. Brown, "The Magnificent Robert Mondavi," *Market Watch*, vol. 8, no. 8 (July/August 1989), p. 35.

222   **French Paradox:** Harvey Posert is quoted in *Harvests of Joy* as explaining the impetus for the *60 Minutes* story like this: "We invited Dr. Ellison to share his knowledge with our Mission Program. Sol Katz and Ellison then made up their minds to approach *60 Minutes*. They convinced Morley Safer to do the story, and Dr. Ellison wound up being one of those interviewed on camera. The rest we know. Looking back now, I think it's fair to say that Bob Mondavi was really the father of that famous *60 Minutes* segment." Robert Mondavi, *Harvests of Joy: My Passion for Excellence: How the Good Life Became Great Business* (New York: Harcourt Brace and Company, 1998), p. 263. Morley Safer stated, "I'm afraid the story had nothing to do with Mondavi. I saw a report of research being done in France and Massachu-

setts and decided to investigate. No Wine company or Vintner had anything to do with the story. Sincerely, Morley Safer." Morley Safer, e-mail to Catherine Thorpe, September 12, 2006.

222   **fears that some Mondavi employees:** Dr. R. Curtis Ellison, interview by Catherine Thorpe. At the time of the interview, Dr. Ellison was a professor of medicine and public health at Boston University.

222   **its financial support of the study:** Ibid.

223   **"I like to educate our country":** Emma Lipp, age six, school project dated March 18, 1993.

224   **late-night field trips:** Billy Cross recalled that Robert made an appearance at a party in Bordeaux dressed as a Marilyn Monroe look-alike; interview with the author. The former tour guide Lili Thomas remembered Robert donning similar female garb at a party hosted by the winery's public relations staff; interview with the author.

224   **so drunk they could barely stand:** Brad Warner, interview with the author.

224   **he shouldn't "push it":** Cliff Adams, interview with the author.

224   **never took any formal legal action:** Deep background interview.

224   **There were other instances:** Michael Mondavi said, "[Attorney] Mike Byers handled the other sexual harassment cases;" interview with the author. In addition, a prominent Napa Valley lawyer confirmed in July 2006 on background that there were numerous such allegations against the Mondavi men over the years, all of which were settled out of court. Mr. Byers declined to be interviewed.

224   **other women in the valley:** Deep background interview.

225   **infatuated with Nina Wemyss:** Margrit Biever Mondavi, interview with the author, March 3, 2006. Nina Wemyss declined to be interviewed.

225   **"I'm out of gas":** Michael Mondavi, interview with the author.

225   **Robert's habit was well-known:** Ibid.

225   **unscrupulous or needy females:** Margrit Biever Mondavi, interview with the author.

226   **as a way of adding the prestige:** Joe and Elsa Maganini, interview with the author. Holly Peterson declined to be interviewed.

226   **leading employees to wonder:** Brad Warner, interviews with the author.

227   **more than three years later:** "Tim contends that the date of separation was June 1, 1992; Dorothy contends separation occurred on or about August 1, 1995." Marriage Settlement Agreement, December 2000, attached to Judgment, September 18, 2001, *Timothy Mondavi v. Dorothy Mondavi,* case no. C-77159, Superior Court of California, Napa County, p. 1.

227   **"committed monogamous relationship":** Divorce records, *Holly Mondavi v. Timothy Mondavi,* p. 2854. case no. 26-17232, Superior Court of California, Napa County.

227   **Robert voiced his criticism:** Cliff Adams, interview with the author, October 25, 2005.

227   **shouts of "Jerreeee, Jerree":** Don Clark, "Chips Are Down: Intel's Monopoly Faces an Attack from a Perennial Gadfly," *Wall Street Journal,* October 21, 1994, p. A-1.

228   **recruited the Baroness:** Baroness Philippine de Rothschild, interview with the author.

228   **the group's stated goal:** "Family Ties for Top Wine Firms," *Off License News,* February 11, 1993, p. 2.

228   **That message rang false:** Heather Jane Pyle and David Lucas, interview with the author.

229 **solid, reliable image that Wall Street valued:** Michael Mondavi cannot recall exactly when he had cut off his ponytail but says it was sometime in the early 1990s. He says that his decision had nothing to do with what the bankers might have expected at the time of the IPO.

229 **For Robert, who had hated Michael's rat's tail all along:** Cliff Adams and Harvey Posert, interviews with the author.

230 **"something to cheer yourself up with":** Rita Koselka, "A Pox on Stox," *Forbes*, v. 151, no. 12 (June 7, 1993), p. 47.

230 **at the insistence of Robert:** Philip Greer, interview with the author.

231 **had not gone according to plan:** Michael Mondavi, interview with the author.

231 **At the time of the IPO:** Prospectus, Robert Mondavi Corporation, June 9, 1993, p. 46.

231 **"Bob Mondavi and his sons":** L. Pierce Carson, "Auction Action: Wine Auction kickoff events warm up, get hot," *Napa Valley Register*, June 11, 1993.

232 **spend his time with Peterson:** Harvey Posert, interview with the author, October 26, 2005.

232 **loss of his family's respect:** Timothy Mondavi, interview with the author

PART THREE: EXPANSION

Chapter Fifteen: Regency's End, 1993–1994

236 **examined his heart:** Robert Mondavi, *Harvests of Joy: My Passion for Excellence: How the Good Life Became Great Business* (New York: Harcourt Brace and Company, 1998), p. 286.

236 **painful rebuff from investors:** Michael Mondavi, interview with the author. Kim Marcus, "The Rising Son," *Wine Spectator*, vol. 22, no. 11 (October 31, 1997), p. 74.

237 **under his wing:** This characterization is based on interviews with both Timothy and Michael Mondavi.

238 **"the economic difficulties":** "Robert Mondavi Winery announces financial projections" (press release, Robert Mondavi Corporation), December 1, 1993.

239 **"My name is Robert Mondavi":** Descriptions of testimony by Robert, Michael, and Timothy rely heavily on Moira Johnston's account in *Spectral Evidence: The Ramona Case : Incest, Memory, and Truth on Trial in Napa Valley* (Boston: Houghton Mifflin, 1997), and are used with her permission.

239 **company's counsel had advised Robert:** Bruce Miroglio, interview with the author, November 4, 2005.

240 **"limited by his weaknesses":** Johnston, *Spectral Evidence*, p. 333. This view is also reflected in Timothy's deposition; Deposition of Timothy Mondavi, *Gary Ramona v. Stephanie Ramona, Marche Isabella, et al.*, case C61898, Superior Court of the State of California, Napa County, May 22, 1992.

241 **"I was ineffective":** Deposition of Timothy Mondavi, *Gary Ramona v. Stephanie Ramona, Marche Isabella, et al.*, case C61898, Superior Court of the State of California, Napa County, May 22, 1992, p. 20.

241 **Wearing his black hair . . . :** Johnston, *Spectral Evidence*, p. 334.

242 **The jurors, when asked later:** Bruce Miroglio, interview with the author; Johnston, *Spectral Evidence*, p. 336.

243 **Dr. Barry Grundland, the psychiatrist:** Deposition of Michael Mondavi, *Gary Ramona v. Stephanie Ramona, Marche Isabella, et al.*, case C61898, Superior Court of the State of California, Napa County, May 22, 1993, p. 48, states that by then Dr. Grundland had been eased out of his role as a consultant to Mondavi. Information

on the dispute over Dr. Grundland's support payments comes from *Barry Grundland v. Nan Grundland*, case C55487, filed March 14, 1998, Superior Court of California, Napa County.

244   **distributed Jackson's wines:** In September of 1996, Jackson dropped Southern and began distributing its wines to retailers in California on its own. According to the *Santa Rosa Press Democrat*, the split occurred after K-J told Southern it planned to distribute directly to restaurants. Ted Appel, "K-J to Distribute Wines Itself; Move Affects Only Sales in State," *Santa Rosa Press Democrat*, September 11, 1996, p. E-1.

244   **"You're getting hammered":** Ted Simpkins, interview with the author.

244   **rolled out against his objections:** Timothy Mondavi, interview with the author.

244   **weakening his power base:** Ibid.

245   **Holly eventually left:** Timothy Mondavi, interview with the author, December 15, 2005. Holly resigned from her job at Mondavi in 1996, a year before she and Timothy wed, but the issues surrounding their relationship had simmered for several years before her resignation.

245   **Michael had initiated the ouster:** Michael Mondavi, interview with the author.

245   **"they'd lie down in front of a train":** Alan Schnur, interview with the author.

246   **failing to agree even on an agenda:** Philip Greer, interview with the author.

246   **exactly the same recommendation:** Frank Farella, interview with author.

247   **"But I just can't stay on the board":** Philip Greer, interview with the author.

247   **Greer advised him to choose Michael:** Ibid.

247   **urged his father to pick:** Kim Marcus, "The Rising Son," pp. 71–72.

247   **the potentially explosive matter:** A shake-up at Mondavi had been rumored for weeks beforehand and when it was finally announced, in June of 1994, George Starke, the wine columnist for *The St. Helena Star*, wrote, "Whassa [sic] mean? I dunno. Maybe the change was to emphasize the best talents of each." George Starke, "Up and Down the Wine Roads," *St. Helena Star*, June 23, 1994, p. 5.

Chapter Sixteen: Disinherited, 1994–1996

250   **"wine is made in the vineyards":** Manny Martinez, interviews with Catherine Thorpe.

250   **a project with NASA:** Prospectus, Robert Mondavi Corporation, June 9, 1993, p. 34. There were several newspaper stories about this program, as well.

251   **it would donate the amount:** George Starke, "Up and Down the Wine Roads," *St. Helena Star*, December 8, 1994, p. 8.

252   **became an instant pariah:** Alan Schnur, interview with the author.

252   **advanced management at Harvard:** George Starke, "Up and Down the Wine Roads," May 4, 1995, p. 5.

252   **he seemed to be skipping classes:** Cliff Adams, interview with the author; Alan Schnur, interview with the author.

252   **halfhearted effort:** Timothy Mondavi, interview with the author.

252   **turn Mondavi into a leader:** Ray Goldberg and Thomas Urban, "Robert Mondavi Corporation," case study, Harvard Business School, October 17, 1995, pp. 1–2.

252   **Antinori had led a rebirth:** Piero Antinori, interview with the author, April 9, 2005; Frank Prial, *Decantations: Reflections on Wine by* The New York Times *Wine Critic* (New York: St. Martin's Press, 2002), p. 86.

253   **reluctant to move as fast:** Piero Antinori, interview with the author. Antinori added during the interview that he felt "particularly lucky not to have done it," referring to not entering into a joint venture with the Mondavis.

253   **mutual courtship:** Lamberto Frescobaldi, interview with the author; Vittorio Frescobaldi, interview with the author.

254   **hire a university professor:** The anecdote about the Frescobaldis hiring a university professor as a family advisor comes from Piero Antinori; interview with the author.

255   **"If you think it is right, just do it":** Lamberto Frescobaldi, interview with the author.

255   **play him off his brother:** Frank Farella, interview with the author, Timothy Mondavi, interview with the author, Michael Mondavi, interview with the author.

256   **a packaging revolution:** "Market Drives Wine Bottle Revolution," *Wines & Vines,* October 1, 1995 by Larry Walker.

257   **one-third, one-third, one-third:** Michael Mondavi, interview with the author.

257   **stock their mother Marjorie had given them:** Frank Farella, interview with the author. Michael Mondavi in an interview with the author confirmed that the vast majority of his and his siblings' stock in Robert Mondavi Corporation came from their mother: "I don't know how astute my mother was, but she was more about her children and her grandchildren than herself and she was almost clairvoyant in the fact that she knew she had to protect them [by making sure they inherited company stock]."

257   **his sweat equity in the business:** Michael Mondavi, interview with the author.

257   **he had the right to choose:** Michael Mondavi, interview with the author, and Timothy Mondavi, interview with the author.

258   **possibility that seemed remote:** Cliff Adams, interview with the author.

258   **still be divided equally:** Timothy Mondavi, interview with the author.

258   **putting his own interests first:** Ibid. Timothy suggested that Marcia shared his view.

258   **his children had been well provided for:** Margrit Biever Mondavi, interview with the author. Cliff Adams, interview with the author.

258   **Michael, in turn, suspected:** Michael Mondavi, interview with the author.

258   **Robert seldom discussed financial matters with his wife:** Cliff Adams, interview with author.

258   **"the happy victims of success":** Michael Mondavi, interview with the author.

259   **Edmunds . . . was particularly incensed:** Edmunds is deceased. This account is based on interviews with Cliff Adams by the author.

259   **"Cliff loved power":** Robert Mondavi, *Harvests of Joy,* p. 265.

Chapter Seventeen: Michael's Show, 1996–1997

262   **deepening the schism:** Cliff Adams, interview with the author.

263   **"It does if I have anything to do with it":** Peggy A. Loar, interview with the author.

264   **such new techniques:** Mark Chandler, executive director of the Lodi-Woodbridge Winegrape Commission and a grape grower under contract to Woodbridge since 1997; interview by Catherine Thorpe.

265   **the Wild West of France:** Reporting on Mondavi's venture in Languedoc by William Echikson, used with his permission.

265   **the number-one French wine:** Annual Report: 1998, Robert Mondavi Corporation, p. 5.

265   **a deal with foreign growers:** Sewell Chan, "Mondavi Uncorks Strategy to Build on Surging Demand—Winery Takes a Bold Step by Looking Overseas to Fill in Product Lines," *Wall Street Journal,* Eastern edition, July 15, 1996, p. B-3.

266   **it had 475,000 gallons:** Annual Report: 1998, Robert Mondavi Corporation, pp. 40–41, note 10.

267   **reminded him of the potential:** Eduardo Chadwick, interview with the author.

267   **the Chilean industry's sales:** Much of the information in the section on Caliterra is drawn from Brian R. Golden, Henry W. Lane, and David T. A. Wesley, "Mondavi: Caliterra" (case study, Richard Ivey School of Business, University of Western Ontario, 1999); Alan Schnur, interviews with the author; and John Adriance, who represented Mondavi in Chile, and was interviewed by Catherine Thorpe.

268   **drinking oxidized white wine:** Eduardo Chadwick, interview with the author.

269   **"Have you looked in the mirror?":** Golden, Lane, and Wesley, "Caliterra," p. 1; Alan Schnur, interview with the author.

270   **Mondavi's bottling manager discovered:** John Adriance, interview by Catherine Thorpe.

270   **whose egos, he felt, were bigger than their experience:** John Adriance, interview by Catherine Thorpe.

271   **nearly tripled its sales volume:** Golden, Lane, and Wesley, "Caliterra," p. 16.

271   **build an entirely new winery from the ground up:** Eduardo Chadwick, interview with the author.

271   **he needed legal paperwork:** Declaration of Timothy Mondavi, attached to Request for Judgment of Dissolution, March 21, 1997, *Timothy Mondavi v. Dorothy Mondavi*, case C-77159, Superior Court of California, Napa County, p. 1

272   **five courses of beautiful food:** According to Heidi Peterson Barrett, who attended the Positano wedding; interview with the author.

272   **more than $70,000:** Divorce records, *Holly Mondavi v. Timothy Mondavi*, p. 2854. Case no. 26-17232, Superior Court of California, Napa County.

272   **roared up to Opus One:** Ted Simpkins, interview with the author.

272   **Michael grinned widely:** Photo courtesy of Ted Simpkins.

272   **Michael would tenderly kiss Rob:** Alan Schnur, interview with the author.

272   **"It was five thirty A.M.":** Hilary Rosenberg, "Cigars before Wine," Q & A–style interview, *Business Week* 3642 (August 16, 1999), p. F14.

273   **"I'm going to take the kid out back":** Background interview.

273   **employees did outside consulting:** David Lucas, interview with the author; Glenn Carnahan, interview with the author.

273   **embraced such status symbols:** From Eduardo Chadwick's description of Michael in recounting the Sena launch; interview with the author.

274   **"Our objective":** Kim Marcus, "The Rising Son," *Wine Spectator*, October 31, 1997, p. 70.

274   **"You're having too much fun":** L. Pierce Carson, "Mondavi Shareholders Equate Fun with Profits," *Napa Valley Register*, November 5, 1997.

274   **"Prohibition would be a disaster":** Dan Berger, "Taking Stock at Mondavi," *Santa Rosa Press Democrat*, December 3, 1997, p. D-2.

275   **"had finally had enough":** Cliff Adams, interview with the author, January 10, 2006.

Chapter Eighteen: Waterloo, 1998–2001

278   **"the best Chilean wine":** Anthony Dias Blue, "Mondavi's Big Chilean Venture," *San Jose Mercury News*, January 28, 1998, Wine section, p. 1.

278   **gifts made of lapis lazuli:** John Adriance, interview by Catherine Thorpe.

278   **"a Goofy Gewürtztraminer":** Victoria Colliver, "Mondavi, Disney Team Up," *San Francisco Examiner*, April 30, 1998, p. B-1.

278   **"The 'Happiest Place on Earth'":** "Mondavi Teams Up with Disney," Associated Press, May 20, 1998.

278   **"a promotion I can't help hating":** Sumi Hahn, "Table Hopping," *Seattle Weekly*, May 14, 1998, p. 31.

278   **the plan's biggest internal booster:** Mondavi director Sir Anthony Greener, interview with the author.

278   **over the initial hesitations:** Nancy Light, interview with the author.

279   **a quick swing through the Golden State:** Leslie Dolinger, interview by Catherine Thorpe.

280   **the stores preferred:** Gregory S. Miller, "The Chardonnay Shortage at Mondavi" (case study, Harvard Business School, September 23, 2004), p. 2.

280   **a standing invitation:** Final Report of the Independent Counsel Donald C. Smaltz in re: Alphonso Michael (Mike) Espy, filed January 30, 2001, U.S. Court of Appeals for the District of Columbia Circuit, Washington, D.C.,

280   **a mere slap on the wrist:** Robert Mondavi Corporation press release, July 21, 1998, "Robert Mondavi Announces Settlement in Espy Investigation." According to several stories in *The Wall Street Journal*, Mr. Espy was acquitted by a federal jury of corruption charges in December of 1998, but Tyson plead guilty in 1998 to giving Mr. Espy illegal gifts and agreed to pay a $6 million fine.

281   **wept as they left:** Axel Fabre, interview with the author.

282   **"a marriage without love":** Vic Motto, interview with the author.

282   **buy it at Costco:** Former Opus One co-CEO George Scheppler, who represented the Rothschild side of the partnership; interview with the author.

283   **"user-friendly":** Diane Brady, "Good Life: Scions of the Vine Do Asia," *Asian Wall Street Journal*, March 20, 1998, p. 15.

283   **"What the hell is this?:** Story related by Greg Evans, interview with the author, and a background source, interview with the author; both were present at the dinner.

284   **a venture down under:** Christopher Hancock, interview with the author. Mondavi announced a fifty-fifty joint venture with Rosemount about eighteen months later.

284   **the idea was abandoned:** Background interview with a senior Mondavi executive who was closely involved in the negotiations.

284   **"it made a hell of a lot of sense":** Philip Greer, interview with the author.

284   **"governance issues":** Greg Evans, interview with the author.

284   **why he should bother:** Philip Greer, interview with the author.

284   **a new nine-thousand-square-foot house:** "Mondavi Residence, For Michael & Isabel Mondavi, 5593 Silverado Trail," architectural floor plan (Sonoma, Calif.: Forrest Architects, 1998), obtained by Catherine Thorpe.

284   **welcome gift to the Yountville fire department:** Jason Martin, interview by Catherine Thorpe.

285   **$4 million–plus estate:** Napa County assessor, record for parcel 039-040-047.

286   **"Disney is good at certain things":** Steve Rubenstein, "Disney's Virtual California," *San Francisco Chronicle*, February 8, 2001, p. A-1.

287   **about $2 million more:** Account based on Kevin Yee, "Mondavi's Hangover," http://www.mouseplanet.com/chef/mondavi.htm, March 8, 2001.

287   **the most popular purchase:** Leslie Dolinger, interview by Catherine Thorpe.

288   **he'd relinquish control:** Peter Mondavi Sr. announced at least twice that he was handing over control to his sons. According to Paul Wagner, who worked for Charles Krug for five years in the late 1980s and early 1990s and recalls preparing a press release about a management transition to the next generation during that time. Paul Wagner, interview with the author. A *Wine Spectator* article announcing the transition from father to sons also appeared March 31, 1996: Jeff Morgan, "Peter Mondavi Lets Sons Take Charge at Charles Krug," *Wine Spectator*, March 31, 1996.

288   **Peter senior continued to work:** William F. Heintz, "A History of the Charles Krug Winery: The Mondavi Family, 1943–1997" (St. Helena: Napa Valley Wine Library, William Heintz Collection), p. 60.

288   **"re-Pete":** Paul Wagner, interview with the author.

288   **"We're going to bury you":** Kenneth Drost, a Krug production worker from 1981 to 2003; interview by Catherine Thorpe, May 30, 2006. Drost said he witnessed this particular scene, and other former Krug employees also say they witnessed blow-ups between Marc and Peter senior.

289   **"You people are ruining my life!":** Statement of Kenneth Drost, Case #01-1172-04, St. Helena Police Department, September 5, 2001. In the statement, Drost alleged that Marc Mondavi had tried to run him down, and indicated that he wanted to file charges. The police subsequently investigated, taking the statements of several witnesses to the incident, who largely corroborated Mr. Drost's account. Mr. Mondavi's statement as part of the case file claims that Mr. Drost was standing in front of Mondavi's Jeep, blocking the way. The investigating officer, T. J. Scott, forwarded his report to the district attorney's office, but no charges were filed.

290   **"L'Affaire Mondavi":** Amy B. Trubek, "Incorporating Terroir: L'Affaire Mondavi Reconsidered," in *Gastronomica*, vol. 4, no. 3, summer 2004, pp. 90–99.

291   **the company's "Mr. Outside":** Philip Greer, interview with the author.

291   **simply proper corporate governance:** Sir Anthony Greener, interview with the author.

291   **"We need you to become chairman":** Michael Mondavi, interview with the author.

291–92 **hadn't gone into detail:** Philip Greer, interview with the author.

292   **"a bait-and-switch game":** Michael Mondavi, interview with the author.

292   **convincing sales job:** Philip Greer, interview with the author.

292   **his tireless cheerleading and, at worst, was misleading:** Jonathan Smiga, interview with the author.

293   **drawing on average about 4,500:** Attendance figures from a *Los Angeles Times* article by Marc Ballon and Kimi Yoshino, October 2, 2001, citing an unnamed Disney official.

293   **a contract that did not protect it or penalize Disney strongly enough:** Jonathan Smiga, interview with the author.

293   **a $12.2 million charge:** Note on Special Charges, Annual Report: 2002, Robert Mondavi Corporation, p. 20.

PART FOUR: DEMOLITION

Chapter Nineteen: Mondaviland, 2001–2003

297   **concerned that it would be a showcase:** Peggy Loar, interview with the author.

298   **a pediatric intensive care unit:** Michael Mondavi, interview with the author.

298   **another $15 million:** Frank Farella, interview with the author.

298   **"We were in a race":** Michael Mondavi, interview with the author.

298   **"cream de la pooh pooh":** Geoffrey Tomb, "A Vintner's Vision," *San Jose Mercury News*, April 13, 1999, p. 1A.

300   **"they show up for everything":** Cliff Adams, interview with the author.

300   **"Age doesn't matter unless you are wine":** Nancy D. Holt, "Workspaces," *Wall Street Journal*, eastern edition, August 9, 2000, p. B-10.

302   **"Never forget":** Robert Mondavi Winery, *Robert Mondavi Winery 2001* (Oakville, Calif.: Robert Mondavi Winery, ca. 2001), p. 5.

302   **"All those black tie events":** Professor Michael A. Roberto, "Robert Mondavi and the Wine Industry" (case study, Harvard Business School, March 15, 2002), p. 10.

303   **a tangle of suits and countersuits:** Cases No. C-02-5311 and C-02-5473, U.S. District Court of the Northern District of California, San Francisco. The suits and countersuits were eventually settled.

303   **another example of the Mondavi's overexpansiveness:** Andy Beckstoffer, interview with the author.

303   **quality shortcuts to save money:** Brad Warner, interviews with the author.

303   **racked four times instead of five:** Manny Martinez, interview by Catherine Thorpe.

303   **to organize a companywide research group:** Brad Warner and Greg Evans, interviews with the author.

303   **frequently jet-lagged:** Timothy Mondavi, interview with the author.

303   **bursting at the seams:** Manny Martinez, interview by Catherine Thorpe.

303   **wrong varieties planted on the wrong soil:** Greg Fowler, interview with the author. Fowler later became senior vice president of winery operations at Icon Estates, owned by Constellation Brands, and in that job oversaw Mondavi's vineyards.

304   **"indifferent, innocuous wines":** Robert Parker, *The Wine Advocate*, Issue 132 (December 2000), p. 28.

304   **MOND dropped fourteen points:** Elin McCoy, *The Emperor of Wine: The Rise of Robert M. Parker, Jr., and the Reign of American Taste* (New York: Ecco, 2005), p. 207.

304   **the enological equivalent:** McCoy, *The Emperor of Wine*, p. 2.

304   **"We're passionate about wine":** James Laube, "Mondavi at the Crossroads," *Wine Spectator*, vol. 28, no.10 (October 15, 2003), pp. 63–64.

305   **taken their eyes off Oakville:** James Laube, interview with the author.

305   **The rumors in the valley were flying:** Part of material about the rumors comes from Walter Links, interview with the author.

305   **involved with other people:** Timothy Mondavi, interview with the author.

305   **counseling for more than a year:** Declaration of Timothy J. Mondavi, divorce records, *Holly Mondavi v. Timothy Mondavi*, p. 2854. case no. 26-17232, Superior Court of California, Napa County.

305   **a line of credit he'd been using:** Supplemental Declaration of Petitioner re: Spousal Support and Attorney's Fees, p. 3. Divorce records, *Holly Mondavi v. Timothy Mondavi*, p. 2854. case no. 26-17232, Superior Court of California, Napa County.

306   **no substantial income:** Holly Peterson Mondavi's Declaration of Support, August 16, 2002, p. 2640. Divorce records, *Holly Mondavi v. Timothy Mondavi*, p. 2854. case no. 26-17232, Superior Court of California, Napa County.

307   **"Mr. Nasty":** Lindsay Vincent, "Sharp End—Tony Greener—New Head at Guinness" *The Observer*, January 17, 1993, p. 33.

307   **dour, arrogant and aloof:** various British publications described Anthony Greener in such ways. Hashi Syedain, "Profile—Tony Greener, Chairman of Guinness," *Management Today*, September 1, 1993, p. 48. Patrick Hosking, "Boy from the Black Stuff," *Independent on Sunday*, March 15, 1992, p. 11. Andrew Leach, "Greener's Touch of Genius," *The Scotsman*, May 17, 1997, p. 25.

307   **resigned in 2000:** James Barksdale declined to be interviewed.

309   **a $2.5 million fine:** Judgment and Commitment issued as to Fred Franzia, by Honorable William B. Shubb, October 12, 1994, *USA v. Bronco Wine Company et*

al., U.S. District Court, Eastern District of California (Sacramento) Criminal docket for case #93-CR-508-ALL.

310 **"Fred, I just don't know":** Harvey Posert, interview with the author.

311 **largest single private gift:** Larry Vanderhoef, interview with the author.

311 **to drop the Biever name:** The only other large charitable project with Margrit's name on it at the time was the Margrit Biever Mondavi Theatre at the Napa Valley Opera House.

311 **"I learned to make wine":** "$35 Million Gift to Benefit Institute for Wine and Food Science and Center for the Performing Arts" (press release, University of California at Davis), September 19, 2001, news.ucdavis.edu/search/news_detail.lasso?id=5895.

312 **deeply worried:** Frank Farella, interview with the author.

312 **he ... faced insolvency:** Terry Eager, interview with the author. Eager, who is Robert's tax advisor, says that although Robert was not technically insolvent in early 2003 because he had other non-stock assets to rely upon, he faced the threat of becoming insolvent if the stock price continued to decline. Ted Hall and Frank Farella, in interviews with the author, also support the view that Robert was under severe financial pressure.

312 **try to renegotiate:** Frank Farella and Terry Eager, interview with the author. Timothy Mondavi, interview with the author.

312 **if Robert reneged on his pledge:** Larry Vanderhoef, interview with the author.

313 **spelling help:** Margrit Biever Mondavi, interview with the author.

313 **with his coordination failing:** Margrit Biever Mondavi, interview with the author.

313 **"they weren't hearing":** Alan Goldfarb, "Robert Mondavi: We Lost the Image," *St. Helena Star,* December 26, 2002, p. A-6.

313 **"when you have to make money":** Corie Brown, "The Patriarch in a Storm," *Los Angeles Times,* June 11, 2003, p. F-9.

Chapter Twenty: The Board Coup, 2003–2004

315 **a "reign of terror":** Timothy Mondavi, interview with the author.

315 **a "Come to Jesus" gathering:** Greg Evans, interview with the author.

316 **tipped off:** Michael Mondavi, interview with the author.

317 **Timothy's proposal was futile:** Greg Evans, interview with the author, and Brad Alderson, interview with the author.

317 **suffocated dialogue:** Timothy Mondavi, interview with the author.

317 **"you are a one-note fanatic":** Timothy Mondavi, interview with the author.

318 **"I'm going to get you":** The quote was confirmed with both Greg Evans, interview with the author, and Timothy Mondavi, interview with the author.

318 **fly to the Mayo clinic:** Michael Mondavi, interview with the author.

318 **Namenda:** Margrit Biever Mondavi, interview with the author.

318 **he had disrupted the meeting:** Clay Gregory, interview with the author, and Timothy Mondavi, interview with the author.

318 **Threatening to quit:** Philip Greer, interview with the author.

318 **"Am I running the place or not?"** Sir Anthony Greener, interview with the author.

319 **his shorn head:** Timothy Mondavi, interview with the author.

320 **Timothy had to agree:** Greg Evans, interview with the author.

321 **believed that he'd found a powerful ally:** Timothy Mondavi, interview with the author.

321 **"do more better" plan:** Ted Hall, interview with the author. Michael Mondavi, interview with the author.

322   **Michael's insistence that he should get a discount:** Philip Greer, interview with the author.

322   **"This is the appraised value":** Ibid., and also based on the recollection of Greg Evans, interview with the author, and Michael Mondavi, interview with the author.

322   **"We've talked about this ad nauseam":** Michael Mondavi, interview with the author, and Philip Greer, interview with the author.

322   **He bought the property:** Proxy Statement, Robert Mondavi Corporation, December 2, 2004, p. 97. The record for parcel 039-040-048-00 from the Napa County Assessor's Office says the assessed value of the home and land was $1.976 million.

323   **"You're now blessed":** Michael Mondavi, interview with the author.

323   **act as his son's ombudsman:** Greg Evans, interview with the author.

323   **for around $800,000:** The deed for the sale , R1998-0006293, March 13, 1998, Napa County Recorder's Office, listed a document transitory tax for the property of $870.65, which translates into a purchase price of $791,500 according to the assessor's office formula of (T/1.10)1000 where T= the transitory tax. The office keeps on file only the current year's home sales prices, in addition to the latest sale price for any property; therefore, the formula is the only way to determine older sale prices. According to Deed of trust, R1998-0006295, March 13, 1998, Napa County Recorder's Office, Rob borrowed $554,050 to help bankroll the purchase.

324   **Robert had long enjoyed:** Timothy Mondavi, interview with the author.

324   **describes as his grandfather's own "colossal" home:** Robert Mondavi Jr. (Rob), interview with the author.

324   **seemingly arrogant handling:** Margrit Biever Mondavi, interview with the author.

325   **"antiquated":** Robert Mondavi Jr. (Rob), interview with the author.

325   **"He needs to learn humility":** Ibid.

325   **it became a matter of principle:** Michael Mondavi, interview with the author.

326   **Michael had to go:** Sir Anthony Greener, interview with the author.

326   **brought up the subject with Marcia:** Ibid.

326   **she did not relish her role:** Marcia Mondavi Borger, interview with the author.

326   **the possible humiliation:** Mrs. Borger declined to comment on her father's philanthropic bind. This statement is based on interviews with Timothy Mondavi, Michael Mondavi, and outside directors.

326   **starting petty fights:** Timothy Mondavi, interview with the author, suggests that Marcia shared his views on Michael's choosing the wrong battles to fight.

326   **even though she'd lost confidence:** Marcia Mondavi Borger, interview with the author.

326   **did not try to stop them:** Philip Greer, interview with the author.

327   **reluctant to upset them on their vacation:** Timothy Mondavi, interview with the author.

327   **"Heads up":** Michael Mondavi, interviews with the author.

327   **"We'll figure it out":** Michael Mondavi, interview with the author. Philip Greer, interview with the author.

327   **He grew pale from the shock:** Philip Greer, interview with the author.

327   **Farella, too, felt pained:** Frank Farella, interview with the author.

327   **urged her husband to quit:** Philip Greer, interview with the author.

328   **Marcia's betrayal:** Michael Mondavi, interview with the author.

328   **how . . . would he tell people:** Michael Mondavi, interviews with the author.

328   **last-minute attempt to install his sister . . . as chairman:** Ted Hall and Timothy Mondavi, interviews with the author.

329   **suggested . . . Michael that take a sabbatical:** Timothy Mondavi, interview with the author.
329   **"Don't let the bastards get you down":** Michael Mondavi, interview with the author.

Chapter Twenty-one: Brothers, 2004
331   **rumored to have been a bootlegger:** Based on information from a longtime wine writer. Richard Sands denied his grandfather was a bootlegger in a conversation in July of 2006.
334   **despite the talk of nepotism:** The issue was raised in profile of Agustin Huneeus Jr.: Tim Fish, "California's New Generation," WineSpectator.com, July 31, 2003.
335   **They listened politely:** Philip Greer, interview with the author.
336   **unaware of Timothy's efforts:** Greg Evans, interview with the author.
336   **perhaps even mentally unstable:** Background comment, December 14, 2005, that reflects views of several other directors as well.
337   **symbolic of the heavy-handed proceedings:** Timothy Mondavi, interview with the author.
339   **"Where did you get these ideas":** Greg Evans, interview with the author.
339   **"the nuclear option":** Tony Greener, interview with the author.
339   **mistake to view the Mondavis as a family**: Ted Hall, interviews with the author.
339   **source of leverage**: Michael Mondavi, interview with the author. Michael and Timothy later came to believe that Hall and the outside directors had used scare tactics to divide the family members, arguing that unless they went along with their plan, the stock was likely to plunge further and Robert could be forced to file for bankruptcy protection. Even though all three siblings had pledged fifty thousand shares of their stock as a way to try to cushion the risks their father was facing, and several directors believed Marcia would step in if her father's financial bind became too severe, that wasn't enough to counter what Michael claims were the board's "fear tactics," including citing the tougher Sarbanes-Oxley rules on corporate governance to them.
339   **hoping it would put more money in his pocket:** Ibid.
340   **"holding a gun to our father's head":** Timothy Mondavi, interview with the author.
340   **brought tears to their eyes:** Michael Mondavi, interview with the author.
340   **a saga of the Gallo family's tragic problems:** The book: Ellen Hawkes, *Blood and Wine: The Unauthorized Story of the Gallo Wine Empire* (New York: Simon and Schuster, 1993).
341   **"I never thought":** Ted Hall, interview with the author.
341   **offspring would find a way:** Frank Farella and Terry Eager, interview with the author. Margrit Biever Mondavi, interview with the author.
341   **He felt deeply betrayed:** Timothy Mondavi, interview with author. Cheer confirmed by Greg Evans, interview with the author.
342   **a betrayal of the family:** Margrit Biever Mondavi, interview with the author.
342   **urged them to move swiftly:** Frank Farella, interviews with the author.
342   **"try harder":** Philip Greer, interview with the author.
343   **$749 to $929 million within a year:** Presentation by Greg Evans, Bank of America Investor Conference, September 20, 2004, slide 21 of 24.
343   **closer to $320 million:** Note, D. A. Davidson Research, September 22, 2004.
343   **had unintentionally put a price tag on the company:** Greg Evans insists his

intention was not to put a price tag on the company; Constellation's advisor insists that this is what he inadvertently did at this presentation.

343   **ramping up their efforts:** William D. Rifkin, speech to the Association for Corporate Growth—New Jersey Chapter, January 18, 2005, transcript p. 5.

344   **"obviously you want me out":** Robert Mondavi Jr. (Rob), interview with the author.

344   **"This is one harvest":** Jerry Hirsch, "Winemaker Is Hoping for High-End Harvest," *Los Angeles Times*, September 27, 2004, p. C-1.

345   **proxy reported that he resigned:** Proxy Statement, Robert Mondavi Corporation, December 2, 2004, pp. 20–21.

Chapter Twenty-two: The Takeover, October–November 2004

350   **trying to ambush him:** Ted Hall, interview with the author.

350   **"your stockholders would be surprised":** Proxy Statement, Robert Mondavi Corporation, December 2, 2004, p. 23.

351   **a $50,000 monthly retainer fee:** Proxy Statement, Robert Mondavi Corporation, December 2, 2004, p. 96.

352   **"We are very concerned":** Event Brief of Constellation Brands, Inc. Conference Call to Discuss the Proposed Acquisition of the Robert Mondavi Corp., Fair Disclosure, October 19, 2004.

356   **around $70 million:** author's estimates, confirmed with board members.

358   **"Carlo, you have to do this":** Carlo Mondavi, interview with the author.

358   **who had always been his boss:** Michael Mondavi, interview with the author. Robert F. Howe, "The Fall of the House of Mondavi," *Business 2.0*, vol. 6, no. 3 (April 2005), pp. 98–104.

358   **spent as little time with his father as possible:** Michael Mondavi, interview with the author.

359   **Michael was determined:** Michael Mondavi, interview with the author.

359   **psychological effects:** Margrit Biever Mondavi, interview with the author.

359   **shutting out the painful realities:** Ibid.

359   **Timothy had gone to Hawaii:** Margrit adds that she and Robert typically spent Thanksgiving with her family and Christmas with Robert's.

359   **had not shared holidays:** Michael Mondavi, interviews with the author.

359   **"He was a man without a family":** Ted Hall, interviews with the author.

360   **"Can't anyone salvage something here?":** Margrit Mondavi, interviews with the author.

360   **go on cruises:** Ted Hall does not recall making this comment regarding flying first class or taking cruises, but Margrit Biever Mondavi recorded it in her diary entry for that day.

360   **people who operated more like calculating machines:** Margrit Biever Mondavi, interview with the author.

Chapter Twenty-three: Damage Control, December 2004 to April 2005

362   **"I personally never thought":** Author's reporting at the hearing, based on digital recording.

364   **received several threats:** Ted Hall and Greg Evans, interviews with the author.

364   **felt as if he were at a funeral:** Philip Greer, interview with the author.

365   **worth $12.35 million:** Proxy Statement, Robert Mondavi Corporation, December 2, 2004, pp. 99–102.

365   **"Calistogans have great admiration":** Michael Dunsford, "Here's Why Calis-

toga Voted No on Naming Highway for Mondavi," letter to the editor, *St. Helena Star*, January 27, 2005, p. A-9.

367   **a painful and ultimately unsuccessful attempt:** This interview, on March 28, 2005, with the author, was the last formal interview given by Robert Mondavi, according to Harvey Posert in an interview with the author.

367   **no experience in manufacturing or selling:** Confidential Private Offering Memorandum, Davi Skin, Inc., November 1, 2004, p. 6.

368   **the site also featured:** The Web site's address is daviskin.com; the original images have been taken down, but are visible at http://www.viking-media.com/davi/davi.html.

368   **Carlo brought a group of potential investors:** Timothy Mondavi, Margrit Biever Mondavi, and Carlo Mondavi confirm that this visit took place in interviews with the author.

368   **seemed to imply the family still owned and operated:** According to allegations in a Complaint filed in Superior Court of Ca., Los Angeles, *Nelson v. Davi Skin*, filed September 20, 2005, item 91, pp. 7–8, 18.

368   **relied on others in the group to translate:** Plaintiff's attorney Erwin Shustak, interview with the author.

368   **Ted Hall and the rest of the board were briefed on Carlo's plans:** Ted Hall, interview with the author.

369   **"If Carlo asks you":** Timothy Mondavi, interview with the author.

369   **vulnerable to unscrupulous people:** Michael Mondavi, interview with the author.

369   **Michael didn't go:** Michael Mondavi, interview with the author.

Chapter Twenty-four: Billionaires' Ball, June 2005

378   **"You of all guys":** Fred Franzia, interview with the author.

378   **"I love you":** Michael Mondavi, interview with the author, confirmed in interview with Margrit Biever Mondavi, who had been told of the meeting by her husband.

378   **their estrangement continued:** Michael Mondavi, interview with the author, Cliff Adams, interview with the author.

378   **briefly said hello:** Michael Mondavi, interview with the author. Margrit Biever Mondavi recalls that Michael did not speak to her husband at the party.

379   **pitching her memoir of the Mondavis:** Serena Mondavi Ventura, brief interview with the author.

379   **the first article:** Frank Prial, "Two Brothers, One Barrel of Wine," *New York Times*, January 25, 2005, p. C-2.

379   **The family tattle:** Elsa and Joe Maganini, interview with the author.

379   **it was time to move:** Marc Mondavi, interview with the author.

380   **reluctant to partner with a publicly traded company:** Peter Mondavi Jr., interview with the author.

381   **a "billionaires' ball":** Auction cochair Dan Duckhorn, interview with the author.

382   **purple balloons were bunched together:** Robin Daniel Lail, interview with the author.

383   **a single word: "Time":** Peg Melnik, "Leno Works Wonders: *Tonight Show* Host, *Desperate Housewives* Star Push Bidding to Record $10 Million," *Santa Rosa (Calif.) Press Democrat*, June 5, 2005, p. B-1.

388   **worried that the auction:** Margrit Biever Mondavi, interview with the author.

Interviews

The interviews listed here were conducted by Julia Flynn Siler (JFS) and Catherine Thorpe (CT). Only key interviews are noted out of the more than three hundred that were done between February of 2004 and November of 2006. With very few exceptions, all interviews were conducted on the record and most were digitally recorded.

Adams, Cliff, 5/3/04, 12/28/04, 2/21/05, 9/1/04, 9/6/05, 10/6/05, 10/25/05, 1/10/05, 10/13/06, 11/30/06 (JFS)
Adriance, John, 11/17/05, 12/8/05 (CT)
Alderson, Brad, 11/15/05, 9/19/06, (JFS)
Alioto, John, 5/11/05 (JFS)
Antinori, Piero, 4/8/05 (JFS)
Barajas, Dorothy, 11/10/05 (JF)
Beckstoffer, Andy, 8/29/05 (JFS)
Bernstein, Arlene, 9/21/05 (JFS)
Borger, Marcia Mondavi, 11/5/06 (JFS)
Brown, Ken, 5/13/04 (JFS)
Chadwick, Eduardo, 6/30/06 (JF)
Carnahan, Glenn, 1/26/05 (JF)
Chandler, Mark, 4/9/06 (CT)
Cortese, Bobbe Serlis, 8/31/05 (JF)
Cross, Billy, 11/20/05 (JF)
Daniels, Charles, Sr., 5/15/05, 5/24/05 (JFS)
Deutsch, Cindy, 12/15/04 (JFS)
Dolinger, Leslie, 4/11/06 (CT)
Drost, Kenneth, 5/30/06 (CT)
Evans, Gregory, 9/12/06 (JFS)
Fairchild, Robert, 5/23/06 (CT)
Farella, Frank, 6/6/05, 11/14/05, 10/05/06, 11/28/06 (JFS)
Franzia, Fred, 4/21/04, 8/04, 5/16/06 (JFS)
Frescobaldi, Vittorio, 4/7/05 (JFS)
Frescobaldi, Lamberto, 4/6/05 (JFS)
Greener, Anthony, 4/18/15 (JFS)
Greer, Philip, 10/6/06, 10/9/06 (JFS)
Grgich, Miljenko, 3/15/05 (JFS)
Gregory, Clay, 5/28/04 (JFS)
Hall, Ted, 3/9/05, 3/30/05, 6/2/05, 12/14/05, 11/7/06 (JFS)
Hancock, Chris, 7/1/06 (JFS)
Harrison, Stuart, 8/18/05 (JFS)
Heintz, William F., 1/10/05 (JFS)
Jackson, Jess, 2004 (JFS)
Johnson, Martin, 4/04 (JFS)
Johnston, Moira, 12/15/04, 1/24/05 (JFS)
Kalvaria, Leon, 4/14/05 (JFS)
Kornell, Marylouise, 9/27/05 (JFS)
Lail, Robin Daniels, 1/23/05, 1/24/05 (JFS)
Lawson, John, 1/26/05 (JFS)
Laube, James, 11/21/05, 3/16/06 (JFS)
Light, Nancy, 1/18/05 (JFS)
Lipp, Gary, 8/17/05 (JFS)
Loar, Peggy, 6/15/05 (JFS)

Long, Zelma, 3/29/05 (JFS)
Lucas, David, 11/15/05 (JFS)
Lutz, Regina, 3/11/04 (JFS)
Maganini, Joe and Elsa, 3/16/05, 5/25/05 (JFS)
Martel, John, 4/19/05 (JFS)
Martin, Hilary, 11/4/05 (JFS)
Martinez, Manny, 8/1/06, 8/2/06, 9/20/06 (CT)
Martini, Michael, 3/6/05 (JFS)
Miroglio, Bruce, 11/4/05 (JFS)
Mondavi, Carlo, 9/26/06 (JFS)
Mondavi, Marc, 11/30/04, 12/01/06 (JFS)
Mondavi, Margrit Biever, 6/9/05, 9/9/05, 3/3/06, 9/25/06, 11/29/06 (JFS)
Mondavi, Michael, 3/10/06, 6/29/06, 9/22/06, 11/29/06 (JFS)
Mondavi, Peter, Jr., 11/8/04, 9/22/06 (JFS)
Mondavi, Peter, Sr., 4/04 (JFS)
Mondavi, Robert, 3/28/05 (JFS)
Mondavi, Robert Michael Jr. (Rob), 11/28/06 (JFS)
Mondavi, Timothy, 11/4/05, 12/15/05, 9/25/06 (JFS)
Motto, Vic, 9/7/05 (JFS)
Pate, Susan and Dwight, 9/12/05, 9/30/05 (JFS)
Pearson, David, 5/13/04, 12/7/04, 8/31/05 (JF)
Posert, Harvey, 3/11/04, 5/6/04, 8/4/05, 9/9/05 (JF)
Pyle, Heather, 11/15/05 (JFS)
Rifkin, William, 9/15/05 (JFS)
Rothschild, Baroness Philippine de, 9/22/05 (JFS)
Sands, Richard and Robert, 9/19/05 (JFS)
Sands, Robert, 11/14/05 (JFS)
Schnur, Alan, 11/9/05, 12/7/05 (JFS)
Scheppler, George, 8/18/05 (JFS)
Silacci, Michael, 9/22/05 (JFS)
Simpkins, Ted, 11/16/05 (JFS)
Smiga, Jonathan, 12/7/05 (JFS)
Staevert, Joyce, 3/2/05 (JFS)
Sullivan, Charles, 1/12/05, 1/13/05 (JFS)
Thomas, Charles and Lili, 9/29/05 (JFS and CT)
Valette, Jean-Michel, 2/04, 6/29/06 (JFS)
Vanderhoef, Larry, 3/20/06 (JFS)
van der Vord, Andrew, 4/14/05 (JFS)
Ventura, Peter, 12/1/04, 12/8/04, 1/11/05, 8/11/05, 10/18/06, 12/02/06 (JFS)
Warner, Brad, 3/17/05, 11/30/05 (JFS)
Watson, Doug, 12/28/04, 1/5/05, 2/21/05 (JF)
Weis, Michael, 2/28/05 (JFS)
Williams, Charles, 11/10/05 (JFS)
Winiarski, Warren, 4/3/05, 8/17/05 (JFS)

SOURCES AND BIBLIOGRAPHY

This book drew on the shared knowledge and recollections of hundreds of people. I would like to thank them all and to acknowledge a few whom I interviewed repeatedly and who were willing to look deeply and sometimes painfully into their lives. Through them, I came to understand the remarkable history of the Mondavi family. I am grateful to Margrit Biever Mondavi, Michael Mondavi, Timothy Mondavi, Peter Ventura, Peter Mondavi Senior, Peter Mondavi Junior, Marc Mondavi, Warren Winiarski, Cliff Adams, John Martel, Frank Farella, Ted Hall, Sir Anthony Greener, Philip Greer, Jean-Michel Valette, Greg Evans, Brad Warner, Clay Gregory, and Harvey Posert. I was privileged to use the St. Helena Public Library as my home away from home and would like to thank the professionals there, as well as Nancy Light and the staff of the Wine Institute in San Francisco and the Bancroft Library at the Univeristy of California at Berkeley. Victor Geraci, the food and wine historian at the Bancroft's Oral History Office, was particularly helpful, as was the research staff of the Napa Superior Court. I am also indebted to Linda Reiff and the Napa Valley Vintners, David Pearson and Roger Asleson at Opus One, and Peter Marks and Lauren Ackerman at Copia, Jane Laube of *Wine Spectator*, Susan and Dwight Pate of Pate International for sharing their treasure trove of images with me, and Paul Wagner, who helped smooth the way for my reproting in Italy. I worked with three researchers during the course of this book: Amy Lyman, Aleta George, and, for the longest period, Catherine Thorpe. I wish to especially thank Catherine, the daughter of a grape grower and a novelist in her own right, who brought her great intelligence and perseverance to this project.

Adams, Leon D., *The Wines of America*. New York: McGraw-Hill, 1973, rev. 1985.

Amerine, Maynard. "The University of California and the State's Wine Industry." By Ruth Teiser. Berkeley: University of California, Bancroft Library, Regional Oral History Office, 1972.

Amerine, Maynard. "California Wine Industry Affairs: Recollections and Opinions." By Ruth Teiser. Berkeley: University of California, Bancroft Library, Regional Oral History Office, 1988.

Benson, Robert. *Great Winemakers of California: Conversations with Robert Benson*. Santa Barbara, Calif.: Capra Press, 1977.

Bernstein, Arlene. *Growing Season: Life Lessons from the Garden*. San Francisco/Tulsa: Wildcat Canyon Press, 2004.

Birmingham, Stephen, *California Rich*. New York: Simon and Schuster, 1980.

Bonetti, William. "A Life of Winemaking at Wineries of Gallo, Schenley, Charles Krug, Château Souverain, and Sonoma-Cutrer." By Carole Hicke. Berkeley: University of California, Bancroft Library, Regional Oral History Office, 1998.

Bottles and Bins: Uncorked and Poured From Time to Time by Charles Krug Winery, St. Helena, California. Edited by Francis L. Gould. St. Helena, Calif.: Charles Krug Winery, 1960–1975.

Bowen, Robert M. "The Robert Mondavi Corporation." Case study, University of Washington Business School, 2001.

Caen, Herb. *The World of Herb Caen: San Francisco 1938–1997*. San Francisco: Chronicle Books, 1997.

California Wine Greats: Pioneers in Building the Wine Industry of California. California: M. Shanken Communications, Inc., 1984.

Collier, James W. *Wealth in Families*. Harvard University, 2003.

Conaway, James. *Napa*. Boston: Houghton Mifflin, 1990.

Davies, Jack, and Jamie Peterman Davies. "Rebuilding Schramsberg: The Creation of a California Champagne House." By Ruth Teiser and Lisa Jacobson. Berkeley: University of California, Bancroft Library, Regional Oral History Office, 1990.

Echikson, William. *Noble Rot: A Bordeaux Wine Revolution*. New York: W. W. Norton & Co., 2004.

Gallo, Ernest, and Julio Gallo. *Our Story*. New York: Times Books, Random House, 1994.

Golden, Brian R.; Henry W. Lane; and David T. A. Wesley. "Mondavi: Caliterra." Case study, Richard Ivey School of Business, University of Western Ontario, 1999.

Gomberg, Louis. "Analytical Perspectives on the California Wine Industry, 1935–1990." By Ruth Teiser. Berkeley: University of California, Bancroft Library, Regional Oral History Office, 1992.

Grgich, Miljenko. "A Croatian-American Winemaker in the Napa Valley." By Ruth Teiser. Berkeley: University of California, Bancroft Library, Regional Oral History Office, 1992.

Hargrave, Louisa Thomas. *The Vineyard: The Pleasures and Perils of Creating a Family Winery*. New York: Viking, 2003.

Hawkes, Ellen. *Blood and Wine: The Unauthorized Story of the Gallo Wine Empire*. New York: Simon and Schuster, 1993.

Heintz, William F. *California's Napa Valley: One Hundred Sixty Years of Winemaking*. San Francisco: Scottwall Associates, c. 1999.

Johnston, Moira. *Spectral Evidence: The Ramona Case : Incest, Memory, and Truth on Trial in Napa Valley*. Boston: Houghton Mifflin, 1997.

Kramer, Matt. *Making Sense of California Wine*. New York: William Morrow, 1992.

Lansberg, Ivan. *Succeeding Generations: Realizing the Dream of Families in Business*. Boston: Harvard Business School Press, 1999.

Lapsley, James. *Bottled Poetry: Napa Winemaking from Prohibition to the Modern Era*. Berkeley: University of California Press, 1996.

Laube, James. *California Wine*. New York: Wine Spectator Press, 1995.

Littlewood, Joan. *Baron Philippe: The Very Candid Autobiography of Baron Philippe de Rothschild*. New York: Crown Publishers. 1984.

Lukacs, Paul. *American Vintage: The Rise of American Wine*. Boston: Houghton Mifflin, 2000.

MacNeil, Karen. *The Wine Bible*. New York: Workman Publishing Company, 2001.

McCoy, Elin. *The Emperor of Wine: The Rise of Robert M. Parker Jr. and the Reign of American Taste*. New York: Ecco, HarperCollins, 2005.

Miller, Henry. *Big Sur and the Oranges of Hieronymous Bosch*. New York: New Directions Publishing Corporation, 1957.

Mondavi, Margrit; Annie Roberts; Laurie Smith; and Victoria Wise. *Annie and Margrit: Recipes and Stories from the Robert Mondavi Kitchen*. Berkeley: Ten Speed Press, 2003.

Mondavi, Peter. "Advances in Technology and Production at Charles Krug Winery, 1946–1988." By Ruth Teiser. Berkeley: University of California, Bancroft Library, Regional Oral History Office, 1990.

Mondavi, Robert. "Creativity in the California Wine Industry." By Ruth Teiser. Berkeley: University of California, Bancroft Library, Regional Oral History Office, 1985.

Mondavi, Robert. *Harvests of Joy: My Passion for Excellence: How the Good Life Became Great Business*. New York: Harcourt Brace & Company, 1998.

Morton, Frederic. *The Rothschilds: A Family Portrait*. New York: Atheneum, 1962.

Napa Valley Register, 1943–2006.

Neubauer, Fred, and Alden G. Lank, *The Family Business: Its Governance for Sustainability*. London: MacMillan Press, 1998.

Pellegrini, Angelo M. *Americans by Choice*. New York: Macmillan Company, 1965.

Posert, Harvey, and Paul Franson. *Spinning the Bottle: Case Histories, Tactics, and Stories of Wine Public Relations*, St. Helena, Calif.: HPPR Press, 2004.

Prial, Frank. *Decantations: Reflections on Wine by The New York Times Wine Critic*. New York: St. Martin's Press, 2002.

Ray, Cyril. *Mouton-Rothschild : The Wine, The Family, The Museum*. London : Christie's Wine Publications, 1977.

Ray, Cyril. *Robert Mondavi of the Napa Valley*. Novato, Calif.: Presidio Press, 1984.

The Redwood. Santa Clara, Calif.: Santa Clara University. Yearbook. 1961–1970; 1994; 1998.

Roberto, Michael A. "Robert Mondavi and the Wine Industry." Case study, Harvard Business School, 2002.

Rosano, Dick. *Wine Heritage: The Story of Italian-American Vintners.* San Francisco: The Wine Appreciation Guild, 2000.

Rothschild, Baron Philippe de. *Vivre la Vigne: Du Ghetto à Francfort à Mouton-Rothschild, 1744–1981.* Paris: Presses de la Cité, 1981.

Santa Clara, newspaper of Santa Clara University, August 1962–June 1969.

Soul of the Vine: Wine in Literature: A Selection. Edited by Nina Wemyss. Oakville, Calif.: Robert Mondavi Winery, 1998.

Starr, Kevin, *Land's End.* San Francisco: McGraw-Hill Book Company, 1979.

Starr, Kevin, *Coast of Dreams: California on the Edge, 1990–2003.* New York: Alfred A. Knopf, 2004.

St. Helena Star, 1943–2006.

Stuller, Jay, and Glen Martin. *Through the Grapevine.* New York: Wynwood Press, 1989.

Sullivan, Charles. *Napa Wine: A History from Mission Days to the Present.* San Francisco: The Wine Appreciation Guild, 1994.

Taber, George M. *The Judgment of Paris: California vs. France and the Historic 1976 Paris Tasting That Revolutionized Wine.* New York: Scribner, 2005.

Teiser, Ruth, and Catherine Harroun. *Winemaking in California.* New York: McGraw-Hill, 1983.

Topolos, Michael; Betty Dopson; and Jeffrey Caldewey. *Napa Valley Wine Tour.* St. Helena, Calif.: Vintage Image, 1977.

Ventura, Serena Mondavi. "Crush: A Memoir of My Mother, the Mondavis, and Me." Thesis, M.F.A.-Writing, University of San Francisco, 2005.

Wilsey, Sean. *Oh the Glory of it All.* New York: Penguin Press, 2005.

Winiarski, Warren. "Creating Classic Wines in the Napa Valley." By Ruth Teiser. Berkeley: University of California, Bancroft Library, Regional Oral History Office, 1994.

Zraly, Kevin. *Kevin Zraly's American Wine Guide.* New York: Sterling Publishing Co., 2006.

INDEX

MONDAVI

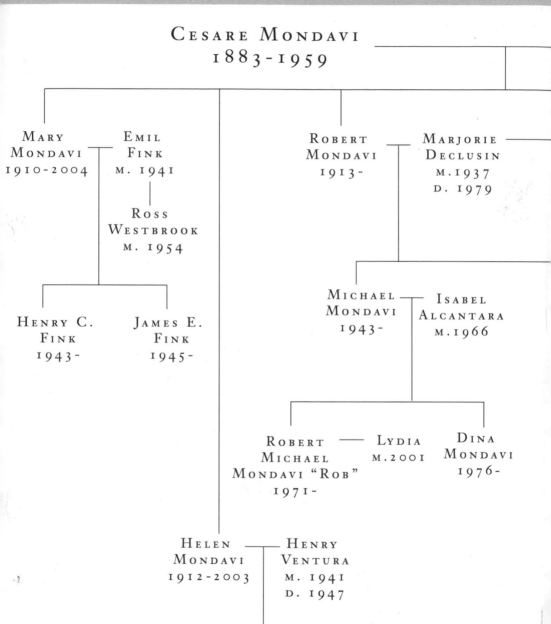

CESARE MONDAVI
1883-1959

MARY
MONDAVI
1910-2004

EMIL
FINK
M. 1941

ROBERT
MONDAVI
1913-

MARJORIE
DECLUSIN
M.1937
D. 1979

ROSS
WESTBROOK
M. 1954

MICHAEL
MONDAVI
1943-

ISABEL
ALCANTARA
M.1966

HENRY C.
FINK
1943-

JAMES E.
FINK
1945-

ROBERT
MICHAEL
MONDAVI "ROB"
1971-

LYDIA
M.2001

DINA
MONDAVI
1976-

HELEN
MONDAVI
1912-2003

HENRY
VENTURA
M. 1941
D. 1947

SERENA
VENTURA
1946-

PETER
VENTURA
1943-